I NEVER KNEW WHEN I MIGHT BE TAKING MY LAST RIDE. With so many ways to bust my butt flying research aircraft, I knew better than to think that any test flight was routine. Even so, on the morning of October 27, 1947, I was feeling confident in the cockpit of the X-1 research rocket airplane. On the previous flight, the bullet-shaped X-1 had zoomed me into the history books by cracking through the sound barrier. I always had butterflies before being dropped from the belly of the B-29 mother ship, but my tensions this day were minor compared to the sound barrier mission.

"Are you ready, Chuck?" they ask from the mother ship.

"All set," I reply.

The release cable pops and we plunge clear from the shadows of the mother ship, falling fast. I reach for the switch to ignite my engine. It clicks. Nothing happens.

"Hey, I've got total electrical failure," I report. My words travel no further than the cabin because my radio is powerless, too.

The ship is dead and I'm dropping like a bomb, certain to blow a giant crater into the desert floor 20,000 feet below. . . .

YEAGER: AN AUTOBIOGRAPHY

"Ever since Tom Wolfe's book was published, the question I'm asked most often and which always annoys me is whether I think I've got 'the right stuff.' I know that golden trout have the right stuff, and I've seen a few gals here and there that I'd bet had it in spades, but those words seem meaningless when used to describe a pilot's attributes. I don't deny that I was damned good. If there is such a thing as 'the best,' I was at least one of the title contenders. I've had a full life and enjoyed just about every damned minute of it because that's how I lived."

—General Chuck Yeager

YEAGER

An Autobiography

GENERAL CHUCK YEAGER
&
LEO JANOS

BANTAM BOOKS
TORONTO · NEW YORK · LONDON · SYDNEY · AUCKLAND

YEAGER: AN AUTOBIOGRAPHY

A Bantam Book
Bantam hardcover edition / July 1985
23 printings through March 1985
A selection of Book-of-the-Month Club, September 1985.

Serialized in Aerospace America, October 1985; Cosmopolitan,
December 1985; Reader's Digest, October 29, 1985, Family
Weekly, July 7, 1985; Literary Cavalcade magazine, December
1985; and Toronto Globe and Mail, October 14, 1985.

Bantam paperback edition / September 1986

A portion of this work originally
appeared in Playboy magazine.

Grateful acknowledgment is made to the U.S. Air Force, the
White House, Northrup Corporation, and the Ladd Company,
producers of the movie The Right Stuff, *a Warner Brothers*
release, for making available some of the photographs that
appear in this book.

ISBN 0-553-25674-2

Published simultaneously in the United States and Canada

Bantam Books are published by Bantam Books, Inc. Its
trademark, consisting of the words "Bantam Books" and the
portrayal of a rooster, is Registered in the United States Patent
and Trademark Office and in other countries. Marca Registrada.
Bantam Books, Inc., 666 Fifth Avenue, New York, New York
10103.

PRINTED IN THE UNITED STATES OF AMERICA

O   0 9 8 7 6 5 4 3 2 1

Contents

ACKNOWLEDGMENTS

The authors wish to acknowledge the contributions of various friends and former colleagues who enriched the pages of this book with their perspectives and recollections. Among them: Clarence "Bud" Anderson, Bob Hoover, Maj. Gen. (retired) Fred J. Ascani, Russ Schleeh, Richard Frost, Charles K. Peters, William R. O'Brien, Bill Overstreet, Robert H. Smith, Carl Bellinger, Aldene Tarter, Vi Strauss-Pistel, Margaret Ann Curlin, George Hupp, Emmett Hatch, Don Jacques, Dr. Robert S. "Buck" Buchanan, and Don Emigholz. Particular thanks to Glennis Yeager for her patient insights, to Del Riebe for his friendship and support, to Ian Ballantine, the wise and resourceful father of this project, and to Betty Ballantine for her skilled editing.

ALWAYS THE UNKNOWN

I never knew when I might be taking my last ride. With so many ways to bust my butt flying research aircraft, I knew better than to think that any test flight was routine. Even so, on the morning of October 27, 1947, I was feeling confident in the cockpit of the X-1 research rocket airplane. On the previous flight, the bullet-shaped X-1 had zoomed me into the history books by cracking through the sound barrier. That first Mach 1 ride launched the era of supersonic flight. I always had butterflies before being dropped from the belly of the B-29 mother ship, but my tensions this day were minor compared to the sound barrier mission, when I was scared, knowing that many of my colleagues thought I was doomed to be blasted to pieces by an invisible brick wall in the sky. The X-1 proved them to be wrong, and I breathed easier knowing what to expect on my second attempt to fly faster than the speed of sound.

"Are you ready, Chuck?" they ask from the mother ship.

"All set," I reply.

The release cable pops and we plunge clear from the shadows of the mother ship, a thirteen-thousand-pound load, falling fast. I reach for the switch to ignite my engine. It clicks. Nothing happens.

I try another engine switch. Nothing happens.

"Hey, I've got total electrical failure," I report. My words travel no further than the cabin because my radio is powerless, too.

The ship is dead and I'm dropping like a bomb, loaded with five thousand pounds of volatile fuel, certain to blow a giant crater into the desert floor 20,000 feet below. Without power, I can't ignite my engines or actuate the propellant valve to blow out my fuel. The X-1 can't land with fuel on board; its landing gear would buckle under the weight, and we'd dig a trench into the lakebed and blow up.

My mind races. I've got only a couple of seconds to find a way to save my airplane or risk a dangerous parachute jump. I remember an emergency valve above and behind my seat that manually opens the jettison valve to slowly blow out my fuel. I have no idea how long it will take and the force of gravity is relentless. I'm down to 5,000 feet and turn toward the lakebed. A chase plane is keeping up with me, but without radio contact I have no way of knowing whether the pilot can see the escaping fuel vapor streaming from my engine, the sign that the emergency valve is working.

The lakebed fills my windscreen and I reach for my landing gear release, but with no internal power the only way to lower my gear is by gravity. All I can do is rock the ship and pray. My only chance is to come in fast and high over the lakebed, keeping the nose up and those wheels off the deck until the last possible moment. I need time, every precious second I can manage to squeeze out of a delayed landing, to blow out that fuel. My fuel gauge is as dead as everything else, and I can only go by feel. We feel lighter by the second, but we're almost out of seconds. The ground is sweeping by as we glide in for a touchdown. My eyes are on the *ship's raised nose. In a moment we are going to stall; I can sense it.*

Inches from the lakebed I feel the X-1 shudder slightly. We've slowed into a stall, and the ship's nose lowers. Instinctively I hunker down, bracing for the impact. If there's still fuel in those tanks, I'm finished.

The wheels hit hard.

STARTING FROM SCRATCH

$\mathbf{W}$hen President Truman presented me with the Collier Trophy in 1948 for breaking the sound barrier, my dad attended the White House ceremonies, but refused to shake hands with the President. He glowered at Truman, acting like a revival preacher trapped into meeting the pope. As far as Dad was concerned, the first good Democrat had yet to be born. Mom had battled to get him to the ceremony, then chewed him out glory for being so rude. But Dad wasn't going to shake that damned Democrat's hand; hell, he hated Truman. Mom tried to cover up by exchanging corn bread recipes with the President, while Air Force Secretary Stuart Symington and Gen. Hoyt Vandenberg saw what was happening and fought against the giggles. "My husband is a little firm in his ways," Mom explained to Symington. He broke up.

There were two Methodist churches in Hamlin, West Virginia: one was for the Southern Methodists, all Democrats; the other congregation was Northern

Methodists, the hardcore Republicans of Lincoln County. You can guess which church we belonged to. On election day, Dad traveled the hollers armed with two-dollar bills and pints of whiskey, trying to buy votes for the GOP. But there wasn't enough booze or bucks to beat FDR Democrats, and Dad fumed.

Albert Hal Yeager had plenty of Dutch and German blood. He was stubborn and opinionated about what he believed and didn't care who knew it. He stood only about five feet, eight inches, but weighed two hundred pounds—about half that weight in each of his two powerful arms. Dad's word was his binding contract; if he said he'd do something and shook hands on it, that was his unbreakable commitment. Susie Mae Yeager was a couple of inches taller than her husband, a big-boned, no-nonsense churchgoer who lowered the boom on any of us if we got out of hand. Mom was half-Dutch with some French ancestry in her family. Like the Yeagers, her kin were West Virginia country people, small farmers planted in the hollers of the Appalachians since the early nineteenth century. Dad's family name was originally "Jäger," but it was changed phonetically; in German, Yeager means "hunter."

My parents were in their mid-twenties when I was born on February 13, 1923, the second of their five children. My brother Roy, a year-and-a-half older, was in every way my big brother: he would grow up to be six feet, four inches and weigh about 250 pounds. My wife Glennis called him "the gentle giant," but as a kid, I gladly trailed behind a big brother twice my size. Nobody picked on me.

We lived in Myra, on the upper Mud River, which was just a few farmhouses, a post office, and a country store. Our white clapboard house stood next to a cornfield. When I was about three, we moved to Hubble, where Dad went to work for the railroad. I remember him coming home with his face and hands bandaged from a flash fire when he shoveled coal into the firebox. As young as I was, that incident

made a deep impression: I realized for the first time
how hard he struggled to shelter us from the cold.
Until then, I had no idea what Dad was up against,
how tough life really was. But Dad wasn't a brooder
or a complainer. In fact, he was a great prankster,
and a real marksman with a slingshot. An old lady
neighbor had a milking cow and every evening she'd
come out and milk it in a field next to the railroad
tracks. Dad would sit on the porch and shoot pebbles
at that cow; the old lady milking on the other side
couldn't figure out why Bessie kept kicking over her
bucket.

Dad made home-brew with yeast and malt, and
wine in grape season. I worked the bottle-capper, the
first mechanical thing I ever understood. Mom got
all over him because he stored his bottles in the
basement to keep them cool and they were always
blowing up. West Virginia was a dry state, and you
either made your own or got mighty thirsty.

I was still a preschooler when we moved to Hamlin, which seemed to me like a big city, with a main
street and a bunch of stores, schools, and churches.
Hamlin was a town of four hundred. We moved because Dad began work as a natural gas driller, con-
tracting out with a string of tools in southern West
Virginia and Kentucky. We lived in a three-room
house across from the grade school. Roy and I slept
in the family room on a studio couch that opened
into a bed. By then we had a two-year-old baby
sister, Doris Ann. Shortly before Christmas, when I
was four-and-a-half and Roy was six, we were sitting
on the floor in the family room playing with Dad's
12-gauge shotgun. Roy found some shells and loaded
the gun; he accidentally fired and the baby was killed.
For our little family it was a time of terrible shock,
loss, and suffering. I suppose some parents would've
locked away any guns following such a tragedy, but
Dad didn't. Shortly after the funeral, he sat down
with Roy and me. "Boys," he said, "I want to show
you how to safely handle firearms." I'm sure Roy

carried this heartbreak with him until his own early death from a heart attack at age forty-one. He and I never again discussed it, nor did my parents. Years later, Glennis asked my mother about the accident, but she just didn't want to talk about it. That's the Yeager way; we keep our hurts to ourselves.

Those were tough times with Dad just starting a new occupation. If you've ever seen two growing boys wolfing down food, then you know what Mom was up against. She cooked us mush for breakfast, which was plain boiled white cornmeal served in a bowl with milk and sugar. She made more than we used and set it aside until it got rubbery, then she sliced it, fried it, put butter on it, and that was supper. Some evenings we'd have only corn bread and buttermilk. When the weather turned cold, rats nested in that little house, and I once chased an enormous rat running off with Mom's pan lid. Around that time, I also started school. We were seated alphabetically, and I sat back in daydreamer's row with the other Ys. I lived for vacations and weekends. We kids spent most of our free time running around in the hills. We made walking stilts from tree limbs or spent whole days up in trees, jumping like monkeys from one sapling to the other to see how far we would get. We built log forts and staged wars, using slingshots and rubber-band guns. By the time I was six, I knew how to shoot a .22 rifle and hunted squirrel and rabbit. I'd get up around dawn, head into the woods, and bring back three or four squirrels, skin them and leave them in a bucket of water for Mom to cook up for supper. Sometimes I got so engrossed in hunting, I was late for school and got chewed out by the principal. I also used to fish for suckers and bass in the Mud River.

We ran barefoot all summer. On Saturday night, Mom made us wash our feet, getting ready for Sunday school. On Sunday night, our feet were sore and blistered from wearing shoes, and our family joke was that the first pair of shoes we had, we wore out

first from inside out. In summer, Mom canned black-
berries and made jelly and jam; Roy and I sold black-
berries for ten cents a gallon, a source of additional
income. Dad was gone all week, but sometimes when
he came home on the weekends, he brought a canta-
loupe—a real treat—or a watermelon, which you could
buy in those days for a nickel.

The Great Depression began when I was eight,
but it had no real impact when you were already so
low on the income scale. Dad got regular work in the
gas fields. When a family named Baker was forced
into foreclosure on their mortgage and lost their home,
the bank approached Dad, and we moved into what I
thought was a palace on a hill—a two-story, four-
bedroom house with a big parlor and a smokehouse
in back. Dad got the place, plus two small city blocks
that went with it, for signing a note for $1,800. He
worked hard, was known for his integrity, and the
bank figured he'd manage somehow to keep up on
his monthly payments.

Now we had a garden and a cow, slopped hogs,
and raised chickens. I could wring off a chicken's
neck when I was six. Mom pickled corn and beans
and made sauerkraut. In the fall she made apple
butter in a thirty-gallon copper kettle, and as a treat,
she added sprigs of peppermint. We kids had the job
of keeping the fire going. She also boiled sorghum
molasses, a source of syrup all winter. We had no
refrigeration, but we used the smokehouse when Dad
slaughtered a hog. One time, he and a neighbor teamed
up to kill a five-hundred-pound hog. The guy shot it
between the eyes and Dad walked up to it to slit its
throat and bleed it, when that hog suddenly got up
and ran off. Dad jumped on and rode it through the
streets as if it were a runaway horse. It carried him
two hundred yards before he succeeded in slitting its
throat.

After a hog was killed and bled, we kids covered
it with burlap sacks and poured steaming water over
it, to set the hair before scraping it off. Dad did the

butchering. The hams were cured with salt and hung in the smokehouse; meanwhile, Mom cooked and canned souse meat (better known as Philadelphia scrapple). She also cured bacon, rubbing sides with salt and pepper and hanging them in the smokehouse. Vines of Concord grapes grew out back, and we kids harvested hickory nuts and black walnuts in the woods, as well as berries and wild persimmons. Mom used the nuts in cakes and candies. We also brought back pawpaws, an almost tropical fruit that grows only along the western edge of Appalachia, in West Virginia, and tastes halfway between a banana and a peach.

From time to time, Dad let me go on hunting trips with some other local men, shooting deer, bear, quail, and wild turkeys. To us, hunting was like harvesting nuts or fruit; we never killed more than we could use. Every kid in Hamlin was raised with a gun and there were few, if any, poor shots; even so, I was pretty good. Shooting is a matter of good eyesight, muscular control, and coordination. Roy, for example, was a little more high-strung: his hands shook before he squeezed the trigger. I never got excited or flustered sighting on game; that wasn't my nature. And somehow I was usually able to spot a deer hidden in brush before anyone else. I had exceptional 20/10 vision.

My sister Pansy Lee and younger brother, Hal, Jr., were born in the house on the hill. But for a long time, Roy and I did all the chores. With Dad being gone so much, Mom raised us. If we got too rambunctious, she told Dad about it when he got home, and he brought out the heavy artillery—his leather strap. I got my first licking for calling a neighbor "McCoglin," instead of "Mister McCoglin." Roy and I ran errands, weeded in the garden, slopped the hogs, and milked the cow twice a day. I cannot remember a moment when there wasn't something to do. I wasn't big enough to be a rowdy kid, but I wasn't above mischief either.

We spent so much time in the woods, we got to be like little animals, knowing everything that went on. Once Roy and I watched a moonshiner named Bill Lawson hiding jugs of white lightning in a hollow log. We stole his jugs and sold them in town for a quarter a gallon. But even Roy was plenty scared of ol' Bill Lawson, so we never did that again. Of course, we had to drink some and it nearly killed us—pure alcohol. Dad grew some tobacco for his smoking; I tried chewing some and it wiped me out. In summer, we swam up the river to steal watermelons in the bottomlands, where they grew best. We'd roll those big melons into the river and float them downstream, where we could feast in safety; the farmers kept shotguns loaded with rock salt to sting the butts of kids like us.

When I was nearly thirteen, I climbed into a '33 Dodge truck belonging to our neighbor, Mr. Sites. Dad let us fool around with his truck, and I thought I knew how to drive it. I decided to drive Mr. Sites's truck off our hill. I kicked it out of gear and took off, going fifty-five with no brakes on. I tried, but failed, to get into low gear and barely turned the corner at the bottom of the hill, where there was a vacant lot loaded with empty asphalt drums from recent road paving. I hit those drums with a crash that was heard for miles. Man, I got out of there using my own two feet.

I was a competitive kid. Whether it was swinging from vines over the swimming hole or skiing down hills on barrel staves during the first snowfall, I always tried to do my best. We made and raced our own bobsleds too, so I knew what a skid was when I first learned to fly. Students skidded in the sky when they didn't properly coordinate aileron with rudder. I had plenty of experience fighting ice skids down steep hills on sleds and homemade skis; that's probably the reason I flew coordinated and kept the ball in the middle.

Dad was an expert mechanic; he had clever hands

with generators and motors and was always tinkering with his old Chevy truck or his drilling equipment. Roy and I inherited his mechanical ability. I was only seven when I helped Dad in the gas fields. He was drilling on the side of a hill, and I helped him rig up a series of single-cylinder engines to pump water uphill to a big tank. My job was to keep feeding gasoline into those small engines, which had magnetos for spark-control that knocked me on my fanny every time they stopped or started. When we were older, Roy was a bigger help to Dad than I was. I was just too small; Roy could easily move a section of four-inch drill pipe; I couldn't even lift one. But when I encountered dome regulators flying in the X-1, I knew more about them than the engineers, from working with Dad's regulators as a kid.

By the time I reached high school, I excelled at anything that demanded dexterity or mathematical aptitude. My best grades were in typing and math. My geometry teacher, Miss Gonza Methel, considered me one of her better students. But my English and history teachers had to search for excuses to pass me. In sports, I was terrific at pool and ping-pong, good in basketball and football. I played trombone in our high-school marching band, and would've been a damned good trombone player if only I practiced. But in high school, I discovered girls, and between them, chores, homework, and hunting and fishing, I was stretched thin. We teenagers hung around the recreation center in town, called "The Chicken House," playing ping-pong and listening to records. In those days nobody went steady. Guys played the field and made sure we always carried rubbers—the big thing to do. I carried mine in my watch pocket; when it got worn out being in there so long, I bought another. But through a combination of trial and error, my luck changed in my senior year, and Mom began raising hell when I came home at two in the morning. She locked me out, so I began

climbing a tree and crawling into an upstairs bedroom window.

West Virginia still leads the country in unemployment and Lincoln County, where I was raised,
remains one of the poorest counties in the state, but I
never thought of myself as being poor or deprived in
any way. Like most everyone else in town, we managed to scrape by. Kids learned self-sufficiency from
their parents and made their own toys and invented
their own fun. Life was basic and direct: people said
what they meant and meant what they said. I learned
face value. We wore our moods right on our faces;
trying to deceive somebody to make a sale, for example, was nonexistent in the hills. For openers, you
might get your ass shot off. By big-city standards, we
might seem raw and uneducated, but we knew right
from wrong and could spot a phony even before he
said his first words.

Mom and Dad taught us by example. Mom worked
as hard as any of the pioneer women, from dawn to
dark, cooking and mending and cleaning. Dad got
home late Friday and left on Sunday; in between he
worked like a dog. They never complained. We country people had our own way of life. We didn't sit
around worrying and were contented with the little
we had. We didn't know any better or any different.
The mountains kept us isolated from the rest of the
world, and we didn't wonder much whether things
were better or worse over the next ridge.

It was only when some of us traveled out into
the world that we realized everyone wasn't like us.
Once you began talking, people looked at you in
amazement, wondering what in hell you were trying
to say. I discovered fast that not everyone said "bidy"
when they meant "body," "paper poke" instead of
"sack," "simon" for "salmon," "hit" for "it," and so
on. But, like Dad, I had certain standards that I lived
by. Whatever I did, I determined to do the best I
could at it. I was prideful about keeping my word
and starting what I finished. That's how I was raised.

I never got into fights, but nobody pushed me around, either. Mountain people are damned stubborn about their grudges and don't easily forgive or forget. If I thought I was being put down unfairly, I was one mean son of a bitch.

I never thought about going to college; Dad just wasn't that well off. I wasn't much of a scholar, but I was always eager to acquire practical knowledge about things that interested me. That was a big reason for my success as a pilot. I flew more than anybody else and there wasn't a thing about an airplane that didn't fascinate me, down to the smallest bolt. And I was blessed with a sharp memory for detail. I was that way as a kid, too. J.D. Smith was the town lawyer and a former state senator. I liked to visit with him on his porch; his wife served me lemonade and cookies while Mr. Smith talked to me about hunting and fishing and the habits of different animals. We small-town kids mixed easily with people of different ages: old guys like Mr. Smith had reputations, and we wondered how they got them. When I got married, I asked Mr. Smith to fill in for Glennis's dad, who couldn't be there and give away the bride. Grandpa Yeager fascinated me, too. He was a tough little guy with a glass eye, who farmed deep in a holler. He showed me how to hunt bear and wild turkey, and how to stalk game so it didn't run and lower the quality of the meat.

Although Mom raised us, I think I was more "turned" like Dad, which is West Virginia for "taking after." I'm stubborn and strong-willed too, and opinionated as hell. My folks weren't well-educated, but they never lacked country wisdom and common sense. As hard as Dad worked, he enjoyed it, and that was an important lesson, too. Tramping alone through the woods with a rifle, or in a cockpit with a throttle in my hands—that's where I was happiest. And that's how I've lived my life.

My beginnings back in West Virginia tell who I am to this day. My accomplishments as a pilot tell more about luck, happenstance, and a person's destiny. But the guy who broke the sound barrier was the kid who swam the Mud River with a swiped watermelon, or shot the head off a squirrel before school.

TAKING WING

Y ou're whipping through a desert canyon at three hundred miles an hour, your belly just barely scraping the rocks and sagebrush, your hand on the throttle of a P-39 fighter. It's a crystal-clear morning on the desert of western Nevada, and the joy of flying—the sense of speed and exhilaration twenty feet above the deck—makes you so damned happy that you want to shout for joy. A hillock rises ahead, and you ease back, skim over the top of it, dropping down above cottonwoods lining the bank of a stream. You feel so lucky, so blessed to be a fighter pilot. Nearly one hundred of us are testing our skill and courage by leaving prop marks on the dirt roads, stampeding grazing cattle (a few angry ranchers even take pot shots at us), and raising the shingles off ranch houses. Swooping over the desert like a horde of metal locusts, we practice for strafing runs, the most dangerous missions that will eventually kill many of us. Our instructors warn us to get down on the deck as low as we can, staying

15

below the treeline, where enemy machine guns can't target a clear shot.

That was Tonopah, where thirty fledgling pilots began six months of intensive training to become a combat fighter squadron—the 363rd. We lived surrounded by Nevada sand dunes in tarpaper shacks belching black smoke from the oil-burning stoves that only warmed themselves on cold desert nights. The wind never stopped blowing and the chow was awful, but none of us complained. We flew from dawn to dusk, six flights a day, six days a week, dogfighting, buzzing, and practicing gunnery. We crawled exhausted into the sack at ten and straggled to breakfast at 4:30 A.M., taking off on our first flight of the day just as dawn broke. I logged one hundred hours of flying that first month. Hog heaven.

No matter what happened later, the war had already changed my life forever. Unlike others in the squadron, I had never dreamt of being an aviator. Even as kids, guys like Bud Anderson and Jim Browning used to hang around airports and wash old Boeing tri-motors to get a free ride. Me, I was a pool hustler from the West Virginia hollers. I saw my first airplane close-up when a Beechcraft bellied into a cornfield on the Mud River, and I went to look at it to see what all the excitement was about. I was fifteen, and stopped by on my bike to see the wreck before heading out to the county poor farm where I helped out on Saturday afternoons, giving shaves to the old codgers. Between running chores, playing kelly pool in the poolhall or poker under a covered bridge at the edge of town, and catting around with three or four different gals, there wasn't a helluva lot going on in my life in the summer of 1941. I had my diploma from Hamlin High School tucked in a drawer somewhere, and I fished it out, together with my birth certificate proving I was eighteen, when an Army Air Corps recruiter came to town. I enlisted for a two-year hitch. I thought I might enjoy it and see some of the world. Dad never preached at us, and I can recall him giving me only two pieces of advice: never buy a pickup truck that wasn't built by General Motors, and, much later, on the day I left for the service, he said, "Son, don't gamble." He hadn't been pleased with a job I had had sweeping up and racking the balls at the poolhall for ten bucks a month, and especially he hadn't liked it when I picked up side money hustling games.

I became an airplane mechanic. Growing up around truck engines and drilling equipment generators, I was one of the few kids in town who could take apart a car motor and put it back together again. Dad was an expert mechanic, and I just understood motors—a natural ability, like having exceptional eyes and the coordination to be a crack shot. Hand a rifle to a hillbilly and he'll hit a bull's-eye every time. So, without knowing or even caring, I had the talents needed for flying in combat. But after taking my first airplane ride, I'd rather have crawled across country than go back up. I took off for a spin with a maintenance officer flight testing a ship I had serviced, and I threw up all over the back seat, staggering out of that damned thing as miserable as I'd ever been. But teenagers blot out the past when the present seems appealing. I saw a notice announcing a "Flying Sergeant" program. I'd take my chances with flying to become a sergeant. Three stripes and you were out of pulling K.P. and guard duty. I applied.

The war was only a few months old when I was accepted. There were only a few of us enlisted men; the rest were college boys, cadets who would become commissioned officers when they received their aviator's wings. At first I worried about keeping up with guys who were a little older and a whole lot better-educated than I was, but once we took off in a trainer, we were all created equal. I got sick the first few flights, but quickly overcame it. Because I was well-coordinated, I had less trouble than most handling a stick and rudder. But it was hard work learning to fly, and like everyone else, I sweated through my first solo and bounced in for a landing in one piece. But rather soon, the differences between students began to show. After fifteen hours of flying, an instructor complimented me by assuming I had flown a lot in civilian life. He was damned impressed when I told him I was just a learner.

Flying became fun. I knew what I was doing in the cockpit and understood the airplane. In only a month, I graduated from being air-sick even while flying level to actually enjoying spins and dives. I was lucky; some cadets never made it past the air-sick phase. Being cocky and competitive, I began bouncing other students and staging mock dogfights. I could line up on air or ground targets before others in the class even saw them. My instructor knew who was best in the group, and in the end, I was the one he recommended to become a fighter pilot. I was thrilled.

Dad and my kid brother, Hal, Jr., came to Arizona to see me get my wings, but I didn't report to the 363rd Fighter Squadron as a flying sergeant. By then, the regulations had changed, and those of us receiving our wings as enlisted men were made noncommissioned flight officers, wearing blue bars instead of gold. I didn't care. In fact, I felt damned lucky that because of the war mobilization, my military records had not caught up with me. Otherwise, I would have probably been bounced from flight school when they discovered I had been court-martialed as a corporal for shooting a horse with a thirty-caliber machine gun. On guard duty one night, I showed a guy how to fire the gun by shooting bursts out into the desert. I saw the horses grazing, but thought I would fire short; I didn't, and an angry rancher demanded that the Air Corps pay for his dead horse.

In Nevada, we trained in the Bell Airacobra, the P-39, a compact tricycle-geared fighter, with the engine mounted behind the cockpit and a 37-millimeter cannon barrel protruding through the prop shaft. You entered the cockpit through a car-type door,

which made you wonder how quickly you could get
out if the ship spun in. But I was excited to be flying
in a real fighter plane. I remember my first morning
there, Bill "Obie" O'Brien, one of the squadron leaders, with three hundred hours more flying time than
the rest of us, checked me out in the Thirty-Nine.
Obie was tough and demanding. I sat in the cockpit
while he explained all the switches. "Okay, Yeager,"
he said, "when you take off, raise the nose-gear at
sixty miles an hour—it'll get airborne about ninety
or one hundred. Then, raise your landing gear and
keep the son of a bitch wide open until you get out.
Then, cut the power back. Same way on landing.
Hell, it's no problem." Then he slammed the cockpit
door and signaled for me to fire up my engine. Instruction over.

There were three squadrons in our fighter group,
and among all those pilots, I was one of the few who
loved the Thirty-Nine and would have gladly flown it
off to war. The British refused it, and so did our own
Air Corps, except for instruction, so we gave P-39s to
the Russians to fight in. Our guys even sang a song
about it:

> Don't give me a P-39
> With an engine that's mounted behind.
> It will tumble and roll
> And dig a big hole—
> Don't give me a P-39.

Well, it was true that the drive shaft ran right up
the center of the cramped cockpit, that the airplane
performed beautifully at low altitudes, but was
underpowered up high, and that if you stalled it, you
might wind up boring a deep hole because it spun
like a top going down. But once you had a feel for the
ship and understood it, the Thirty-Nine was a fun
airplane to fly. Another problem was maintenance.
We flew so much, yet there were few old hands among
the ground crews working on the airplanes. There

was a lot of trial and error, both on the flight line
and in the sky.

"Crash" is not a word pilots ever use. I don't
really know why, but the word is avoided in describ-
ing what happens when several tons of metal plows
itself and its pilot into the ground. Instead, we might
say, "He augered in." Or, "He bought the farm."
However you chose to describe it, we were doing it.
Hell, the sky was filled with green pilots practicing
night landings, dogfighting, and strafing, so accidents
were inevitable, although our kill-rate cost the group
commander his job. We lost thirteen pilots in six
months. And in nearly every case, the worst pilots
died by their own stupidity—making a low-altitude
turn that dropped them into the ground, or waiting
too long to come out of a dive. One pilot dropped out
of formation for no apparent reason and plunged like
a boulder into the ground; guys snapped wings off
their planes doing crazy power dives, or buzzed into
the side of a hill. And if something went wrong, they
made the wrong decision about whether to jump or
stay. I saw a guy try to land with his engine on fire,
flames streaming, doing at least 150 mph, skidding
off the runway in flames and smoke. The crazy bastard hit the ground on the run just as his tail melted
off.

A gruesome weeding-out process was taking place.
Those who were killed in Nevada were likely to have
been the first killed in combat. But those of us who
did survive the training were rapidly becoming skilled
combat pilots and a cohesive team. I turned my back
on lousy fliers as if their mistakes were catching.
When one of them became a grease spot on the tar-
mac, I almost felt relieved: it was better to bury a
weak sister in training than in combat, where he
might not only bust his ass, but do something (or,
more than likely, fail to do something) that would
bust two or three other asses in addition to his own.

But I got mad at the dead: angry at them for
dying so young and so senselessly; angry at them

for destroying expensive government property as stupidly as if they had driven a Cadillac off a bridge. Anger was my defense mechanism. I've lost count of how many good friends have augered in over the years, but either you become calloused or you crack. By the time we flew combat in England, most of us had reached a point where, if a pilot borrowed our Mustang on our day off and was shot down, we became furious at the dead son of a bitch. The dead pilot might have been a friend, but he wasn't as special as our own P-51 that loyally hauled our own precious butt through the flak and tracers. Some losses, of course, tore into your guts as if you'd been shot. Then there was nothing left to do but go out and get blind drunk—which is exactly what we did. Those who couldn't put a lid on their grief couldn't hack combat. They were either sent home or became a basket case.

Death was our new trade. We were training to be professional killers, and one day at Tonopah, we crowded into the day room to hear an early combat veteran in the Pacific, named Tex Hill, describe his dogfights against the Japanese. Man, we were in awe. Shooting down an airplane seemed an incredible feat. I had no idea why the German people were stuck with Hitler and the Nazis and could care less. History was not one of my strong subjects. But when the time came, I would hammer those Germans any chance I got. Them or me. Even a "D" history student from Hamlin High knew that it was always better to be the hammer than the nail.

Those six months of squadron training were the happiest that I've ever been. Now that I was a fighter pilot, I couldn't imagine being anything else. We were hell-raising fighter jocks with plenty of swagger. When we weren't flying, we zipped on our leather flight jackets that told the world who we were and crowded into Anderson's 1939 Ford convertible or

Willet's Essex and drove into Tonopah, a wide-open silver-mining town. On paydays, we crowded around the blackjack tables of the Tonopah Club, drank ourselves blind on fifths of rotgut rye and bourbon, then staggered over to the local cathouse. Miss Taxine, the madam, tried to keep a fresh supply of gals so we wouldn't get bored and become customers of Lucky Strike, a cathouse in Mina, about thirty miles down the road. But we went to Mina anyway, wrecked the place, and the sheriff ran us out of town. The next morning, a P-39 strafed Mina's water tower.

My roommate and closest buddy was the only other flight officer in the squadron, a lanky Texan named Chuck McKee; I called him "Mack." Being the only two guys in the squadron who hadn't gone to college and weren't commissioned officers, we thought of ourselves as a different breed of cat. We were both rural boys who loved to hunt and fish, and we wore the blue flight officer's bars on our leather jackets as a badge of honor. So, it was natural that we paired off. On Sundays, we would drive jeeps out into the desert and hunt rabbits with Springfield rifles. We raced our jeeps through the sage and rocks, and why we weren't killed right then and there, I'll never know. But one Sunday we went roaring up a dirt road into a canyon we had buzzed a few days earlier, causing a herd of cattle to stampede, and to our embarrassment the rancher happened to be on his front porch that morning. Instead of grabbing his shotgun, he signaled to us to stop and say hello. His name was Joe Clifford. His place was called the Stone Cabin Ranch. He invited us to stay for Sunday dinner and introduced us to his two boys, Joe, Jr., and Roy. Ma and Pa Clifford and their boys became like family, not only to Mack and me, but to all the other guys in the squadron. Ma cooked on a wood stove for sometimes as many as ten or fifteen hungry fighter jocks. I remember huge roasts, mounds of mashed potatoes, three different pies and cakes. We'd waddle out of that place.

We buzzed the ranch all the time, and if Pa Clifford came out and waved a bed sheet, it meant yo'all come over tonight for Ma's chow. Mack and I used to fly over and drop the Clifford boys all kinds of ammo for their hunting, whole belts of thirty-ought-six, since bullets were hard to come by in wartime. There was a dry lakebed about a hundred yards from the house, and we would practice dive-bombing over that lakebed, dropping practice bombs, while Pa Clifford, down below, watched and laughed like hell.

One day I heard Pa mention that he'd like to get rid of a tree that stood near the roadway to the house. The next day, I buzzed that tree in my P-39 and carefully topped it with my left wingtip. I enjoyed that kind of challenge, but when I landed there was hell to pay. The maintenance officer demanded to know why my smashed wingtip looked as if it were taking root—hunks of wood were rammed into it. "I hit a bird," I told him. "Well," he replied, "that son of a bitch must've been sitting in one helluva nest." I was grounded from flying P-39s for a week. But there were several BT-13s available, and I flew them instead. A few nights later, when most of the squadron was seated around Ma Clifford's table, I came in on them in a BT-13, raised the shingles on the roof from my prop wash, while the guys inside never doubted who was buzzing them. "I wonder which crazy hillbilly did that?" I was always up to something.

In late June, we left Nevada to begin training in bomber escort and coastal patrol operations at Santa Rosa, California. The morning we left from the train depot, Taxine and the gals from the local cathouse came down to see us off with sandwiches, doughnuts, and hot coffee, and gave us a heroes' send-off. For us, the war was drawing ever closer.

But I unexpectedly found myself close to home. Travel orders sent me to Wright Field, in Ohio, to be—of all things—a test pilot. The assignment was temporary: to do accelerated service testing on a new propeller developed for the P-39. I was chosen because of my maintenance background and flying ability, and all I had to do was fly as much as possible and keep careful records. And because I couldn't keep my hands off airplanes, I managed to get checked out in the P-47 fighter, and began to fly that big old fighter regularly.

Early one morning, I took off thinking that my hometown of Hamlin was only 130 miles away and I could make it down there in only half an hour. I had about two hours of fuel. I followed the Ohio River into Huntington, West Virginia, then banked south across the thickly-wooded rolling hills. Hamlin looked a lot smaller from the air, although even on the ground it was only a few city blocks. I could pick out streets and my high school, but I had trouble finding my house. It was about seven in the morning when I kicked everything wide open on that P-47 and dived on Main Street, shooting across town at 500 mph. Then I pulled up, did some rolls, and came in again just over the tree tops. That night, back at Wright Field, I called home. I think if I had been there, my folks would've shot me. I was accused of wrecking the town and causing such fright to one old lady that she had to go to the hospital. One farmer claimed I blew down his entire crop of corn; another complained that I terrified his horse while he was plowing, and ruined his crop. God knew how many cows and sows miscarried because of me. One old guy even insisted that I flew underneath his pasture fence. And everyone knew who was flying; I was Hamlin's only fighter pilot.

Anyway, I didn't stop. I buzzed Hamlin regularly and people gradually got used to it and actually began to enjoy the air show. Once, I even buzzed Grandpa Yeager's place. He lived on a small farm so deep in a holler that you had to pipe in sunshine. I spent a summer up there once slopping the hogs and hoeing in his garden. I flew to his place in a P-47, but

that damned holler was so crooked and narrow, I
couldn't get down in it. Finally, I discovered that if I
turned extremely tight around the hilltops and kept
my wing pointed straight at Grandpa's house, I could
corkscrew my way down. And sure enough, I saw
Grandpa standing on the front porch, shading his
face from the sun. I found out later, he called into the
house for Grandma to come out. "Adeline," he said,
"come out here. There's an airplane up there with no
wings on it." My wing was pointing straight at him
and he was looking only at the fuselage.

I got back to California on the day my squadron
flew from Santa Rosa to Oroville, the next stop on
our training schedule. That first day in Oroville, Mack
and I went over to the local gymnasium to try to
arrange a USO dance, a way for our guys to meet the
local girls. I remember walking the length of an enormous gym to a small office where a *very* pretty bru-
nette was seated behind the desk. Her name was
Glennis Dickhouse. She was eighteen, had just graduated from high school, and was holding down two
or three jobs, including social director for the town's
USO. I asked her if she could arrange a dance that
evening for about thirty guys. She looked so annoyed
I thought she might throw me out. "You expect me
to whip up a dance and find thirty girls on three
hours' notice?" Glennis exclaimed. I said, "No, you'll
only need to come up with twenty-nine, because I
want to take you."

Glennis did it. The Elks Club gave her their hall,
and it looked as if every available woman in Oroville
showed up. I took her, and she was both the sharpest-
looking and the best dancer there. I could two-step,
but we sat out anything faster; so we sat out a lot,
and it was tough to make small talk with her because she complained that she couldn't understand
my West Virginia accent. *"That's* how they talk in
your neck of the woods?" She couldn't believe it. But
I made her laugh, and that's always a good start.

I asked her out again, but I had to wait my turn.

She didn't lack for dates, including our squadron's physical training officer, "Muscles" Muldoon. Glennis was too young to take to a bar (I was underage, too, but being in an officer's uniform, nobody asked to see my I.D.), so we went to the movies and ate popcorn, and discovered that we had similar backgrounds and interests. She had been raised on a small ranch, and her Dad taught her how to shoot, hunt, and fish to help put food on the table. She was a great shot. Not only was she a champion swimmer and dancer, but she was also as tough and gutsy as she was good-looking.

Glennis was living alone. She stayed behind to finish high school when her parents moved to Oakland, where her Dad found a job in the shipyards. She held down three jobs—as secretary to the superintendent of schools, as bookkeeper for a drug store, and as social director at the USO. Hell, I couldn't help getting serious about a girl as pretty as a movie star who made more money than I did.

Mack dated her girlfriend, and the four of us spent the weekends together going on picnics, swimming in the Feather River, or hiking in the hills. Glennis had her own apartment, but some people in town did not think too highly of local girls who dated fighter pilots. Working for the school superintendent, she had to be careful, especially living alone without her parents. So, it wouldn't do for her landlady or anyone else to see me visiting. I used to climb out the back window and shimmy down a tree. One night, I slipped and crashed on to the back porch below, knocking over two garbage cans and scattering half a dozen cats.

By the time the squadron left Oroville (we were there only two months), Glennis gave me her picture, and we promised to write. We never talked about the future because in a few months I'd be in the middle of World War II. We would wait and see what happened, and try to get to know each other better through the postal service.

Sorry as I was to be leaving Glennis, I was glad to be leaving Oroville. I was in trouble at the base. There was a basic training school for cadets about twenty miles away, at Chico, and I flew over there one day and bounced those cadets right in the traffic pattern and began waxing their fannies in dogfights. They flew BT-13s, and one of them followed me back to Oroville and landed right behind me. I thought, "What now?" when out charged a furious bird colonel. He was Chico's commanding officer and he wanted me drawn and quartered on the spot. He accused me of busting through the traffic pattern, endangering the lives of his cadets, and disrupting his training program. Boy, he chewed on me. Then he blasted into base headquarters and began chewing on all our squadron's officers for allowing a menace like me to fly without proper supervision. So, moving on to Casper, Wyoming, for the final phase of our training, was welcome to me: I needed all the mileage that I could get between me and Chico airspace.

At Casper, the group commander led us in a simulated attack on a box of bombers, but instead of turning to the left, as he instructed us, he turned right and had his tail chewed off by another P-39. We were in such a tight formation that the tail pieces nearly knocked us out of the sky; but all of us chuckled watching the old man bail out.

We lived in drafty barracks with coal stoves. One freezing day, I came in and saw a bunch of guys sitting around the stove shooting the breeze. I walked up to the stove as if I had some coal in my hands and dumped it in. It was actually a handful of fifty-caliber bullets. I put the lid back on and then began to walk fast to get out of there. The guys detected something wrong in my actions and scrambled in every direction. One dove under a bunk, but the others ran for the door just as that ammo knocked off the lid in a big cloud of soot. They never trusted me after that. The word on me was, "Keep your eye on Yeager and your back to the wall."

Wyoming was great hunting. The ranges were full, and because of the war, no one was hunting those big herds of deer and antelope. We went out with carbines in weapons carriers. That's how I lost Ed Hiro, one of our squadron leaders. It was night, and we had about six deer in the back that I had shot. I cleaned them and piled them in the back of the carrier, and I was driving like a son of a bitch to get back to the base for chow. Hiro was sitting next to me when we skidded out, bounced across a ditch, and nearly turned over. I finally recovered and began talking to Hiro, but he didn't answer me. Damned if his seat wasn't empty. So, I stopped and turned around. I found him doubled up, holding his side, madder than hell about falling out and busting a couple of ribs. We laughed about that episode for months afterward. Ed was later shot down and killed over Holland.

Sergeant Miller, who ran the flight line, knew how to make antelope roasts and steaks. One day, I drew a map for Miller and a few other enlisted men, who left base before dawn, armed with knives, carbines, and a map showing the backroads to a place where I had seen thick herds of antelope. I took off in a P-39 and began herding the antelope toward the road where Miller and his boys stood waiting. I charged one of the guns to fire one shot at a time and laid about ten antelope right at their feet. Roast would be the main course at the big squadron blowout before we left for Europe.

But before then, I almost bought the farm. Our fighter group staged a mock attack on a box of B-24s. I was indicating about 400 mph when there was a roaring explosion in the back. Fire came out from under my seat and the airplane flew apart in different directions. I jettisoned the door and stuck my head out, and the prop wash seemed to stretch my neck three feet. I jumped for it. When the chute opened, I was knocked unconscious. A sheepherder found me in the hills and tossed me across his burro, face down.

I remember the date: Friday, October 23, 1943. I was supposed to fly to Reno later in the day and meet Glennis at the Kit Carson Hotel. Instead, I was moaning and groaning in a damned hospital bed. My back was fractured and it hurt like hell.

OTHER VOICES:

Glennis Yeager

This was to be a great adventure. I bought my round-trip ticket to Reno a few days ahead, went out and bought myself a cute red hat and a striped gray skirt and jacket. I wore white gloves and self-consciously carried an overnight case. I got down to the depot just as the train pulled in, and, to my horror, I discovered that it was a freight train. I approached the station master, showed him my ticket, figuring the freight train would pull out, and a passenger train, most likely right behind it, would pull in. Instead, he took me by my dainty gloved hand and walked with me down the station platform to the last car attached to the freight. It was a caboose. I was furious. "You sold me a ticket to ride in *that*!" I shouted. He had. There were no passenger trains between Oroville and Reno; it was a caboose or walk. So I sat in the caboose with an elderly brakeman, who must've thought I was crazy, but who shared his egg-salad sandwiches and thermos of coffee through the long, six-hour ride.

We arrived in Reno about three in the afternoon. I took a taxi to the Kit Carson Hotel, where I had reservations in my own name. I was very nervous and self-conscious, half expecting to meet somebody I knew from Oroville. The room was nice. I unpacked, and with time on my hands before Chuck arrived, I decided to go out and take a walk. There was a jewelry shop down the street from the hotel, and I bought myself a small pair of aviator's wings, with tiny jewel chips in it. (I still have it.) Then I went back to the room to wait. Five o'clock, no Chuck. Six o'clock, no Chuck. He told me he'd be there before five. By seven, I was fuming, beginning to wonder if he would arrive at all. I thought, "How low can you sink, standing up a girl who has suffered through a six-hour ride in a caboose to shack up with you for a weekend?" Shortly before eight, I telephoned to his base in Casper. I got the runaround. No one would tell me anything about him because I wasn't a relative. Somehow, I got through to one of the boys in his squadron, and he told me what had happened that day: Chuck bailed out and was in the base hospital. He hurt his back, but he was okay.

I really don't know why Chuck appealed to me so much, but obviously he did. He was very skinny in those days, although my girlfriends thought he was cute. At first he was unsure of himself around me, quite shy and a little intimidated. And his grammar was just atrocious; with his West Virginia accent, I barely understood every third word he spoke. Of course, I was very young, and those were dramatic times—all those young men preparing to go off to war. I had dated a few soldiers, but never a fighter pilot. I think that really impressed me, even if he was the most junior officer in his squadron. But, also, I sensed that he was a very strong and determined person, a poor boy who had started with nothing and would show the world what he was really made of. That was the kind of man I hoped one day to marry.

What to do? I called the Reno train station and found that a train for Oroville would be leaving in an hour. I was so low, so disappointed and upset, that I couldn't endure the idea of spending the night in that hotel room—our little love nest—without Chuck. So I checked out and took a taxi to the station. There it was: the same freight and caboose, waiting for me. That train ride home was the longest, most awful and miserable experience of my young life.

A few weeks later, we finally got together on his final weekend at Casper, before they shipped out for overseas. I flew up on a commercial airliner. The entire group, all three squadrons, had a big party in a downtown hotel in Casper. Chuck's back was still bothering him quite a bit, but he made light of it and we had a great time. He had gone hunting and killed nearly a dozen antelope, and they served antelope steaks. I danced with everyone in his squadron. The men were quarantined, confined to the base following the party until they shipped out on Monday morning. Chuck sneaked out to stay with me. When I returned home and went to work, one of the girls looked at me rather strangely. "What on earth happened to you?" she asked. "Look in the mirror." My face was a mass of tiny red pimples. I had chicken pox. I had to laugh thinking that through Chuck I had spread chicken pox among all those quarantined fliers.

Chuck called me the day he left. As the maintenance officer, he stayed behind for a few days to help pack and move equipment. He said he had loaded five hundred pounds of Christmas candy to give to children into the washing machines they were taking to England. Then he left for New York to catch up with the squadron. He wrote from England to say they had sailed over on the *Queen Elizabeth*. He wrote regularly, telling me he had named his fighter, *Glamorous Glen*. He sent me his paychecks in war bonds to hold for him. We both agreed to see other people, but the only one special to me was in England.

ON THE RUN

Free-falling. Flat on my back. Spinning from 16,000 feet. Velocity doubling each second. Hold off. Get below clouds where krauts can't see chute. Yank that cord now, you're dead. Germans strafe guys floating down. Clouds whisk past. French countryside filling horizon. Even so, wait, goddamn it. Ground rushing up. Occupied territory.

Two fingers grip chute ring.

A canister of carbon dioxide hooked to my Mae West bangs close to my head. It's tethered to the dinghy we sit on in the cockpit, and the dinghy, which the CO_2 inflates if we go down in the Channel, flaps in the wind like an enormous doughnut. I unclip the canister and the dinghy; they fall away.

Corner of my eye—ground closing in. Smell forests and fields below.

Now.

I yank the ripcord ring.

The parachute blossoms, braking my fall, and I'm rocking gently in the winter sky. Below me, the hills and fields are crawling with Germans. I see the black smoke from my airplane wreckage and sweat the slow ride down. I'm easy target practice from the ground.

I hear a dogfight raging far above me—the chattering machine guns and roaring engines of dozens of fighter planes spinning across the sky above a dull gray cloud deck. I'm dropping down over southern France on a deceptively peaceful countryside. I work the shroud lines toward a pine forest.

Trees rush up at me. I reach out and grab on to the top of a twenty-foot pine. I bounce a couple of times on that limber sapling, leaning it over to the ground, just as I did as a kid in West Virginia, when we'd ride pines for miles through the woods. In only seconds, I'm six inches from the ground; I step down, gather in my parachute to use later as a shelter, and limp off into the woods. There's blood on my pant leg, blood on my torn leather gloves, and blood dripping down the front of my flying jacket from my head.

The woods are dark and still, but even as I move deeper into them, I hear the distant rumble of army vehicles and the sounds of voices shouting in German. They pick you up fast in occupied territory, before the locals can hide you. The bastards saw me coming down.

It is slightly past noon on Sunday, March 5, 1944, and I'm a wounded, twenty-one-year-old American fighter pilot, shot down and on the run. After only eight combat missions, I'm now "missing in action," World War II shot out from under me by the twenty-millimeter cannons of a Focke-Wulf 190. The world exploded. I ducked to protect my face with my hands, and when I looked a second later, my engine was on fire, and there was a gaping hole in my wingtip. The airplane began to spin. It happened so fast, there was no time to panic. I knew I was going down; I was barely able to unfasten my safety belt and crawl over the seat before my burning P-51 began to snap and roll, heading for the ground. I just fell out of the cockpit when the plane turned upside down—my canopy was shot away.

I treat my wounds in deep brush. There are shrapnel punctures in my feet and hands from the shells that hit around my cockpit; I've got a hole in the lower part of my right calf from a fragment that tore through my fleece-lined boot, and a gash on my forehead from banging against that CO_2 canister when I fell out of my dead airplane. I sprinkle sulfa powder on the leg wound and bandage it, then study a silk map of Europe that is sewn into our flight suits. I'm about fifty miles east of Bordeaux, near the town of Angoulême, where our bombers had blasted a German airdrome five minutes before I was shot down.

Man, I can't believe how fast luck changes in war. Just yesterday I landed back in England after scoring my first kill over Berlin. The weather was stinking, but I spotted a Messerschmitt Me-109 below me, dove on him, and blew him to pieces. Today some kraut is drinking mission whiskey, celebrating hitting me. Flying as tail-end charlie, I never had much of a chance. Our squadron of eighteen Mustangs took off from our base on the British coast to escort B-24s on their bombing run. Sixteen Mustangs, four flights of four, provided air cover; the two extras joining the mission only if there were aborts. I was an extra and when a Mustang from Captain O'Brien's flight of four turned back over the Channel with engine problems, I pulled in as the fourth plane— the tail-end charlie. Krauts attack from above and behind, and it's the last tail that gets hit first. I saw the three Focke-Wulf fighters diving at me, and radioed a warning to O'Brien, "Cement-Green leader, three bogies at five o'clock. Break right." We turned sharply to meet the bastards head-on. As I turned, the first Focke-Wulf hammered me.

I study my escape map, trying to figure my best route across the Pyrenees into Spain. The deep mountain snows should begin melting by late spring; if I can stay clear of the Germans, I might be able to contact the French underground for help. There would be no help if these were German woods. I'd wind up a POW, or, worse, fall into the hands of angry farmers who'd rather use axes and pitchforks than take prisoners. All of us carry forty-five-caliber automatics; mine is gripped in my right hand.

Even now, in shock from being shot down, cold and scared, I figure my chances are good for coming out of this alive. I know how to trap and hunt and live off Mother Nature. Back home, if we had a job to do, we did it. And my job now is to evade capture and escape.

I can survive in these woods for as long as it takes to keep the damned Germans from finding me and hauling me off to a POW camp. But whatever happens, for me the war is over. If I make it over the Pyrenees and manage to get back to England, I'll be sent home. No more combat—a rule meant to protect the French underground from pilots they assisted, who might later be shot down again and tortured by the Gestapo into revealing escape networks. So far, none of the guys shot down in my squadron have been able to make it back.

Our commanding officer, Capt. Joe Giltner, was shot down on a strafing run near Antwerp. Joe bailed out, tried to evade the Germans and get to the coast. But his wounded foot hurt so much he was forced to hobble. Finally, he sat down, undid his boot, and discovered the cause of his pain when his shot-off big toe plopped on the ground. The Germans captured him. Because I was a junior officer, but a good pilot with exceptional eyes, I flew my first missions as wingman to the group commander, Col. Henry Spicer, a daring pilot with bristling mustaches, who loved to dogfight and could care less about the personal risks. Spicer smoked a big briar pipe, and on the return home, he always dropped down to below 12,000 feet, unhooked his oxygen mask, and had himself a smoke. As his wingman, I dropped down with him right over

Paris. German flak guns began pounding at us, but I could see Spicer in his cockpit tamping his tobacco and lighting his Zippo. We were practically over the rooftops when tracers flashed by my canopy. I spoke up into my mike: "Christ, Colonel Spicer, we're gonna get shot down." I saw him chuckle through a cloud of pipe smoke. "Relax, laddie," he replied. "Those bastards couldn't hit a billboard." Colonel Spicer was later shot down by a burst of white flak near the French coast, after he had descended to 12,000 feet to light that damned pipe. He bailed out over the Channel, but the Germans picked him up.

I decide to stay put in the heavy brush until dark. Several times I hear low-flying planes—Germans hunting for me. I'm sweating, but stay well-hidden under thick brush. I saw a lot of farmland coming down, and at night I'll pop out of these woods long enough to raid some turnips and potatoes. I figure a French farmer is no match for a hungry hillbilly. Before dark, it begins to rain, and there are no more search planes. I eat a stale chocolate bar from my survival kit. Then, wet and cold, I huddle under my parachute and try to sleep. I doze on and off but at first light, I'm wide awake, gripping my pistol.

I peek out and see a woodcutter shouldering a heavy ax. I decide to rush him from behind and get that ax, killing him if necessary. I jump him and he drops the ax, almost dead with fright. With eyes the size of quarters, he stares at the pistol I'm waving in his face. He speaks no English, so I talk at him like Tarzan: "Me American. Need help. Find underground." He jabbers back in excited French, and if I understand right he tells me he will go get somebody who speaks English. I read his face, which is scared but friendly. He grins and nods when I say I'm an American. Puts a finger to his lips to whisper, "Boche," then hurries off into the forest, after signaling to me to stay hidden and wait for him to get back. I keep his ax and watch him run off; then I move across the path into a stand of big trees, wondering if I should take off or wait for him. Can I trust the guy?

Long before I see them, I hear returning footsteps. Definitely more than one person, but whether they are more than two, I can't tell. It's been more than an hour since that woodcutter took off. I move back into the stand of trees and drop down. My pistol is pointing at the path. I won't get very far if he's brought a squad of German soldiers. I'm burrowed into the wet ground, my heart thudding like a five-hundred-pound bomb as the footsteps stop. My impulse is to turn tail and run, but I check it. Then I hear a voice calling to me in a whisper. "American, a friend is here. Come out." I can't see them and it takes all my courage to slowly pick myself up. I'm on the opposite side of the path from where the woodcutter left me. My .45 is aiming at the back of an old man staring into the brush. The woodcutter is with him. Silently, I move forward.

OTHER VOICES:

Glennis Yeager

Chuck wrote regularly from England a couple of times a week. There were long delays getting his squadron combat-ready and he was frustrated. But after three months or so, he began seeing action. I had one letter in which he said they had finally flown over the Channel on a routine sweep to get combat experience, but then his letters stopped. I had no word from him for many weeks. Then one day his mother called to tell me they had been notified by the War Department that he was missing in action. She was a religious woman and said she was praying as hard as she knew how that he would be all right. She called me because Chuck had written to her saying that I was the girl he planned to marry. He had never told me that. The fact that the telegram said he was missing, not killed, was at least something to cling to. After that, I called her every week, eager to hear news, trying to bolster her spirits and mine. But I didn't have much hope. I figured Chuck was gone.

The old man leads the way through the deepest, darkest part of the woods. German patrols are all around us, hunting for me. Several times we think we hear distant voices and scramble to hide in the brush. But soon we are circling a clearing, staying in the shadows of the pines, and I see a two-story stone farmhouse. The old man nudges me, bends low, and runs across the open field toward the house. I follow him, expecting to hear rifle shots any moment. I forget my wounded leg and *move*. He leads me to the back of the house and I follow him into a barn, and up a ladder to the hayloft. He opens a door to a small room used to store tools and pitchforks, and pushes me in. Then he shuts the door, locks it, and begins pitching hay against my hiding place. I'm drenched in sweat. The small room is almost airless and pitch dark with barely room for me to sit. I'm trapped in this damned place and begin to wonder whether or not I've been trapped by the old guy: made a prisoner while he runs to get the Germans and maybe pick up a cash reward. I argue with myself about that lousy possibility, but not for long: there are German voices in that barn, and I hear them climbing the ladder to the hayloft.

My automatic is out, my finger on the trigger. The sounds are muffled but definite: they're rummaging in the hay, maybe stabbing into it with bayonets like in a war movie. I don't know how long I sweat it out, but straining to hear, I hear nothing. I never hear them leave—if they have. Maybe they are just sitting out there, having a smoke, and playing a nasty game with me.

They come for me several hours later. I hear the sounds of hay being moved; by then, the .45 feels like it weighs fifty pounds and it takes both of my aching hands to hold it. Before he opens the door, the old man wisely whispers: "It's me. You're okay. They're gone."

When he unlocks the door, I don't know whether to hug him or shoot him. I've no idea what's going on. We move quickly from the barn into the farmhouse, and I'm amazed to see it is already dusk. He leads me up a flight of wooden stairs to the second floor, and we enter a bedroom where a woman is sitting up in bed, wrapped in a shawl and surrounded by medicine bottles. She's about fifty-five, with keen, intelligent eyes, and when she sees me, she begins to chuckle. "Why, you're just a boy," she exclaims. "My God, has America run out of men already?" I tell her most pilots are young and that I'm twenty-one. She speaks perfect English and begins to question me—my name and background. I shake my head when she asks me if I'm married, and her eyes narrow. "What about that?" she asks, pointing to my high-school ring, which I wear on my right hand, where Europeans wear wedding rings. I explain and she seems satisfied. "We must be very careful," she says. "The Nazis are using English-speaking infiltrators to pose as downed American fliers."

She's satisfied that I'm not a German, although my West Virginia accent puzzles her. "Our people will help you," she says, "but you must do exactly what you are told." If the Germans catch us, I would be sent to a prison camp, but they would be pushed against the stone wall of the farmhouse and shot on the spot. I'm taken down to the kitchen where a young girl feeds me soup, bread, and cheese, my first meal in more than twenty-four hours; I wolf it down. Later that night the village doctor climbs the ladder to the hayloft and I'm let out of my dark little cell long enough for him to pick the shrapnel from my hands and feet. The shrapnel puncture in my lower calf is not very deep. When he's done, the doc makes a little speech in French, probably saying, "Hey, kid, your wounds are the least of your problems."

I stay in the tiny store room in the hayloft for nearly a week, although each day I spend more time outside than in. The Germans have seemed to lose interest in finding me; there are fewer patrols now. Maybe they're hoping that if they stop looking so hard, I'll become careless and fall into their net. And it nearly happens that way. One sunny morning, I climb down the ladder and venture out of the barn only to dive for cover when a Focke-Wulf comes roaring over the treetops.

It's a pretty farm, and I feel homesick. Late one night the doctor returns, hands me civilian clothes, and tells me to put them on. "We take a little journey," he says. We set out on bikes; I have an ax strapped to my back like any other French woodcutter. We travel for hours in the dark on empty country roads. I have forged identity papers and if stopped by a German patrol, I'm to let the doctor do the talking. We travel together for two days, biking most of the night, resting in various farmhouses during the day, until finally we reach the village of Nerac, a few miles from a more famous town named for its cheese, Roquefort. It's dark when we enter a farmhouse. The farmer's name is Gabriel, a huge guy with a thick, black mustache. The doc says good-by, and Gabriel takes me out back to a shed that will be my home for the next few weeks. If my kids ever ask how I spent the war, I'll have to tell them the truth: hiding in closets and sheds. Gabriel has a wife and a young son, and from time to time, I'm allowed to sneak into the house and share their family meal.

"We loove Americains," his wife tells me. I think she learned that piece of English just for me.

Gabriel's farm is right on a main road. As the days drag, I begin to get restless and bored—and a little careless. One day, fed up with my shed, I sit under a sycamore tree in the front yard, and before I can get up or get away, a troop of German soldiers marches around the bend. They pass not ten feet from where I'm sitting under that tree. Gabriel sees this and nearly dies from fright. He says the French equivalent of "God almighty, fella, what in hell are you doing?" In English, he says, "Stay in hide. Otherwise, me and you." He scrapes a finger across his throat. I nod and apologize. His young son likes to play ball and sometimes we kick the ball to one another behind the shed. But mostly I just stay in hiding, wonder what's happening to my squadron, write letters to Glennis in my head, and sleep a lot.

One night, well after dark, I leave by foot with Gabriel as my guide. We move deep into the pine forests, and after two days of mostly steep uphill climbing, Gabriel tells me to wait while he goes on alone. I wait for him most of a day and begin to wonder whether I've been deserted. But when he finally returns, he's with a group of heavily-armed men wearing black berets and bandoliers of rifle cartridges strapped across their chests. I don't have to be told who these guys are. These are the Maquis, the French resistance fighters who live and hide in these mountain pine forests by day and blow up trains and bridges by night.

I'm to stay with them, Gabriel tells me, until the snow thaws in the high mountains. Then they will help me cross over into Spain. Until then, they have work that I can do to help them.

Robert is the commander of our Maquis group. He speaks fairly good English. He tells me he's a lawyer from the town of Eauze and has been in the resistance for two years, most of them spent hiding from the Germans in these pine forests. I count twenty-six guys in his group, including a few really tough old birds with rosy cheeks who can hike longer and carry heavier loads than many of the younger men. Practically none of the group speaks any English, and I can understand only a few words of French, but they are friendly toward me, smiling and nodding each time our eyes meet. They know these deep forests the way I know the woods back home: all of them were born and raised in this area and knew each other before they joined the Maquis.

It's a tough, dangerous life. Most of the time, I have no idea where we are. We are constantly on the move, making camp twice a day to eat and sleep, but never staying in any one place longer than a few hours. The Germans are always hunting for us, their Fiesler Storches skimming in low over the forest while we rush for cover under the biggest trees we can find. We're well-armed—British Sten guns, Spanish .38 Llama automatics—and I'd love to fire off a couple of bursts at one of those damned Storches, hit the radiator in its belly, and bring it down. But if the pilot radioed our location, we'd have the German air force bombing hell out of these woods in fifteen minutes. Of course, we never know for sure when we've been spotted by one of these recon planes, and our position reported. So, we stay as alert as deer, knowing that every step can lead to a German ambush. It has happened before in these woods, although it has usually been the Maquis, not the Germans, who have staged the ambushes—getting the drop on a German foot patrol, or wiping out a small motorized convoy.

The Maquis hide by day and hit by night, blowing up bridges, sabotaging rail lines, hitting trains carrying munitions or military equipment. Through the French underground, dozens of Maquis contingents like ours, hidden in the forests and mountains, are wired in to most of the towns and villages in southern France. Their people in the marshaling yards and train depots keep them fully informed on the latest movement of troops or munitions. But it is tricky because every village has its informers or double-agents. And from time to time, assassinations are carried out against these people, supporters of the pro-Nazi, Vichy French government. I wonder whether there are any double-agents in our group. Running around in the French woods in civilian clothes is not exactly safe duty for a downed American flier. If I were caught, I'd probably share the same fate as any of these Maquis—turned over to the Gestapo for torture-questioning, then shot. Traveling around with the Maquis, the Geneva Convention on the treatment of prisoners of war would not apply to me. But I need these guys if I'm to get out across the Pyrenees.

I'm not included in any of their nighttime operations. They are a close-knit bunch, and I'm definitely an outsider. Most of the time I don't even know what they are up to. I'm left behind with an old man who's the cook and a few others guarding the camp. My first day with them, for example, I led a tethered cow, which a couple of the guys had "borrowed" from a farm, while we hiked to a new camp. Later, I helped in the butchering, which somehow amused the Maquis. I'm the first American pilot they've encountered, and they're curious about what I think of the German air force. I tell them that the Focke-Wulf 190 is a damned good fighter, probably on a par with our own P-51 Mustang; but the Mustang, using 108-gallon wing tanks, can escort bombers and dogfight deep into Germany, and that is a tremendous advantage to the American daylight precision-bombing campaign. Although our intelligence has warned us that the Germans have recalled their best fighter pilots from the Russian front to fight against us over Germany, I tell them that the difference between the respective fighters is not nearly so important as the difference between the abilities of the pilots flying them, and that so far, the Americans have proved their superiority with a ten-to-one kill ratio.

Robert translates this, and everyone is smiling and nodding at what I've said, except for one moon-faced guy I didn't like the first moment I saw him. This moon-face I don't like or trust. He asks a question in French that causes Robert to frown and argue with the guy for even asking it. Finally, Robert puts moon-face's question to me in English: "If you Americans are as good as you say, then why do we see American planes falling out of the sky like hailstones—and why are you here with us?"

The son of a bitch!

We eat under the trees, our table a long board. They've made a huge kettle of beans and beef, from the cow we slaughtered. I look down the table and see moon-face stuffing himself with stew, his beret pushed down to his eyebrows. I get up, walk over to him, take off his damned hat, and put it down on the table. He's furious. He reaches to his belt, takes out his Llama pistol, cocks it, places it next to him on the table, and puts on his hat. I get up, pick up a Sten gun, unlock the safety, and stick the barrel against moon-face's nose. One flick of the trigger would fire off about thirty rounds. Moon-face turns chalk white. I grab the beret off his head and slam it on the table. The others choke not to laugh, because moon-face is a general pain in the ass, but finally everyone explodes. Moon-face manages a sick smile. His hat is on the table, and it stays there, too.

Robert invites me to take part in a supply drop operation. We walk for hours in the dark, and it's well past midnight when we stand in an open field, looking up at the sky. The guys light flare pots to illuminate the field. It's cold and overcast, and I hear the drone of a four-engine RAF Lancaster. The bomber makes a low pass while one of the Maquis signals with a flashlight. Then the Lancaster circles to the west, gains altitude, and on the next pass overhead, drops a fifteen-hundred-pound canister that floats down to us under two billowing parachutes. It lands with a thud. We rush to it, gathering in the chutes, and hoist the canister onto a wagon pulled by two oxen. The drop operation takes less than five minutes.

An hour later, we are crowded inside a barn, working by lanterns, as the canister is opened. We separate the contents: Sten guns, .38 Llama pistols, boxes of ammunition, packages of counterfeit franc notes, bread and meat ration stamps, bundles of plastic explosives, and all kinds of fuses and timing devices. I tell Robert: "I can help you with this stuff." As a kid, I helped Dad shoot gas wells with plastique explosives. To me, sears and fuses are a piece of cake. There are printed instructions in English attached to the fuse packages, but first the weapons caches have to be hidden in various haystacks and root cellars around the countryside. I'm put in charge of the explosive fuse devices. I take them with me back to camp and show Robert how to set them for different timings—two, four, six, or eight hours. And that will be my assignment for as long as I'm with these guys: Maquis fuse man. When they see I know what I'm doing, I'm put in charge of cutting up cords of plastique and attaching them to fuses—a terrorist bombmaker. The work is fun and interesting.

The Maquis live off the villages, not off the woods. The villages are dangerous, crawling with Germans and Vichy police, but guys slip into town to buy food, cigarettes, and medicine, using phony ration stamps and money. I'm amazed that no one is ever caught, or if they are, maybe I'm not told about it. But on a very wet afternoon in late March, Robert takes me aside to tell me that I'm to accompany two of the guys into town. He grins and slaps me on the back. "Don't worry," he says. "Just stay with the men." Then he turns his back and walks away. I'm not happy about it, but the two guys I am to accompany start walking into the woods, and I hurry to catch up.

We don't walk very long. There's a van parked

along a dirt road used by loggers; as we approach,
the back opens and a young guy motions for me to
climb aboard. I reach for his hand, climb in, and we
take off.

It's pitch black in the back, and my companion
speaks no English, but I don't have to be told that
this is it: we're driving south, heading toward the
Pyrenees. We drive for several hours before the van
lurches to a stop. It is early evening, but dark and
drizzly, and we are parked against a wall in what
seems to be a backstreet in some village. A Frenchman
quickly takes me across the street where another
truck is parked, its engine idling. The moment I hop
in the back, the truck takes off. There are four or five
other guys seated on benches, and nobody says a
word, mostly because they are too busy hanging on
while the driver barrels down twisting backstreets,
doing fifty or better. I hear the guy seated next to me
mutter, "Jesus Christ." I'm figuring I'm in with a
bunch of bomber guys who will be crossing the
Pyrenees together.

Soon the gears up front are constantly switching
between second and first as we begin to travel up
steep grades. It would be nice to be driven across the
mountains into Spain. A flashlight is switched on by
a guy seated at the end of one of the benches. He
hunches down on the floor between the rest of us.
He's a Frenchman who speaks good English. "We're
just outside Lourdes," he tells us, "heading into the
foothills." He distributes hand-drawn maps to each
of us, detailing our routes up and over. "You can
either go together as a team, or pair off. It will
probably take you four to five days to cross, depend-
ing on the weather. It's been rather mild, so I don't
think you'll encounter any blizzards. But it will be
rough—I won't deceive you about that. The most
dangerous part will be just before you cross the Spanish frontier. It's heavily patrolled by the Germans,
and there are all sorts crossing over—smugglers, ref-
ugees, military personnel like yourselves. Your best

bet is to cross over at night, as late as possible. We've mapped out a southerly crossing—the farther south, the better, because the Spaniards up north have a nasty habit of turning in American pilots to the Gestapo and collecting a few hundred francs reward. If that should happen, you can expect to be tortured to tell all that you know about us, then taken out and shot. So, please be careful."

I notice a pile of bulging knapsacks stashed against the wall of the cab. When we finally stop, well past midnight, in the middle of nowhere, each of us grabs a knapsack and climbs out. "You're at the starting point," the guy tells us. "There's a woodsman's shed about a hundred yards directly ahead. You can use that. But no fires and no talking. This place is patrolled. Start out at first light. Today is March twenty-third. With luck, you can expect to be in Spain by the twenty-seventh or twenty-eighth." He wishes us well and then takes off in the truck.

We spend what's left of the night shivering in the dark hut. By the first light, we set out in the rain, deciding to at least start out together and see how it goes. By noon, two of us have made it to the timberline in gale winds. The other two are lagging far behind, not even in sight. My companion's name is Pat. He's a lieutenant, a navigator on a B-24 shot down over France. The French provide bread, cheese, and chocolate in our knapsacks. Pat and I eat and wait for the others to catch up. We agree that if they can't hack it and reach us in half an hour, we'll go on without them. Pat is big and strong; we wait more than forty minutes, then push on together.

The Pyrenees make the hills back home look like straightaways. We are crossing slightly south of the central ridge that forms the boundary line between occupied France and neutral Spain. The highest peaks are eleven thousand feet, but we figure we won't get higher than six or seven thousand; the trouble is we are up to our knees in wet, heavy snow. We cross ridges so slick with ice that we cross them on the seat of our pants. At first, we rest every hour, then every half-an-hour; but as we climb into the thinning air, we are stopping every ten or fifteen minutes, cold and exhausted. The climb is endless, a bitch of bitches, and I've got to wonder how many of our guys actually make it across these mountains and how many feed the crows that caw overhead.

We sleep and rest when we can, using outcroppings to protect us somewhat from the constant, freezing wind. Our feet are numb, and we both worry about frostbite. The French have given us four pairs of wool socks. We wear two pair at a time, but our boots leak. By the end of the second day, we're not sure how long we've been up here; by the third day, we wonder if we are lost; late into the fourth day, we're almost ready to give up. We should be near the frontier, but low clouds restrict visibility to less than fifty feet. It's four in the afternoon, and we are so exhausted that we catnap between each step we take, staggering like two drunks. I'm thinking that this is the kind of situation that produces fatal accidents, when we reach the top of a ridge and practically bump into a lumberman's cabin. We approach the front door cautiously, my pistol out, but my finger is so numb that I doubt I could squeeze the trigger. The place is empty.

I just crumple on the floor. Pat takes off his shoes and hangs his soaked woolen socks on the branches of a bush. The two of us sleep side by side on the bare wooden floor. And while we sleep, a German patrol passes in front of the cabin. They see Pat's socks hanging on the bush out front. The bastards ask no questions. They just unsling their rifles and begin firing through the front door. The first bullets whine above my head and thud into the wall; I leap through the rear window, Pat right behind me. I hear him scream, and I grab hold of him and yank him with me as I jump on a snow-covered log slide. I'm spinning around, ass over teakettle, in a cloud of snow, and it seems like two miles down to the bot-

tom of that flume. We splash straight down into a
creek.

Fortunately, the water is deep. I surface and so
does Pat. I grab him and paddle across to the other
side. Christ, he's gray. He's been shot in the knee,
and he's bleeding to death. I tear away his pant leg,
and I can't believe it. It looks to me like they hit him
with a nine-millimeter soft nose bullet, a dumdum,
because it blew away everything. His lower leg is
attached to his upper leg only by a tendon. Using a
penknife, I cut off that tendon. In my knapsack is a
silk shirt that Gabriel's wife had made for me out of
my parachute, before I left their farm to join the
Maquis. I tear off a piece and tie it tightly around the
stump. Then I take the shirt and wrap it two or three
times around the stump and tie that. Pat is unconscious, but still breathing, and we're pretty well hidden from the Germans up above. I decide to wait till
dark and then somehow drag both of us back up that
mountain and get us into Spain.

Night falls early in the mountains that time of
year, and thick clouds bury the stars. I can barely see
the reflected ice and snow of the steep mountainside.
The going is rough and treacherous, dragging both of
us up that steep slope. At one point, not even halfway
up, I lose both my footing and my grip on the collar
of Pat's jacket, and we slide backwards more than
fifty feet, slamming against a boulder. If the slope
had been extreme, that would have been it for both
of us, but it was gradual and we weren't sliding fast.
It's very cold, but the low cloud deck prevents the
temperature from really dropping and glazing the
wet snow into a sheet of ice. And at least there is no
wind. I stop dozens of times to hear if Patterson is
still breathing. The truth is, I would be glad to let go
of my one-hundred-seventy-pound bundle, but his
breathing is regular, although weak. A few times I
hear him moan softly.

I think, "He's the lucky one. He's unconscious."
Every muscle in my body is hammering at me. I just

want to let go of that goddamn bomber guy and drop in my tracks—either to sleep or to die. I don't know why I keep hold of him and struggle to climb. It's the challenge, I guess, and a stubborn pride knowing that most guys would've let go of Pat before now, and before he stopped breathing. I keep going on anger, cursing the mountain that's trying to break my hump. The mountain isn't exactly trembling, but getting mad at it at least keeps my blood warmer. It's too dark to do anything but inch up, mostly crawling and hauling. I have no idea how far I am from the top, which is just as well, because if I did know I would probably quit right then and there. I decide not to stop and rest; I can't trust myself not to fall asleep and let go of Pat.

The strange thing is, I think I did go to sleep. One moment it is night, and the next, I panic, thinking I'm bleeding on the snow. But I check again and see that it is the rosy glow of sunrise firing the world. I haven't let go of Pat. It happens that fast: dark one minute, light the next. What happened in between, I'll never know, or care. Because we make it to the top. I can let go of him and stand up. We're on top of a glazed snowcap at sunrise.

I walk to the far edge and look down at a long sloping draw. Off in the distance, through the mist, I see the thin line of a road that must be in Spain. I'm standing near a rocky ledge and a cluster of dwarf pines. I break off a bough, then go back and fetch Pat. I haul him to the edge, check once more to make sure he's still breathing, then shove him over the side and watch him slide down the draw until he's barely a small dot in the snow. Then I hunch down, holding the bough between my bent knees, just as I did when I roller-skated down the steep hill behind my house, using a broomstick as a brake. I'd sit against that stick, and it kept me from breaking my neck. And that's what I do now. I hunch down as low as I can get, put my weight against that bough, and push off down the draw.

When I stop, I'm only about thirty feet from Pat. I crunch through the glazed snowfield, check him out, then give him another shove. He spins down another twenty feet. The draw slopes all the way to the road, so I keep shoving him down until the last fifty yards, when I haul him to the side of the road. By now, he is so gray that I figure he is dead. But there's nothing more that I can do for him. So, I leave him where the first passing motorist would see him. Then I take off, walking south. (I found out later that he was picked up by the Guardia Civil only an hour or so after I left him and was taken to a hospital where they amputated most of the stump. Within six weeks Pat went home.)

I walk south for another twenty miles until near dusk I reach a small village and turn myself in to the local police. I don't expect a hero's welcome, but I don't expect to be locked into a small, filthy jail cell, either. I want a hot bath, a hot meal, and a warm bed to sleep in for forty-eight hours; and as tired as I am, I'm just not going to spend this night locked in jail. They don't bother to search me, and I'm carrying my survival kit. It contains a small saw for just this kind of situation. The window bars are made of brass, and that good American steel blade zaps through the brass like butter. I find a small pensione a few blocks from the police station. The police know where I am, but ignore me. I eat two portions of steaming chicken and beans, soak for an hour in a hot tub, sleeping with my head propped on the enamel rim. Then I stagger to the bed and dive into it, asleep before I hit the mattress.

I was still sleeping two days later when the American consul knocked on my door. It was early afternoon on March 30, 1944.

THE ULTIMATE HIGH

OTHER VOICES:

Clarence E. "Bud" Anderson

(LEADING ACE OF THE 363RD, WITH 17 KILLS)

Chuck Yeager is my closest friend. Our bonds are firm and deep and were forged while flying together in combat. Flying Mustangs in World War II was the top of the mountain for Chuck, and for me as well. If you're a military pilot, that's why you're there—to fight and to fly.

He was a stand-out pilot and character from the day I met him in Tonopah. He flew like a demon and was always taking calculated risks that are the essence of his personality. We all liked to buzz, but Chuck buzzed a few feet lower than the rest of us. I saw him top off Pa Clifford's tree, a helluva flying feat, because green as he was in the cockpit, he knew exactly what he was doing. Any other young pilot would have probably augered in right then and there. He was aggressive and competitive, but awfully skillful, too. In combat, he didn't charge blindly into a gaggle of Germans, but with the advantage of having sharp eyes that could see forever, he set up his attack to take them by surprise, when the odds were in his favor. And when Yeager attacked, he was ferocious. But he was also a superb team player; he saw everything taking place around him, and in his calm and confident manner, helped a lot of guys out of tough moments. There wasn't a pilot in the squadron, including a few who didn't like him, who didn't want Yeager close by in a dangerous mission.

He once introduced me to Jack Ridley, his engineer on the X-l research rocket plane, as the only fighter jock who ever whipped him in a dogfight; well, if that ever happened, I'd enjoy remembering when. Yeager was the best. Period. No one matched his skill or courage or, I might add, his capacity to raise hell and have fun. His combat record is incredible: he was the first USAAF pilot I'm aware of to become an ace in a single mission—five victories. He was the first in our squadron to shoot down a German jet. And these and other feats were possible only because he was the first in our group to somehow make it back as an evadee.

It was at that point, when he returned from Spain and I came back from leave to volunteer for a second tour, that we roomed together and became close friends. Chuck certainly has his faults, but strangely, they often became strengths. I doubt whether any other evadee could have avoided being sent home. But Chuck is the most stubborn bastard in the world, who doesn't dabble in gray areas. He sees in black and white. He simply said, "I'm not going home."

Our friendship, in part, began as a natural gravitation between the two best pilots in the squadron, especially the two who were the most aggressive in combat and who had the keenest pairs of eyes. During our training days, I watched Chuck shoot a rabbit from about fifty yards with my pistol. You have to see the enemy to get them, or to want to get them. We'd see them coming from fifty miles away—the dimmest specks—minutes before anyone else. I'm proud to have been the leading ace in the squadron, but the truth is that once you begin running up a string of victories, the final total is largely a matter of luck, of being in the right place at the right time. Chuck never missed when he fired his guns. If the enemy was gettable, he got them.

When I think of what we lived through, and how young, wild, and crazy we were (we really thought that someone twenty-five was an old man), it seems to me a miracle that any of us survived. I never got over some of the friends I lost; I named my son James Edward Anderson, after Jim Browning and my wingman, Eddie Simpson. I still have bad dreams about the horror I witnessed and some of the close calls that left my feet shaking on the rudder pedals. Yet, in honesty, I admit that I enjoyed it, and so did Chuck. Maybe "enjoy" is the wrong word, but there was a total need for us to be in that place and with those guys at that particular time. Neither of us were war-lovers, but we loved to dogfight. We didn't mind killing German pilots, but we didn't relish it, either. The thrill was in shooting down his airplane.

Combat was the high point of both our lives. Chuck made his mark on history breaking the sound barrier. But deep down I think his combat experiences and accomplishments in World War II meant more to him. If he had done nothing more in his life as a man and a military pilot, he could have been satisfied with that.

When I returned to England in the middle of May, 1944, the guys in the squadron couldn't believe what they saw. Not only did they never expect to see me again, but I was twenty pounds heavier and brown as a hog in mud. I was the first evadee to make it back. "Yeager," Obie said, greeting me, "when are you gonna do things right? When you're shot down, you're supposed to stay down." My shoulders were peeling from the Spanish sun, while the guys were pale and skinny. Flying daily above the weather, they got sunburn circles around their eyes—contoured around the outlines of their oxygen masks and flying helmets—and looked like a pack of damned raccoons. When I handed out a bunch of ripe bananas I brought back for them, man, they were speechless; they hadn't seen a banana since we left the States. That's how I got so fat, I told them, eating bananas in Spain, while soaking up sunshine at a resort hotel. All expenses were paid by Uncle Sam, including civilian clothes, room, food, and booze. By the time I was finished, they couldn't wait to bail out over Spain.

Mostly, I was telling the truth. About Spain at least; I really didn't spend my time in France hidden out on the second floor of a whorehouse in Lyon. But I did have a room with a balcony in a resort hotel in Alma de Aragon, where there was nothing to do but sunbathe, eat, and flirt with the chambermaids for six weeks while the American consul tried to free six of us downed airmen from our hellish existence. Because of the war—which I heard about from time to time—the Franco government was short of gasoline, and that's how we were negotiated out: so many gallons of Texaco per evadee.

I was sent back to England to pack my bags: I was going home. No more combat. The regulations were strictly enforced to protect the underground in occupied countries who assisted Allied airmen. German intelligence kept dossiers on most of us and knew who had been shot down before; they'd go right to work on your fingernails if you were shot down again.

Of course you had to be crazy to want to stay and shiver at Leiston, which was three concrete runways surrounded by a sea of mud, and cold and clammy Nissen huts. The Eighth Air Force had stuck us where the sun never shines, sixty miles up the coast from London with only two miles of land between us and the gales blowing in from the North Sea. We huddled around coke stoves and shivered in sleeping bags. The locals in the nearby village of Yoxford resented having seven thousand Yanks descend upon them, their pubs, and their women, and were rude and nasty. Who would want to fight to stay in such a miserable place where you flew off every day to get your ass shot off, and existed mainly on beer and greasy fish and chips? Well, much to my surprise, I did.

In Spain, I looked forward to going home and marrying Glennis. But from the moment I arrived back at Leiston, I knew that this was where I belonged until I had done my share of the fighting. I felt like a bug-out artist. And the idea of sitting out the war as a damned flight instructor in Texas or somewhere tore me up. Guys like Bud Anderson and Don Bochkay were already double aces who completed their tours and then volunteered for more. I was raised to finish what I started, not slink off after flying only eight missions. Screw the regulations. And when I said as much to friends like O'Brien and Browning, they looked at me as if my brains had been boiled into oatmeal by the Spanish sun. Group put me in for the Bronze Star for helping Pat to make it over the Pyrenees, and my friends told me to take my medal and run. I was scheduled to fly to New York on June 25.

"No way," I said.

I sat alone in my room, staring at the empty bed across from mine, where a bare mattress was rolled, waiting for a new occupant. My roomie was gone;

Mack McKee had been shot down over Germany a few weeks after I was. Mack and I had stuck together all the way, from Nevada on. We even shared the same eight-decker bunks aboard the *Queen Elizabeth* and kept things interesting by sawing through the ropes holding those bunks, so when the top sleeper crawled in the sack, he broke through and started a chain reaction pileup that landed six others on top of the bottom sleeper. At Leiston, we outsmarted the gamekeepers and poached His Majesty's rabbits and pheasants in the nearby woods, frying them on our small coke stove. We bought a couple of wire-haired terriers from a kennel; I named mine Mustang; he named his Ace. The dogs were gone; because we both had our asses shot off, the guys thought they were jinxed. Mack was a bloody mess when he bailed out. He left one of his arms in the cockpit.

I told myself, "Well, that's war. That's how it is." But that wasn't much comfort. I felt like I had lost a close brother, which, in a way, I had. He had flown more than twenty missions and fought the good fight, which was a lot more than I could say for myself. Evadee rule or not, I figured the war had been cut out from under me before I could make worthwhile all those hard and expensive months of combat training. There wasn't a rule ever invented that couldn't be bent. So I marched on group headquarters and began my fight.

Without realizing it, I was about to take charge of my life and push it in a direction where everything that happened in later years was a logical outcome for a career fighter pilot who had compiled an outstanding combat record. If I had submitted to being sent home, I doubt whether the Army Air Corps would have been interested in retaining my services when the war ended. I would've been just another noncommissioned officer who had spent most of the war instructing young fighter pilots how to fly. Not very impressive. I would probably have been mustered out and my flying career abruptly ended. But I wasn't

consciously thinking about my future; I was just being
stubborn about the present. I knew the odds were
stacked against me, but in the end events and luck
came together for me, and one man—the only one
who could—decided my fate: Gen. Dwight D. Eisenhower.

I was brassy and pushed my way up the chain of
command at group headquarters, arguing my case.
And because I was the first evadee to make it back,
the majors and colonels I talked to were kinder than
they might have been and helped me to keep climbing the ladder by allowing me to go to London and
talk to the brass at Supreme Headquarters. Everyone
I saw told me I couldn't stay, but the brass enjoyed
meeting a very junior officer who refused to go home.
"We'd like to help," I was told, "but the regulations
won't allow it." While I was being passed around
among colonels and generals at SHAPE, the Allies
launched the invasion of Normandy on June 6, and
the London newspapers reported that the French Maquis were now openly battling the Germans in the
hedgerows of Normandy, behind the lines. "Well,
there you go," I remember telling a colonel at SHAPE,
"the Maquis are out in the open now, and there's no
way I can blow them to the Gestapo if I were shot
down again."

On June 11, I had an appointment with a two-
star general and was joined by a bomber captain
named Fred Glover, who had evaded back through
Holland, and didn't want to be sent home, either.
The general listened to our arguments, sighed, and
finally told us that only General Eisenhower could
decide the matter. "I think Ike would like to meet
you two," the general said. "I'll see what I can do."
He got us an appointment for eleven the next morning.

I woke up scared to death. My hotel room was
shaking from a roaring *putt putt putt*, and I rushed to
the window thinking I would see one of those German jet fighters I had heard about in trouble and
about to crash over central London. Instead I saw a

German V-1 buzz bomb directly overhead; even as I watched, the engine quit and the damned thing nosed over from fifteen hundred feet and began to fall. I hit the deck. There was a jarring explosion only a few blocks away. The first V-bomb attack on London had begun, and I figured that my appointment with Eisenhower would be canceled. But exactly at eleven, Glover and I were saluting smartly in front of the Supreme Allied Commander's desk in his map-lined office.

"I just wanted to meet two guys who think they're getting a raw deal being sent home," he said with a grin. I was so in awe, I could barely talk. "General," I said, "I don't want to leave my buddies after only eight missions. It just isn't right. I have a lot of fighting left to do." Glover, who was a pretty sharp college boy, did most of the talking, and Eisenhower kept nodding in agreement. Finally, he said, "I just don't have the authority to keep you here. That's a War Department regulation, not mine. But I can ask Washington if they will give me the authority to make the decision. That's all I can promise."

I returned to Leiston not knowing what to think. The guys were impressed that I had actually seen Eisenhower, and they figured that the odds were now in my favor. Meanwhile, they let me fly above England, practicing dogfighting with new replacements. Through attrition and losses, there were only about a dozen of us left from the original gang, and I was considered one of the old heads. I was flying over the base with three new guys when the control tower ordered me to lead the others out over the North Sea, near Heligoland, to provide air cover to a couple of shot-down B-17 crewmen in a dinghy awaiting rescue by a patrol boat. We headed out and found them bobbing in the swells. We began circling above them when I spotted a Junkers JU-88 approaching from the east. He was heading for us, probably to strafe the crewmen, and without even thinking or saying a word to the others in my flight, I turned toward him; when he finally spotted me, he turned tail, but I cobbed my engine and caught up with him right on the coastline of occupied Heligoland. German ground gunners were firing flak by him trying to scare me off, but I closed on him at about two hundred yards and opened up. He burst into flames and rolled up on the beach. I got spectacular gun camera film as the JU-88 exploded. And I received a spectacular ass-chewing when I landed.

I reported in to Ed Hiro, now a major and our squadron's operations officer. When I told Ed what I had done, he reminded me I was under strict orders to avoid combat. "Goddamn it, Yeager," he shouted, "can't you do anything right?" Ed took the gun camera film from my plane and gave it to Eddie Simpson, who had four kills. Eddie wrote up a claim and became an ace. We gave the combat time to a young guy in the squadron. As for me, I was grounded. I kept a low profile for a day or two, and then was summoned back to Hiro's office. I remember thinking, "Christ, what now?" Ed handed me a message filtered down from group. My travel orders home were rescinded. The War Department had allowed General Eisenhower to decide whether or not I could stay, and he decided in my favor.

Within two weeks, my tan was gone and I had lost the twenty pounds I gained in Spain. I was back to being skin and bones with two sunburnt circles around my eyes, a Leiston raccoon. But I couldn't care less. For me, the real war had begun.

On mission days, you're up at five-thirty splashing icy water on your face because there is no hot, trying to shave close to avoid any stubble that will chafe your face beneath the tight-fitting oxygen mask you'll be wearing for nearly six hours. It's cold and dark as you stumble out the door and grab your bike to pedal through the mist to the group briefing hut, where the pilots from all three squadrons are assembled—like you, barely awake. Another "Ram-rod" mission—escorting heavy bombers deep into Germany. The group leader briefs you and you jot down on the back of your hand three vital numbers: takeoff time, rendezvous time with the bombers, and the average course coordinates back to base. Then the intelligence officer takes over, telling us to expect heavy flak and possibly vicious fighter opposition in the corridor between Bremen and Berlin. We hope he's right about meeting fighters. The weather officer is always grim. The weather is seldom good, but no matter how bad, he predicts even worse, just covering his bet so that we can't later complain that we weren't warned about fifty-foot visibility or head-winds that blow you backwards. When the weather is really unflyable, we just don't go.

You bike over to the squadron operations shed to suit up. You put on your flying suit, your two pairs of wool socks, and then a pair of fleece-lined boots. You strap on your forty-five, then your leather flight jacket and your Mae West. You draw your parachute pack from supply, put on your leather flying helmet and goggles, then stand around and drink a couple of cups of coffee and eat a piece of hard dark bread spread thickly with peanut butter and orange mar-malade: your breakfast. No one talks very much. Before a mission, guys are pretty well closed into themselves, like players before a big game. We know that this lousy snack could well be our last meal.

You remember to pee—very important, because you'll be sitting in that cockpit for more than six hours, and it gets so cold at high altitudes that the elimination tube usually freezes solid. You're already cold and weary before the day has even begun as you climb up on a weapons carrier for a lift out to the flight line. *Glamorous Glen* always looks beautiful. She's a P-51 Mustang, the best American fighter in the war, equal to anything the Germans can put up against her. With her two-thousand-mile range, she is turning around the air war against Germany by protecting our bombers over the deepest targets. Her Packard-built Rolls-Royce Merlin engine with a two-stage, two-speed supercharger provides terrific speed and maneuvering performance—a dogfighter's dream. Loaded with fuel and ammo, she's a tricky airplane to fly, and also vulnerable. Get hit in your radiator and lose your coolant, and you are going down. That's all there is to it.

Sergeant Webber, your crew chief, is up on the wing, leaning into the cockpit. You ask him if anything is wrong, but there never is, so you crawl in and strap yourself to your seat. A thick piece of armor plating protects your back; behind that is an eighty-five-gallon tank of high-octane aviation gasoline. You look up at the sky, thickly overcast as usual, and check out the instruments and especially the oxygen system. You'll be flying at 30,000 feet most of the day. You're alert now for engine-start, hoping what you always hope in the moments before taking off: that the sky will be crowded with German fighters, that you and your buddies will shoot down all of them. You always get butterflies before a mission, although by now it is almost routine.

Our first mission, on February 11, 1944, we were all scared to death, even though it was a routine sweep along the French coast. I remember looking down and thinking, "Jesus, that's occupied territory down there." It looked really evil as the flak rose to meet us; I heard the drone of German radar on my own VHF radio and it sounded to my ears as if they were zeroing in on me personally. We didn't encounter any fighters that day, and I don't think we were too disappointed. But now, a mission without a dog-fight is like going to London only to find that all the women have been evacuated.

We take off at 8:00 A.M., taxiing by twos to the edge of the runway where the ops officer stands and waves a red flag every eight seconds. *Go.* I'll take off climbing straight ahead, while the guy on my wing will turn ten degrees for ten seconds to parallel me and provide space between us as we come up through the low clouds, bouncing around in prop wash and struggling to break out on top before ramming into one another. We all climb at the same power, 2,600 rpm, indicated airspeed of 120. We're all carrying the same full weight of fuel and ammo, so climbing at the same rate, we all begin popping out of the clouds together. The morning sun is dazzling, and Mustangs are forming up into flights of four. Your wingman slips in next to you, slightly to the rear, a new guy, and you hope he's good and knows what he's doing. His job is to protect your rear, stick with you no matter what, while you hammer German fighters. We are spread across the sky, three squadrons of four flights of four airplanes each, and to maintain radio silence you use visual signals to tighten up your four-plane flight. You rock your wings and the guys move in closer.

You clip your oxygen mask into place and begin climbing to 28,000 feet. The sun warms your face and shoulders, but outside it is sixty below zero, and the lower half of your body, in the shadows, is already cold and stiff. The small cabin heater keeps your right foot warm but your left foot is numb. You're sitting on that damned dinghy, which is a genuine pain in the ass. The cabin isn't pressurized, and at 30,000 feet you fatigue easily. You adjust your silk scarf, making sure its edges are higher than the rough collar of your leather jacket. You'll be looking back constantly to check your tail. "The German who gets you is the one that you'll never see." That's been drummed into us from the first day of squadron training.

We cross the North Sea, following the group leader in the lead formation whose responsibility is to get us to the rendezvous point with the bombers we will be escorting. The bombers take different routes to avoid flak concentrations. Exactly on time, flak begins drumming up at us. Without even looking down, you know you are over the Frisian Islands, off

the Dutch coast. They always fire four-burst patterns
that hit at the same moment. Over Dummer Lake,
farther south, they fire vertical clusters at increasing
altitudes. Once you know the flak patterns in various
places, you can practically navigate by them. You
can't hear the flak exploding over the drone of your
engines; and if you ever do hear it, you'll probably be
blasted.

We pick up our bombers southwest of the Zuyder
Zee, three boxes of lumbering B-24s, and provide top
cover. The bombers chug along at 200 mph, while
we, going at twice that speed, weave back and forth
above them, staying alert for any bogies diving at us
from above. The bomber boys claim to be winning
the war by blasting German industry to rubble; while
we claim to be winning it by an almost ten to one
kill ratio over the Luftwaffe. Big egos are at work on
both sides, although until recently we were not allowed to go lower than 12,000 feet to chase German
fighters. Stick with those bombers, were the standing orders. So, we're not exactly fond of bomber
boys, but we respect their guts. They take a terrible
pounding, and when one bomber goes down, ten crewmen buy the farm.

You know how it is going to be for this bomber
box this day. They're in the second or third wave,
hitting fuel storage facilities, and by the time they
reach the target there will be a dark cloud hanging
in the sky, looking just like a thundercloud—old flak
smoke—and those B-24s will fly straight and true,
lining up their bomb sights on the target, disappearing into that black cloud to catch hell. There's nothing they can do about it. And after they drop their
bombs and begin to turn toward safety . . . that's
when they get bounced by the Focke-Wulfs and Mes-
serschmitts. Then those bomber boys worship us
fighter jocks.

You stay alert, checking the skies above and behind. You're over German soil now, the most likely
place to be bounced. On your right is a P-51D, the

latest model, with six fifty-caliber machine guns instead of the usual four, and a slightly faster and more maneuverable airplane. *Daddy Rabbit* is painted over the engine cowling. The airplane is flown by Capt. Charles Peters, a buddy from New Orleans, who's flying his last mission. "Daddy Rabbit" is his nickname, and he's agreed to turn that beautiful P-51D over to you when this mission ends. Tomorrow it will fly as *Glamorous Glen III*. You keep Daddy close and check his tail almost as often as you check your own, which is why he agreed to let you have his airplane. "I know you, you son of a bitch," he laughs. "You won't let anything happen to me on my last ride. You want my airplane too much." Ol' Daddy is right.

A cloud of dark smoke looms above the target. The bombers head straight for it. One of them suddenly blows up in a fireball of bombs and gasoline. No chutes. You turn and catch a glimpse of hundreds of bomb flashes through the smoke and clouds, a moment of maximum alertness because those bombers will soon be turning and the squadron commander orders us to drop our wing tanks. You can't dogfight with wing tanks. You pull the release cable, but the damnedest thing happens: your tanks drop away but so does *Daddy Rabbit*. He drops like a damned rock, right out of the formation. Nothing hit him, you're certain of that, but he's falling to earth. You dive after him. "My engine quit," he says. It's one of those moments in war that is so horrible that it's actually funny. Daddy is falling to below 5,000 and you're right with him, on his wing, and the flak is coming up. His last mission and he's about to auger in. "Christ, I'm thinking about leaving this thing," he says. "Hold off," I tell him. "I'm gonna ride in that thing tomorrow. Let's figure this out." We go around the instrument panel, checking every possibility, while the damned ground fills the windshield. Machine gun tracers are flashing by.

"Hey, what about your fuel mixture? Go to emer-

gency rich and see what happens." He does, and his
engine suddenly comes alive; ol' Daddy zooms upstairs as fast as that Packard Merlin will carry
his homeward-bound butt. "I must've accidentally
knocked back my mixture control when I pulled the
wing tank release cable," he says when he can talk
again. It was a close call, but we laugh about it.
"Damn it, Daddy, you park that thing and hand over
the keys." My voice is shaky, too.

No enemy fighters are sighted this day, but no
combat mission is ever routine; by definition, the
outcome of any mission is unknown until you safely
land, and often the worst part is making it home in
terrible weather, sometimes in a crippled airplane,
fighting against fatigue and exhaustion. It's early
afternoon when you drop down to 3,500 feet above
the North Sea and unfasten your oxygen mask. The
cabin stinks of gas, oil, and your own sweaty body.
You've got a headache and you're starved. You reach
for a D ration chocolate bar that's hard as a brick
from the cold. You use the side of your jaw to bite
into it, and it tastes wonderful. Those damned gravel-
crunchers back at the base already had their lunch,
and by the time we land the chow hall will be closed.
We have an hour of mission debriefing with the intelligence officers before we are off for the day. By then
it will be three-thirty. If it isn't raining and we aren't
too tired, we'll pedal off on our bikes to Yoxford and
fill up on fish and chips. The chow hall situation
always pisses us, but we're usually worse to deal
with when we come back without scoring any victories.

You're about forty miles from the British coast
when you call in and request a compass steer. Sometimes Leiston is so socked in that we land at other
fields. Bud Anderson was once forced to land at a
bomber base that had the luxury of fifty feet of visibility; he came in, leading a flight of four, groping
for the runway lights, when he saw two Flying
Fortresses directly ahead and below. He almost landed

right on them. It can be terrifying, but you get used to it; like a motorist who makes it home safely in terrible weather, you just forget about it the minute you walk in the door. Anyway, you know the surrounding countryside like the back of your hand, so you line up your descent with landmarks like a lighthouse or a road or a plowed field. When it's really bad visibility, they shoot up flares and you corkscrew down to the edge of the runway. The miracle is we've only lost one guy landing—a stupid accident. He came in after finishing his last mission, shouted over his radio, "Tell Ma I'm coming home." He did a victory roll over the field and augered into a tree.

This time you've got a hundred yards of visibility and a light crosswind—a piece of cake. You taxi up to the hardstand, where Sergeant Webber is waiting, and turn off the engine. You see his disappointed look when he glances at the gun ports which are still taped shut. Another dry run. Your twenty-first mission since returning to combat without encountering an enemy airplane. It's like hunting for six hours in the woods and not even seeing a damned chipmunk. But you crawl out of that cockpit as stiff and tired as if you had taken on the whole damned Luftwaffe. Tomorrow, you might bag three or become a German's victory, but the routine of these long, tiring days is always the same. Yet, you enjoy it. Hard to believe, maybe, and harder to explain, but you really do.

That summer of 1944 was a dry gulch for those of us eager to mix it up with the Germans. The real fun of combat was at the end of a day of action, when we'd sit around in the Nissen set aside as an officer's club, drinking Scotch and eating Spam sandwiches while chattering like a bunch of bluejays—refighting our dogfights or refiring our high angle deflection shots that nailed a 109. Now, all we talked about was whether or not the air war was over. Paris was liberated and it seemed as if the Germans were ready to call it quits, at least in the sky. All they were sending up were buzz bombs, many of them fired from the Dutch coast and passing right over Leiston, en route to London. Some of them came in so low that they blew up against the hills near our base. It was an awesome weapon, but it couldn't win the war. Ed Hiro and a few others thought the Germans were biding their time, building up their strength to sock it to us in a few big punches. Whatever the truth, I was frustrated. I still had only one air victory officially credited to me, which was really amusing because I was now one of the four squadron flight leaders, the only one who wasn't an ace with at least five victories, and the only one not a commissioned officer. My new roommate was Bud Anderson. Andy was the best fighter pilot I've ever seen, with the eyes of an eagle and the instincts of a mongoose. We had the best eyes in the group, and could pick up specks in the sky from fifty miles away. And as he said, "Chuck, if we don't see 'em, they just ain't up there." Well, they weren't up there, and Andy and I were left to dogfighting each other to see who got to lead the flight home.

But we were still taking losses. Because there was no action upstairs we were ordered down on the deck to find targets of opportunity like trains and barges and motor convoys. That's how we lost Ed Hiro in early September. He was strafing German positions in support of the airborne invasion in Arnheim, Holland, when he was shot down on his last mission. We lost Eddie Simpson when he collided with another Mustang on the deck over France. I remember Andy and me climbing on the wing of Col. Don Graham's Mustang after a really hairy strafing run. Graham was our group commander and he looked in shock. Stubby Gambel was Graham's wingman and our friend. "Where's Stubby?" Andy asked. Graham shook his head. "I don't know," he said. "There were all these tracers. . . ." He stopped and stared at his propeller blades. One of them had a bullet hole the size of a silver dollar. He turned white. So, we lost Stubby, too; and by now there were only a handful left who had joined the 363rd the day it originated in Tonopah. Each loss of one of the original guys drew together those of us who were left; in fact, we were living together under the same roof, and we became so close that it was as if we were flying in our own separate squadron.

Don Bochkay was the old man. He was about twenty-five, a Californian who loved to tinker with cars. Silk panties or nylons were impossible to get in wartime London, and he had his mother send him some to use as bait. One night, five of us were in a West End pub getting drunk, while Ol' Boch made a play for one of the barmaids by giving her a pair of fancy silk panties. "Honey," Boch said to her, "you stick with me and you'll be fartin' through silk." That line became famous throughout the entire Eighth Air Force. London had nightclubs, and we'd stay in a hotel and chase girls and get drunk. We'd go there whenever Doc Tramp, the flight surgeon, thought we needed a rest. He watched over us like a damned mother hen. You'd have thought we'd race to London every chance we got, but we were afraid of missing something—like a big dogfight—on our days off. But once we did go, we had ourselves a blast. One time, Andy and I, more drunk than sober, raced down the platform to catch the last train to Leiston, which was just pulling out. We managed to toss our bags on board, but the damned train left without us. Doc Tramp would just shake his head when we got back from a three-day "rest" in London. We were in sorry shape.

Not that we didn't keep ourselves amused back at the base. We'd finish a night of boozing by dog-fighting on our bikes in the pitch dark until the night when Jim Browning went ass over teakettle and almost broke his back. Then the C.O. threatened court martial. All the Nissens attracted rats, and all of us had .45s, so it was worth your life to wander around at times. Obie O'Brien's Nissen was like a damned sieve, bullet holes everywhere. Obie was quick on the draw with a temper to match, and one night, after polishing off a bottle of Scotch with a few buddies, he marched on the chow hall, shot the lock off the food locker, and helped himself to a couple of hunks of corned beef. If I got hungry, I'd sneak out in the woods and shoot the head off a rabbit. And if the truth be known, I made a few "emergency landings" that summer in parts of France occupied by our troops. Once I flew back to base with a case of champagne in my lap. To a country boy it tasted like sody pop; I drank it celebrating my promotion to lieutenant. After turning me down three times because of the court martial on my record, a board of colonels finally agreed that I was commissioned-officer material.

I was still the most junior officer in our squadron because any other second lieutenant had seniority over me; rank meant nothing in combat, or should've meant nothing, but by early fall I was actually leading our entire squadron on missions, and there were several captains who were rubbed wrong being led by a new lieutenant. One of them was assigned to my flight of four, and refused to follow my orders. Flying combat is deadly serious, life-and-death stuff, and a flight leader is like a captain of a ship. His job is to spot the enemy fighters and order when to drop wing tanks, how and when to attack, and so forth. We were over Germany and this guy was flying as tail-end charlie, but lagging too far back in the rear, and ignoring my order to close up. So far back, he could be picked off by a 109 sneaking up on us and we'd never know it. Man, I got hot. I did a big barrel roll and came in behind him; he never saw me. Then, I fired a burst right over his canopy. The bastard saw that. He closed up immediately, and did what he was told. But I couldn't understand a guy like that: without discipline and teamwork, we'd all be killed.

On September 18, I led two squadrons in support of airborne landings in Holland. Our assignment was to provide top cover to C-47s towing gliders filled with combat troops. German flak and small arms fire were intense, and we sat up there watching those slow-moving C-47s getting hammered. Ten of them were blown out of the sky in minutes, and the ground was littered with smashed gliders. It was a bloodbath, and a part of me ached to get down on the deck and strafe hell out of those German guns; but another part of me was damned glad that our orders were to stay at 5,000 feet, well above the murderous flak, and escort the surviving C-47s out of there.

I was really shocked when group headquarters chose me to lead the entire group on a mission. I was only twenty-one, a new second lieutenant, not even worth mentioning when it came to kills. By then, there were more than twenty aces in the three squadrons comprising the 357th Fighter Group—I wasn't even close. But group noticed me. The captain filed a complaint against me for firing warning shots at him; we were both called on the carpet. He was sent packing, and I was complimented. I was aggressive and reliable, and while fighter jocks don't lack egos and a few guys might've thought they could outfly me, there was nobody in the entire group who claimed they could outsee me. Being out there in front, your job is to see the enemy ahead of anybody.

A few days later, I was assigned as group leader and led all three squadrons on a bomber escort mission over Germany. Andy ragged me by calling me "colonel." The group leader is usually the group's commanding officer. Although I acted pretty matter-of-fact about it (actually there wasn't that much to it: I was responsible for getting us to the rendezvous point with the bombers and positioning each squadron) I did manage to squeeze off a quick prayer we all used in tight spots: "Lord, just don't let me screw up." Anyway, I figured that as group leader, if there were any Germans in the sky, at least I'd get first crack at them. And that's exactly what happened.

On October 12, leading the group on a bombing escort over Bremen, I scored five victories—the first ace in a day.

I take credit for being plenty lucky. We picked up our two boxes of B-24s over Holland, and I positioned two squadrons to escort them, then took off with my own squadron to range about one hundred miles ahead. We were over Steinhuder Lake when I spotted specks about fifty miles ahead. "Combat vision," we call it. You focus out to infinity and back, searching a section of sky each time. To be able to see at such distances is a gift that's hard to explain, and only Andy and I could do it. The other guys, who had excellent eyesight on the ground, took it on faith that the two of us actually saw something far out there. This time, I didn't even radio to the others, but just kept us heading toward the German fighters from out of the sun. We were at 28,000 feet and closing fast. Soon, I was able to count twenty-two individual specks. I figured they were Me-109s, just sitting up there, waiting for our bombers. And I was right.

They were just circling and waiting and didn't see us coming at them out of the sun. We closed to about a thousand yards, and if their leader saw us, he probably thought we were additional 109s because he made no effort to scramble out of our way. In the lead, I was the only one yet in firing range; I came in behind their tail-end charlie and was about to begin hammering him, when he suddenly broke left and ran into his wingman. They both bailed out. It was almost comic, scoring two quick victories without firing a shot. But, apparently, the big shortage in Germany was not of airplanes, but of pilots, and they were probably under orders to jump for it in tight spots. (After the war, it was learned that a few of their leading aces had flown more than a thousand combat missions and bailed out more than twenty times.) By now, all the airplanes in that sky had dropped their wing tanks and were spinning and diving in a wild, wide-open dogfight. I blew up a 109 from six hundred yards—my third victory—when I turned around and saw another angling in behind me. Man, I pulled back on my throttle so damned hard I nearly stalled, rolled up and over, came in behind and under him, kicking right rudder and simultaneously firing. I was directly underneath the guy, less than fifty feet, and I opened up that 109 as if it were a can of Spam. That made four. A moment later, I waxed a guy's fanny in a steep dive; I pulled up at about 1,000 feet; he went straight into the ground.

That night at the officer's club, I took a pounding. The other squadron leaders were furious because I didn't invite them in for the kill, which totaled eight, all by our squadron. They sat fifty miles back with the bombers, listening to our radio chatter: "He's in flames," "Watch your tail," etc., while I ignored their request for our vector. Over beers, I told them the damned truth: "There just weren't enough krauts to go around." And Bochkay didn't let me forget that two of my victories were scored without firing a shot. He presented me with a pair of silk panties. He wrote across the bottom: HILLBILLY PARACHUTE. DROP THESE WHEN YEAGER GETS ON YOUR TAIL.

But the *Stars and Stripes* said it better in their front page headline: FIVE KILLS VINDICATE IKE'S DECISION. Group recommended me for the Silver Star.

Obie O'Brien

I was a flight leader, an ace with 5½ kills, and being young and competitive, I'd have given a lot to have eyes like Bud Anderson and Chuck Yeager. Hell, we heard them over the radio. "A gaggle of bogies coming in from down south," Andy might say. And you'd hear Yeager's flat twang: "Rhat, I been watchin' 'em." The others would be asking: "What! Where?" Five minutes later we'd see them. I'd ask that son of a bitch, "Chuck, how do you do it?" He'd grin and say: "Well, goddamn it, Obie, you should've seen them, too. They were practically dropping their wing tanks right on your canopy."

The guys trusted Chuck because he always knew what he was doing. He knew the difference between being aggressive and reckless. I remember flying back from a mission one day, and this green kid got on the radio, excited because he spotted a German fighter base below. Well, Chuck got on the horn with that kid and said, "You want to go down and hit it, I'll give you top cover." The rest of us laughed. The only way to survive strafing a fighter base was to take the flak gunners by surprise. Yeager might be a hell-raiser on the ground, but he was cunning in combat, with good instincts about what was a risk worth taking, and what was a no-win, impossible situation. If he said, "Let's give it a try," we went with him.

He knew he was damned good, but was low-key about it. If the weather was terrible and new kids were clutched about landing, Chuck would get on the horn and say, "Hey, no sweat. I know the way if you want to follow me in." And sometimes, when you were going balls-out—at full-throttle—in a dogfight and concentrating on shooting down an enemy, you'd suddenly hear, "Blue flight leader, visitor on your tail, break right." Hell, he wasn't Superman, but he kept his concentration and alertness in that cockpit. Nothing got by him. And in a dogfight, if he got on a German's tail, that son of a bitch might as well recite the Lord's Prayer.

The better pilots were all highly motivated to shoot down German planes; hell, that was the name of the game. We had more balls than brains and figured being outnumbered ten to one were acceptable odds. If you were good and lucky enough to be in the right place at the right time, you'd score victories. For quite a while Chuck was low man on the victory scoreboard, but then his luck changed; the Germans began to come up to challenge us and ran into a goddamn West Virginia buzzsaw. He'd never let up: as long as he had a few belts of ammo left in those guns, he was always looking for more.

ON THE DECK

"Blow jobs," the bomber crews called them, but no one was eager to be on the receiving end of the twin-engine German jet fighters that screamed down on our formations to quickly hit and run. The jets had a 150 mph speed advantage over the Mustang, but their pilots tried to avoid dogfights, concentrating instead on hammering the bombers. So, rarely did we encounter any jets. The word on them was that they were wing-heavy; the Mustang, with its laminar flow wing, could easily turn and dive with them, but in a level chase there was no contest; the Me-262 easily sped beyond gun range. Andy, for example, waxed the fanny of a 262, and was just about to open fire when the German pilot spotted him and left him in the dust.

German jet pilots were probably under orders not to get shot down in a dogfight. Some of their pilots were damned arrogant and didn't bother about dropping their wing tanks in a chase. They just teased around, let a Mustang get close, then cobbed the throttle and thumbed their nose. If one of our pilots got off a shot, it was a quick burst at long range. So, I could hardly believe my good luck when I looked down into broken clouds from 8,000 feet and saw three jets cruising about 3,000 feet below. I was leading a flight of four Mustangs, just north of Essen, Germany, and I dove after them. I fired a few bursts before losing them in the cloud deck. My gun camera recorded that I put a few bullets into two jets. Chasing those guys, I was a fat man running uphill to catch a trolley. I was doing 450, but they zoomed out of sight. I climbed back to 8,000 feet to search for my flight, but I couldn't find them, so I headed north, figuring I'd pick them up over the North Sea on the return home.

Meanwhile, I kept watch below, hoping I'd spot those jets again and get another chance at them. Instead, I saw a large airdrome with a six-thousand-foot runway and a lone jet approaching the field from the south at 500 feet. I dove at him. His landing gear was down and he was lining up the runway, coming in at no more than 200 mph, when I dropped on his ass at 500 mph. He never saw me, but the damned control tower did. Ground gunners began blasting at the lunatic American swooping right at them, who was trying to line up a quick burst and pull out of there. I came in full-throttle at 500 feet and fired above and behind the jet from four hundred yards. My hits slapped into his wings and I pulled up 300 feet off the ground with flak crackling all around me. Climbing straight up, I looked back and saw that jet crash-landing short of the runway, shearing off a wing, in a cloud of dust and smoke. I'd rather have brought down the son of a bitch in a dogfight, but it wasn't exactly an easy kill—one quick, accurate burst, with flak banging all around me. Group apparently thought so, too, because they recommended me for the Distinguished Flying Cross.

I was elated flying home, but shaky, too. That flak was damned close, and I always figured that if I busted my ass, it would be down on the deck rather than up in the sky. Dogfighting, there were thousands of feet of sky in every direction to outmaneuver an enemy airplane determined to destroy you. There wasn't much room for ducking on the deck, where one lucky shot could blow the radiator in your belly and bring you down. With only sporadic fighter resistance against our bombers, we had full ammo to strafe targets of opportunity on the way home. But the strafing missions I most dreaded were hitting airfields. Then, you had to hit fast, come at them from different directions and varying altitudes, and take them by surprise. God help your ass if you were a tail-end charlie in the last wave. By then, those ack-ack guns were ready.

A few days after shooting down that jet, I was assigned to lead the entire group on a strafing mission against Rechlin, the most heavily defended air base in Germany. Located in the suburbs of Berlin, it was the German Wright Field, where all of their latest aircraft were tested and maintained. Bombing operations had been ineffective; I was ordered to lead our three squadrons onto the deck to destroy their service hangars and any airplanes caught on the ground. The place was swarming with antiaircraft batteries, and we were relying on the element of surprise plus predicted low visibility to make it through. I wasn't a worrier; after months of flying combat, I was fatalistic. Hell, if I took off with a rough engine, so what? It would probably smooth out, but if not, I'd cope somehow. But the Rechlin assignment scared me to death.

I remember sitting in my airplane, warming up for takeoff, feeling clammy with a real premonition that I was taking my last ride. The weather was terrible at both ends, rain squalls and turbulent winds; and I had to figure a way to get to the target and then get out in one piece. I knew I was leading a lot of guys to their death, and there wasn't a damned thing I could do about it. Andy was scheduled to lead

the final wave of Mustangs in the attack, probably
taking the worst pounding of all. I was usually confident and gung-ho, but I found myself praying for a
mission abort. Man, I had the shakes: I did not want
to fly into the sky that day. And that morning, at
least, God turned out to be a West Virginia Methodist: we got an abort just as I began to taxi out to the
runway. Zero visibility at the target. I never wore a
bigger grin, and when I saw Andy, I hugged that son
of a bitch and we began to laugh like two crazy men.
We had the rest of the day off and all of us went out
and got falling-down drunk. Reichland was never
rescheduled.

It's a very different war at 50 feet off the ground;
you see everything, especially in winter, when cars
and trucks and people are easily spotted against a
blanket of snow. Coming in so low, my eyes once met
with the driver of a German staff car. I was coming
straight at him; one quick burst and that car disintegrated, four bodies tossed out on the icy road like rag
dolls. Another time, I spotted a five- or six-truck
German troop convoy; by the time I swooped down
on them, the troops had jumped out and were hun-
kered down in a roadside ditch. I opened up with my
six fifty-caliber machine guns and watched those sparkling butterflies dance right up the line in that ditch.
Before leaving, I hit their trucks. It was the first time
I had ever strafed troops, and I was surprised at how
quick and easy it was to take out an entire battalion.
Enemy troops were fair game: a driver in a jeep—
zap him. A soldier running through the snow—zap
him. But we weren't always scrupulous about our
targets.

Atrocities were committed by both sides. That
fall our fighter group received orders from the Eighth
Air Force to stage a maximum effort. Our seventy-
five Mustangs were assigned an area of fifty miles by
fifty miles inside Germany and ordered to strafe anything that moved. The object was to demoralize the
German population. Nobody asked our opinion about

whether we were actually demoralizing the survivors or maybe enraging them to stage their own maximum effort in behalf of the Nazi war effort. We weren't asked how we felt zapping people. It was a miserable, dirty mission, but we all took off on time and did it. If it occurred to anyone to refuse to participate (nobody refused, as I recall) that person would have probably been court-martialed. I remember sitting next to Bochkay at the briefing and whispering to him: "If we're gonna do things like this, we sure as hell better make sure we're on the winning side." That's still my view.

By definition, war is immoral; there is no such thing as a clean war. Once armies are engaged, war is total. We were ordered to commit an atrocity, pure and simple, but the brass who approved this action probably felt justified because wartime Germany wasn't easily divided between "innocent civilians" and its military machine. The farmer tilling his potato field might have been feeding German troops. And because German industry was wrecked by constant bombing, munitions-making was now a cottage industry, dispersed across the country in hundreds of homes and neighborhood factories, which was the British excuse for staging carpet bombing and fire bombing attacks on civilian targets. In war, the military will seldom hesitate to hit civilians if they are in the way, or to target them purposely for various strategic reasons. That's been true in every war that has ever been fought and will be fought. That is the savage nature of war itself. I'm certainly not proud of that particular strafing mission against civilians. But it is there, on the record and in my memory. Early in my tour, I heard that one of the guys had seen a 109 strafe an American bomber crew in their chutes. I thought it was bad practice in every way. Both sides at least gave lip service to a gentleman's agreement not to do it. And if I had to jump for it again, I could hope the agreement was being honored that day.

You didn't sit around brooding, because if you did, you'd never get through it. It could be tough playing God down on the deck, picking and choosing who or what to target in your gun-sight. For example, during D-day operations, Andy and a few others spotted a German Tiger tank entering a small French village. They strafed the damn thing, but their bullets just bounced off that thick armor plating. The tank pulled up next to a little hotel. Our guys were carrying bombs and one of them told Andy, "I think I can dive bomb and get a direct hit." Well, he missed and blew that hotel into the next province. He was sick about it; that incident haunted him for a long time. Don Bochkay came in on a freight train as it was passing through a French village. Just as he began to strafe, he saw the engineer jump down from the locomotive and run for his life. That train was packed with munitions and when it blew, the village was demolished.

Targets of opportunity meant legitimate military targets, which should have been a clear mandate, but often wasn't. Three of our guys came in over a clearly marked German hospital train. They were passing overhead when the sides of one car slapped down and machine guns opened up, knocking down one of them. During the Normandy invasion, the Germans used church belfries as observation posts, and stored ammo and bivouacked troops in school houses. They were ruthless about hiding behind civilians in occupied territory, while we became calloused in order to get the job done. And over Germany, where you would be killed or taken prisoner if forced to bail out, there were hundreds of scared young pilots free-lancing down on the deck every day—hitting fast and getting the hell out, and maybe not being too particular about what they shot at.

That's why I loved to dogfight. It was a clean contest of skill, stamina, and courage, one on one.

FLYING HIGH

On rainy nights in the flight leader's Nissen, we'd listen to Glenn Miller records on the phonograph and toast grilled cheese sandwiches on the coke stove. If we had a good day at work, we heated a poker red hot and branded another swastika on the front door. Each swastika represented a dogfight victory, and by the end of my tour, that door displayed fifty. Four of us accounted for more than half the squadron's total number of kills. During the last week in November, I became a double ace with eleven kills by shooting down four German planes during an historic dogfight—the greatest single American victory of the air war.

Andy was leading the squadron and I was leading one of the flights of four. Our job that day was to escort Mustangs carrying a bomb and a drop tank under their wings for attacking underground fuel facilities near Poznań, Poland. We provided top cover, flying at 35,000 feet, while the bomb-carrying Mustangs cruised below. On German radar we were mis-

taken for a fleet of unescorted heavy bombers, and
the Luftwaffe scrambled every available fighter in
East Germany and Poland. Andy and I were the first
to see them coming; at fifty miles or more, they were
a dark cloud moving toward us. "God almighty, there
must be a hundred and fifty of them," Andy exclaimed. We couldn't believe our luck. Andy called
for a turn left that put me in the lead; we punched
our wing tanks and plowed right into the rear of this
enormous gaggle of German fighters.

There were sixteen of us and over two hundred
of them, but then more Mustangs from group caught
up and joined in. Christ, there were airplanes going
every which way. I shot down two very quickly; one
of the airplanes blew up, but the pilot bailed out of
the other. I saw him jump, but he forgot to fasten his
parachute harness; it pulled off in the windstream
and he spun down to earth. To this day I can still see
him falling.

A dogfight runs by its own clock and I have no
idea how long I was spinning and looping in the sky.
I wound up 2,000 feet from the deck with four kills.
Climbing back to altitude, I found myself alone in an
empty sky. But for as far as I could see, from Leipzig
to way up north, the ground was littered with burning wreckage. It was an awesome sight.

We found out later that we hadn't even attacked
their main force: the Germans put up 750 fighters
against what they thought was a huge bomber fleet.
They ran into two hundred Mustangs from three different fighter groups and lost ninety-eight airplanes.
We lost eleven.

I climbed to 35,000 feet and saw three small
specks way off and slightly higher. I still had plenty
of fuel and ammo, and I just began to turn toward
those specks, when I heard a familiar voice: "Bogie
down south." Only one pair of eyes could've spotted
me the moment I began my turn. "Andy," I asked,
"is that you?" It was. And crazy bastards that we
were, we raced toward each other and began to dog-

fight, happy as clams. He had shot down three. Andy led us home and it turned out to be one of the funny moments of our friendship.

We encountered unusually powerful headwinds, and after a couple of hours Andy assumed we were over the Channel and began his descent. We followed him down into a thick cloud cover and found ourselves directly over the antiaircraft emplacements on the Frisian Islands. I mean we could've walked home on that flak; the sky was black with it. And there we were, only 500 feet above those big guns. Man, did we cuss poor Andy. By the time we landed his ears were purple. And we kept at it for days. Hell, I still haven't let him forget that one.

That day was a fighter pilot's dream. In the midst of a wild sky, I knew that dogfighting was what I was born to do. It's almost impossible to explain the feeling: it's as if you were one with that Mustang, an extension of that damned throttle. You flew that thing on a fine, feathered edge, knowing that the pilot who won had the better feel for his airplane and the skill to get the most out of it. You were so wired into that airplane that you flew it to the limit of its specs, where firing your guns could cause a stall. You felt that engine in your bones, felt it nibbling toward a stall, throttle wide open, getting maximum maneuvering performance. And you knew how tight to turn before the Mustang snapped out on you, a punishment if you blundered. Maximum power, lift, and maneuverability were achieved mostly by instinctive flying: you knew your horse. Concentration was total; you remained focused, ignoring fatigue or fear, not allowing static into your mind. Up there, dogfighting, you connected with yourself. That small, cramped cockpit was exactly where you belonged.

You fought wide open, full-throttle. With experience, you knew before a kill when you were going to score. Once you zeroed in, began to outmaneuver your opponent while closing in, you became a cat with a mouse. You set him up, and there was no way out: both of you knew he was finished. You were a confident hunter and your trigger finger never shook. You picked your spot: slightly below, so you could pull up, lead him a little, and avoid being hit by metal when he disintegrated. When he blew up, it was a pleasing, beautiful sight. There was no joy in killing someone, but real satisfaction when you outflew a guy and destroyed his machine. That was the contest: human skill and machine performance. You knew when you killed a pilot in his cockpit from the way his airplane began to windmill, going straight down. Then, you followed him to the deck, flipping on the camera to record the explosion and document your kill. The excitement of those dogfights never diminished. For me, combat remains the ultimate flying experience.

Tactics? Keep the sun at your back and as much altitude advantage as possible; bounce the enemy out of the sun. Not always possible, of course, and sometimes you were the one being bounced. For every action there was a possible reaction, and with experience I learned to anticipate and outguess my opponent. I knew, for example, even while I was cutting him off that he would probably try to reverse himself, so I led him a little; if I was right, I had him. If I was wrong, I had to go back to work to get him. But, really, my biggest tactical advantage was my eyes. I spotted him from great distances, knowing he couldn't see me because he was only a dim speck. Sometimes he never did see me when I bounced him out of the sun; or when he did finally see me, it was too late.

In a sky filled with airplanes, I needed to keep my neck on a swivel to avoid getting hit, being shot down, or running into somebody. The best survival tactic always was to check your tail constantly and stay alert. Dogfighting was hard work. You needed strong arms and shoulders. Those controls weren't hydraulically operated, and at 400 mph they became extremely heavy. Without cabin pressurization, flying

at high altitude wore you out. And so did pulling Gs
in sharp turns and steep dives. (A two-hundred-pound
pilot weighs eight hundred pounds during a 4-G turn.)
After a couple of minutes of dogfighting, your back
and arms felt like you had been hauling a piano
upstairs. You were sweaty and breathing heavily.
Sometimes you could see a German's exhaustion from
the way he turned and maneuvered—another advantage if you were stronger.

Dogfighting demanded the sum total of all your
strengths, and exposed any of your weaknesses. Some
good pilots lacked the eyes; others became too excited and lost concentration, or lost their nerve and
courage; a few panicked in tight spots and did stupid
things that cost them their lives. The best pilots were
also the most aggressive, and it showed.

We quickly learned basic do's and don'ts. If the
enemy was above, we didn't climb to meet him because we lost too much speed. When in a jam, we
never ran. That was exactly what he expected. It was
important to always check your back when popping
out of the clouds: you could have jumped out in front
of a 109. We avoided weaving around cumulus clouds;
they're like boulders and you could have been easily
ambushed. And we were particularly alert while flying
beneath high thin cirrus clouds. Germans could look
down through them and see you, but you couldn't
see up through them. Whenever possible, we carefully timed our turns in a head-on attack, to avoid
being caught sideways and becoming a direct target.
We also tried to avoid overshooting an enemy plane,
which put you in front of his gun-sights; it was like
shooting yourself down. One of the guys once asked
Colonel Spicer, our group commander, what to do if
caught by a large force. "Rejoice, laddie," the old
man said, "that's why you're here."

Some of our guys fought that way. In the middle
of a vicious dogfight, I heard one of them say: "Hey,
I've got six of them cornered at two o'clock. Come on
up and have some fun." But one time I also heard the

most horrifying scream blast into my headphones. "Oh, God, they got me. My head, my damned head. I'm bleeding to death." That night at the officers' club, the shrieker showed up wearing a Band-Aid, a goddamned Band-Aid, taped to the back of his neck. He had been nicked by a piece of Plexiglas. So, our squadron ran the gamut. If you wanted to stay alive, you kept an eye on the weak sisters as carefully as you watched for Germans. The worst of them would get so shaken in a dogfight that they'd shoot at anybody, friend or foe. I remember how pissed we were when the worst pilot in the outfit became the first of us to score a victory and won a bottle of cognac. He was in a flight of four that got bounced by some Germans and crawled in behind his leader, only to discover he was on the tail of a 109 hammering his leader. He closed his eyes and pulled the trigger.

There were guys who became so terrified being in the same sky with krauts that they began to hyperventilate and blacked out; a few actually shit their pants. Some were honest about their fear and asked to be relieved from combat duty. There were others who talked big during training, but once in combat turned tail at critical moments. Of course, they were screwing the rest of us. We also had a few abort artists, guys who would fly with you until a gaggle of Germans was sighted and then radio they were turning back with engine trouble. There were still others who would fire a burst, then quickly break off; or watch somebody else hammer an airplane, then, when the German was already windmilling and going down, dive in and fire a quick burst, then try to share credit for the kill. I had a guy do that to me. Believe me, he never did it again. Worst of all were wingmen who left you naked in a tight spot. A wingman's job was to stick like glue to his leader's tail, while his leader did the shooting. He was your damned life insurance, his reliability a matter of your life or death. If he failed you, there was no second chance. You got rid of him in a hurry. Eddie Simpson was

Andy's wingman until Eddie got shot down. Before
they flew together, Eddie said to Andy, "Let's go to
London and get drunk together. Then, I'll follow you
into hell." I had five or six wingmen during my tour;
some had better eyesight or more discipline than
others, but since I never got shot down flying as an
element or squadron leader, they were competent
enough, I guess.

The special closeness between the best of us—
Anderson, Bochkay, Browning, O'Brien, and myself—
existed because we fought the same way. Andy
especially. On the ground, he was the nicest person
you'd ever know, but in the sky, those damned Germans must've thought they were up against Franken-
stein or the Wolfman; Andy would hammer them
into the ground, dive with them into the damned
grave, if necessary, to destroy them. So would I. We
finished what we started every time. That's how we
were raised. We did our job. We were over there to
shoot down Germans, and that's exactly what we
did, to the best of our ability and training. We were a
pack of untested kids who grew up in a hurry. Andy
called it the college of life and death. I don't recommend going to war as a way of testing character, but
by the time our tour ended we felt damned good
about ourselves and what we had accomplished. Whatever the future held, we knew our skills as pilots, our
ability to handle stress and danger, and our reliability in tight spots. It was the difference between thinking you're pretty good, and proving it.

WINDING DOWN

Clarence Emil Anderson, better known as "Bud" or "Andy," was now a twenty-three-year-old major, while I was promoted to captain a few months short of my twenty-second birthday. Wartime promotions came fast, and we figured that if the war lasted another year or more, the Air Corps would have a bunch of baby generals on its hands. In addition to flying, I was now squadron maintenance officer, which meant that I checked out all of the overhauled Mustangs; Andy was now the squadron's operations officer, and he woke me at six one morning to tell me I made captain. I reached into my bag and found a bottle of champagne I'd been saving. We were smashed before seven, hung over before lunch—a first for us.

"Chuck," Andy said, "we're gonna need new livers if we make it through this damned war." I don't think any of us actually flew missions in a falling-down condition, but flying with a hangover was not unknown. You'd die when your engines cranked and swallow a couple of aspirins, swearing you'd never do it again. We sent guys up to Scotland on whiskey runs, and when that ran out we drank rotgut rye or British beer. There was always something to celebrate: a friend's kill or the fact you were still alive.

We threw a blast the last week in November to mark our first anniversary in England that nearly wrecked the officer's club. We brought in London strippers and maybe a few local amateurs, too. Those twelve months in Leiston seemed a century, and I found it hard to believe that only a year had gone by. So much had happened, so much adventure and hell-raising since we stepped off the *Queen Elizabeth* as green and eager fighter jocks. Of the original thirty who arrived at Leiston as a squadron, a dozen had been killed, and eight more were missing in action. Six others had finished their tour and gone home. Four of us were left from the original group, and without saying so, I wondered whether all of us would actually make it back. As it turned out, one didn't; Jim Browning was shot down a few days short of going home.

My own tour was winding down. I had only eight more missions to complete. Being a short-timer was a strange feeling. I wanted to score as many victories as possible in the time remaining, but somehow avoid getting my ass busted at this late date. And from time to time, we all had nasty reminders that the war was far from over. One night, we had just turned out the lights to go to sleep when we heard an airplane coming in low. We knew the sound of American and British fighters, but this deep-throated roar was different. Man, we hit the deck. That German was directly above our little Nissen when he began firing into the roof of the empty mess hall. We waited for the bomb, but it was never dropped. When it was over we giggled nervously, because there was Obie O'Brien flopped under his mattress, pointing his forty-five at the ceiling.

I wrote to Glennis a couple of times a week and received a couple of letters back. Andy was also writing regularly to his childhood sweetheart, Eleanor. Both of us planned to get married as soon as we got home. I had already written to my mother telling her that, but I didn't tell Glennis. I didn't have to because our letters said everything we were feeling about each other, and, to tell the truth, I was a little superstitious. There were still combat missions to fly. I knew I was getting married, but that's about all I knew about the future. At twenty-two, my idea of heaven was to be reassigned to the same base as Andy, where the two of us could dogfight every day. Being in the Air Corps was all he ever wanted since boyhood. I loved to fly, but whether the Air Corps would want to keep me, I had no idea. About all I could promise Glennis was a cabin in a holler. Things usually worked out in their own way, and I wasn't one to spend much time planning a future. I tried to make the most of each day, get through a mission in one piece, and leave some time for fun. I might be getting married before long, but there were still a few girls to chase, a few bottles left undrunk, and more than likely a few krauts to shoot at and some bullets to duck until then.

Meanwhile, Andy and I worked it out that we would complete our missions on the same day, go home together, and try to be reassigned to the same place. I admired him totally and just felt good in his company. We shared the same background and interests. He was a rural boy from northern California who loved to hunt, fish, and fly as much as I did. Whenever we had a quiet time together, we were always dreaming up hunting trips or going through gun catalogs his folks sent him.

Our personalities meshed, too. We both loved fun and blowing off steam, although he was a helluva lot more tolerant than I was. I was impulsive and headstrong—something is either right or wrong; I didn't spend any time in between. We saw eye to eye on rights and wrongs, but Andy saw the other side; I wasn't interested. That wasn't my nature, but friends— real friends—don't have to always agree or try to cover over their differences. We found our harmony from mutual respect and just plain liking one another.

God, we had fun during those last months in England. As Andy put it, "Captain Yeager may be very busy, but somehow he will manage to fit into his daily program both dogfighting and hell-raising." Andy, Bochkay, and I complained a couple of times to the base ambulance crew, who parked their damned meat wagon next to our Nissen and woke us up gunning that engine to warm it. Finally we rigged a string of whistle bombs and attached it to the motor. You could've heard that racket in Glasgow; that crew's ears didn't stop ringing for weeks. We'd go out and poach pheasants and rabbits and have ourselves a feast. A Texan named G.I. Carlisle was a genius at making Texas white gravy to pour over our fried hares. One time I got myself invited to a legitimate hunt on the estate of a local lord. We shot grouse, and he used Italian prisoners of war as beaters. I was standing next to our host when he fired twice and missed. I turned around and shot that bird and it dropped behind him. Somebody whispered to me: "Don't ever wipe the governor's eye like that."

A few weeks before Christmas, I received an unexpected vacation from the British. Group sent me off to Switzerland; the assignment was so hush-hush, I wasn't even told why I was going. I flew over to Lyon, where we now had advanced fighter bases, and was driven over the Alps to Lake Annecy, just south of Geneva, and put up at the Beaurivage Hotel. At Leiston, we slept in sleeping bags on a G.I. mattress, and this bed was so comfortable I couldn't get used to it. I quickly learned what my trip was about when Peter De Paolo, a famous racing car driver, now the American air attaché in Switzerland, arrived at my room and took me to dinner. As a former evadee who had escaped from France by climbing the Pyrenees, I was asked to help in an escape plan for eight hundred American fliers who were interned in neutral Switzerland. There were also sixteen hundred Americans interned in Spain.

"We want to do some discreet smuggling," Pete said. "Maybe set up a mountain-climbing expedition one of these moonless nights. We can't just ask the neutral Swiss to let them go home. The Germans would see this as a hostile act." He asked my advice about the ideal size of a group trying to get across, the best time to try it, and so on. Frankly, it sounded to me like a better war movie than a practical plan. Those Alps were mighty big, even compared to the Pyrenees. I told Pete I'd help plan it, but not help climb it.

Between Christmas and New Year's, we planned a small smuggling operation, bringing in canvas covers to protect a half-dozen American airplanes that had force-landed at Swiss air bases, shot-up but still serviceable, if we could get them out. As far as I know, the escape plan was never attempted.

It was amusing when I left, because I gave a lift to an O.S.S. guy. He sat on my lap when I took off from France in my Mustang. I carried him, his bag, and a case of champagne, in that tiny cockpit. We flew back low with the canopy opened.

OTHER VOICES:

Bud Anderson

Chuck and I flew eight missions in January, beginning with New Year's Day, and a couple of them worried us—strafing operations in support of the U.S.

counterattack during the Battle of the Bulge. But
finally, on the morning of January 15, 1945, the great
day dawned—our last mission. We both flew as spares
on an escort mission over Leipheim. We flew with
the squadron over the Channel, and when no other
Mustang was forced to abort with engine problems,
we left the squadron and went off by ourselves.

Where we were headed, I really didn't know.
Chuck had planned the day for both of us. I followed
him to Switzerland. The weather over Europe had
been dreadful for weeks, but on this day at least, it
was a dazzling sunlit winter morning, and the Alps
were majestic and glorious, sparkling in snow. We
buzzed the peak of Mont Blanc and dropped our
wing tanks near a stone shelter. Now, over the years,
I've heard Chuck tell this story dozens of times. In
his version, we strafed those tanks and set them on
fire. The truth is, we used up all of our ammo trying
to set them on fire, but couldn't. But, as Chuck says,
it's a slightly better story if the darned things burned.

Anyway, with Chuck, you never knew what might
come next. I was feeling nostalgic, my last flight in
Old Crow, my loyal Mustang that had pulled me
through just about everything imaginable without a
scratch on me or her. So, I just followed my leader
into Switzerland. He wanted to show me Lake Annecy
and the hotel he had stayed at, and show me he did.
We came in at 500 mph, practically blew the shingles off the rooftop of that place, and swept over the
lake, our props a few feet off the water. "Look, Andy,"
he said, "isn't it beautiful?" It was. But we were in
the middle of a war; Switzerland was a neutral country, and we were buzzing its lakes and cities. I had to
figure we could be at least court-martialed, maybe
drawn and quartered. But, hell, Chuck would not be
denied. He showed me Geneva, a small restaurant
where he had dined at Christmas, and gave me a
blow by blow description of all he had done and seen
as we roared over the rooftops.

The next stop was the south of France. We came

in over the woods where he had bailed out, swooped over the farmhouse where he was first hidden, then the one in Nerac, where he had lived in a shed. Then, we traced his route over the Pyrenees and actually found the wooden shack where Germans fired their rifles at him and the other fellow. Then we turned around and headed for Paris. Neither of us had ever been there, but we knew all the landmarks, and we buzzed in over the Arc de Triomphe.

It was a wonderful day. And time and again I was struck with the thought that if the entire Luftwaffe, or whatever was left of it, had decided to take to the air and finally get even with the two of us, Chuck and I would have busted the ass of every last one of them. When I said this to him over the radio, he laughed and said he had been thinking the same thing.

Now, this story has a special ending. We were the last two Mustangs to come back in at Leiston. It was already dark, exactly at 6:00 P.M. We taxied up to our hard-stands and turned off our engines for the last time. Our wings were seared from all the heavy gunning we had done in the Alps and the ground crews came running up excitedly. "How many did you guys get?" my crew chief asked. He saw the black around my guns, and my own puzzled look. "The group ran into more krauts than they had ever seen," he said, "and shot down fifty-seven of them." The two squadron hotshots, the last to come in, their wings all smoke-stained, everyone figured we had shot down about fifty of our own. The real dogfight occurred just around the time that Chuck and I were trying to ignite those damned wing tanks with our tracers. Man, we were sick.

We received Government Issue whiskey, mission whiskey that was parceled out after completing a flight. We saved all of ours for this last mission, then stood back to back, and drank a full canteen cup of this rotgut rye—Old Overholt, I think it was. Then we filled up a second cup. We drank his sixty-one missions' worth, then started on my allotment that included two full tours. Chuck collapsed first. I vaguely remember hitting him over the head with my canteen cup to make him stand up and keep going. "Andy," he said to me, "look at it this way. We could have had our asses shot off today. Isn't that so?" I said it was, and in war anything was possible, but neither of us really believed that. "We'll just have to make do," I said. Seventeen for me and twelve for him. That wasn't too shabby, friend.

The two of us woke up the next morning lying in an open ditch in the pouring rain. Chuck was wearing a parka that he had promised to give Bochkay. He had, I noticed, thrown up all over it.

We flew home together. In fact, he didn't go home to West Virginia, but went out to California to pick up Glennis and get married. He stayed overnight at my place. It was his twenty-second birthday that day, and my mom baked him a birthday cake. I drove him down to the train depot the next morning and said good-by. Both of us were kind of in a daze. We couldn't believe that our days at Leiston were really over, and that a whole new life was about to start. We had left behind a helluva lot in England—friends we'd never see again, wonderful fun times, terrible ordeals, the lot. But we had also left behind our youth. The next time we saw each other, we were both married men.

THE RIGHT PLACE

WRIGHT FIELD, DAYTON, OHIO, 1945–1946

Glennis Yeager

Chuck never did propose, but that didn't keep me from wondering what my life would be like as an Air Corps wife. He wrote regularly from England, enclosing most of his pay. "Here," he wrote, "bank this for us." His letters were short, but nobody could say more in a few words than Chuck. He wished the war would be over soon, but he would not have minded dogfighting forever. Flying came with the marriage license, and I had no problem with that. Being a military pilot's wife seemed exciting, especially with a husband like Chuck, who loved action, whether it was flying or hunting or fishing. So, I was primed to say "Yes!" if and when he ever proposed. He arrived

at my door in California straight from the war in
Europe and told me to pack my bags.

"I'm taking you back home to meet my folks."

"What for?" I asked.

"What do you think?" he replied.

Now, that sounded promising. So, we boarded a
train to West Virginia and played like honeymooners
on the sleeping car for three whole days—darned
racy for that era, wartime or not. I turned around my
high-school ring while slinking past the train con-
ductor. I was very nervous, a young girl on the big
adventure of her life, but Chuck looked great in his
officer's uniform with a chest full of combat ribbons
and decorations. Alone on the train, we talked about
the future. The Air Corps was definitely his calling.
Although only a high-school graduate, he was already a captain and a pilot. I had no qualms about
marrying him; what scared me was going off alone
and being a stranger in a strange land. I pictured
West Virginia as a foreign country where I couldn't
understand the spoken language. Chuck laughed about
it. "Oh, hell, hon, we all just speak the king's English, same as you do. If you understand me, you can
understand anybody, I reckon."

Chuck's reception back home caught both of us
by surprise. He was Lincoln County's personal war
hero, its only double ace, and Hamlin greeted him as
if he were General Eisenhower. We rode in a home-
coming parade right down Main Street, and they
packed the high-school gym to stage a civic celebra-
tion. The local papers had reported all his exploits,
which is how I found out about most of them. "Did
you really do all those things?" I asked him. "Hell,
no," he laughed. But, of course, he had.

The people of Hamlin gave us all kinds of presents, including a starter set of sterling silver. They
weren't rich and their generosity was wonderful. Every time we turned around there was another reception or church supper. My face ached from smiling,
and although everyone was very nice, the local girls

really eyed me, wondering what was so special about me that Chuck couldn't find the same, or better, in his own backyard.

We stayed at his parents' house, in separate rooms. The Yeagers were a prideful family, strong and independent-minded. His parents were friendly, but reserved; Chuck's older brother Roy was away in the Navy, but both his kid brother Hal, Jr., and his teen-age sister, Pansy Lee, clearly hero-worshiped Chuck. I was the shy, uncertain outsider trying to make a good impression. I think his family was kind of dazed by Chuck's war exploits; at that point, I doubt whether any bride he chose could have measured up in their eyes. I was so proud of him I could bust, but I thought he was darned lucky, too. And in the middle of this hectic week, we learned that we couldn't get married unless I received my parents' permission, because at age twenty, I still wasn't legal. My parents wired their blessings, and on the eve of the wedding, I went with Chuck to Huntington to buy our rings and my wedding dress, a nice pale green dressy suit. His mom and sister helped me pick it out.

The night before the wedding, he finally proposed, in his own way. "I don't have much, so I can't promise you much except maybe a little cabin up in some holler." Being young and in love, that seemed enough for us both.

We were married at home in the family parlor, the room they kept the doors shut on all the time. A local lady sang "Always," and the family preacher married us. J.D. Smith, a local attorney whom Chuck very much admired, gave me away. He was very old and very ill, but his presence at our wedding meant a lot to Chuck. Everyone in town seemed to have sent flowers and the parlor was crammed with them. It was a crisp, sunny winter day, February 26, 1945.

We spent our wedding night in a hotel in Huntington, then boarded the train back to California—this time with our marriage certificate in our suit-

case—to honeymoon at an Air Corps recreation and
rest center at Del Mar. We went up to our room, put
on our bathing suits, and bounced out onto the beach.
The first couple we saw on the sand was Bud Anderson and his new bride, Eleanor. He was Chuck's
closest friend from the war and had beaten us to the
altar by three days. Chuck was amazed and delighted.
He didn't know that Bud was getting married so
soon. But before leaving Europe, he had claimed
California as his residency to try to get stationed
together with Bud.

We had a glorious two weeks together at Del
Mar, at the end of which I went back alone to Oroville
to pack my things and start my new life as an Air
Corps wife, while Eleanor and the guys drove off to
Texas, where they were going to serve together at
Perrin Field.

By the time I caught up with them, the honeymoon was definitely over. Housing was nonexistent,
and we, like the Andersons, were forced to rent a
bedroom in a private home, with kitchen privileges. I
didn't know anything about cooking, and the first
time I invited the Andersons over for dinner, I served
fried chicken. I fried and fried, but I still couldn't get
a fork into it. They had sold me an old stewing hen
that should've been boiled for a day, and Chuck and
Bud bravely chewed until their jaws ached, smiling
and complimenting me. Finally I said, "This is awful. I know you guys are starved. Let's go out and get
a decent meal." They practically jumped from the
table, and we wound up in a very fancy restaurant.
They were both in uniform, and those two crazy
coots start acting as if they were shell-shocked, twitch-
ing and shaking so that the silverware rattled and
everybody stared at us. Eleanor and I almost died,
but a rich Texan picked up the bill.

That was about the only laugh we had at Perrin.
Chuck and Bud encountered a lot of jealousy against
a twenty-two-year-old captain and a twenty-three-
year-old major, both hot-shot combat pilots, from

other officers who had spent the war in Texas. They were assigned as pilot instructors, and they hated every minute of it. It was a far cry from combat excitement, and they took out their frustrations on the poor cadets who flew with them by tossing out rolls of toilet paper and then slicing the paper with their wings, or dogfighting each other so wildly that cadets passed out and refused to fly with them again.

We were there a month when Eleanor discovered she was pregnant. Two weeks later, I learned I was pregnant, too. She was sick and I was sick and the guys were sick of us being sick all the time. Chuck was glad, but like many men of his generation, he was blasé about having children. When they were born he got a big kick out of them, but raising them was my job. Like his dad, he wouldn't know the difference between a diaper and a hand towel.

I wanted a family, but this was rather quick. When the baby was born, I figured that everyone in Hamlin would be counting on their fingers to see if it was legal. Coping with sick wives did nothing to improve Bud and Chuck's blues. They were really down. Then a new regulation was announced that allowed former prisoners of war or evadees to select an assignment at the base of their choice. Chuck opened a map of the United States and measured with a string to find the closest base to Hamlin, West Virginia. It turned out to be Wright Field, in Dayton, Ohio. He filled out the forms and we were transferred. Poor Bud was stuck, although he finally got transferred out by volunteering to go into recruiting work. We hated to part with the Andersons, but we left Texas without looking back. And when we arrived at Dayton, we learned that housing in wartime was impossible. There wasn't an apartment available in a hundred square miles. Chuck could live on the base, but there was no room anywhere in town for his wife.

I wound up in Hamlin, moving in with my in-laws because we didn't know what else to do. Chuck bummed airplane rides in on the weekends, when he could. His parents and sister were working, so I kept that big house and cooked for all of them. That's where I learned how to cook. Mrs. Yeager taught me all of her West Virginia recipes, including fried chicken, corn bread, and biscuits and beans. Our first son, Donald, was born in a hospital in Huntington, in January 1946, one month after little Jim Anderson arrived in the world. At the time, Chuck was at Muroc in California. The baby was two weeks old before his dad finally saw him. We figured that during our first year of marriage we were together less than half the time—par for the course over the years.

I was a self-sufficient and independent person; I did all of our banking and budgeting, found our housing, took care of our purchasing and home needs, and raised our kids. As a young bride, I had to learn how to cope with loneliness, living without my husband for weeks and months at a time. I wasn't a complainer or a worrier, but the adjustments were not easy, and Chuck was not the only member of our household constantly facing the kinds of challenges that test courage and character. "Well, hon, you knew what you were getting into when you married me," he said. I'm sure that many exasperated pilots' wives heard that sentence, although it was only partially true. My own daydreams about what it would be like being married in the military were rather naive. Chuck and I would share some marvelous experiences during his career, but being an Air Corps wife was tough duty.

I got to Wright Field on a fluke. Because Glennis was pregnant and sick, I figured we needed to be close to West Virginia, where Mom could give us a hand. As a former evadee, I could be stationed at the air base of my choice. I knew I'd be gone a lot—that's the pilot's life—and we both agreed that being near Hamlin was a smart move with a baby on the way. To have Glennis move in with my folks was not our idea of married life. Right from the start, we were a typical military couple: we never could find housing or enjoy any real family stability. Whenever Glennis needed me over the years, I was usually off in the wild blue yonder. Yet, she never griped, not even when we lived out on a dry lakebed in the Mojave, drawing our water from a damned windmill pump, and the nearest store or doctor was forty miles away.

If another air base had been closer to Hamlin than Wright Field, I would not have been at the right place at the right time. I had no idea that I had stumbled into the most exciting place on earth for a fighter pilot. Not only were Wright's huge hangars crammed with airplanes begging to be flown, but it would soon be the center of the greatest adventure in aviation since the Wright brothers—the conversion from propeller airplanes to supersonic jets and rocket-propelled aircraft.

I reported into Wright in July 1945, a few weeks before the atomic bomb ended the war. I had eleven hundred hours of flying time and a background in maintenance. I was a perfect candidate for what they needed: a fighter pilot to run functional test flights on all the airplanes after engine overhauls and other repairs. I was assigned as an assistant maintenance officer to the fighter test section of the flight test division, the hub, over the next decade, for the testing of a radically new generation of powerful airplanes that would take us to the edge of space and change aviation forever. These tremendous changes occurred in the age of the slide rule, before computers were born or advanced wind tunnels existed. We would discover by dangerous trial and error what worked and what didn't. That cost lives, but for the pilots who survived, it was the most thrilling time imaginable. I was in on the beginning of a Golden

Age. Two weeks after arriving at Wright, I was flying the first operational American jet fighter.

I had no idea of what the future might hold when I reported in. All I knew was that Wright Field was a fun place to be, loaded with every airplane in the inventory, and there was plenty of gasoline. It was like Aladdin's lamp with unlimited rubs. I could fly as much as I wanted, building flying experience on dozens of different kinds of fighters. The first chance I got I flew to Hamlin and buzzed Glennis. I called her that night and said, "I miss you, hon, but I'm in hog heaven."

I wasn't an ambitious kid, but I was competitive. I had a small office between Hangars Seven and Eight, where all the fighters were kept, and got to know some of the test pilots. It never occurred to me that I could be one of them; I lacked the education. All of them were college grads, mostly with engineering degrees. There were about twenty-five fighter test pilots, and they weren't exactly shy about their status. They were the stars of the show. I thought, well, fair enough. If they're fighter test pilots, they must be hotter than a whore's pillow. It would be interesting to see how well I could do against the best fighter jocks in the Air Corps.

So, every time I took off in a P-51 on a test hop, I climbed to 15,000 feet and circled over Wright, waiting for one of those guys to take off. They were all fair game for a dogfight, and I lived and breathed dogfights. That was a way of life ever since my squadron training days. As soon as a test pilot climbed to altitude, I dove at him. I went through the entire stable of test pilots and waxed every fanny. A few of them fought back halfheartedly, but none of them had any combat experience, and when they saw I was merciless, they just quit. The test pilots couldn't fly an airplane close to the ragged edge where you've got to keep it if you really want to make that machine talk. And they weren't amused by being shown up by an assistant maintenance officer.

One of them told me, "We weren't trained to do acrobatics. We're precision fliers. If I handed you a test card and told you to go test an airplane, you couldn't do it. You'd bust your ass." That was probably true, but I kept after some of the sore losers, waxing their tails every chance I got.

I flew six to eight hours a day; I flew everything they had, including most of the captured German and Japanese fighter planes. (The Focke-Wulf 190 was the only one in the same league with the Mustang.) I checked out in twenty-five different airplanes. I never did understand how a pilot could walk by a parked airplane and not want to crawl in the cockpit and fly off. I could not honestly claim to be the best pilot, because as good as you think you are, there is always somebody who is probably better. But I doubt whether there were many who loved to fly as much as I did. Nobody logged more flying time. My feet touched ground just long enough to climb out of one airplane and service check another. I even flew the first prototype jet fighter, the Bell P-59, which had been secretly tested out on the California desert in 1942. Its crude engines were vastly underpowered, so there wasn't an exhilarating sense of speed, but I marveled at how smooth and quiet it was compared to prop airplanes, and I flew that first jet right down the main street of Hamlin.

If you wanted to fly in those days, you had only to ask a crew chief to check you out in an unfamiliar cockpit, brief you on the systems and characteristics, and then fire the engine. Everything about airplanes interested me: how they flew, why they flew, what each could or couldn't do and why. As much as I flew, I was always learning something new, whether it was a switch on the instrument panel I hadn't noticed, or handling characteristics of the aircraft in weather conditions I hadn't experienced. Unlike many pilots, I really learned the various systems of aircraft. A typical motorist is content to drive without knowing a spark plug from a crankshaft; a typical pilot is much the same. The gauges in the cockpit tell him as much as he wants to know about his machine. You've got to love engines and valves and all those mechanical gadgets that make most people yawn to have an eager curiosity about an airplane's systems. But it was a terrific advantage for me when something went wrong at 20,000 feet. Knowing machinery like I did, and having a knowledgeable feel for it, I knew how to cope with practically any problem. I knew what was serious or manageable. All pilots take chances from time to time, but knowing—not guessing—about what you can risk is often the critical difference between getting away with it or drilling a fifty-foot hole in mother earth.

And it also set me on a path that would change my life.

It was my feel for equipment that first brought me to the attention of Col. Albert G. Boyd, head of the flight test division.

The Jet Age arrived for me the day when I was seated in the cockpit of the Lockheed P-80 Shooting Star, the first operational American jet fighter. What a breathtaking ride—like being a pebble fired from a slingshot. Cruising straight and level, I flew at 550 mph, faster than I had in a full-throttle power dive in my Mustang. I felt like I was flying for the first time. I greased that thing in on landing, happy as a squirrel hunter who had bagged a mountain lion. The life of an engine in those early jets was practically nothing; after only three or four hours an engine would burn out, and we had so many fire-warning lights in the cockpit that I finally unscrewed the bulb. But since the Shooting Star was always being repaired, I logged more jet time than anyone else: the airplane couldn't go back into service until the maintenance officer checked it out in the sky. So, right from the start, I was probably the most experienced jet pilot in the Air Corps.

Flying those primitive jets was tricky. You had to be cautious opening the throttle because the engine temperature would climb enormously. So, you'd ease up on the throttle slowly, making sure you didn't go over the red line on the temperature gauge. The landings were even trickier. Flying faster than ever before, you had to line up your approach faster and more accurately than with props. The Shooting Star didn't decelerate very quickly, and its rate of acceleration was even worse, so if you came in too slow, you couldn't get your power back for nearly twenty seconds, and by then you might be heading into the ground. We lost several jets and pilots that way. Like somebody said, it was like trying to learn how to ride a race horse after riding only on elephants.

But I adjusted quickly, and in August 1945, I accompanied Colonel Boyd and a detachment of fighter test pilots out to Muroc Air Base in the Mojave Desert to conduct service tests on the Shooting Star. I was the detachment's maintenance officer. Muroc, about seventy miles from Los Angeles, was the site of ancient lakebeds that were six miles wide and eight miles long, perfect landing fields in the middle of nothing but scrub and Joshua trees. During the war it was used for practice bombing and secret test work. The place looked like the ass-end of the moon, and little did I know at the time that I would spend sixteen years of my life there.

We flew off the north end of the lakebed. There were six pilots and six or seven jets, working in temperatures way over 100 degrees. And we worked our fannies off. Especially the ground crews. The jets were constantly breaking down, which meant that the maintenance officer was logging more flying time than anyone else in test hops. Colonel Boyd watched me fly, and he also saw that I was on top of the maintenance and the mechanics. At the end of a week of testing, he ordered one Shooting Star flown back to Wright, while the others were returned to the factory. He chose me to fly it back, which really frosted the major in charge of the fighter test section. "Colonel," he said, "I think a test pilot should fly it back." Boyd said no. "Yeager is a maintenance officer who knows the airplane and understands the system, and he'll get it back there." And I did.

If you love the hell out of what you're doing, you're usually pretty good at it, and you wind up making your own breaks. Other than being forced by circumstances to live apart from Glennis, I was as happy as I ever was. If I could fly and hunt and fish, I had nine-tenths of it all. Rank didn't mean a whole helluva lot, except that I needed more money. If they had decided to make me a general, my first question would've been: Do generals get to fly? I wasn't a deep, sophisticated person, but I lived by a basic principle: I did only what I enjoyed. I wouldn't let anyone derail me by promises of power or money into doing things that weren't interesting to me. That kept me real and honest. Job titles didn't mean diddly. Assistant Maintenance Officer might not be a title that would really impress Aunt Maude, but if it meant that I could fly more than anyone else, I'd stick with it for as long as I could. I loved being in the Air Corps because I was a trained combat pilot, and that's where all the airplanes were. But I wasn't thrilled by all the regulations, orders, and chains of command; and over the years, I bent most of their rules into pretzels if they ever got in the way of what I wanted, especially when it came to flying off somewhere to hunt or fish. In the end, though, I figure they got more out of me than I got out of them.

I wasn't a saint, for sure. I could raise hell with the best in the bunch. But pride was a big part of me, and I never tried to be who I wasn't. I thought I was as good as the rest of them. And when it came to flying, I was better.

I was self-conscious about my lack of education, especially in comparison to the test pilots. With jets coming into the picture, flying would get more complex and technical, and I worried about keeping up without an engineering background. I wasn't particularly impressed with the skills of the fighter test pilots, and after the service tests at Muroc, they felt even worse about me. That the old man had chosen me to fly back the P-80 really stuck in a few craws. When I detected that kind of petty jealousy, I couldn't resist rubbing their noses in it, so I became ruthless in my dogfight tactics against the test pilots, waxing them so often they had to sit on pillows.

One day I took off in the Bell jet, the P-59. It was only my second flight in it, and I really didn't know the systems. Suddenly, a P-38 prop fighter dove in on me. I couldn't believe it! None of the test pilots had ever started a dogfight, but this guy seemed determined to bounce me. I whipped that jet around and pulled up in a vertical climb—not really understanding what in hell I was doing—and I stalled going straight up. I was spinning down and that damned P-38 was spinning up, both airplanes out of control, and when we went by each other, not ten feet apart, my eyes were like saucers and so were the other pilot's. We both fell out of the sky, regained control down on the deck, engines smoking and wide open. Finally he said, "Hey, man, we'd better knock it off before we bust our asses." I didn't know who he was. We landed, and I went over to meet this tall, lanky first lieutenant. His name was Bob Hoover. I told him, "You're really hot in that airplane." He said, "You are, too. I didn't know a P-59 could swap ends like that." I told him the truth: "I didn't either, till I tried it."

Bob was a combat pilot, had been shot down, and spent time in one of the worst German stalags. He was assigned to the fighter test section, and from then on, we would dogfight every chance we got, in any airplane we happened to be flying, and neither of us ever won. As soon as our wings would pass we'd go right into a vertical climb, spin down, and break off so low to the ground, that it was either give up or crash. A stand-off every time. Bob became a legend: he had about twenty major accidents, all equipment failure, and once made it back into Wright on a dead engine by bouncing his wheels off a passing truck to give himself altitude over a chain link fence.

He loved practical jokes. He went over to a little airport in Dayton and signed up for flying lessons. He took the course taught by a really sharp-looking blonde, and when the time came for him to solo, a bunch of us went out to watch. He took off, climbed above the field, then dove straight down, did a roll and barely missed the hangars, looped and spinned, and turned everything loose. His instructor hid her face in her hands and almost passed out, but when she saw us standing in our uniforms and laughing like hell, she knew she'd been had.

Bob and I became pals and called each other "pard." One Friday, I said to him, "Hey, pard, how about dropping me off down at Hamlin? We have an airplane that needs some service testing and there's a little strip up there on the side of a hill." The truth is, I had got other pilots to fly down there, but when they saw the small strip that stopped just short of a steep cliff, they chickened out of landing. But Bob was game, and made it in with a couple of yards to spare. I got out and he took off wide open and dropped right off the edge of that damned cliff, engine racing. Down he went into the valley, roaring around down there to build up speed. It was a ten-minute walk to my front porch in Hamlin, and when I climbed those steps, I could still hear ol' Bob grinding away in there.

In the fall of 1945, Hoover and I began putting on air shows together. Air shows were very popular around the country after the war, and tens of thousands of people would show up at a local airport to watch military airplane demonstrations. At Wright, we had the only jet fighters flying, the P-80 Shooting Star, and when the requests began to pour in from local groups, some of the senior test pilots felt they couldn't be bothered, but Bob and I would fly anywhere, anytime, because we loved it. So, off we went—Michigan, Wisconsin, Alabama, New York. We were the stars of the show; the public hadn't seen a jet airplane, and there were no restrictions about what we could do: we could fly as fast or as low as we wanted, buzz Main Street, anything, nobody cared. It was great fun, and, man, you'd come in and break real crisp and grease it in, then taxi to a ramp in front of all those people, and think, well, I might not be the world's greatest, but maybe the second greatest.

People would come up and stare at your airplane and wonder how it could fly with no propeller. I'd get a volunteer to stand behind the tail pipe and light a newspaper. Then I turned on the igniter and *whoosh*, the engine fired up. The crowd really thought that guy had lit the engine. One day at a show in Philadelphia, I noticed two gals staring at my jet. "You gals ever seen a jet before?" I asked. They said no. I helped them up on the wing, and one of them told me she was flying air shows, too. She pointed nearby and said, "That's my P-39." I hadn't seen one since my early days of squadron training at Tonopah. I told her I had five hundred hours in the Thirty-Nine and thought it was the best airplane I ever flew. She asked me if I wanted to fly it. "Yeah, man," I replied, "I'd give my right arm." So we concocted a little deal.

She was scheduled to fly the show the next morning. She was an ex-WASP, and the P.A. announcer told the crowd all about her just before take-off. We parked her Thirty-Nine away from the crowd. She had outfitted me in a woman's wig, a white jump suit, and a blue cap, and off I went. I put on a helluva acrobatic show, doing Immelmanns and Cuban eights, thrilled to be back in a Thirty-Nine again. I landed and parked far from the crowd, where she replaced me in the cockpit and then taxied up to the main ramp to receive the cheers.

Those air shows were wonderful fun and good flying, as long as you kept your nose clean and didn't have any accidents. That's all that mattered. Those Shooting Stars were tricky; Hoover had a bad accident flying into Boston for a show; his engine exploded at 40,000 feet, and he somehow dead-sticked in the fog. The test pilots would fly the Shooting Star to an air show and after the first day they would fly back on a commercial airliner, leaving behind a malfunctioning P-80. We would send a crew out to fix it, and then I would go get it and bring it back. But I knew the P-80 systems cold; if anything went wrong, I could usually fix it myself. I had a crew chief along to service the airplane and help. The point was, that of all the guys who flew in air shows, I was one of the very few who always came whistling back in without any problems.

I know that impressed Colonel Boyd because he ordered me to stage an air show with a Shooting Star for the open-house at Wright Field in early November 1945. Twenty-five fighter test pilots prayed that I'd bust my ass. Here I was, a damned maintenance officer, being the star attraction at an air show at their own base. And I wasn't even a test pilot. But anyone who knew my combat background understood that doing acrobatics was my piece of cake. For the Wright Field show, I took off with jet assists on each wing and water injection into the engine for additional power boost, and that P-80 shot straight up in the sky. Then I dove low over the crowd, did a few slow rolls, shot back up, then down again to do acrobatics. It really was an impressive show, and I flew real crisp that day. The test pilots looked grim after that.

A few days later, the old man sent for me and asked me if I wanted to be a test pilot. I told Colonel Boyd that I was interested, but that I wasn't very well educated. "You shouldn't have any problem," he said. "If you do, there are a lot of test pilots around here who would be glad to tutor you." Nothing got by Colonel Boyd. He knew damned well that Hoover and I were beating the asses off his test pilots in dogfights every day, and it amused the hell out of him.

Boyd's office was on the second floor of the head-quarters building, his windows facing the flight line. He was six feet, two inches, lanky and balding, with thick dark eyebrows, and a thick hard jaw. Think of the toughest person you've ever known, then multiply by ten, and you're close to the kind of guy that the old man was. His bark was never worse than his bite: he'd tear your ass off if you screwed up. Everyone respected him, but was scared to death of him. He looked mean, and he was. He might have the most responsible job in military aviation, heading flight tests of all new airplanes, and you might be his star test pilot, but Lord help you if you stood in front of his desk with an unpolished belt buckle. That's the way he was. There were some tough characters among the pilots at Wright, but when the old man sent for any of us, we stood at attention with sweaty palms and knocking knees.

And he was one helluva pilot. He flew practically everything that was being tested at Wright, all the bombers, cargo planes, and fighters. If a test pilot had a problem, you could bet Colonel Boyd would get in that cockpit and see for himself what was wrong. He held the three-kilometer, low-altitude world speed record of 624 mph, in a specially built Shooting Star. So, he knew all about piloting, and all about us, and if we got out of line, you had the feeling that the old man would be more than happy to take you behind a hangar and straighten you out. In later years, he and I would fly together a lot doing test work, and we developed a warm relationship. But one thing had nothing to do with another: whenever I got out of line, he swatted me down. I've got the scars to show for it. Outside of Glennis, he became the most important person I've known. He completely changed my life in ways I never could imagine.

In January 1946, the skies over Wright Field were finally quiet. That's because Bob Hoover and I were sitting in class at the test pilot school on base, taking a six-month course. By far the smartest guy in our class was a skinny little bomber pilot from Oklahoma named Jack Ridley. He had studied at Caltech, and was about ten steps ahead of the others, and a lot more than that ahead of me. The course was a bitch, and it took me a while to get with it because I lacked the academic background. We were taught to reduce data, plot graphs and charts using calculus and algebraic formulas. When I didn't understand something, I'd go to Ridley for help, and he always explained a problem in ways that made it clear for me. As it turned out, Jack would do that time and again in the years ahead, saving my life many times.

The point was to teach you to fly in extremely precise ways, then prepare technical reports reducing the data of your flight into charts and graphs. As test pilots we would be investigating extremely specific performance characteristics of a particular airplane to determine whether or not it met its military specifications. Half a day of classroom work and half a day of flying. The flying part was for me a breeze. We'd crawl into a prop trainer with a test card to record our measurements. The assignment might be to find out the best climbing speed of the airplane. You'd start at 90 mph, hold it exactly, and record the rate of climb—about nine hundred feet a minute at a certain altitude. Then you'd increase to 100 mph and record that rate of climb. Then 110 mph. . . . Back on the ground, you'd record these three points and calculate a curve that showed the best airspeed—110 mph in that particular airplane. On board your aircraft was a barograph, a smoked drum rotating with two needles showing time and altitude. The barograph paper revealed how accurately you flew. If you performed a perfect rate of climb and descent, the graph looked like the teeth in a saw, and it was called a saw-tooth climb. It meant perfect precision flying. The instructor showed my graph to the class and said, "This saw-tooth climb belongs in a textbook." Because of my flying ability, they took mercy on my academics.

But I came within an inch of being bounced out of test pilot school and out of the service. I took off with my instructor one day in a two-seat T-6 prop trainer to run a power-speed test at 5,000 feet. Suddenly, the master rod blew apart in the engine, and the ship began to vibrate as if it would fall apart. I cut back on the power and began looking down to see where I could make an emergency landing. We were over Ohio farmland with plenty of plowed fields. I didn't want to bail out unless it was absolutely necessary. My instructor, a lieutenant named Hatfield, hadn't done much flying, and I looked back at him in the mirror and saw that his teeth were sticking to his lips. I said, "No sweat. Lock your shoulder harness and make sure your belt is tight because I'm gonna try and make it into one of these fields."

There were two fields on either side, and I started to set myself up on one of them. But I was sinking too fast coming in on a dead stick to make one field, and was really too high to use all of the other field, so we came in between the two, directly in the path of a farmhouse, a chicken house, a smokehouse, and a well. Wheels up, we hit the ground, slithering along and went through the chicken house in a clatter of boards and a cloud of feathers. As the airplane skidded to a stop, the right wing hit the smokehouse, turning us sideways, and the tail hit the front end of the farmhouse porch, flipping us around. We came to rest right alongside the farmwife's kitchen window. She was at the sink, looking out, and I was looking her right in the eye through a swirl of dust and feathers. I opened the canopy and managed a small smile. "Morning, Ma'am," I said. "Can I use your telephone?"

Because there was a loss of civilian property, a board of inquiry was held. One of the witnesses was a councilman in a nearby village who claimed that before I crash-landed, I had buzzed down Main Street. Lieutenant Hatfield, who was my passenger, supported my denial, but those four majors on the board seemed hostile in their questioning, and I was scared to death. I could easily have been court-martialed. But the barograph aboard my airplane was my best defense. It clearly showed my altitude at the time of the engine problem, and what we were doing before I hit. Without that thing aboard, I'd probably be back in Hamlin digging turnips.

I was stuck at this damned hearing when my son, Donald, was born and because of it I couldn't get home for a couple of weeks. Andy was also gone when little Jim was born a few weeks earlier. He was off recruiting somewhere while Elly had the baby back in California. The military was the pits for things like that, but there was nothing you could do about it except get out. It was exciting, though, being a father, even if the news came long distance; I told Glennis on the phone that if I were flying at this moment, I'd do three slow rolls down on the deck. When I finally did get back and held Don in my arms, it was one of the big moments of my life. I figured that our lives would settle down as soon as I got test pilot school behind me. Little did I know.

A few months after I graduated from school, Colonel Boyd selected me to be the principal pilot to fly the X-1 and try to break the sound barrier.

FROM NOBODY TO SOMEBODY

German pilots dove for their lives in dogfights—wide-open, straight down power dives—in a desperate gamble to get us off their tails. Sometimes they never did pull out and plowed into the ground. More than once, I almost followed them in. Diving at more than 500 mph, my Mustang began to shake violently and my controls froze. I nearly bent that damned stick straining to pull out. I was lucky that Mustangs were slightly more resistant than the German airplanes to shock waves that form at the speed of sound (Mach 1). Air travels faster across the top curved surface of a wing than across the flat bottom, producing lift. In a steep dive, turbulent air was ripping past my wings at 700 mph or better, while shock waves slammed against my ailerons and stabilizer. At sea level, the speed of sound is 760 mph; at 40,000 feet, it is 660 mph. This buffeting in power dives was called "compressability" and led to a widely held belief in the existence of a "sound barrier," an invisible wall of air that would smash any airplane that tried to pierce it at Mach 1.

The early jet fighters I had flown were all subsonic; but shortly after test pilot school, I flew a new and more powerful fighter, the P-84 Thunderjet, a single-seater capable of nuclear bomb delivery. Flying straight and level at .82 Mach number, the Thunderjet began to shake violently, and its nose pitched up. I got the message and eased back on the throttle. It was hard to believe that there wasn't a wall out there. But all of the major aircraft companies were competing to design more powerful engines and aerodynamically sleeker aircraft that would push us right up against that barrier in the sky. Yet there were a lot of engineer brains who thought that the laws of nature would punch the ticket for anyone caught speeding above Mach 1.

The famous British test pilot, Geoffrey De Havilland, Jr., was blown to pieces trying it when his tailless experimental aircraft called *The Swallow* disintegrated at .94 Mach. That happened early in 1947, during a practice dive in his attempt to break the barrier. So the British packed it in, giving up on their supersonic experiments.

Breaking the sound barrier was a very complex undertaking, and I knew next to nothing about it. Twice during quick trips out to Muroc to pick up airplanes and ferry them back to Wright, I saw the X-1 being shackled beneath a B-29 bomber prior to taking off on a flight. It was a small ship, painted bright orange and shaped like a fifty-caliber machine-gun bullet. Somebody told me it was rocket-propelled with six thousand pounds of thrust, designed to fly at twice the speed of sound. That was beyond my understanding, and I let it go at that.

The pilot was a civilian named Chalmers "Slick" Goodlin, and I saw him around. He was a sharp-looking guy, rumored to be making a fortune from Bell in these risky flights. I heard he was real hot and had to be to walk away from a few of those X-1 tests.

Bell really pumped out the publicity on him, and you couldn't open a magazine without reading about Slick, who seemed destined to become America's first supersonic pioneer. In those days, civilians did all of the research flying, so they could be paid risk bonuses; nobody wanted to ask an Air Corps pilot to risk his neck on a military paycheck.

Goodlin and his orange beast belonged to another world from mine. Glennis was expecting again, and we had scraped up enough money to make a downpayment on a small house in Hamlin; Dayton was just too expensive. So I was still commuting home on the weekends. I was busy doing air shows and flight test work; being the most junior test pilot in the shop, I was lucky to be asked to make coffee, but I did manage to get a few interesting jobs. One of them was comparison testing between the Shooting Star and a captured German Me-262 jet fighter. I was among the first Mustang pilots to shoot one down in the war, so I was fascinated to discover that the 262 and the Shooting Star performed identically— the same range, top speed, acceleration, and rate of climb. We had four P-80s in Europe in 1945, but they never did tangle with the 262. After that, I was sent to Long Island to test fly the Thunderjet at the Republic plant there, and was gone about six weeks. When I returned to Wright in May 1947, I attended a meeting of all the fighter test pilots, requesting volunteers to fly the X-1. Hoover, Ridley, and I raised our hands, along with about five others. It was probably a good thing that I wasn't very close to the flight test engineers who worked in the section, because they had warned some of the pilots to stay away from the X-1 project if they wanted to stay alive.

Hoover and I were renegades who were gone a lot of the time and definitely weren't part of the clique, so all we heard was that the X-1 research program was in some sort of trouble, and that the Air Corps was planning to take it over from Bell and

Slick Goodlin. I said, sure, put my name down, knowing there were at least a dozen others with more seniority in the section; then I flew off to Cleveland to do an air show. The old man was also there, and I flew back on his wing. When he landed, I remarked on the radio, "Not bad for an old man." Colonel Boyd wasn't amused. "Who said that?" he barked. There was absolute silence, although I figured my drawl gave me away. Colonel Boyd had just bought a new car, and he was the kind who kept meticulous records about its performance. So, a couple of us decided to put some pebbles in his hub caps and make his life more interesting. We watched from a window when he began to drive home. He backed up, stopped, got out, looking puzzled, got back in, drove a little more, stopped, got out. We laughed until we almost wet our pants.

But a few days later, he sent for me, and I thought, oh, God, here we go! It was either the pebbles or my remark when he landed that had caught up with me. Colonel Boyd never looked sterner, and when I saluted in front of his desk, he kept me standing at attention for nearly half an hour, while we talked. I left in a state of shock. He didn't exactly offer me the X-1, but he sure moved around the edges. He asked me why I had volunteered, and I told him it seemed like an interesting program, something else to fly. He said, "Yeager, this is *the* airplane to fly. The first pilot who goes faster than sound will be in the history books. It will be the most historic ride since the Wright brothers. And that's why the X-1 was built." He told me there were all kinds of incredible planes on the drawing boards, including an aircraft that could fly six times faster than the speed of sound and a supersonic bomber powered by an atomic reactor. The Air Corps was developing a project that would put military pilots into space. But all these plans were stuck on a dime until the X-1 punched through the sound barrier. "I haven't any doubt it will be done," Colonel Boyd told me, "and that an Air Corps pilot will be the one to do it."

He asked me if I knew why the Air Corps was taking over the program. "No, sir," I replied, "and until now, I could care less." He told me that Slick Goodlin had contracted with Bell to take the X-1 up to .8 Mach, which he did. Then he renegotiated his contract and demanded $150,000 to go beyond Mach 1. Point-eight Mach was phase one of the program. Phase two was to take it on out to 1.1 Mach—supersonic. Slick completed twenty powered flights, but felt that things were getting too thrilling and tried to renegotiate his bonus by asking that it be paid over five years to beat taxes. Bell brought in their chief test pilot, Tex Johnson, to take a test flight and verify the dangers involved. He flew around .75 Mach and reported that Slick deserved every dime he asked for. But the Bell lawyers turned down Slick's payment on the installment-plan idea, and until the matter was resolved, Slick refused to fly. The Air Corps lost patience with all the delays and decided to take over the X-1 project.

I asked the old man if he thought there was a sound barrier. "Hell, no," he said, "or I wouldn't be sending out one of my pilots. But I want you to know the hazards. There are some very good aviation people who think that at the speed of sound, air loads may go to infinite. Do you know what that means?"

"Yes, sir," I said. "That would be it."

He nodded. "Nobody will know for sure what happens at Mach 1 until somebody gets there. This is an extremely risky mission, and we're not going to take it one step at a time, but one inch at a time. This is our first crack at being allowed to conduct research flying, and we are not going to blow it like the British." Then he asked, "If I did choose you to fly the X-1, and left it up to you to select your backup pilot and flight engineer, who would you pick?"

I told him I'd pick Bob Hoover as backup because he was a fabulous stick-and-rudder man, and

Jack Ridley as flight engineer, because he was one helluva brain and a good pilot, too.

That night, Ridley, Hoover, and I were ordered to fly to the Bell plant at Buffalo, New York, and be briefed on the X-1 and crawl around a backup ship there. I was in a daze; the job wasn't mine yet, and both Ridley and Hoover had also been interviewed by Colonel Boyd, so all we knew was that the three of us were in the running. That was amazing to us, because we were three of the most junior test pilots at Wright. Before we saw the ship, Bell's engineers took us up to the labs. Liquid oxygen and alcohol powered the four X-1 rockets, and the lab was right out of a horror movie, with big vats smoking mist. Liquid oxygen was a tad chilly, like minus 290 degrees, and to illustrate the point, they picked up a frog with tweezers, dipped it into the vat, then dropped it on the floor. The frog broke into five pieces.

Larry Bell was a great salesman. He was a self-made man, in love with aviation all his life, and by the time he got through selling us on the beauty of his orange beast, we were ready to believe that the X-1 could punch its way through the Pearly Gates and make it back covered with angel's feathers. A lot of what his engineers had to tell us sailed over my head, but not Ridley's: he sat there scribbling notes like teacher's pet. But I understood enough. It was reassuring to learn that the ship was built to withstand stress of eighteen Gs, or eighteen times the force of gravity. But the thin wings were razor-edged to dissipate shock waves, so if you had to jump for it, the only way out was through a side door that positioned you to be cut in half. Crammed inside that small ship were a dozen round fuel containers, stored from nose to tail, making that thing a flying bomb. And you didn't take off in the X-1: you were dropped like a bomb from the B-29 mother ship at 25,000 feet, giving the pilot time to jettison the fuel and dead stick in for a lakebed landing if something went wrong.

"Without fuel aboard, she handles like a bird," Larry Bell told us.

"A live bird or a dead one?" Hoover asked.

Late in the day, we stood in a hangar, open at one end, for a close look at the X-1, which was chained to the ground. I crawled in the cockpit and was invited to fire the engines. You could light them one at a time. I threw a switch, and, my God! a sheet of flame shot twenty feet out the back door. I clapped my hands over my ears against the loudest manmade noise ever heard on earth. I threw a second switch, and that damned plane began surging against its chains; the hangar was shaking, and plaster and dust rained down on us. The noise was so fierce I thought my eyes would pop out. Hoover and I laughed in awe. We didn't walk too steady when we left that hangar. I told him, "Pard, I don't know about you, but that sumbitch scares me to death." He agreed it was a damned monster. But not Ridley. He wore that engineer's smile, and on the ride back to Wright, he said, "God almighty, what a brute-force machine! Those Bell guys have it figured just right. That sound barrier ain't got a chance." Then, for the two high-school graduates aboard, he translated into simple English what the Bell engineers had tried to explain.

So I had some idea of what I was talking about when Colonel Boyd sent for me to hear my impressions. "Sir," I said, "that's the most tremendous airplane I've ever seen." He asked me if I wanted to fly in it, and when I said yes, he said, "Okay, Yeager, it's your ride."

Maj. Gen. Albert G. Boyd

(FROM AN INTERVIEW TAPED SHORTLY BEFORE HIS DEATH
IN 1976)

Selecting the X-1 pilot was one of the most difficult
decisions of my life. If the pilot had an accident, he
could set back our supersonic program a couple of
years. Looking back, I'm amazed at the freedom given
to me to select the crew. I had full authority and
didn't have to defend my decision to anyone. And I
was well aware that the decision could be historic, so
I asked my deputy, Col. Fred Ascani, to sit down with
me and review all of the 125 pilots in the flight test
division and see what kind of list we could compile.
We informed each pilot we interviewed that this was
definitely a high-risk project, that most scientists
believed that at Mach 1 shock waves would be so
severe that the airplane would break up in flight.
Our own Air Corps engineers thought it could be
done, but at a very high risk.

I wanted an unmarried man with no family ties,
eliminating that part of the risk. I wanted a pilot
capable of doing extremely precise, scientific flying.
Above all, I wanted a pilot who was rock-solid in
stability. Yeager came up number one.

He had a couple of children at the time, but
there was no doubt in our mind that he was the one,
because of his ability to perform and his stability
and willingness to follow instructions, and, of course,
his tremendous ability as a pilot. We put Chuck under heavy pressure to test his reaction. We interviewed him for more than an hour, with him standing
stiffly at attention the whole time. I told him, "Now,
Captain Yeager, tell us why you want to be selected
and why you think you can succeed." Well, he had

thought it through and said, "Sir, I'm sure I can do it
if it can be done. And I wouldn't be standing here if I
didn't believe the Air Corps could do it." To me,
Chuck was the ideal candidate, and I still feel that
way twenty-seven years later. We had several other
outstanding pilots to choose from, but none of them
could quite match his skill in a cockpit or his cool-
ness under pressure. About the only negative was his
lack of a college education. That placed me in a
defensive position, if my superiors would ever second-
guess me—but, fortunately, they didn't. Jack Ridley
provided the engineering backup for Chuck, and those
two were so close that we knew Chuck would rely
heavily on Jack. I've never seen anyone who could
explain engineering concepts better than Ridley, who
was one helluva engineer and a test pilot himself.

I really did sweat out the crew selection, but in
the end I felt we had the best group available to try
to do what many thought was impossible. Over the
years, I've often been asked if Chuck were the only
one who could've successfully flown the X-1. I don't
know, but I can't think of anyone who could've done
a better job.

Maj. Gen. Fred J. Ascani

I was Colonel Boyd's executive officer in Flight Test
back in 1947. Boyd agonized over selecting the X-1
pilot, and uncharacteristically brought me in as a
participant while he pondered for three whole days.
He treated it like the momentous decision it was.
Fighter pilots are the most egotistical bunch in the
business. But flight test fighter pilots are a couple of
orders of magnitude higher than that, so we didn't
lack for candidates who thought they were the logical choice. Nor were fighter pilots ignorant of military rank, and most of them assumed that the senior
people in the test pilot stable had the inside track.
There was a definite pecking order, and junior men

like Yeager had to wait their turn. The competitiveness and rivalry among test pilots was such that, for example, in the short landing phase of a flight test, if a pilot were able to land, say, in five hundred feet, you could bet that there would be a series of accidents as other pilots tried landing in three hundred. It was dog-eat-dog.

Well, we all wanted to be somebody, but some got to be somebody more than others. In those days, Chuck wasn't quite a nobody but he wasn't a somebody either, and I mostly knew him by reputation, which was as an extremely proficient pilot, who flew with an uncanny, instinctive feel for the airplane. He's the only pilot I've ever flown with who gives the impression that he's part of the cockpit hardware, so in tune with the machine that instead of being flesh and blood, he could be an autopilot. He could make an airplane talk. Boyd thought that Chuck was the best instinctive pilot he had ever seen.

Piloting and dependability were the two principal criteria in making his decision. Education was not a factor, or else Yeager would have been quickly eliminated. Chuck was very unpolished. He barely spoke English. I'm not referring to his West Virginia drawl; I mean grammar and syntax. He could barely construct a recognizable sentence; the Chuck Yeager who does A.C.-Delco commercials nowadays bears no resemblance to the Chuck Yeager back then. We knew that our choice would become world-famous breaking the sound barrier, and Boyd fretted about the Air Corps' image if its hero didn't know a verb from a noun. He decided that before Chuck would meet the public, I would give him English lessons.

Boyd began his Air Corps career in the thirties as a pilot instructor and had the highest student wash-out rate of that era. He was demanding, but he knew pilots and flying, and I'm convinced that Chuck was his first choice right from the start. We talked in depth about all the others, but we kept coming back to Yeager. At one point, Boyd asked me which of our men I would choose to fly with on a dangerous combat mission. I replied, "Yeager, sir. He'd be there when I needed him in a life-and-death situation. He's cool and doesn't panic. And he has integrity. He wouldn't let me down to save his own hide." He nodded in agreement.

Yeager was a choice that insisted on itself on the basis of demonstrated skill and ability, but it wasn't an easy choice to make. It was Boyd's decision entirely, but life is never that simple in a decision of this magnitude. His superiors could easily second-guess him if something went wrong, and wonder why he chose the most junior test pilot available for the most important test project. My own choice would've been the easiest for him to make: Maj. Ken Chilstrom, head of the fighter test section. I chose Ken only because I knew him better than any of the others. But Boyd had seen Yeager fly in air shows, had watched him carefully when Chuck was maintenance officer during a test flight session at Muroc, and was tremendously impressed. I think, too, that Boyd saw a lot of his younger self in Chuck. Like Yeager, he was a southern boy who had come up the hard way. I remember him saying of Chuck's background, "You can't throw a kid like that who's taken so many hard knocks long before he ever got here. That's what makes him a great fighter pilot."

Picking Chuck was the right decision, but it was also courageous because it was unorthodox. Boyd had me sit in when he sent for Yeager. There was an electric atmosphere in that office. Each of us knew that history was being made right then and there. Bob Hoover as backup pilot and Jack Ridley as flight engineer completed the team.

Al Boyd's biggest concern was whether the structural integrity of the X-1 could withstand the extreme stress loads likely to be encountered at Mach 1. He told Chuck, "This is highly dangerous work. If you decide you want to quit this program at any time, it will not be held against you in any way. If you feel that way, I expect you to call me and say so. We can afford that kind of failure, but we can't afford to hurt anybody." There were two long meetings with Chuck, and throughout, Boyd forced him to stand at attention and called him "Yeager." But at the very end, he stood up and warmly shook hands and said, "Chuck, God speed and good luck. I have every confidence in you. But, Chuck, if you let me down and do something stupid out there, I'll nail you to the cross." And Chuck flashed that grin and said, "Colonel Boyd, I'd rather face the sound barrier any day than one of your chewings." And off he went to the Mojave, leaving behind a few shocked and jealous senior test pilots, who would wait impatiently for Yeager to fall on his ass.

PILOTING THE X–1: 1947

The airplane was officially called the X-S-1. The "S" was dropped about three years later. "X" meant research; "S" meant supersonic, and number one meant that it was the first Air Corps contract for a research airplane—this one to investigate high speed at high altitude. I would be flying higher (around 45,000 feet) and faster than any military pilot had yet flown, and the Air Corps medical labs decided that Hoover and I would be perfect specimens for experiments to learn about the limits of human endurance under maximum G loads and extreme high altitude. Hoover and I were now the first Air Corps research pilots, so we were fair game for all the torture that the astronauts would later suffer. The X-1 was back at the Bell plant in upstate New York being outfitted with a new tail. That spring of 1947, I was being strapped onto centrifuges or locked into altitude test chambers, testing different kinds of pressure suits.

That was really stepping into the unknown. Just terrifying. Hoover and I wore primitive pressure suits, looking like damned deep-sea divers, and got locked into sealed chambers where they'd rupture the diaphragm on the door, and in two-tenths of a second you would be at 70,000 feet. Papers flew around and the window fogged. The first time that happened, they forgot to hook up Hoover's oxygen supply inside his pressure suit, and he couldn't exhale or inhale or communicate, and turned dark purple inside his helmet.

They took us up to 105,000 feet, which is the most air they could pump out of those chambers, then nearly did kill us on the centrifuges. As experienced fighter pilots we could routinely withstand the pull of four Gs without any "G" suits, but they put tremendous loads on us, while strapped standing up and lying down. God, it was miserable, and we got sick as dogs. Bob said, "You know, pard, these tests are more traumatic for me than sitting in that damned X-1 cockpit and running the rocket even though the whole thing might have blown us sky-high." I agreed.

David Clark, a corset manufacturer in Worcester, Massachusetts, received an Air Corps contract for the first high-altitude pressure suits, so Bob and I flew there in a B-25 bomber to be outfitted. We would be the first pilots to wear them; these first models were so cumbersome that we looked like the Pillsbury Doughboy. There was no way we could eject from an airplane wearing them. The company was in the bra and pantyhose business, and I returned home with boxloads for Glennis. We came within an eyelash of going down on the return flight to Ohio, and investigators would have searched our wreckage to find two fighter jocks and a ton of bras and panties. Colonel Boyd ordered us not to fly in bad weather, but we hit an unexpected electrical storm. We were bouncing all over that sky. Hoover was flying when we were struck by lightning, a first for both of us. I mean a severe strike that blasted out the Plexiglas nose of the airplane. There was a rush of air and a terrible burning smell. We were both blinded by the flash. When our vision returned, we glanced at one another. Bob said, "I'm surprised you're still with me, pard." I told him, "I was just waiting for you to move to the exit and I'd be right behind you." Man, that was the truth.

We left for the Mojave in early July. I was officially TDY from Wright Field. That was military jargon for "temporary duty" at Muroc Air Base in California. Because I was TDY, I was not entitled to any on-base housing for my family; nor could Glennis use any base facilities, including its hospital or emergency room. Unless I was being permanently relocated, I would have to pay to move my family out to Muroc, and there would be no housing allowance if I did. I was disgusted. Glennis was back in West Virginia, having just given birth to Mickey, our second son, and we had yet to really live together. I wasn't around for Mickey's delivery, either. All this time, I was coming home on weekends, and now they were sending me to the West Coast to risk my neck and giving me nothing in return. It was a rough deal, and we were both sick of living apart. I told Glennis that we'd find a place at Muroc even if it meant putting up a tent on the desert. And it almost came to that.

Meanwhile, I'd leave California late Friday afternoon and fly all night to West Virginia in a T-6, which was a single-engine prop trainer. Many times I fell asleep in that damned cockpit, only to wake up not knowing where I was and find the airplane circling. It's a wonder I lived so long. Bud Anderson arrived in Dayton as I was preparing to leave for California. He was TDY, too, and Elly was with her folks near Sacramento. We flew out a few times together in a C-45 cargo plane. We'd take off at the end of a long day of work and put that thing on autopilot. Andy slept in the aisle in the back and I slept in the cockpit seat. Once I woke up just in time to find us flying up a box canyon in the Sierras. Another time, we both fell asleep and ran a fuel tank dry. Two big red lights were flashing on the panel, with both of us scrambling around. So, he was either flying all night for me, or I was doing it for him. It was a stinking way to live, but that is the life we chose. We once drove from Wright out to see Elly in Andy's 1946 Ford when we couldn't take off in bad weather. We drove out nonstop, taking turns sleeping in the backseat. And all this breakneck traveling gave us one full day at home with our families.

On one of these trips, I showed Andy the X-1. He still talks about it. Here was a Top Secret, six-million-dollar-research plane, and the two of us slid back the hangar door and walked in. No guards, no nothing. There were only thirteen of us working on the project, and we were off by ourselves at the south end of the lakebed. There were two big hangars and a few shacks and Quonset huts shimmering in the summer desert sun. The base commander, a bird colonel, ignored us completely. There isn't a film record on any of my first rides because no one bothered to install movie cameras. We weren't exactly warmly welcomed. Colonel Boyd had told me that no one would know that I existed unless or until the flights were successful. I didn't have to be a genius to figure out that they were putting plenty of distance between their own hides and south base to see whether or not the only thing I'd break was my own precious neck.

Dick Frost

(BELL X-1 PROJECT ENGINEER)

Yeager, Ridley, and Hoover arrived at Muroc in mid-July. The rumor I heard about the two pilots was that they were the most junior guys in the flight test section at Wright and therefore the most expendable in a catastrophe. That was the kind of sour-grapes rumor that I didn't believe. What I did believe was that they were supposedly two of the hottest fighter jocks in the Air Corps, who always flew balls-out. Having been a fighter test pilot myself, that description fit.

The military test pilots were very macho; in some it didn't show as aggressively as in others, but inside they were all the same. They'd rather fly a fighter than do anything else in the world, and they were awfully good at it. They flew daringly, surviving a lot of close shaves that killed some of their buddies. Each was convinced that he was better than a friend who bought the farm. When that happened, one part of them was sorry, another part contemptuous—the idea being that busting one's ass doesn't happen to those who know what they're doing. "Dumb bastard should've known better" was a common attitude. Supreme self-confidence is a big part of a fighter test pilot's baggage, a real cockiness. But they saw enough buddies die to know that what they were doing was a dangerous way to live. So all of them adopted the eat, drink, and be merry attitude, even if they had never heard the cliché. Being a wild character was part of their trade, and there were always plenty of women drawn to their bravery. I'd been around fighter pilots all my life, so I figured I knew Chuck and Bob even before I met them.

Ridley told me that Yeager had made the most perfect saw-tooth climb barograph record ever seen at Wright Field and that Hoover was simply a magician in the cockpit. My first impressions of the two were very different. Hoover was a happy-go-lucky stick-and-rudder man, a helluva good pilot, but Chuck Yeager was all test pilot. He was intent and serious. My job was to hold class every day for two weeks and teach them all that I knew about the X-1. I had been with it from the beginning and knew that airplane inside and out.

I was project engineer on all of Slick Goodlin's flights. Like Chuck, Slick was a superb pilot with all the courage in the world. They also shared an identically cool response to dangerous situations—completely cool to save themselves and their airplane. They were both only twenty-four, but Chuck had more native good sense and didn't care a damn about fame or wealth. The biggest difference between them was Slick's lack of interest in learning about the airplane and its power system. He knew how to fire the rocket engines or how to handle problems by common sense and overall pilot experience. But he depended entirely on the fact that I was in the sky with him, flying chase, and it never occurred to him that the radio might go out. In a pinch, he counted on me to tell him what to do. Yeager would rely on himself. I couldn't teach him enough.

Chuck didn't say much. He sat in class listening, and I could tell from his eyes that he understood everything. When he asked a question, it was always to the point. The guy was an instinctive engineer, born to an innate understanding of mechanics and mechanical systems. He told me that the pressure valve system on board was exactly the same as the one he had worked with helping his Dad in the gas fields of West Virginia. Those first days in the classroom, he was sizing me up. There was a certain skeptical look in his eyes, probably from the feeling that people looked down on him because he lacked their education and background, but, by God, he'd show them. He was immensely competitive and beat my ass off by the hour playing ping-pong. But any feeling of inadequacy he had about being only a West Virginia high-school graduate was nonsense. He used Ridley and me as his professors and wound up knowing nearly as much as we did.

I recall him as a loner—both gregarious and a loner, who needed space by himself, but also needed fun with others. I've seen this loner quality often in those who were topnotch test pilots.

We'd talk during lunch and coffee breaks, and I was amazed to learn about some of the independent research flying he had done, strictly out of his own curiosity. He was fascinated by ground effect. His opinion was that you couldn't fly the Shooting Star jet fighter into the ground while flying just over it. He knew because he had tried it! He flew ten feet or less over the ground to test his theory. No one would ever ask a pilot to try that stunt, but Chuck was sufficiently curious and skilled to pilot that P-80 over a flat lakebed and feel the ground effect for himself—the pressures that build up beneath an airplane as it approaches ground-level. Air compresses under it and it flies differently. He did it carefully; he wasn't about to kill himself, but he wanted to know. On flying and airplanes, his curiosity was endless, and it was his accumulated experience and knowledge that saved his life on several occasions. Yeager could always find that extra option in a critical situation that another pilot didn't know about.

The X-1 was a complex airplane. It was only thirty-one feet long with a twenty-eight-foot wingspan. It had a high tail with a stabilizer in the fin, well above the wake of turbulent air off the wings at transonic speeds. It had a straight, extremely thin wing to delay the onset of shock waves as long as possible. It was a beautiful airplane to fly, but at least half the aviation engineers I had talked to thought it was doomed. Chuck raised a few questions that I answered uncomfortably, but frankly. He asked whether I thought he could survive a bail-out. I told him, no way. He'd be sliced in half by those thin wings. But he never did ask me if I believed in an impregnable sound barrier. At best, I was ambivalent about it, and the only honest answer would have been that if any airplane could do it, it would be the X-1.

Dick Frost taught me all the systems, but without Jack Ridley, the X-1 probably would never have succeeded. Jack looked like a little elf with big ears that stuck straight out from the sides of his head. He was in his late twenties, but his skin was already weathered from the sun and wind, and when Glennis met him, she said, "Jack could pass for a man who is a hundred and three." That was true. He had an Oklahoma drawl and a dry Sooner wit, smoked like a fiend, and was always burning holes in his shirt and tie because he forgot to flick his cigarette ashes. He was small and tough; in college he had been a bantam wrestling champion, and although he was as sweet-natured as any man I've ever known, put a couple of drinks in him and he'd want to take on the biggest and toughest pilots he could find. Andy was the same, and because of those two, we were forever getting bounced off barroom walls. Jack loved to raise hell, but it was a chore getting him going because he pretended to be henpecked. "Jesus, Nell will kill me," he'd protest. But he always went along. He once went out with test pilot Pete Everest and got blasted. Jack was a complete mess when he staggered up on his front porch. Nell greeted him by hurling out a pillow and blanket, then slammed the door in his face.

I trusted Jack with my life. He was the only

person on earth who could have kept me from flying
the X-1. As committed as I was to the program, and
with all that was riding on these flights, if Jack had
said, "Chuck, if you fly in that thing, you're not
gonna make it," that would have been it for yours
truly. Jack was brilliant. He had been the prize pupil
of Dr. Theodore Von Karman, the great Hungarian
aerodynamicist, while a graduate student at Caltech.
But he was also one sharp cookie who could spot a
flaw in a flight profile or an engineering design before anyone else. Colonel Boyd told me, "Use Ridley.
I'm sending him out there with you because you can
always trust his judgment." And I always did.

At Muroc, we had to deal with a high-powered
team of scientists and engineers from the National
Advisory Committee for Aeronautics (NACA), the forerunner of the space agency. Those guys were in charge
of the five hundred pounds of monitoring instrumentation aboard the X-1 and ultimately had a lot to say
about the pace of our flights—how quickly we attempted to breach the barrier. It was clear that the
NACA guys had expected Boyd to send out his most
senior people, both in experience and education. Instead, Jack and I were just captains, Hoover a
lieutenant—and the two pilots had never had any
college. NACA wasn't thrilled.

I'd attend these highly technical NACA preflight
planning sessions and postflight briefings and not
know what in hell they were talking about. But Jack
always took me aside and translated the engineers'
technical jargon into layman's terms. There was no
way I could communicate with Walt Williams, who
headed the NACA team. He had a reputation for
being pompous. But when Jack spoke, it was the only
time that any of Walt's colleagues ever saw him
listen intently to somebody else. Everyone listened to
Jack that way. He had a lot more practical knowledge of what we were doing than any of the others.
So, Jack is the one I relied upon; I really felt that he
was my life-insurance policy. When he explained some-

thing, I usually kept asking why until I understood it thoroughly. If I had my own opinion, we'd discuss it and argue until we both agreed. Because he was also a good pilot and was so practical, we were always on the same wavelength. Ridley knew me so well that when I described something that was happening with the X-1, he knew immediately what we were getting into. Without having him close at hand, I'd have been lost.

There was one incident with Jack that cemented my trust in him. We had only been at Muroc a few days, when a training command pilot out of Luke Air Force Base had run out of fuel and made an emergency landing on a small strip out on the desert somewhere. These little strips were all over, constructed during the war as a hedge against a Japanese invasion of the West Coast, and were designed as emergency strips for prop fighters. The airplane that had run out of fuel was a P-84 Thunderjet, needing a longer runway to take off again with a load of fuel aboard. So, Jack said to me, "Come on, let's go out there and see what we can do about it." I can still see him standing next to that jet on that small runway, working his slide rule. He calculated exactly how much fuel we'd need to get the jet back to Luke, then he carefully paced off the exact spot where I should fire jet boosters to lift off, driving in a stake at that point. He said, "I've given you ten feet of runway to spare. That should be plenty." A crew brought in the boosters and the fuel, and I took off, fired the boosters at the marker, and was airborne with ten feet to spare. After that, if Jack had told me, "No sweat, Chuck, I've left you three inches," that would've been fine by me.

Jack was so convinced that the sound barrier was breakable that he eased my own fears. He said flat out, "The only barrier is bad aerodynamics and bad planning. Bell has designed the perfect ship for this program, and we're not gonna make any mistakes getting there." Period. Sure, I was nervous. But it was a good kind of nervousness—the nervousness of flying a completely different kind of airplane for the first time, of wanting to learn everything about it before I crawled inside, and psyching myself not to screw it up. It was the tension of wanting to get it over with as quickly as possible and getting back in one piece. I was intimidated by that orange beast, but Jack put me right about that too. He said, "Aw, bullshit, Chuck. You make quick friends with every new airplane that you fly. After a couple of flights in the X-1, you'll be in love. She won't bite you without any warning." He knew what he was talking about.

There was another guy who knew what he was talking about too, because he had already flown the X-1 twenty times. Slick Goodlin was still around, and Pancho Barnes, who ran the Fly Inn bar and restaurant at the edge of Rogers Dry Lake, arranged for Hoover and me to meet Slick at a dinner at her place, and have him brief us about flying the X-1. We had a steak and a couple of drinks. I said, "I was hoping you could tell me a few things to know about flying that bugger." Slick said he'd be glad to check me out in the X-1 as soon as the Air Corps made out a thousand-dollar contract. I told him, "Well, Slick, if you flew that thing, I guess I can, too." Pancho was really ticked at him.

The first flights would be nonpowered, familiarization flights, scheduled for the middle of August. I'd be dropped at 25,000 feet from the B-29 mother ship, without any fuel aboard, and glide back down and land on the lakebed. That way, I could get a feel for the ship and its handling, as well as practice glide landing, which is how we landed even on powered flights. Any remaining fuel was jettisoned, and I glided in. Dead-sticking in was a must because of a lightweight landing gear that could not withstand the heavy load of a ship carrying fuel. And it was also safer that way. X-1 fuel was volatile.

I didn't eat much breakfast the morning of that first flight. I was out early watching them load the

X-1 under the B-29, by backing it into a cross-shaped pit and pulling the bomber over it. Then the X-1 was hoisted up and hooked to the B-29's bomb bay with a bomb shackle. I'd fly in the B-29 until we got to altitude, then climb down a ladder to enter the X-1. Ridley would lower the cabin door, which I locked into place, then I would settle into the tiny cockpit and wait to be dropped like a goddamn bomb. The cockpit was pressurized with pure nitrogen that was nonflammable, so I had to be on 100 percent oxygen at all times. We had no backup oxygen system; that's how you did business in those days. A lot of the times, you'd get a leaky oxygen mask and land groggy. And we had only one battery to activate the radio, the propellant valves, the instrumentation, and the telemetry system. No backup battery, either. So, I guess that Colonel Boyd wasn't out of line when he suddenly sent for me just before I left for Muroc. Because I lived on base and Glennis wasn't around, he just assumed I was a bachelor. Somehow he learned I was married and a father and he really looked perturbed. I told him because I had a family I would fly more cautiously than an unmarried pilot.

"This is a highly risky project," he said. "Have you considered what might happen to your family?"

"Yes, sir," I said, "I plan to bring them to Muroc as soon as we can find some housing."

I was good at watching out for myself in a cockpit. The only trouble was that with the X-1, there was so much to watch out for.

How we dropped the X-1 never varied from the first glided flight to the final powered run. Once everything was squared away on the ground, I stored my helmet inside the cockpit because I didn't want to carry it coming down the ladder. The first hardhat helmets had yet to be built, so I made my own by cutting the top out of a World War II tank helmet, which fit like a protective dome on top of my skull, and put four straps and a snap on my pilot's leather helmet, which was fitted around the dome. Then I carried my parachute and boarded the mother ship. I would sit on an apple box behind Maj. Bob Cardenas, the pilot, and Ridley, the copilot, as we taxied out and took off. We took off early in the morning, so that the sun would not be in my face when I landed on the dry lakebed. Cardenas kept his climb within gliding distance of Rogers Dry Lake. His flight plan called for him to climb to 25,000 feet, then back off for some forty miles to pick up speed, but always stay within gliding distance of the lakebed. He then dropped the nose into a twenty-degree diving angle until he reached 240 mph indicated. Then he gave me a countdown of ten and dropped me.

When Cardenas reached 12,000 feet I headed for the ladder in the bomb bay. The reason that I didn't sit in the shackled X-1 cockpit was that if we had an accidental shackle release, or had to drop the X-1 anywhere under 10,000 feet, I would end up in a fatal spin. In fact, loaded with fuel, the X-1 stalled at anything below 240 mph, and the climbing speed of the B-29 was only 180 mph. We figured that if I were dropped at a slow speed in a stall, I would probably have time to recover and fire off the rocket engines, as long as I was above 10,000 feet.

So, at 12,000 feet I headed for that ladder, with Ridley behind me. Climbing down into the X-1 was never my favorite moment. The ladder was on the right side of the bomb bay opposite the entrance door on the right side of the X-1. The wind blast from the four bomber prop engines was deafening, and the wind-chill was way below zero. I wore a leather jacket and my flight suit, but no gloves so I could grip the rungs. I had to bounce on the ladder to get it going, and be lowered into the slipstream. There was a metal panel to protect against the wind blast, but it was rather primitive, and that bitch of a wind took your breath away and chilled you to the bone. I would slide into the X-1 feet first, wearing a seat-type parachute, primarily to sit on, because once you were in, the only way out was to land safely.

With those thin wings only six feet behind the door, jumping was pointless.

Once I was safely inside, the crew above would lower the door on a pulley to Jack, who had followed me down the ladder. Jack would hold the door in place while I locked it from the inside. Still shackled to the B-29, it was dark as night in that cockpit.

I'd put on my helmet and oxygen mask and hook into the communications systems so I could speak with the mother ship and the two Shooting Star chase planes that were only now taking off from Muroc. Dick Frost flew low chase, sticking with me for the drop-out because he knew the systems so well. Hoover flew high chase. In powered flights, he'd position himself about ten miles ahead at 40,000 feet, giving me an aiming point. Once I ignited the rockets, I whistled past him in a few seconds, but he tried to keep me in sight as long as he could in order to position himself as an escort when I glided in for a lakebed landing.

On this first flight, I was going over my check-list, when that damned Hoover buzzed me! He flew by so close that his jet exhaust almost knocked me loose from the B-29. Christ, I was rocking and swaying, scared to death. "Hoover, you bastard!" I was really hot. I said, "If this thing carried guns, I'd shoot your ass out of the sky." Ol' Bob laughed. "Come and get me," he said. Well, I didn't try on this first glide flight. But on the third, when I saw him turning toward me, I turned into him and we had a dogfight down to the deck, just like at Wright, only this time I almost stalled the damned X-1 waxing Bob's fanny true and good.

Man, the adrenaline was pumping as I sat in that cockpit, waiting to be dropped for the first time. The cockpit floor sloped up toward the ship's nose, so I sat on my seat-type parachute to get as high as I could to see out. The plexiglass windshield provided only marginal visibility on landings because it was flush with the fuselage, to eliminate drag. Squeezed in there, my knees were higher than my shoulders, and my feet rested on the X-1 rudder pedals. I drove with an H-shaped control wheel on which the rocket thrusters and key instrumentation switches were located; I didn't have to move my hands at critical moments, which is the reason I was able, later on, to fly with broken ribs.

"All set, Yeager?" Ridley asks.

"You bet," I reply. "Let's go to work."

At altitude, Cardenas begins a shallow dive and starts his countdown from ten. Inside the X-1, I brace myself.

". . . Two. One."

The sound of a sharp pop, like snapping cable, and a jolt that lifts me off the seat and strains my shoulders against the safety harness. The X-1 falls free.

Bright sunlight blinds me. I blink rapidly, my eyes shocked after long minutes in the dark hole of the bomb bay. I push the control wheel out of neutral, and without even thinking, do two pretty slow rolls. Larry Bell was right: the X-1 glides like a bird. I'm flying in total silence, aware only of the sound of my own breathing through the oxygen mask, and my ship is graceful, responsive, and beautiful to handle. It's a fabulous ride that I wish would never end, but in less than three minutes, I begin a banking turn at 5,000 feet above the lakebed, and with Bob Hoover riding on my wing, lower the landing gear at 250 mph and line up with Rogers Dry Lake, which stretches before me almost to the horizon. Lakebed landings can be damned tricky; they weren't marked in those days, and without experience, a pilot's depth perception ran into trouble against all that open space—like landing on a calm ocean. But I had been landing on these lakebeds since 1945. I whistle on in, delaying touchdown as long as possible, and grease it down at 190 mph. When I crawl out into the hot sun, I'm wearing a grin that almost breaks my face. "Best damn airplane I ever flew," I tell Dick Frost.

I'm ready to load her with fuel and go for the sound barrier that afternoon.

On the second glide flight, she handles so wonderfully that I actually allow her to fly herself, and startle Frost, looking down at me from the chase plane above, by raising my arms in the air and exclaiming, "Look, Ma, no hands." The final glide test, the following day, I dogfight Hoover down to the lakebed, merciless in an airplane that is lighter than his and more maneuverable.

Now we are ready for the "big boy" flights: load her with fuel and take off like a bullet for the dark part of the sky.

We needed a week to prepare the X-1 and plan our first powered flight. Colonel Boyd came out from Wright to confer with us. "Start out easy," he said. "Don't stretch the program by getting too eager on this thing. Find out what the hell is going on with the airplane." Ridley and I had already talked it over and agreed that since Goodlin had taken the X-1 to .8 Mach, we would start by going out to .82 Mach. The old man approved. "Okay," he said, "we'll let you go up in increments of fifteen or twenty mph on each flight, but no more than that."

I felt almost cocky about my ability to master the orange beast and make her do exactly what I wanted. What I knew for certain was that the X-1 would never play any dirty tricks on me without giving me fair warning. And I was right about that in terms of flying her. But I was wrong about other unexpected problems that gave me nightmares.

AGAINST THE
WALL

Glennis Yeager

Absence may make the heart grow fonder, but when Chuck was sent out to Muroc, it was a turning point for us. Instead of being three hundred miles apart, we were three thousand miles, and trying to get home on weekends was practically killing him. We just decided that this was it; even though he was out there temporarily, with no idea whether it would be a few months or years, I was coming out with the children. After two years of marriage, we had lived together only a few months, and that was no way to build a solid foundation. So we agreed not to be practical, not be frugal, and just do it.

If I had to do it over again, I would have waited longer to have my children. I had my four one after another and it made a tough situation much tougher. I was always sick when I was pregnant, and I was always pregnant. Chuck would come home for a few days and, whammo!—I'd be expecting. That's how it seemed. We weren't exactly testimonials for efficient birth control.

I left Mickey, who was only a few months old, with my mother-in-law, and took two-year-old Donald with me to California. Chuck met us at the Los Angeles airport and drove us out to Muroc. Well, a garden spot it definitely wasn't. I was raised in the pine forests of the Sierra foothills, and living out on the high desert would take getting used to. Chuck drove us straight to Muroc, and we went past the guarded gate and drove for miles and miles and there was absolutely nothing there but scrub and lakebeds and Joshua trees. Twenty-eight thousand acres of nothing. The place was used during the war for practice bombing, and I could see why. I said to him, "Where's the base?" Chuck laughed. "Hell, this is the busy part." Well, there really wasn't much to Muroc in those days—a few hangars and buildings shimmering in the sun. The wind never stopped howling. The desolation took your breath away.

The nearest town was twenty miles from the base, and we had left our car back in West Virginia. Don and I stayed in a room at the guest house on base, which was a barracks for dependents. You could only stay three nights, then had to pack your bags, walk out the door, then sign back in. The men could not visit their wives there. And the wives could not visit their husbands in the bachelor officers' barracks. Cohabitation must've been against Air Corps's policy in those days, so I would sneak over to Chuck's room after Don fell asleep.

We'd get angry as hornets, but usually wound up laughing at the ridiculous situations; our spirits were high because at least we were together. We borrowed Jack Ridley's car to go house-hunting, but homes out there were sparser than vegetation. For example, one day Colonel Ascani came out from Wright to confer with Chuck and Jack. The three of them were standing near the lakebed, when Ascani suddenly saw a spiral of black smoke far off in the distance. "Looks like a fire," Ascani said. Jack ran to his car and took off across the lakebed. His house was on fire, and he knew it because there was nothing else out there. That old clapboard place burnt to the ground, and he and Nell lost everything they owned. There was some housing on the base, but the X-1 crew wasn't eligible because they were at Muroc on temporary duty. So, we'd haul little Donald around with us on long treks across bumpy dirt roads, looking for anything with a roof.

We got so desperate that we almost rented a rancher's chicken house. But then someone told us about a place available at the Zabrowski Ranch, about thirty miles from the base. And that's where we ended up. It was a one-bedroom adobe guest house, much too small for a family of four, but by then it seemed like a palace. We had a kitchen and a living room, but no facilities, like a washing machine, and I did all the diapers and laundry in the bathtub. Donald slept on a daybed in the living room, and little Mickey slept in a playpen in our bedroom. Chuck laughed. He said, "Well, this ain't much, but it's better than that cabin up in a holler I promised you."

Chuck and Bob Hoover flew back east together. Bob was getting married in Dayton, and Chuck went to West Virginia to bring back the baby and our car. He left Hamlin for California on September 17, the day that Bob and Colleen were married, arriving at the church in Dayton with little Mickey strapped into one of those porto-chairs. Hoover, who is six-three, and his new bride piled into our Ford coupe and drove all the way across country with our five-month-old baby. Now, that was a honeymoon! Somewhere around Kansas, they decided to rest for a while, so in the middle of the night, they pulled into a graveyard next to the highway and slept among the tombstones. Only Hoover and Yeager would do that.

My mother-in-law had made up a traveling formula of Karo syrup and boiled water to mix in with the baby's canned-milk feedings. But with all the sloshing around, the Karo fermented, and the baby got plastered. Mickey wore a silly grin and giggled clear across the country. When they finally arrived at our front door, I came running out, so glad they had made it safely. Chuck handed me the baby. There was a terrible smell in the car. Mickey had messed his pants about a half-an-hour earlier, and Colleen had wanted to stop and change him, but Chuck said, no, let Glennis think we never changed him at all. So, he handed me the baby and I said, "Well, at least you could've changed him." And Chuck said, "Hell, no. We just wrapped another blanket around him to keep down the smell."

What an introduction to the military life for Colleen!

When I first got out there, I had no idea what Chuck was doing with the X-1. It really didn't register. What's the sound barrier? Oh, I think he may have told me that a British test pilot was killed trying to fly faster than sound, but the reason for the accident, he said, was an improperly designed airplane. I said, if there is a barrier, it must exist for a reason. Why try to break it? He explained that then planes could go faster. The X-1 was the best airplane he had ever flown, and he didn't anticipate much of a problem accomplishing the mission. If he was at all apprehensive, he certainly didn't transmit those concerns to me. Chuck never was a worrier. He could fall asleep in ten seconds. So, I certainly had no appreciation for the dangers involved in his flights, and neither of us had any idea about the fuss that would be made later on when he flew at Mach 1.

Only rarely over the years did he ever tell me about his close calls; those I had to find out about for myself. He only brought home good news. He en-

joyed telling me about a good day of flying. Any
bragging he ever did was for my ears only.

So, I was never nervous about his work. Maybe I
would've been if I were told more about it. I know
there were some wives who died a thousand deaths
every time their test pilot husbands walked out the
door. But Chuck was so matter-of-fact, so confident,
that I was convinced there was no way he would
allow himself to get killed. He was doing exactly
what he wanted to do. And it would not have made
much difference to me whether he was a fighter pilot
or a test pilot, or whatever description was ahead of
that word "pilot." Flying was flying, and that was
his life. And in later years, when I became a veteran
air force wife and actually witnessed several crashes
and lost count of all the memorial services I attended, I think I became fatalistic as well as philosophical about the risks. I knew that if the worst did
happen, then it was the price he was willing to pay
to do what he loved.

When I first moved out to Muroc, I was practically the only wife there. Later on, some of the wives
came out, so when we had parties, the men talked
flying and the women talked babies. I was a loner,
anyway, and didn't need hen parties. Taking care of
two babies out on the desert, I had plenty to do and
all the work I needed. I was like a pioneer wife out
there; the nearest stores were thirty miles away. There
was so much to get used to, including living full-time
with my husband. Chuck wasn't easy for an orderly
person to live with. He never picked up his clothes,
left them all over the house, no matter how much I'd
nag. So, one day I decided to teach him a lesson. I
began picking up his clothes and just dumped them
on the floor in the hall closet. I dumped and dumped
until that closet bulged. Finally he asked me where a
blue windbreaker was. My big moment! I said, it
must be in the hall closet. He opened the door and
this enormous pile of clothes just dumped out on
him. He kicked through the pile, found the jacket in

the mess, put it on, and left. That man showed no surprise and never said a word. I was so damned mad I could've spit nails.

Life was basic out there, but we had fun, too. We'd hunt jack rabbits or drive over to Pancho Barnes's place and ride horses. She served a nice steak, and we had good times—parties and dances and barbecues. The Zabrowskis had a daughter who babysat for us on Saturday nights, which was a great treat for me. Chuck, too. He couldn't stand sitting around. It drove him crazy. He needed action, otherwise he got antsy and bored. And it had to be constant: something going on all the time. And he is still that way. With him, even driving home from a party could be an adventure. If we spotted a coyote in the headlights, off we'd go across a lakebed, chasing the darned thing—and they could run about 50 mph. We'd no sooner gain on the little devil than he'd stop in his tracks and take off in the opposite direction.

Shortly after we settled in, Chuck drove us to the base to show us the X-1. He purposely hadn't told me he named the plane *Glamorous Glennis*, but there it was, written on the nose. He did that with his Mustang in England, but this was an important research airplane, and I was very surprised. And proud. He said, "You're my good-luck charm, hon. Any airplane I name after you always brings me home." I really think that's why the Air Corps allowed my name to stay on the X-1. Chuck didn't ask permission to do it, and they weren't delighted that he had (the official pictures of the ship had my name air-brushed out), but none of the brass wanted to interfere with his good-luck charm and perhaps jinx the mission. So, Chuck got his way and I had a namesake that one day would be displayed in the Smithsonian, near another famous airplane, the first one flown by the Wright brothers.

FIRST POWERED FLIGHT: AUGUST 29, 1947

Shivering, you bang your gloved hands together and strap on your oxygen mask inside the coldest airplane ever flown. You're being cold-soaked from the hundreds of gallons of liquid oxygen (LOX) fuel stored in the compartment directly behind you at minus 296 degrees. No heater, no defroster; you'll just have to grit your teeth for the next fifteen minutes until you land and feel that wonderful hot desert sun. But that cold saps your strength: it's like trying to work and concentrate inside a frozen food locker.

That cold will take you on the ride of your life. You watched the X-1 get its 7:00 A.M. feeding in a swirling cloud of vapor fog, saw the frost form under its orange belly. That was an eerie sight; you're carrying six hundred gallons of LOX and water alcohol on board that can blow up at the flick of an igniter switch and scatter your pieces over several counties. But if all goes well, the beast will chug-a-lug a ton of fuel a minute.

Anyone with brain cells would have to wonder what in hell he was doing in such a situation—strapped inside a live bomb that's about to be dropped out of a bomb bay. But risks are the spice of life, and this is the kind of moment that a test pilot lives for. The butterflies are fluttering, but you feed off fear as if it's a high-energy candy bar. It keeps you alert and focused.

You accept risk as part of every new challenge; it comes with the territory. So you learn all you can about the ship and its systems, practice flying it on ground runs and glide flights, plan for any possible contingency, until the odds against you seem more friendly. You like the X-1; she's a sound airplane, but she's also an experimental machine, and you're a researcher on an experimental flight. You know you can be hammered by something unexpected, but you count on your experience, concentration, and instincts to pull you through. And luck. Without luck . . .

You can't watch yourself fly. But you know when you're in sync with the machine, so plugged into its instruments and controls that your mind and your hand become the heart of its operating system. You can make that airplane talk, and like a good horse, the machine knows when it's in competent hands. You know what you can get away with. And you can be wrong only once. You smile reading newspaper stories about a pilot in a disabled plane that maneuvered to miss a schoolyard before he hit the ground. That's crap. In an emergency situation, a pilot thinks only about one thing—survival. You battle to survive right down to the ground; you think about nothing else. Your concentration is riveted on what to try next. You don't say anything on the radio, and you aren't even aware that a schoolyard exists. That's exactly how it is.

There are at least a dozen different ways that the X-1 can kill you, so your concentration is total during the preflight check procedures. You load up nitrogen gas pressures in the manifolds—your life's blood because the nitrogen gas runs all the internal systems as well as the flaps and landing gear. Then you bleed off the liquid oxygen manifold and shut it down. All's in order.

Half an hour ago, we taxied out to takeoff in the mother ship. Because of the possibility of crashing with so much volatile fuel, they closed down the base until we were safely off the ground. That's the only acknowledgment from the base commander that we even exist. There's no interest in our flights because practically nobody at Muroc gives us any chance for success. Those bastards think they have it all figured. They call our flights "Slick Goodlin's Revenge." The word is that he knew when to get out in one piece by quitting over money.

One minute to drop. Ridley flashes the word from the copilot's seat in the mother ship. We're at 25,000 feet as the B-29 noses over and starts its shallow dive. Major Cardenas, the driver, starts counting backwards from ten.

C-r-r-ack. The bomb shackle release jolts you up from your seat, and as you sail out of the dark bomb bay the sun explodes in brightness. You're looking into the sky. *Wrong!* You should be dropped level. The dive speed was too slow, and they dropped you in a nose-up stall. You blink to get your vision, fighting the stall with your control wheel, dropping toward the basement like an elevator whose cable snapped. You're three thousand pounds heavier than in those glide flights. Down goes that nose and you pick up speed. You level out about a thousand feet below the mother ship and reach for that rocket igniter switch.

The moment of truth: if you are gonna be blown up, this is likely to be when. You light the first chamber.

Whoosh. Slammed back in your seat, a tremendous kick in the butt. Nose up and hold on. Barely a sound; you can hear your breathing in the oxygen mask—you're outracing the noise behind you—and for the first time in a powered airplane you can hear the air beating against the windshield as the distant dot that is Hoover's high chase P-80 grows ever bigger. You pass him like he's standing still, and he reports seeing diamond-shaped shock waves leaping out of your fiery exhaust. Climbing faster than you can even think, but using only one of four rocket chambers, you turn it off and light another. We're streaking up at .7 Mach; this beast's power is awesome. You've never known such a feeling of speed while pointing up in the sky. At 45,000 feet, where morning resembles the beginning of dusk, you turn on the last of the four chambers. God, what a ride! And you still have nearly half your fuel left.

Until this moment, you obeyed the flight plan to the letter: firing only one chamber at a time, to closely monitor the chamber pressures; if you use two or more, there's too much to watch. If you fire all four, you may accelerate too rapidly, be forced to raise your nose to slow down, and get yourself into a high-speed stall.

Now the flight plan calls for you to jettison remaining fuel and glide down to land. But you're bug-eyed, thrilled to your toes, and the fighter jock takes over from the cautious test pilot. Screw it! You're up there in the dark part of the sky in the most fabulous flying machine ever built, and you're just not ready to go home. The moment calls for a nice slow roll, and you lower your wing, pulling a couple of Gs until you're hanging upside down in zero Gs and the engine quits. As soon as the X-1 rights itself it starts again, but you've been stupid. At zero Gs the fuel couldn't feed the engine, and you might have been blown up. But the X-1 is forgiving—this time.

You know what you're supposed to do, but you know what you're gonna do. You turn off the engine, but instead of jettisoning the remaining fuel, you roll over and dive for Muroc Air Base. We blister down, shit-heavy, .8 Mach in front of the needle, a dive-glide faster than most jets at full power. You're thinking, "Let's show those bastards the real X-1."

Below 10,000 feet is the danger zone, the limit for jettisoning fuel with enough maneuver time to glide down to a safe landing. But we're below 5,000, lined up with Muroc's main runway. And we're still in a dive.

We whistle down that main runway, only 300 feet off the ground, until we are parallel with the control tower. You hit the main rocket switch. The four chambers blow a thirty-foot lick of flame. Christ, the impact nearly knocks you back into last week. That nose is pointed so straight up that you can't see the blue sky out the windshield. We are no longer an airplane: we're a skyrocket. You're not flying. You're holding on to the tiger's tail. Straight up, you're going .75 Mach! In one minute the fuel is gone. By then you're at 35,000 feet, traveling at .85 Mach.

You're so excited, scared, and thrilled that you can't say a word until the next day.

But others said plenty. The NACA team thought I was a wild man. Dick Frost chewed me out for doing that slow roll. Even Jack Ridley shook his head. He said, "Any spectators down there knew damned well that wasn't Slick rattling those dishes. Okay, son, you got it all out of your system, but now you're gonna hang tough." Colonel Boyd fired a rocket of his own. "Reply by endorsement about why you exceeded .82 Mach in violation of my direct orders." I asked Ridley to write my reply. "Bullshit," he said. "You did it. You explain it."

I wrote back: "The airplane felt so good and flew so well that I felt certain we would have no trouble going slightly above the agreed speed. The violation of your direct orders was due to the excited state of the undersigned and will not be repeated."

A few days later, the old man called me. "Damn it, I expect you to stick to the program and do what you are supposed to. Don't get overeager and cocky. Do you want to jeopardize the first Air Corps research project?"

"No, sir."

"Well, then obey the goddamn rules."

From then on I did. But on that first powered flight I wanted to answer those who said we were doomed in the attempt to go faster than sound. My message was, "Stick it where the sun don't shine."

Going out to .85 Mach put the program out on a limb because it carried us beyond the limits of what was then known about high-speed aerodynamics. Wind tunnels could only measure up to .85 Mach, and as Walt Williams of NACA was quick to point out to me, "From now on, Chuck, you'll be flying in the realm of the unknown." Ridley and I called it "the Ughknown."

Whatever happened, I figured I was better off than the British test pilots who had attempted supersonic flights in high-powered dives. If they got into trouble, that was it—especially in a tailless airplane like *The Swallow*. All my attempts would be made in climbs—the power of the rocket over the jet—and that way, if I encountered a problem, I could quickly slow down. But the price of rocket power was flying with volatile fuel. Running four chambers, my fuel lasted only two and a half minutes; it lasted five minutes on two chambers and ten minutes on one. Each minute of climbing we got lighter and faster, so that by the time we had climbed up and over at 45,000 feet, we were at max speed.

Who would decide the max speed of a particular flight? This was an Air Corps research project, but the seventeen NACA engineers and technicians used their expertise to try to control these missions. They were there as advisers, with high-speed wind tunnel experience, and were performing the data reduction collected on the X-1 flights, so they tried to dictate the speed in our flight plans. Ridley, Frost, and I always wanted to go faster than they did. They would recommend a Mach number, then the three of us would sit down and decide whether or not we wanted to stick with their recommendation. They were so conservative that it would've taken me six months to get to the barrier.

I wanted to be careful, but I also wanted to get it over with. Colonel Boyd sided with NACA caution, going up only two-hundredths of a Mach on each consecutive flight. Once I flew back with Hoover to see if I could get the old man to agree to speed things up. We met in the evening at his home. But Bob led off by trying to explain why he had been forced to crash-land a P-80 a few days before. I could tell the old man wasn't buying Bob's explanations; those thick eyebrows were bunching up. But ol' Hoover pushed on, becoming emotional to the point where he accidentally spat a capped tooth onto the old man's lap. I decided to have my say at another time.

So I flew in small increments of speed. On October 5, I made my sixth powered flight and experienced shock-wave buffeting for the first time as I reached .86 Mach. It felt like I was driving on bad shock absorbers over uneven paving stones. The right wing suddenly got heavy and began to drop, and when I tried to correct it my controls were sluggish. I increased my speed to .88 Mach to see what would happen. I saw my aileron vibrating with shock waves, and only with effort could I hold my wing level.

The X-1 was built with a high tail to avoid air turbulence off the wings; the tail was also thinner than the wings, so that shock waves would not form simultaneously on both surfaces. Thus far, the shock waves and buffeting had been manageable, and because the ship was stressed for eighteen Gs, I never was concerned about being shaken apart. Also, I was only flying twice a week, to give NACA time to reduce all the flight data and analyze it. Special sensing devices pinpointed the exact location of shock waves on any part of the airframe. The data revealed that the airplane was functioning exactly as its designers planned.

But on my very next flight we got knocked on our fannies. I was flying at .94 Mach at 40,000 feet, experiencing the usual buffeting, when I pulled back on the control wheel, and Christ, nothing happened! The airplane continued flying with the same attitude and in the same direction.

The control wheel felt as if the cables had snapped. I didn't know what in hell was happening. I turned off the engine and slowed down. I jettisoned my fuel and landed feeling certain that I had taken my last ride in the X-1. Flying at .94, I lost my pitch control. My elevator ceased to function. At the speed of sound, the ship's nose was predicted to go either up or down, and without pitch control, I was in a helluva bind.

I told Ridley I thought we had had it. There was no way I was going faster than .94 Mach without an elevator. He looked sick. So did Dick Frost and the NACA team. We called Colonel Boyd at Wright, and he flew out immediately to confer with us. Meanwhile, NACA analyzed the telemetry data from the flight and found that at .94 Mach, a shock wave was slammed right at the hinge point of the elevator on the tail, negating my controls. Colonel Boyd just shook his head. "Well," he said, "it looks to me like we've reached the end of the line." Everyone seemed to agree except for Jack Ridley.

He sat at a corner of the conference table scribbling little notes and equations. He said, "Well, maybe Chuck can fly without using the elevator. Maybe he can get by using only the horizontal stabilizer." The stabilizer was the winglike structure on the tail that stabilized pitch control. Bell's engineers had purposely built into them an extra control authority because they had anticipated elevator ineffectiveness caused by shock waves. This extra authority was a trim switch in the cockpit that would allow a small air motor to pivot the stabilizer up or down, creating a moving tail that could act as an auxiliary elevator by lowering or raising the airplane's nose. We were leery about trying it while flying at high speeds; instead, we set the trim on the ground and left it alone.

Jack thought we should spend a day ground testing the hell out of that system, learn everything there was to know about it, then flight test it. No one disagreed. There was no other alternative except to call the whole thing quits, but Jack got a lot of "what if" questions that spelled out all the risks. What if the motor got stuck in a trim up or trim down position? Answer: Yeager would have a problem. What if the turbulent airflow at high speed Mach overwhelmed the motor and kept the tail from pivoting? Answer: Yeager would be no worse off than he was during the previous mission. Yeah, but what if that turbulent air ripped off that damned tail as it was pivoting? Answer: Yeager better have paid-up insurance. We were dealing with the Ughknown.

Before returning to Wright, Colonel Boyd approved our ground tests. We were to report the results to him, and then he'd decide whether to proceed with a flight test. Then the old man took me aside. "Listen," he said, "I don't want you to be railroaded into this deal by Ridley or anyone else. If you don't feel comfortable with the risks, I want you to tell me so. I'll respect your decision. Please don't play the hero, Chuck. It makes no sense getting you hurt or killed."

I told him, "Colonel Boyd, it's my ass on the line. I want us to succeed but I'm not going to get splattered doing it."

So, Ridley and I ground tested that stabilizer system every which way but loose. It worked fine, and provided just enough control (about a quarter of a degree change in the angle of incidence) so that we both felt I could get by without using the airplane's elevator. "It may not be much," Ridley said, "and it may feel ragged to you up there, but it will keep you flying." I agreed. But would the system work at high Mach speed? Only one way to find out. Colonel Boyd gave us the go ahead.

No X-1 flight was ever routine. But when I was dropped to repeat the same flight profile that had lost my elevator effectiveness, I admit to being unusually grim. I flew as alert and precisely as I knew how. If the damned Ughknown swallowed me up, there wasn't much I could do about it, but I concentrated on that trim switch. At the slightest indication that something wasn't right, I would break the record for backing off.

Pushing the switch forward opened a solenoid that allowed high-pressure nitrogen gas through the top motor to the stabilizer, changing its angle of attack and stabilizing its upward pitch. If I pulled back, that would start the bottom motor, turning it in the opposite direction. I could just beep it and supposedly make pitch changes. I let the airplane accelerate up to .85 Mach before testing the trim switch. I pulled back on the switch, moving the leading edge of the stabilizer down one degree, and her nose rose. I retrimmed it back to where it was, and we leveled out. I climbed and accelerated up to .9 Mach and made the same change, achieving the same result. I retrimmed it and let it go out to .94 Mach, where I had lost my elevator effectiveness, made the same trim change, again raising the nose, just as I had done at the lower Mach numbers. Ridley was right: the stabilizer gave me just enough pitch control to keep me safe. I felt we could probably make it through without the elevator.

I had her out to .96 at 43,000 feet and was about to turn off the engine and begin jettisoning the remaining fuel, when the windshield began to frost. Because of the intense cabin cold, fogging was a continual problem, but I was usually able to wipe it away. This time, though, a solid layer of frost quickly formed. I even took off my gloves and used my fingernails, which only gave me frostbite. That windshield was lousy anyway, configured to the bullet-shaped fuselage and affording limited visibility. It was hard to see out during landings, but I had never expected to fly the X-1 on instruments. I radioed Dick Frost, flying low chase, and told him the problem. "Okay, pard," he said, "I'll talk you in. You must've done a lot of sweating in that cockpit to ice the damned windshield." I told him, "Not as much as I'm gonna do having you talk me in. You better talk good, Frost." He laughed. "I know. A dumb bastard like you probably can't read instruments."

The X-1 wasn't the Space Shuttle. There were no on-board computers to line you up and bring you down. The pilot was the computer. Under normal flight conditions, I'd descend to 5,000 feet above the lakebed and fly over the point where I wanted to touch down, then turn and line up downwind, lowering my landing gear at around 250 mph. The X-1 stalled around 190 mph, so I held my glide speed to around 220 and touched down at around 190. The ship rolled out about three miles if I didn't apply the brakes. Rogers Dry Lake gave me an eight-mile runway, but that didn't make the landing untricky. Coming in nose-high, you couldn't see the ground at all. You had to feel for it. I was sensitive to ground effect, and felt the differences as we lowered down. There was also that depth perception problem, and a lot of pilots bent airplanes porpoising in, or flaring high then cracking off their landing gears. My advantage was that I had landed on these lakebeds hundreds of times. Even so, the X-1 was not an easy-landing airplane. At the point of touchdown, you had to discipline yourself to do nothing but allow the ship to settle in by itself. Otherwise you'd slam it on its weak landing gear.

So, landing blind was not something you'd ever want to be forced to do. I had survived the Ughknown only to be kicked in the butt by the Unexpected. But that was a test pilot's life, one damned thing after another. Frost was a superb pilot, who knew the X-1's systems and characteristics even better than I did. I had plenty of experience flying on instruments, and in a hairy deal like this, experience really counted. Between the two of us we made it look deceptively easy, although we both knew that it wasn't exactly a routine procedure. Frost told me to turn left ten degrees, and I followed by using my magnetic compass, monitoring my rate of turn by the needle and ball. I watched the airspeed and rate of descent, so I knew how fast I was coming down from that and the feel of the ground effect. I followed his directions moving left or right to line up on the lakebed, which was also five miles wide, allowing him to fly right on my wing and touch down with me.

He greased me right in, but my body sweat added another layer of frost to the windshield. "Pard," Dick teased, "that's the only time you haven't bounced her down. Better let me hold your hand from now on."

Before my next flight, Jack Russell, my crew chief, applied a coating of Drene Shampoo to the windshield. For some unknown reason it worked as an effective antifrost device, and we continued using it even after the government purchased a special chemical that cost eighteen bucks a bottle.

Despite the frosted windshield, I now had renewed confidence in the X-1. We had licked the elevator problem, and Ridley and I phoned Colonel Boyd and told him we thought we could safely continue the flights. He told us to press on. This was on Thursday afternoon. The next scheduled flight would be on Tuesday. So we sat down with the NACA team to discuss a flight plan. I had gone up to .955 Mach, and they suggested a speed of .97 Mach for the next mission. What we didn't know until the flight data was reduced several days later, was that I had actually flown .988 Mach while testing the stabilizer. In fact, there was a fairly good possibility that I had attained supersonic speed.

Instrumentation revealed that a shock wave was interfering with the airspeed gauge on the wing. But we wouldn't learn about this until after my next flight.

All I cared about was that the stabilizer was still in one piece and so was I. We were all exhausted from a long, draining week, and quit early on Friday to start the weekend. I had promised Glennis that I would take her to Elly Anderson's, in Auburn, for a change of scene and to get her away from the kids. As cautiously as we were proceeding on these X-1 flights, I figured that my attempt to break the barrier was a week or two away. So I looked forward to a relaxed few days off. But when I got home, I found Glennis lying down, feeling sick. We canceled the babysitter and called Elly. By Sunday she was feeling better, so we went over to Pancho's place for dinner. On the way over, I said to Glennis, "Hey, how about riding horses after we eat?" She was raised around horses and was a beautiful rider.

Pancho's place was a dude ranch, so after dinner we walked over to the corral and had them saddle up a couple of horses. It was a pretty night and we rode for about an hour through the Joshua trees. We decided to race back. Unfortunately there was no moon, otherwise I would have seen that the gate we had gone out of was now closed. I only saw the gate when I was practically on top of it. I was slightly in the lead, and I tried to veer my horse and miss it, but it was too late. We hit the gate and I tumbled through the air. The horse got cut and I was knocked silly. The next thing I remember was Glennis kneeling over me, asking me if I was okay. I was woozy, and she helped me stand up. It took a lot to straighten up, feeling like I had a spear in my side.

Glennis knew immediately. "You broke a rib," she said. She was all for driving straight to the base hospital. I said, no, the flight surgeon will ground me. "Well, you can't fly with broken ribs," she argued. I told her, "If I can't, I won't. If I can, I will."

Monday morning, I struggled out of bed. My shoulder was sore, and I ached generally from bumps and bruises, but my ribs near to killed me. The pain took my breath away. Glennis drove me over to Rosemond, where a local doctor confirmed I had two cracked ribs, and taped me up. He told me to take it easy. The tape job really helped. The pain was at least manageable and I was able to drive myself to the base that afternoon.

I was really low. I felt we were on top of these flights now, and I wanted to get them over with. And as much as I was hurting, I could only imagine what the old man would say if I was grounded for falling off a horse. So, I sat down with Jack Ridley and told him my troubles. I said, "If this were the first flight, I wouldn't even think about trying it with these busted sumbitches. But, hell, I know every move I've got to make, and most of the major switches are right on the control wheel column."

He said, "True, but how in hell are you gonna be able to lock the cockpit door? That takes some lifting and shoving." So we walked into the hangar to see what we were up against.

We looked at the door and talked it over. Jack said, "Let's see if we can get a stick or something that you can use in your left hand to raise the handle up on the door to lock it. Get it up at least far enough where you get both hands on it and get a grip on it." We looked around the hangar and found a broom. Jack sawed off a ten-inch piece of broomstick, and it fit right into the door handle. Then I crawled into the X-1 and we tried it out. He held the door against the frame, and by using that broomstick to raise the door handle, I found I could manage to lock it. We tried it two or three times, and it worked. But finally, Ridley said, "Jesus, son, how are you gonna get down that ladder?"

I said, "One rung at a time. Either that or you can piggyback me."

Jack respected my judgment. "As long as you really think you can hack it," he said. We left that piece of broomstick in the X-1 cockpit.

NINTH POWERED FLIGHT: OCTOBER 14, 1947

Glennis drove me to the base at six in the morning. She wasn't happy with my decision to fly, but she knew that Jack would never let me take off if he felt I would get into trouble. Hoover and Jack Russell, the X-1 crew chief, heard I was dumped off a horse at Pancho's, but thought the only damage was to my ego, and hit me with some "Hi-Ho Silver" crap, as well as a carrot, a pair of glasses, and a rope in a brown paper bag—my bucking bronco survival kit.

Around eight, I climbed aboard the mother ship. The flight plan called for me to reach .97 Mach. The way I felt that day, .97 would be enough. On that first rocket ride I had a tiger by the tail; but by this ninth flight, I felt I was in the driver's seat. I knew that airplane inside and out. I didn't think it would turn against me. Hell, there wasn't much I could do to hurt it; it was built to withstand three times as much stress as I could survive. I didn't think the sound barrier would destroy her, either. But the only way to prove it was to do it.

That moving tail really bolstered my morale, and I wanted to get to that sound barrier. I suppose there were advantages in creeping up on Mach 1, but my vote was to stop screwing around before we had some stupid accident that could cost us not only a mission, but the entire project. If this mission was successful, I was planning to really push for a sound barrier attempt on the very next flight.

Going down that damned ladder hurt. Jack was right behind me. As usual, I slid feet-first into the cabin. I picked up the broom handle and waited while Ridley pushed the door against the frame, then I slipped it into the door handle and raised it up into lock position. It worked perfectly. Then I settled in to go over my checklist. Bob Cardenas, the B-29 driver, asked if I was ready.

"Hell, yes," I said. "Let's get it over with."

He dropped the X-1 at 20,000 feet, but his dive speed was once again too slow and the X-1 started to stall. I fought it with the control wheel for about five hundred feet, and finally got her nose down. The moment we picked up speed I fired all four rocket chambers in rapid sequence. We climbed at .88 Mach and began to buffet, so I flipped the stabilizer switch and changed the setting two degrees. We smoothed right out, and at 36,000 feet, I turned off two rocket chambers. At 40,000 feet, we were still climbing at a speed of .92 Mach. Leveling off at 42,000 feet, I had thirty percent of my fuel, so I turned on rocket chamber three and immediately reached .96 Mach. I noticed that the faster I got, the smoother the ride.

Suddenly the Mach needle began to fluctuate. It went up to .965 Mach—then tipped right off the scale. I thought I was seeing things! We were flying supersonic! And it was as smooth as a baby's bottom: Grandma could be sitting up there sipping lemonade. I kept the speed off the scale for about twenty seconds, then raised the nose to slow down.

I was thunderstruck. After all the anxiety, breaking the sound barrier turned out to be a perfectly paved speedway. I radioed Jack in the B-29. "Hey, Ridley, that Machmeter is acting screwy. It just went off the scale on me."

"Fluctuated off?"

"Yeah, at point nine-six-five."

"Son, you is imagining things."

"Must be. I'm still wearing my ears and nothing else fell off, neither."

The guys in the NACA tracking van interrupted to report that they heard what sounded like a distant rumble of thunder: my sonic boom! The first one by an airplane ever heard on earth. The X-1 was supposedly capable of reaching nearly twice the speed of sound, but the Machmeter aboard only registered to 1.0 Mach, which showed how much confidence they had; I estimated I had reached 1.05 Mach. (Later data showed it was 1.07 Mach—700 mph.)

And that was it. I sat up there feeling kind of numb, but elated. After all the anticipation to achieve this moment, it really was a let-down. It took a damned instrument meter to tell me what I'd done. There should've been a bump on the road, something to let you know you had just punched a nice clean hole through that sonic barrier. The Ughknown was a poke through Jello. Later on, I realized that this mission had to end in a let-down, because the real barrier wasn't in the sky, but in our knowledge and experience of supersonic flight.

I landed tired, but relieved to have hacked the program. There is always strain in research flying. It's the same as flying in combat, where you never can be sure of the outcome. You try not to think about possible disasters, but fear is churning around inside whether you think of it consciously or not. I thought now that I'd reached the top of the mountain, the remainder of these X-1 experimental flights would be downhill. But having sailed me safely through the sonic barrier, the X-1 had plenty of white-knuckle flights in store over the next year. The real hero in the flight test business is a pilot who manages to survive.

And so I was a hero this day. As usual, the fire trucks raced out to where the ship had rolled to a stop on the lakebed. As usual, I hitched a ride back to the hangar with the fire chief. That warm desert sun really felt wonderful. My ribs ached.

OTHER VOICES:

Glennis Yeager

I saw that flight—what I could see of it, which was mostly the white contrails from Chuck's engine exhaust streaking up in the sky. I didn't hear the sonic boom when he flew at Mach 1 because that happened over Victorville, I think, about forty miles away, so I had no idea that anything special had happened. I recall he drove up in the fire chief's truck, got out, and flopped in our car. "I'm beat," he said. "Let's go home." I turned on the ignition and was about to drive off, when Dick Frost and Bob Hoover came running over and began clapping him on the back and making a big fuss. And that's how I found out that Chuck had broken the sound barrier.

Dick Frost

I didn't learn that Chuck had broken his ribs until a long time later, but it was so typical of him to be matter-of-fact. He was going to go home with Glennis, but we said, "No way." I remember grabbing him and jumping up and down. We were one happy bunch. We went over to the operations office, where I called Larry Bell at the plant to tell him the news. Chuck and Ridley called Colonel Boyd. Then we went over to the officers' club to eat and drink a toast. We planned a big party that night out at Pancho's. Meanwhile, Colonel Boyd's office called back and informed us that the tightest possible security lid had been clamped on the flight. It was not to be discussed or disclosed to anyone. Well, Muroc was a small base, and here we were, rowdy and celebrating in the officers' club—the word was definitely out. But orders were orders, so we decided against holding a party at Pancho's. Instead, we drove out to Chuck's house about thirty-five miles away. It was about four-thirty in the afternoon, and by then none of us was feeling any pain.

Chuck fixed us a pitcher of martinis. Then Ridley took off to go back and write the flight report that had to be sent out to Wright by telex. Around six or so, we decided to go on to my house and continue partying. It really was bizarre being forced to celebrate in secret the most historic flight of the age.

Hoover left his car at Chuck's and drove with me. Chuck had an old motorcycle that Pancho Barnes had given to him—a beat up old thing without a headlight. He cranked up the motorcycle and led the way. We were so damned excited and happy for what we had accomplished that we sat around cackling like geese, insulting the hell out of each other, and by eight or nine o'clock we were definitely pickled.

No one was in any condition to drive, but certainly not to drive a damned motorcycle. Hoover and I urged Chuck to leave his bike at my house and drive back to his place with us in my car. He said, "Aw, shit, I can manage. No sweat." Needless to say, he prevailed. It was decided that I would provide his headlights. It was a moonless night, and he had no illumination on that damned thing. He said, "Yeah, well, I'll keep right in front of you all."

He got on the bike and cranked it up. *RRRRRR-RRRRRRR-RRRRRRR*. It sounded louder than the X-1, and right then I should've known we were in trouble. He roared away. Hoover and I followed in my Chevy coupe. By the time we got on the road, Yeager was way ahead, blazing off in the dark. Now, this is a road out in the boonies, not much traffic, nothing but desert on either side, so the darkness is total. Only somebody with Yeager's incredible eyesight would have dared to drive it without headlights. And he didn't just drive it. That son of a bitch was racing it. He was nowhere in sight.

But just as we approached a right angle turn in the road, Hoover and I saw a big cloud of dust. You never saw two guys sober up any faster than we did. There was Chuck stretched out on the road, underneath that damned motorcycle. He had skidded on sand making his turn. We ran to him, certain that Yeager was dead. And it was sheer terror, because he was the man of the hour who had just broken the sound barrier, and Hoover and I could be held accountable for the death of an American hero.

So, we pulled that bike off him, and saw he was not only still alive, but giggling like a loon. He wasn't even scratched.

Hoover, who was a big guy, had no difficulty picturing what would have happened to the two of us if Chuck had had a fatal accident. I had to restrain Bob by grabbing him around the arms and pulling him away. Chuck got to his feet, still laughing. But he put up his hands in surrender. He said, "Okay, okay, you guys are right. I'll take it easy. I'm sober now." And he started to get back on that bike. "Bullshit," I said. "No way. Get your ass in my car." He shook his head. "No, really. I'm fine now. I'll stay in your lights." Off he went. Hoover and I ran back to my car and took off after him. But there he was, still going balls-out in the pitch dark. We had a brief glimpse of him crouched low over the handlebars and then he just zoomed out of sight. By the time we pulled up at his house, he was already in the kitchen fixing us one more pitcher for the road.

Maj. Gen. Fred J. Ascani

Colonel Boyd came into my office. "Well, they did it," he said, and from the grin on his face I didn't have to wonder what he was talking about. Coincidentally, only a few days before Chuck's historic flight, President Truman declared the Army Air Force to be a separate branch of the service. We were now officially the U.S. Air Force. What better way to celebrate than to crow about this flight? In fact, we had planned to go after every aviation record on the books as soon as the speed of sound was achieved and really give the Navy a run for its money. The Navy always seemed to get all the publicity. So, we were shocked when orders came down from the highest levels in Washington to clamp the security lid on this flight. And it stayed clamped more than eight months. The reason, I suppose, was to give our supersonic fighter production a real leg up over the Russians. But most of us thought Washington had severely overreacted.

The public was kept in the dark, but official Washington knew all about it and everybody wanted to meet the intrepid hero who broke the awesome sound barrier. I recall General Vandenberg getting the word back to us at Wright to "keep that damned hillbilly, Yeager, out of Washington." The general was very Ivy League. But he was whistling in the dark. Everyone wanted to meet Yeager. About a week after he made the flight, we flew him back to Wright and had a top-secret ceremony in the commanding general's office, where he received another Distinguished Flying Cross. I remember him whispering to me afterwards, "I needed that like a hole in the head." But that was only the beginning.

I never gave him English lessons. Hell, as it turned out, he gave all of us lessons. He played his new fame perfectly and knocked Washington on its ear. Very modest, very matter-of-fact, an easygoing, likable country boy with more bravery than Prince Valiant. The Secretary of Defense and the senators who met him were just in awe. They shook their heads in wonder, patted him on the back, and asked him to autograph the pictures he took with them. Chuck wasn't play-acting; he was just being himself. But he was also astute and knew the impact he was making. I don't think any of us had a true appreciation for the contacts he established during those years. He was held in awe by the most powerful people in America. He had big balls and he knew it. But he played the hillbilly to the hilt. "Aw, shucks, I just happened to be at the right place at the right time. It was no big deal. Just another job."

Whether the other test pilots in the flight test division would admit it (and none of them ever would), Chuck was now number one. Their jealousy was immediate. I'd hear comments like, "What's all the fuss? He only did what he was supposed to do. Why be placed on a pedestal for doing your job?" Chuck would be the first to agree, but he wasn't the one making all the fuss. One senior pilot, who prayed that Yeager would fall on his ass, finally got a chance to fly the X-1 and collapsed the nosewheel on landing. Boyd got him out of there, pronto. But the old man was adamant that Chuck would not benefit in promotions or money from that flight. And Chuck agreed wholeheartedly. It took him seven years to be promoted from captain to major.

Boyd thought the world of him as a man and pilot and assigned him very choice testing programs, simply because he believed that Chuck was the best pilot he had. Well, the knives were really sharpened to get Yeager. A lot of test flight people badly underestimated him, fooled by that West Virginia drawl. Their bodies were strewn across the landscape.

When the news finally did get out about his flight, Chuck turned down several lucrative offers for his story. One day he came to see me. He knew Boyd's orders against accepting remuneration, because any pilot worth his salt would've given the world to fly the X-1, and no one should profit that way. "Colonel Fred," he said, "I agree with Colonel Boyd about that. I don't want a damned thing for myself. Not a cent. But what I do want is to buy Glennis a fur coat. Goddamn it, she's earned that much. You've been out to our place and seen how we got to live because the Air Force won't give us any housing. I've saved the government a hundred and fifty thousand dollars by taking over the flights from Slick Goodlin. I don't think it's asking too much to let me make a few bucks from a Hollywood studio to do my story—just enough to get my wife a coat."

He wanted me to take his case to the old man. But I told him he'd lose the esteem of his colleagues in Flight Test if the word ever got out that he took any money. I said, "Hell, Chuck, you're famous. What more do you want?" He replied, "I want to buy Glennis a fur coat."

I was sympathetic. "Glamorous Glennis" she was: a beautiful woman who could've been the double for Vivien Leigh, and a fine, lovely woman as well. But I had to turn him down. I could only imagine how he felt, several years later, when the astronauts signed a lucrative financial deal for their stories with *Life* magazine.

PANCHO'S PLACE

Pancho Barnes and her place were a big part of the sixteen years I spent out on the Mojave. If her little oasis didn't exist, we test pilots would've had to invent something like it, because it was the only place in sight to unwind and have a good time. It was our clubhouse and playroom, and if all the hours were ever totaled, I reckon I spent more time at her place than I did in a cockpit over those years. And I was flying about five different airplanes daily.

At the end of each flight, I'd turn off all the cockpit switches, but there was no way I could so easily turn off all the switches inside myself. Glennis understood that her only serious rivals were not other women, but other pilots like myself, who shared the dangerous life of testing airplanes. The physical and mental stresses were felt by all of us and drew us together in special ways. Often at the end of a hard day, the choice was going home to a wife who really didn't understand what you were talking about, and from whom you kept back a lot so as not to worry her, or gathering around the bar with guys who had also spent the day in a cockpit. Talking flying was the next best thing to flying itself. And after we had a few drinks in us, we'd get happy or belligerent and raise some hell. Flying and hell-raising—one fueled the other. And that's what Pancho's was all about.

I met Pancho Barnes on my first trip out to Muroc in August 1945, when we were testing the Shooting Stars. There were only two places to eat off base, Pancho's and Maw Green's. Maw was a marvelous old salty character, a real desert rat like Pancho, who ran a little restaurant with her husband Angus. You could either eat at Maw's, near Anderson's store on the railroad track, or drive on out to Pancho's, about ten miles farther. Pancho had a real dude ranch operation out there: a twenty-room motel, a swimming pool, stables, bleachers for a rodeo, and, of course, her bar, which was desert-basic—a jukebox, a pool table in back, a battered old piano, some tables and chairs. She also had a landing strip; people would fly up from Los Angeles to party. She raised her own cattle, fed them from her own alfalfa field, aged her own beef, and served a helluva good steak. She called the place "Pancho's Fly Inn." Later on, she changed it to "The Happy Bottom Riding Club," making it a private club so she could get rid of some of the weenies who'd hung around. Gen. Jimmy Doolittle and I got the first two membership cards.

Pancho was forty-six when I first met her. She had black hair and dark eyes, slim hips and broad shoulders. She would never use a five- or six-letter word when a four-letter word would do. She had the filthiest mouth that any of us fighter jocks had ever heard. Now, that's saying a lot, but it's true. She once complimented a general's wife at a party by saying, "For a bitch, you're a pretty nice dame." For Pancho, that was just normal talk. She had to be tough because the only argument about her was

whether she was the ugliest woman we had ever
seen, or one of the ugliest. But that didn't keep her
from being married four or five times and bragging
that she had had more lovers than all of our flying
time put together.

Hell, we liked each other right off the bat. In
those days, most of the fliers who hung out at her
place were Hollywood stunt pilots and civilian test
pilots. She found out I was a fighter pilot, an ace in
the war, and wanted to know all about combat flying.
I'd never met anyone like her. She had been a famous aviatrix, one of the first Hollywood stunt pilots
and winner of a bunch of Tom Thumb races in the
early 1930s. She had flown with Doolittle and Toohy
Spaatz and Paul Mantz, and they often visited her
place.

Her real name was Florence Lowe. Her grandfa-
ther was Thaddeus Lowe, one of the founders of
Caltech, who had used a hydrogen balloon for artillery observation in the Civil War. As a girl, she lived
in a thirty-room mansion in San Marino. She had a
real society wedding and married a Pasadena minister, the Reverend Mr. Barnes. They had a son, Billy,
who died in his thirties, when the Mustang he was
flying drilled a hole not five hundred yards from
Pancho's property. Pancho walked out on Barnes when
Billy was still an infant and took up flying. She
claimed that her husband had only slept with her
once and that produced Billy. So she divorced the
reverend and took off. But she sure as hell made up
for lost time after that.

She became a smuggler and gunrunner, flying
into Mexico during a revolution. She flew rumrun-
ners into Ensenada and Tijuana. She spoke Spanish
and Yaqui better than I talked the king's English.
She had been living in the Mojave since 1933, where
she started her place when the base was little more
than a rat's nest. When I met her, she was married to
a guy named Don Shalita, and she invited me and
another Shooting Star pilot named Johnny Johnson

to go down to Mexico for a day or two with her and
Shalita. So we drove down in an old Cadillac and
spent the day in Tijuana. She knew everybody south
of the border. It was real interesting for me because
it was my first trip to Mexico, even if it was only
right across the border from San Diego.

In the spring of 1947, I again made a trip to
Muroc, and Pancho asked me to fly down to Mexico
with her in her Stinson. She flew it herself and she
was a damned good pilot. We flew into Hermosillo,
where the mayor greeted her like an old pal. They
stuffed us with food and filled our tanks with tequila,
to the point where yours truly fell asleep standing in
a closet. The next morning we set off on horses to a
remote Yaqui Indian village. We rode all day to get
there, and they welcomed her like a queen. The Indians took us out hunting deer on horseback. Every
time I'd shoot, the damned horse would rear, and
while I held on for dear life, it galloped me off into
the brush. The Yaquis thought I was a great clown.
From there, we flew down to Guaymas, where Pancho
had a friend who owned a fishing boat. We went out
and caught marlin. I had a ball, and by the time we
came back from that weekend, we were good friends.
And I was just a maintenance officer. Her liking me
had nothing to do with the X-1.

But when Hoover and I showed up as the X-1
drivers, you can imagine how pleased she was. Hell,
she knew everything that went on at Muroc. Her
place was only a few hundred yards from the lakebed
where we took off from the old south base. She got a
bang out of the idea that we were flying the X-1 for
the kick of flying it, not for some big contract bonus.
She wouldn't let us ever pay for food or drink. She
told Slick right to his face, "Do you know what Yeager
makes? Two-fifty a month. Do you know what he's
getting to fly the goddamn X-1? Two bucks an hour.
And where are you and your hundred-and-fifty-
thousand-dollar bonus? You'll be reading about him

in the paper when he does what you were supposed to do."

One night, she asked Bob, "Hoover, why in hell are you only a lieutenant?" He shrugged and said something about a freeze in promotions. "That's a crock of shit. The Air Force never appreciates real talent." And she picked up the phone by the bar and called General Spaatz on his unlisted number in Washington. "Tooey," she said, "I've got a young lieutenant here named Bob Hoover, who's being fucked over royally. . . ." Hoover liked to have died, and I stopped laughing by the next day.

Just before our first flights in the X-1, Gene May, a civilian test pilot, came over to Hoover and me at the bar, and said, "What makes you young fellas think you can fly faster than sound?"

Hoover said, "Well, Mr. May, Captain Yeager and I happen to have more time flying jets than you or any other ten civilian fliers you can name. So, what makes you think we can't?"

Pancho overheard this and said, "That's right, Gene, these two can fly right up your ass and tickle your right eyeball, and you would never know why you were farting shock waves." That was old Pancho.

If she liked you she was as generous as all outdoors; but, man, if Pancho didn't, she was a tomcat by the tail. For example, if she ever heard anyone say a word against me, out they went. And they stayed out, too. She just thought the world of me, and, as I've said, this was before the sound barrier. She gave me an old Triumph motorcycle, a beat-up old wreck, but I loved to ride around on it. One weekend, before Glennis came out, I took off with Hoover riding on the back to go see Don Bochkay, a pal from my old squadron. Bock lived out at Malibu, and Hoover and I rode right up the steps of that front porch and into the living room.

Pancho liked Glennis. She knew what it was like living on a captain's salary and raising a family, so she'd pack up steaks for us to take home; a couple of

times, she put us all up in her motel for a week or
more, while we were in the process of moving. She
had a Dalmatian named Spot that followed her everywhere and slept right next to her in bed; if any of
her husbands didn't like it, they went, not the dog.
When Spot fathered a litter, she gave a pup to my
kids. We named her "Sug," short for "Sugar," which
is what I used to call Glennis in our courting days.

When Pancho got married for the final time to
Mack McHendry, in 1952, she asked me to be best
man. Albert G. Boyd, our base commander, now a
two-star general, gave away the bride. Glennis helped
her get dressed. It was the damnedest wedding we
ever saw. The bride wore white lace; there were
fifteen hundred guests in a big tent set up behind the
motel. Pigs roasted in a big pit, and she had huge ice
sculptures that melted to the size of ice cream cones
in the afternoon heat. Man, it was a broiler, and we
all about died in there. But Pancho brought in a
bunch of Indian chiefs to do a special bridal dance
that lasted nearly an hour. In the middle of it all, the
bride announced, "Hey, everybody, help yourself to
the food. My ass is killing me in this girdle. I've got
to change into my jeans."

A lot of wives thought that Pancho ran a cathouse and raised hell if their husbands hung around
out there. It wasn't a cathouse, but it sure as hell
wasn't a church, either. She staged some Stag Nights
that would make a Frenchman blush. And all the
women who worked for her were single and good-
looking. A wiseguy friend of hers once called to say
he was coming up for the weekend and wanted a
good-looking gal on toast. Pancho served it to him as
a joke. I helped carry the unhinged door over to his
room. On top was a naked waitress resting on five
loaves of toast.

The rumor was that some of the gals were on the
lam from L.A. for various reasons. I don't really know;
but every once in a while some of the toughest, mean-
est sons of bitches would come out there and hold a

high-stakes dice game at her motel. She warned her
friends to stay away. When she staged her rodeo
shows, she also warned us fighter jocks not to mess
with those cowboys. We didn't listen, and I remember feeling like an actor in a bad western, backing
off, with a pistol pointed at my gut, while walking
backwards out the bar door with my hands in the air
because a cowboy thought I looked too long at his
girl. You'd think, by the way, that a rodeo would be
wholesome family entertainment. Everyone brought
their wives and kids. But for openers, Pancho had a
naked gal with long hair ride bareback around the
stands. She introduced her as Lady Godiva.

Pancho's was the scene of many a wild night.
And it was also the staging area for great adventures.
One of the best (or worst) occurred right in the middle of the sound barrier flights. It was two in the
morning on a Saturday night, and a bunch of us
were still at the bar, when Russ Schleeh, a good pilot
and a great guy (even if he was not only a damned
bomber pilot, but head of the bomber test section at
Wright), suggested we go out on a bear hunt. I had
an old Mauser rifle that my Uncle Bill, a gunsmith in
Hamlin, had made for me. Russ had a thirty-eight
caliber automatic. Bob Hoover and Jack Ridley had
.22s. The four of us piled into Hoover's Roadmaster
convertible and took off for Johnsondale, a logging
camp up on the Kern River.

We arrived around four in the morning; it was
cold, late fall, and we ended up parked at the garbage dump, figuring that's where the bears hung
around. We parked Hoover's car so the headlights
shone on the garbage dump. We had two sleeping
bags between the four of us. We flipped and Hoover
and Schleeh won the bags. They slept out in a raw
wind and spitting snow. Ridley and I were inside
this damned old ragtop convertible on cold leather
seats. Ridley was in the front seat and I was in the
back, shivering in our flying suits, trying to stay
warm on a bottle of Pancho's Mexican sauce. Every

so often Jack would turn on the headlights and call
out to Russ and Bob, "Hey, you guys seen any bears
yet?" But those two were inside the sleeping bags,
dead to the world.

We snoozed, or tried to. Suddenly we heard a
godawful scream and pistol shots. Ridley turned on
the headlights and we jumped out of the car. There
was ol' Schleeh, standing up in his sleeping bag,
looking down into the garbage pit, waving his smoking pistol. "Jesus, I saw a bear and I think I got
him," Russ said. Then we heard a shout from the
bottom of the pit. "Hey, you son of a bitch, what are
you doin'?" Hoover was down there, still inside his
sleeping bag.

The zipper tassel on Hoover's bag had begun
blowing in the wind, tickling his nose while he was
asleep. He dreamt a bear was licking his face. He
woke up, drunk and terrified, forgot about the em-
bankment and that he was inside a sleeping bag, and
rolled down it, screaming. In the dark, he looked just
like a bear to Russ, who emptied his pistol at Hoover. Jack Ridley said it best: "There ain't no future
bear-hunting with this sorry outfit."

I can't recall any rowdy fun that wasn't connected to Pancho's. Of course, she had the most fun
of all. She couldn't care less about making a profit.
Most of the booze was brought up from Mexico (the
good stuff she kept locked away), and many nights I
bartended when all the drinks were on the house.
She loved flying and pilots, understood us and shared
in our code. "Dumb bastard," she'd say, along with
the rest of us, if a friend augered in. If a guy got hurt,
she had her own remedies. When one pilot broke his
back crash-landing, Pancho said, "I know what that
son of a bitch needs. He's going crazy from being
horny and sober." So she marched on the guy's hospital room with a couple of bottles and one of her
prettiest hostesses.

Hell, she was one of us so she knew our natures.
She laughed when we brawled, knowing damned well

there was nothing to it; the only sore feelings would be bumps and bruises. For us, a big part of the fellowship of flying was experienced at Pancho's. Being in our early twenties, we were in good physical shape and at the height of our recuperative powers—which we had to be to survive those nights. That was our Golden Age of flying and fun. By the time we reached thirty, our bodies forced moderation on us.

Pancho's own Golden Age really began when General Boyd came out in 1950 as base commander, moving all of the test division out from Wright Field with him. Her place was jammed every night. On the weekends, guys brought their wives for dances and barbecues, and the place toned down. The old man really liked her, and she took good care of him.

We came right over her place on takeoffs and buzzed the shingles off until the old man issued orders to stop. Around five one Saturday morning, Pete Everest and I took off in a couple of F-86 jets to do an air show for the Navy at Inyo Kern. We buzzed the motel. When I landed late that afternoon, I received two urgent messages: call Pancho and report immediately to General Boyd. Pancho told me that the old man was still at her place when we buzzed and was hopping mad. I reported to him, and the old man really looked the worse for wear. "I thought I issued strict orders not to buzz Pancho's," he frowned.

"Yes, sir."

"Well, why did you disobey my orders?"

I said, "General, how did you know that I disobeyed them? I buzzed that motel at five this morning."

He grinned. He couldn't help it, and that made him only madder. He glared at me for a long minute.

"Goddamn it, Yeager, get out of my sight."

Glennis thought that Pancho lived vicariously through my exploits. Maybe so. She was furious that I never got the recognition she thought I deserved for breaking the sound barrier, and didn't care what visiting general or politician she said it to. When

NASA sent up chimps in the first space capsules, she told me, "Those damn news people don't know a real hero from ape shit." All of the experimental test pilots of that era who had flown supersonic were regulars at her place and she formed a "Blow and Go Club" and hung our pictures on her wall. My picture was in the place of honor, and Pancho sat next to me at a farewell party in 1954 when I left Edwards to take over a fighter squadron in Europe.

I was glad I wasn't around to see Pancho's decline. The commander who replaced General Boyd declared her place off-limits on moral grounds. Pancho sued the Air Force, and after years of legal wrangling, won an out-of-court settlement of $400,000. But she lost her battle to save the place. The Air Force wanted to extend the south base runway, and her bar and motel were condemned. Then the bar burnt to the ground. Pancho gave up and moved fifty miles away. She tried to start another place, but it never caught on.

I visited with her a few times a year. She was living alone with her dog in a mobile home out on the Mojave, a desert rat to the end. She said to me, "Well, goddamn it, we had more fun in a week than most of the weenies in the world have in a lifetime." The saddest part about her passing a few years back was that it was nearly a week before her body was discovered inside her mobile home.

She was my friend.

Russ Schleeh

Camaraderie. We certainly had camaraderie in those days. We all worked hard and lived hard and enjoyed each other to the fullest extent possible. Pancho's was the center of that universe. All the hunts, parties, and fishing trips were planned at her bar and usually started out from there. The week after our bear hunt, we staggered out to go fishing on the Kern River—Yeager, Ridley, Hoover, and I. Well, Chuck was intensely competitive, and I'd challenge him just for the hell of it. We fished in the shadows of an enormous, steep hill. I said, "Chuck, I'll race you up to the top of that sumbitch." God, it was awful. We panted and groaned and struggled up that damned thing. We were hung over and miserable, but neither of us would quit. And I beat him to the top—he won't remember that, I'm sure.

We went out deer hunting. Each of us carried a carload of people. He was driving one car and I was driving the other. We left from Pancho's, and from that moment until we reached Mammoth, more than two hundred miles, it was balls to the wall. The pedal was to the floor and both cars were maxed. One couldn't go any faster than the other; we roared down the highway, going around cars and trucks: he'd go left and I'd go right, or vice versa. That's the way it was in those days: we were addicted to high speeds and risk-taking. That was the damnedest hunting party I've ever been on. The only thing we got— they shot my hat.

Pancho Barnes had a face like a bucket of worms. She had a low, gruff voice, too. Around noon one day, Chuck and I knocked on the door of the cottage she lived in behind the bar. We woke her up. She said, "Who in hell is it?" Chuck told her and she opened the door wearing only bikini panties. Chuck and I exchanged a quick glance: it was far from a turn-on, but that was Pancho: she was crude, rude, and immoral—our kind of gal. The women she kept around there were prime, and I heard a whole lot of scores claimed that I'm not sure were true. I'd have to see the gun camera film on some of them. But Pancho staged wild parties.

The greatest of them all was called "Tonight's the Night." That was the wildest party ever. I mean, *wild*. We had been doing bomber penetration evaluation studies on four new jet bombers. The fighter test pilots tried to intercept us in four new jet fighters. It was tough, demanding work, and we had been at it for three days when the weather people told us that a major storm front was heading for the Mojave and there would be no flying tomorrow. So, we cheered and said, "Tonight's the night. We're gonna raise the roof at Pancho's."

Now, there's no way to mix bomber pilots and fighter jocks in a bar without incidents. The jocks were all small, but that never stopped them from becoming obnoxious, and I've lost count of how many times we were forced to play beachball by tossing around Yeager, Ridley, and Bud Anderson. Jack and Andy were two of the nicest guys flying, but with a couple of drinks they became little Frankensteins. Yeager and Andy showed up in Wichita, where we were conducting some bomber-fighter evaluation tests. The weather was awful, and the hotel was booked solid, so they had to bring in a rolling bed into our room—the bomber pilots' room. There were four bomber pilots. We couldn't fly so we staged a "fog-cutter" party, filled a kettle with vodka, bourbon, Scotch, and a dash of ginger ale. Andy decided it was time to fight; I remember he was wearing only skivvies. So we picked him up, put him in the folding bed, folded and locked it with him inside—one of his arms hanging out the top, I recall—and wheeled him and the bed down to the lobby. Of course, Yeager had to come to the defense of his best friend. He got a bloody nose and was tossed out on the seventh-floor fire escape to cool down. When he started cussing us, we closed the window.

Back to Pancho's. Chuck's parents were visiting, and he brought along his dad, a stout fellow with huge arms. Yeager was nose-to-nose with a bomber pilot, throwing down a straight whiskey, really getting into it, when his dad shoved him aside and took over. Everyone was heaving to, challenging one another. Ridley went behind the bar and mixed together a quart of some horrifying concoction, then challenged one of my guys to drink it. "Goddamn it, drink it!" The guy did and just spun down straight onto the deck. I remember somebody else lying on his back, arcing vomit like a spouting whale. One fighter test pilot, a guy none of us liked very much, tried shoving me. I carried him out and dumped him in Pancho's pool. I went back inside, but the guy drove home to get his gun. He came back waving that damned .45 and threatening to kill me. We looked for a shovel: we were gonna plant that bastard, head first, like a coconut tree.

Near dawn, the bar was a wreck with only a few survivors still standing, and my God, there wasn't a cloud in the sky! It was a perfect, beautiful day! We had to fly!

We never compromised a mission no matter what we had done the night before. Not a hangover, not the weather—nothing ever stopped us. But this was rough. Chuck's dad drove him to the base, watched him throw up then climb into his fighter. He asked him, "Son, you do this often? Puke one minute, take off the next?" Chuck said, "No, Dad. This is the first and last time."

Everyone was sucking oxygen like mad. I was in a pressurized bomber and tried to get up as high as I could—about 43,000 feet. We made our run. The object was for the fighters to try to find and intercept us. On the way up, I was talking to Chuck on the radio, telling him about having sandwiches and asking him, "How ya doin', buddy?" I heard him panting, "You son of a bitch." I grinned and raised my nose even higher. Suddenly I looked up, and there's that goddamn Yeager in an F-86. He came in from behind and was practically sitting in the cockpit with me. He said, "Hey, you weenie, gimme a bite of your sandwich."

There will never be another era like that one. In the sky and on the ground, we lived to the max. Chuck was like most of us: he wasn't ambitious at all; he just stumbled into things. His only ambition was to fly every airplane and fly the hell out of each one. That was about it. But he wasn't easy to know. He and Andy were like close brothers, but with the rest of us, we were Pancho regulars to raise hell with. You had to know Chuck. Certain traits came with the territory. He never did a goddamn thing he didn't want to do, ever. Go hunting with him and he followed his own path. If you wanted to go along, fine; if not, see you around. You make enemies that way, but he never cared. He pissed off Andy and me dozens of times, but if you know Chuck, you know it's coming, and you keep it in perspective because the other side of him really works out; you always have a wonderful time in his company.

Mention his name and I don't think of the sound barrier or any of his other accomplishments. I think of him nose to nose with some bomber pilot at Pancho's. Or racing me for a couple of hundred miles balls to the wall. Or sneaking in booze to me at the base hospital when I was recovering from an accident. I think of him . . . I think of crazy Pancho, and I think how lucky I was to have shared that time and space, with those people and in that place in the middle of nowhere.

THE FIRE NEXT TIME

The plan was for me to continue flying the X-1 until we had exhausted the airplane's research capabilities while flying supersonic at high altitude. Between breaking the sound barrier and my next flight, there was a two-week delay to overhaul the engine. Meanwhile my ribs healed, and I felt good crawling again into that familiar cramped cockpit on the morning of October 27. I was supposed to go out to 1.08 Mach, but when I was dropped from the mother ship, I just plummeted like a thirteen-thousand-pound boulder. All my electrical controls and switches—dead.

While strapped to the B-29's bomb bay, we ran the X-1's electrical system off the mother ship's battery to save power. Only after being dropped do I discover my main battery switch is out. Without power, I can't actuate the propellant valve or ignite the rockets. Loaded with fuel, I'm able to glide, but I'm falling fast, with no way to land safely.

It looked like a sure splat on the deck, with the

only possible way out to jump for it and make it past those razor wings. And that's exactly what would've happened, if not for Dick Frost, who was a great "what if" engineer. He would actually bolt upright in bed, dreaming up "what ifs." And fortunately for me, he is the one who thought, "What if they drop the X-1 and the battery becomes disconnected?" He thought of that before the first powered flight, went out and bought a twenty-five-dollar valve, which he attached to a bottle of nitrogen gas. That way, I could manually open the jettison valve to slowly blow out my fuel.

It didn't take me very long to realize that Dick's valve was all that I had left. It was now or never to expel 604 gallons of fuel. I was down to 10,000 feet and falling, and the emergency jettison was twice as slow as normal. And without radio contact with the mother ship or chase planes, I had no way of knowing whether the emergency valve was really working. I made my turn toward the lakebed at 5,000 feet, and noticed that we were slowing down, which meant I was getting rid of fuel. The question was, how much fuel? All of it or some of it? The landing gear release lever worked, but I had no way of knowing whether or not the wheels were locked down. I needed time to blow out all that fuel; otherwise, I'd land heavy, crack the gear, and probably blow up.

My best chance was to come in at high speed, keep it a few feet above the ground, gradually slow it down, so that if I stalled, I would drop onto the lakebed. And that's what I did: delayed, delayed, delayed while only inches above the lakebed, until I could delay no longer and we bounced in. By the time we stopped rolling, Frost came running up. I got out a little unsteady. "Well, pard, I owe you one," I said. Dick laughed. "You sure as hell do, pard, and don't you forget it."

The cause of the electrical failure on board was a tiny deposit of corrosion between one of the battery terminals and a cable connector. It was so minor that a light pull on the cable reestablished contact, and from then on our preflight check included disconnecting the X-1 from the B-29 electrical supply. But this incident was a reminder of how complicated and potentially dangerous these missions really were. There was no way to be too careful, and even when we were, the X-1 kept finding new ways to bite.

We began having a few heart-thumping problems with the bomb shackle release that dropped me from the mother ship. In early November, the crew forgot to pull the safety pin out of the release mechanism. I heard a loud pop, was dropped an inch or two, then just hung there in the bomb bay, the weight of the undropped X-1 straining that shackle with the safety pin bound into it. I was suspended precariously between mother ship and mother earth. The B-29 couldn't continuously maintain the 240 mph dive necessary to keep the X-1 from stalling, but they kept diving while Ridley and Cardenas wondered what in hell to try next. They dove through 18,000 feet, but the X-1 just wouldn't fall free. Cardenas finally decided we were diving so low that it was becoming dangerous.

No choice but to dump the X-1 fuel and land with the orange beast still attached to the B-29's belly, but not with this test pilot still sitting inside. I had to get back out and up that ladder. That was touchy, too, because the X-1 could've dropped while I was climbing out. I scrambled out in record time, joining the others in the cockpit to sweat out the landing. We made it back without any damage, but not by much.

Despite an overhaul of the release system, on the very next flight the same thing happened. This time the safety pin was released, but for some unfathomable reason, the X-1 wouldn't drop. Cardenas dove below 18,000 and had just pulled out, when the X-1 suddenly lurched free. I was caught by surprise, having just started to unbuckle my safety harness. We fell about twenty miles an hour under the stall speed, and I had to fight against that stall real fast. I finally recovered after dropping five thousand feet and ignited the rockets about twelve thousand feet lower than planned.

That wasn't the end of the release problem, either. In late November, the damned safety pin stuck again. Once again, I sat in there, dangling. This time, one of the crew, a big red-headed sergeant, came down the ladder with a hammer. That dedicated nut stood on the fuselage of the X-1, pounding on the safety pin stuck in the shackle release. He wore a chute and an oxygen mask, but if he did knock out the pin, we were going to drop as a team. I watched him from the cockpit window, thinking, "Man, that guy is pure guts."

On one of those shackle problem flights, I was dropped in a stall, fought it successfully, only to discover that none of my rocket chambers would ignite! I thought, "My God, what next?" I finally got two chambers lit and we rocketed up. One chamber never did fire; nevertheless, I flew out to 1.07 Mach that day. In between these problems, I had already flown out to 1.35 Mach at 48,600 feet—about 890 mph, or twice as fast as I had ever flown in a conventional Mustang during the war. The myth of a sonic barrier was destroyed, but many questions about aircraft stability and control remained. Flying supersonic was becoming almost routine with similar flight characteristics revealed on every mission: light buffet and instability between .88 and .91 Mach; decrease in elevator effectiveness between .94 and .97 Mach, and a single sharp bump, similar to flying through "prop wash," while accelerating through .98 Mach. Decelerating from supersonic speed, I would experience all of these effects in reverse. Meanwhile, we were gaining invaluable data. I was flying the X-1 twice a week, while in between doing all kinds of flight and service testing on other airplanes.

By January 1948, I was outfitted in a pressure suit and began to resemble a spaceman. The plan was now to drop me at 30,000 feet, instead of 20,000 feet, giving me more fuel for higher climbs to 50,000 feet and beyond. Until now, most of our problems had been peripheral to the ship itself. But that quickly changed.

Toward the end of January, I was at 38,000 feet, having just leveled off after achieving 1.10 Mach, when I heard an unusual noise in back. It sounded like an oil stove burning too much fuel. A high frequency vibration began shaking me in the cockpit. I glanced at the instrument panel and noticed smoke hanging in the still air. Even though there was no fire warning light, I quickly turned off the engine, dumped remaining fuel, and landed. Fire is the pilot's terror, especially in the X-1. I sat in the nose just waiting to be blown to pieces because I couldn't see what was happening in the back. After I landed, the crew found a small fire had burnt insulation in the engine compartment. I was shaken. On the next flight, while I was climbing to altitude, I turned on chamber number four and saw the pressures climb too high. I turned it off immediately, but the fire warning light came on, and I quickly aborted the mission. The crew found that the motor cowling on number four was badly burned. I was really worried now. And the following flight, I not only suffered another fire warning light, but the cabin filled with dark smoke.

You're sitting on volatile fuel and if it goes—*pooh*, you're gone with it in a flash. But there was nothing I could do to save myself, except sit there and sweat it out. The fire warning light glaring from my instrument panel means I'm burning back there. If I hit the jettison fuel switch, I've got to worry that my fuel lines are burnt out, so I may be dumping all that fuel directly into an engine fire. So you sweat helplessly, knowing there's a critical point where you've got to make your move to dump fuel. Your engines are shut off and you're losing altitude fast. The chase planes are far below and can't tell you what's pouring out of your engine. You're all alone and nobody is in the position to help you decide what to do. I know more about what's happening up there than Ridley or Frost. Finally, when you can't wait a moment longer, you hit that jettison switch and tense.

Nothing happens. You breathe again. You start setting up your landing pattern and speed. You watch your nitrogen gas pressure because if you use it up, there's nothing left to force out the fuel or blow down the flaps and landing gear. You land soaked in sweat. After three straight flights like this, I marched on Jack Russell, our crew chief. "Hey, Jack," I said, "goddamn, man, fix this thing before I blow to pieces."

This went on flight after flight, through February and March, seven or eight flights in all. Every time I started up an engine, the fire warning light would flash, and the cabin filled with smoke. The problem made no sense. I began to wonder whether or not the X-1 was really designed to do the kind of high-speed, high-altitude testing we were attempting. Frankly, I didn't know what to think, and neither did Jack Russell. He and his crew broke down that engine piece by piece, ground tested it, then Jack stuck his head inside the engine and poked around with a flashlight. He couldn't find anything wrong.

Meanwhile, the problem was really getting to me. I never showed any emotion, and I always stayed cool in these emergencies, so not even Jack Ridley understood what I was really feeling inside. I was scared. I crawled into the X-1 feeling like a condemned man. And I began having really bad nightmares, dreaming I was being burned alive inside the X-1, only to have Glennis shake me awake just as I was trying to jump out of our bedroom window that was shaped like the X-1 door. She would get me calmed down, but she was shaken, too. Until that point, I had never brought my apprehensions home. Seeing me so afraid scared her, even though I purposely didn't tell her what it was all about. Maybe if

Andy were around, I would've confided in him. Ridley was worried enough, and I didn't want to add to his burdens. But I was miserable in secret.

Finally, Bell's engine designer came out and discovered the cause of the problem: the wrong gaskets were installed during one of the engine overhauls. I flew the X-1 a couple of times more, and after my twenty-third powered flight, during which none of the engines ignited because of a short in a cut-off switch, Colonel Boyd thought I'd had enough for a while and ordered me to take a break. I didn't argue. Two other Air Force test pilots flew the X-1 missions for a couple of months. Pard Hoover was out; he broke both legs bailing out of his burning Thunderjet when the air stream slammed him into the ship's tail.

Over the next year, a half-dozen test pilots achieved Mach 1 or better while flying the X-1, and because I knew the systems so well, I flew chase for many of them. Jack Ridley finally got his chance to fly the orange beast, too. I was right behind him in a Shooting Star when he was dropped. He fired up his rockets and smoke appeared around his instrument panel. "Hey, Yeager, I got a fire warning light." I told him, "Hell, Jack, you're in a pure nitrogen environment. Nothing in that cockpit can burn." He replied: "The hell there isn't. I'm in here."

He decided to go for it anyway, and off he streaked, achieving 1.23 Mach. He landed like a little kid who had soloed for the first time on a two-wheeler. He said to me, "You son of a bitch, you made it all look so easy, especially the landings. That lakebed is treacherous."

It was true. Pilots complained about sun glare that blinded them from seeing the instrument panel, and a couple of them dinged the X-1 trying to land it. One pilot dinged it twice. Another had his door fly off as he was gliding in. Still another had his windshield blow out—a very hairy moment. Bad luck and maybe a lack of feel for machinery caused several of these tense moments. And while few of them would ever say so, I think that those who actually flew the X-1 realized that piloting the orange beast was a lot tougher than I had made it appear. Even Colonel Boyd admitted that. The old man came out to fly it. I suggested that maybe he'd want to start with an unpowered glide flight to get a feel for the ship, but he said, "No, I don't have time to waste. We'll go for a powered flight. I want to go as fast as that thing will fly." We developed a flight profile where I would chase him in an F-86 and be in constant communication, positioning myself to be at his side for the lakebed landing.

So, off he went. The old man didn't fool around. The moment he was dropped, he threw the ignition switch and whistled out of sight. But apparently he blew a fuse in his radio, because I could hear him but he couldn't hear me. He got up to 55,000 feet, arcing out over the California coastline, seeing the Pacific far below, and I heard him calling, "Chuck! Chuck! Chuck!" I knew damned well he was worried whether he was too far from the Mojave to be able to glide down to the lakebed, but I picked him up visually after he turned and jettisoned, and flew out to meet him as he dove to line up with Rogers Dry Lake. He, too, landed with a little-kid look. He said, "I think I burnt up more calories than fuel. You're so busy in there. There're so many instruments to watch. And that restricted cockpit visibility. I didn't expect that." I had never seen him so happy and excited; he had reached 1.2 Mach.

In December 1947, *Aviation Week* leaked the news of the sound barrier flight, but it wasn't until the following June that the Air Force confirmed it. I went to Washington and received the MacKay Trophy from General Vandenberg, the Chief of Staff; later that year, President Truman awarded me the Collier Trophy at the White House. Requests for public appearances began flooding in. But there wasn't much I could say about the flights because all details were restricted. But I did attend a top-secret meeting at Wright at which the nation's leading aircraft manufacturers and high ranking officers from various branches of the military were briefed in detail on our flights. The consensus among the experts was that breaking the barrier was much easier than expected, but that many questions remained about whether or not large-size supersonic aircraft could now be built. The X-1 was small, flown at high altitudes where air loads on the structure were less than at lower altitudes. There were plans (soon abandoned) for using the X-1 to research aerodynamic heating and weapons systems for supersonic aircraft. The Air Force contracted with Bell and other manufacturers for four additional X research planes.

The publicity about my supersonic flight really heated the rivalry between the Air Force and the Navy, which had contracted with Douglas for a research airplane of its own. This kind of rivalry was good for aviation (the more research the better), but the Navy began taking cheap shots at the X-1 by announcing that their Douglas D-558-I Skystreak was the first truly supersonic airplane because it could take off from the ground and didn't have to be dropped from a mother ship like a bomb. (Ironically, that is exactly what they would later do with the D-558-II Skyrocket. Ironically again, I flew chase for Navy pilot Bill Bridgeman on many of his Skyrocket test flights.)

Anyway, I was real annoyed at the Navy, and when they brought the Skystreak to Muroc, they invited in the press to see a demonstration flight by the Douglas civilian test pilot, Gene May. He was the same pompous little guy who had challenged Hoover and me at Pancho's about why we thought we could break the sound barrier. Definitely, he wasn't one of my favorites.

The morning of his fly-by demonstration, I took off in an F-86 and climbed to about 40,000 feet, right above the reviewing stands loaded with Navy brass and press people. I sat up there and watched May take off in the Skystreak, heading toward the Antelope Valley, where he was going to turn then rip past those stands flying just under Mach 1. I timed it, then rolled over, came in over the lakebed, roared past those stands ahead of May, did a slow roll, pulled up and left, just as May began his approach over the field. The Navy never knew what hit them. But when I landed, a Navy admiral was standing there, purple with fury. "Captain," he said, "if you were in the Navy I'd have you hung from the yardarm."

"Yes, sir," I said. "But I ain't in the Navy."

But the Navy kept at their publicity campaign by building up the Skystreak at the expense of the X-1, which they called a gimmick. Around Christmas in 1949, I was in New York to receive an award at the Wings Club banquet and had a talk with Larry Bell. I told him the Douglas people were making us look pretty shoddy. He agreed. He said, "Chuck, how would you feel about trying a ground takeoff in the X-1?" I said, "Ridley and I talked about it more than once. That landing gear is really weak, but I think we could do it." So, during cocktails, Larry steered me over to General Vandenberg. "General," he said, "Chuck and I were just talking about all the publicity the Navy has been getting with their Skystreak. I think the time is ripe for the Air Force to put on a show of its own and do a ground takeoff with the X-1."

Vandenberg turned to me and asked what I thought. I told him I thought we could do it successfully. He asked, "What are the risks?" I replied, "Sir, I don't know. The airplane isn't designed for that sort of thing, but if we take off from a smooth lakebed surface and put in maybe half a load of fuel, I think we can do it." The general nodded. Then he buttonholed Secretary of the Air Force Stuart Symington and brought him into our little cocktail-party conference—which was pretty stiff for an Air Force captain. "Mr. Secretary," he said, "Yeager here thinks he can make the Navy chew nails by doing a ground takeoff in the X-1." Symington grinned. "Go ahead and work up the program and do it," he said.

And we did. I sat down with Jack Ridley and asked him what he thought. He scratched his head, scribbled some calculations on a pad, then laughed. "Well," he said, "the worst that could happen is the gear might fall off and you'd bust your ass. But if we keep the fuel light, you can do it." The big problem was trying to measure the amount of liquid oxygen in the fuel tank. The LOX was constantly boiling off, and you couldn't tell whether you had half a tank or three-quarters. So, Jack hit on one of his brilliant ideas. We went to the base hobby shop and bought a couple of two-by-six boards. I sawed them out on a bandsaw to contour to the bottom of the X-1 wings. Jack measured out the mean aerodynamic chord on the wing and the percentage where the airplane's center of gravity would be located with the fuel tanks exactly half-full. We put jacks under the airplane at that spot. Then we measured in half a tank of water alchohol. This went into the rear tank. Then we began filling the front tank with the LOX until the airplane balanced exactly. We let down the jacks and towed the X-1 to the south end of the lake with the jeep. We figured we had fifteen minutes to take off before the LOX boiled off. Hell, if you tried doing something like that today, it would take five hundred engineers and a stack of authorizations ten feet high. But it was just Jack and myself and a couple of ground crew guys in the jeep.

We didn't even have camera coverage. I borrowed a 16-millimeter movie camera from the photo lab and gave it to a friend who was a major. The roar of the X-1 engines almost knocked the camera out of his hands, so the film is a sorry mess. But the flight was fabulous. I was so excited, I forgot to put on my oxygen mask and nearly passed out breathing all that nitrogen. But I hooked it on just in time.

There was no ride ever in the world like that one! I fired all four rockets simultaneously. From a standing start, I just streaked down that runway for about fifteen hundred feet, raised the nose at 200 mph, and we jumped into the air. It was accelerating so rapidly that when I flipped the gear handle up, the actuating rod snapped and the wing flaps blew off. Eighty seconds after starting the engines I was at 23,000 feet at 1.03 Mach! The fuel ran out, so I rolled over and came down. Despite the damage, the X-1 touched down on the lakebed two and a half minutes after taking off. That January 5, 1949, flight occurred the day before the Navy was scheduled to fly its new rocket-powered model of the Skystreak. In Air Force circles, I was a bigger hero for beating the Navy to the punch than for breaking the sound barrier.

But the X-1 program was rapidly winding down. My folks came out for a visit, and Jack Russell drove them out to the lakebed to watch me land. I came in at 500 mph only thirty feet from where they stood. Mom practically died of fright, but Dad got a big charge out of it. In all, I flew the orange beast thirty-three times and achieved the highest speed—1.45 Mach (957 mph). In the summer of 1950, *Glamorous Glennis* was loaded under a B-29 for the last time. Then Ridley, Jack Russell, and I flew it back east. En route, we came in over Main Street at Hamlin at about 500 feet, then pulled back up and delivered the X-1 to the Smithsonian Institution in Washington. At the ceremonies, a Smithsonian official perfectly summed up the role of the X-1. He said, "The X-1 marked the end of the first great period of the air age and the beginning of the second. In a few moments the subsonic period became history and the super-sonic period was born."

ON A PEDESTAL

OTHER VOICES:

Carl Bellinger

(FORMER REPUBLIC TEST PILOT)

Chuck Yeager was a car tinkerer, and I was always tinkering with model trains. I remember driving out to his place one Sunday morning to borrow some tools. We went into his garage, and I was startled to see the Collier Trophy, which he had received at the White House, sitting there on his work bench. He was using the most prestigious award in aviation to store his nuts and bolts.

The X-1 made me famous. The awards, medals, and plaques began piling up, and at first, collecting them was fun. All that was asked of me was to show up at places like the White House in a freshly pressed uniform, smile for the birdie, collect the Collier Trophy from the President, shake his hand, and say thank you. Or go with Glennis, who was dressed to the nines in an evening gown and looked gorgeous, to attend a classy banquet in Dayton, where the International Aviation Federation presented me with a one-pound solid gold medal. We stored it in a bank vault.

The flight was compared in importance to Lindbergh's solo across the Atlantic in 1927, but I received no ticker-tape parade down Broadway—nothing like it. By the time the Air Force announced the flight eight months later, it was old news to official Washington, and a couple of other pilots, including Colonel Boyd, had also punched through Mach 1. But there were big headlines about it, and reporters came out to our house, scaring the hell out of the boys, who were awakened from their nap to have flashbulbs popped in their sleepy faces.

I felt the flight should have received recognition sooner than it did, but figured it was kept secret to give us time over the Russians to develop a moving tail on new fighters then on the drawing boards. I was a little miffed, but not like Larry Bell, who wanted the prestige for his company, or like ol' Pancho, who called pals like General Doolittle and General Spaatz and told them that by the time the Air Force got off its ass, the Navy would probably have flown out to Mach 2.

"Those assholes in Washington are blowing this whole thing," she complained to me. "You're getting a royal screwing." I told her, "Well, up theirs. My flight is in the history books, and that's the whole nine yards for me. All the other crap doesn't mean a thing." That was how I felt about it.

Hell, I was being practical, not modest. Movie

stars put up with all the demands that go with fame because it means bucks. As a blue suiter I wasn't going to get a dime out of the deal. And being famous with the public meant absolutely nothing to a guy living out in the middle of the Mojave Desert. The public wanted heroes, and to me, I was just a lucky kid who caught the right ride. But then, I was naive as could be, living a cloistered life out at Muroc, where the flying was fun and the living was easy.

It was a tight little circle. My life was flying and pilots. I didn't spend a whole helluva lot of time doing or thinking about anything else, unless it was quail hunting at Hansen's Ranch near Jawbone Canyon, or fishing for golden trout high in the Sierras. At a party we were like a bunch of damned doctors, talking a lingo no outsider could understand; our wives would say, "Oh, God, pilot talk again." We were an obsessed bunch, probably worse than other military pilots because we were so isolated. About the only civilians we knew were company test pilots, who flew in to run test programs. The outside world was mostly a place we flew over. But that quickly changed.

Being famous didn't serve any useful purpose for me as far as I could tell. The only compliments that really mattered came from guys like Larry Bell, Dick Frost, and Jack Ridley, who had been intimately associated with my flights. The only reward that really mattered came from Colonel Boyd, who assigned me the testing of the XF-92, the experimental prototype of the first delta-wing airplane. Convair pioneered delta-wing configuration, and if this prototype proved itself in testing, they would proceed with the F-102, the Air Force's first delta-wing supersonic jet fighter.

The old man raised hell with Convair because their own test work proceeded so slowly; their chief test pilot had flown the airplane for almost a year, but was so spooked by the XF-92's supersensitive handling characteristics that he refused to take off if the wind was blowing at more than ten miles an hour. He had only had it out to .85 Mach and landed it no slower than at 170 mph. The Air Force yanked it away from Convair and gave it to me shortly after my supersonic flight.

The controls were the first to be hydraulically operated, so light there was hardly any feel. My comment after flying in it for the first time was that it would be easy to handle if the damned stick were eighteen feet long. It was a tricky airplane to fly, but on only my second flight I got it out to 1.05 Mach, and coming in, I decided to see how slow I could land it, and kept pulling up the nose until it was pointing at a forty-four-degree angle of attack. I was amazed and landed at a speed of only 67 mph, more than 100 mph slower than Convair's pilot—a good example of how experience in high-performance aircraft pays off. I had hundreds of hours more flying time in jet fighters than he did.

In its own way, the XF-92 was as interesting and challenging as the X-1, so I had plenty to keep me busy without worrying about medals or recognition. In fact, I was busy on this program when the Air Force announced my supersonic flight in June 1948. The first trophies and awards meant a lot because they were so prestigious in aviation. I figured there would be a few more awards, then back to business as usual. Then I got a phone call from some colonel at the Pentagon, setting up a personal appearance schedule around the country and telling me I had to make speeches. I said to him, "Colonel, I'm only a fighter pilot. I don't do speeches."

He set me straight in a hurry. The orders to go out and give speeches came directly from the Chief of Staff's office. "And you'd better get used to it, because dozens of business and civic groups are asking for you." Hearing that got me hot. "Sir," I said, "you've got the wrong guy. I'm not some damned preacher. I can't just pick up and go make a talk in the middle of a test program. I'm flying eight hours a day on the new delta-wing."

"I'm not arguing with you, Captain," he replied. "Travel orders are being cut and that's that. You will attend these functions—every one of them."

Give speeches! *Me!* I hated English worse than any other subject because I had to stand in front of the class and give a book report. I thought, "No way, goddamn it. No way I'm gonna do that." I'd rather fight a flame-out on the deck than battle a talk in front of a strange audience. I was self-conscious about my lack of education, my bad grammar; I was just a pilot, not a stump-winding politician. Man, I was terrified, so I called Colonel Boyd at Wright Field, hoping he could protect me against the Pentagon because he wanted to keep me flying instead of running around the country. But he wouldn't take my call. Colonel Ascani told me, "We've already got the word, Chuck. You're going to have to bite the bullet. General Vandenberg thinks you're great p.r. for the Air Force and Colonel Boyd isn't about to argue with *him.*"

I was trapped. I told Ridley, "I wish you had taken that damned ride in the X-1 instead of me." Jack laughed and said, "Me, too, son."

It was summer, boiling hot. We flew early in the morning to keep from being roasted in an airplane left out in the sun, or being scorched from touching its metal skin. So, we finished work early, but while the other pilots headed to Pancho's to splash in her pool and have a cold beer, I took off for Cleveland or Des Moines to make a speech every time the Pentagon blew its whistle. I told Glennis, "I'd rather be ignored than put up with this crap." She said, "Just be yourself. People don't expect a great speech. They just want to see a hero." I looked around. "Where? Where's a damned hero? Show me."

I don't even remember my first speech, or where it was. I'm sure I was scared, kept it short, and made it conversational. One of Bell's p.r. guys who knew me advised me to make eye contact with the prettiest gal in the audience and talk directly to her. He also told me to keep my hands below the rostrum so nobody would see them shaking. Most of these audiences were Kiwanis or Elks or Jaycees and the only gals were the waitresses. I kept my hands behind my back.

I worked up a ten-minute talk, inviting questions from the audience at the end. It took about six or seven speeches before I began to loosen up, but the experience wasn't near as bad as I thought it would be. People liked me for what I had done and liked what I said as long as I kept things light and didn't get too technical. They liked that I was young and just an average person. My talk was simple and patriotic. I said, "You folks can be proud that our country has the best trained Air Force pilots in the world. They took a guy like me, who had never been to college, and trained me to be a proficient pilot. I happen to be the lucky one chosen to fly the X-1. But a dozen other test pilots could've done it as well. All of us receive the same excellent training."

Soon, I was making fifteen to twenty speeches a month, but still the requests for personal appearances continued pouring in, to be king of a winter carnival in upstate New York, or guest of honor at a state fair in the Midwest. A town in North Carolina named its airport Yeager Field, and the Junior Chamber of Commerce named me one of the country's ten outstanding young men. Glennis stored all these awards and trophies in cardboard boxes in the garage, but accepting them could be a fulltime job.

Time put me on its cover, and Pancho hung it right over the bar, just daring any of the regulars to make a wisecrack. The guys gave me a hard time about the speeches and the publicity. "Hey, Yeager, what kind of b.s. you feedin' those damn civilians?" they asked. I said, "Yeah, they rinse the horseshit from their ears when I say you other weenies could have made it through Mach 1, too." It really frosted me that guys were jealous because I made speeches. I wanted to tell them, "Hell, take my place, be my guest." But that would only make it worse. I used reverse psychology, telling them what they wanted to hear—about the motorcycle escort from the airport, the colonel who carried my bags, the good-looking women hot to make it with a hero.

That wouldn't be bad, but the truth was different. I was sometimes taking off at dawn to make it to Topeka for an Optimists' lunch. I'd grab a taxi in from the airport, change out of my flying suit into my uniform in the Holiday Inn john, rush into the banquet room with three minutes to spare to have somebody say, "Oh, you must be our guest speaker," and escort me to the head table and seat me next to some two-hundred-pound honcho who never once glanced my way until dessert was cleared and he lit up a ten-cent cigar. Then, he'd say, "Tell me, son, what is this sound barrier you're famous for? I've got to introduce you in five minutes."

I'd get home at nine o'clock at night just madder than hell. I couldn't see where attending something like that did me or the Air Force a bit of good. It was just a tiring waste of time, but then I'd be told that Congressman X or Senator Y had called the Pentagon and told the Air Force to get me to these functions because their constituents wanted me. And these particular congressmen had clout in getting appropriations or whatever. I thought it stank, but I was only a captain obeying orders.

I recall one occasion where four or five Muroc test pilots flew into an Air Force base in the Midwest for some test work, and I happened to be taxiing in ahead of them because I had a speech to make in town. Whenever I traveled to a local air base, the base commander usually came out to meet me and have his picture taken shaking my hand. The Muroc guys saw this one-star general meet my airplane, which was slightly unusual treatment for a visiting captain, and their eyebrows practically peeled off their heads. They were jealous of me, and I was jealous of them for being the way I was before everything hit the fan. Nobody asked me if I was having any fun.

Big sacks of mail began arriving at my desk in the ops building. Pete Everest asked, "What in hell are you gonna do about that?" I said, "Answer it, I guess." Hundreds of letters a month, requesting autographs and photos. I suppose guys were jealous about that, although no one asked me how long it took to sign all those requests or who paid for the postage when people failed to provide a self-addressed stamped envelope. After John Glenn made his earth orbit, we sometimes appeared together at banquets, and he asked me what I did about all the mail. NASA wanted him to use a mechanical device to sign his name; he wondered if I used one. I said, "John, I don't care if it takes you the rest of your life, but if a kid writes wanting your autograph, sign it yourself." He said, "I know I should, but, my God, they arrive by the thousands." I said, "That's right. By the goddamn thousands. But stay honest. Don't use a signing machine." He agreed.

Then the word got around that I was going to make a movie with John Wayne. That knocked the socks off everybody in flight test. Guys asked me about it. I said, "Well, yeah, but it's no big deal. Just one hot love scene with Janet Leigh." The name of the movie was *Jet Pilot*, starring Wayne and Leigh. The Air Force thought it would be a good movie to publicize itself, so they ordered full cooperation. And they volunteered yours truly to do all the dangerous stunt flying. I never saw Duke or Janet; I spent my time at 15,000 feet, being filmed by the great aviation cameraman, Paul Mantz, chasing me in a bomber, his camera poking out of a special glass compartment.

We went to Kelly Field in Texas because the producer wanted to film big cumulus clouds. The director said to me, "We need the kind of balls-out flying that only you can do, Chuck." I flew for free in an F-86, doing stunts that would've cost them a fortune if I were a professional stunt pilot. They asked me to dive into the overcast inverted at 12,000 feet, with another pilot on my tail, then roll out and pull out down on the deck. I dove too steeply, reaching .92 Mach straight down, and when I tried to pull out, I came back too hard on the elevator and the damned thing ripped right off my tail, taking with it about one-third of my horizontal stabilizer. My wing man shouted, "Get out!"

He hit his speed brakes and pulled up. My instinct told me it was too late to eject myself; I was pulling seven Gs attempting to pull out with only part of my stabilizer left. I leveled off just above the fence posts and climbed back into the overcast. The wingman never saw me and went back to tell them that Yeager went in. The transmission bonding on my radio was also gone, so I couldn't transmit. But I could hear the excited chatter about my "crash." I managed to make it back on what was left of my stabilizer, but it wasn't easy. And a couple of days later, while climbing to altitude to continue the filming, the turbine wheel of my engine came right out the side of my airplane, leaving me sitting at 20,000 feet with no engine. I was feeling good that day, which is why I decided to stay in the airplane and dead-stick it back into Bergstrom Air Force Base. But those were the kinds of deals I was forced into.

Before *Jet Pilot* was released, the Air Force sent me to New York to attend the opening of a British movie called *Breaking the Sound Barrier*. It wasn't about me; supposedly, it was based on the life of Geoffrey De Havilland, Jr., who was killed flying the tailless *Swallow* while trying to break Mach 1. It was a good and very realistic action picture. They used a World War II Spitfire to break the barrier, which was amusing because that airplane wouldn't go faster than .75 Mach in a power dive. When the actor discovered that his stick froze at Mach 1, instead of pulling back, he pushed the stick forward and it somehow released. Any pilot who really tried that stunt would've drilled himself into the ground, but it worked as a dramatic moment in the picture, and I thoroughly enjoyed myself.

When the lights came on, I realized that people seated around me thought they had watched a true story. I overheard one guy say to his wife, "Where in hell was Uncle Sam?" I said to him, "Hey, that was only a movie. We broke the barrier, not the damned British. And I'm the guy who did it." I might have saved my breath. That movie was a hit, and many who saw it believed it was a true story. Even the new Secretary of the Air Force believed the part about reversing the controls. Secretary Finletter stopped me at a Washington dinner and asked me if that's how I had done it in the X-1. I told him, "No, sir. If I tried that, they would've found the X-1's nose poking out the ground in China."

The public really didn't understand the concept of the sound barrier, but the press description of a brick wall in the sky made me seem like a young Captain Marvel. Sometimes I just winced reading stories that credited me with feats that were wildly exaggerated. Glennis saved them all, filling big scrapbooks, but she'd get mad watching me get mad reading them. "Boy, you're hard to please," she said. I told her, "It's hard enough being a test pilot without dragging around a ten-foot reputation that just isn't true. Everyone expects miracles from me and that's a perfect way to get killed."

That ten-foot reputation stuck with me over more than twenty years of my Air Force career, creating a lot of jealousy and enemies. The Air Force insisted on putting me up on a pedestal, and there was no lack of volunteers trying to knock me down. A few of them came damned close to wrecking my career. That was part of the price of having been singled out ahead of the pack to fly the X-1. Being famous got me nothing in the way of promotions or better assignments, but among the intensely competitive pilots in flight test, there were some who would never forgive me for taking that historic Mach 1 flight. The Secretary of the Air Force and the Chief of Staff knew me and called me by my first name, the mail and speech assignments kept rolling in, and powerful politicians asked me for my autograph. Yet, my family and I had gone from bad to worse in our living conditions out on the desert. We lived no better than a damned sheepherder—maybe worse. And I was still outranked by all the senior test pilots. As far as I know, none of those jokers at Pancho's were jealous of that.

OTHER VOICES:

Glennis Yeager

The acclaim didn't change Chuck in the least. We had never really discussed how the sound barrier might affect our lives, which was just as well because, in terms of our home life, I'd have never known it happened. He was gone more making speeches, which he really didn't enjoy very much, although ultimately he became quite good at it. Chuck was Chuck, and fame didn't mean a dog's ear. It didn't interest him. What made him tick were the things that did interest him. Fishing, for example. He loved going out on a boat in the ocean, or frogging on the Mud River, or stream-and-lake fishing, or backpacking in to inaccessible lakes and golden trout fishing—hundreds of ways to fish. Salmon fishing, crabbing—as long as it was challenging and different. Fame meant making appearances. That meant wearing a tie. He hated that.

Well, he was wearing a tie a lot going around the
country for the Air Force, and he was bitter about
the situation. We had been out on the desert more
than two years, and the Air Force still insisted on
carrying him as TDY (temporary duty), which meant
that we were ineligible for base housing. Meanwhile,
I became pregnant with Sharon not long after he
broke the sound barrier. Soon there would be five of
us squeezed in a one-bedroom adobe. We searched
all over, but the best we could find was a weathered
old dump forty miles from the base, at the Wagon
Wheel Ranch. The house was ramshackle and the
wind whistled through every crack, but it had two
bedrooms. On winter nights out on the desert the
temperature dropped well below freezing, and we
darned near froze from exposure. We drew our water
from a windmill pump, and our nearest neighbor
was sixteen miles away. The only road to our front
door was an impossibly bumpy dirt road that ended
at an abandoned silver mine. I lived in terror that I'd
run out of bread or milk out there, because the nearest store meant an hour-and-a-half round trip. It took
Chuck nearly that long to commute back and forth to
work every day.

God, it was awful and it really put a strain on
both of us. I was just stuck. Pancho had given us a
Dalmatian pup, and one day my two little boys wandered off while my back was turned; they got away
from me. My heart was in my mouth because if those
kids got lost out on the desert, that was it. I ran out
into the scrub and Joshua trees, panicked because
anything low to the ground was lost in that rolling
terrain. But then I saw our puppy's white tail wag-
ging way out there. That's how I found them.

I got so tired not having any adult contact all
day long. It was just me, the kids, and a radio. There
was no TV yet, or I'm sure I would've become a game
show addict. Chuck came home from work to be
greeted by an irritable wife sick of hearing baby talk
all day. I wanted him to talk to me about anything, I

didn't care what, as long as they were adult words. But Chuck just isn't a talker. He can't make small talk, and I didn't understand airplane talk. He certainly wasn't interested in my home decoration or my music (we had an upright piano). Normally we understood each other without a whole lot of dialogue. We could tell at a glance whether one of us was mad or glad about something. He knew I was in a tough spot, so he kept asking me to go with him to all those public functions he had to attend, but that wasn't my style. Being in public that way was a strain, and I really didn't enjoy it.

Despite all that Chuck was doing for the Air Force, it was hard to believe that there could be any Air Force family living less high off the hog than we were. One weekend, we went to Pancho's for a family barbecue. I was big and pregnant, and our two boys went off and played by themselves. They drank from some dirty Coke bottles and got trench mouth. Their gums were red and swollen and they could've lost their little teeth. They needed penicillin shots every three hours for three days. Charlotte Wiehrdt, the wife of one of the test pilots, was a registered nurse, and, God bless her, she came out to the house every three hours to give those kids their shots. Their little butts looked like pin cushions, but their teeth were saved.

Chuck, of course, had full hospitalization, but the rest of us could only use the base hospital in an emergency. So, when the time came to deliver Sharon, I went to the town of Mojave, where there was a fourteen-bed hospital, and the baby was born there. It snowed the entire time I was in the hospital, but it let up by the time Chuck came to take me home. We got halfway home, driving out in the middle of the boonies, when the wind picked up, piling huge snowdrifts across the road. Chuck tried to plow through it, but it was no use. We sat there for several hours with our new baby, running the car heater intermittently to keep from freezing. We were becoming real concerned, but fortunately, so was my mother, who was staying with the boys. We were long overdue at home, so she called the air police on base. They sent up search helicopters, which quickly found us because Chuck had thought to keep the car roof clear of snow.

The desert brought hardship, but also provided great beauty and a lot of fun for a couple that loved the out-of-doors. Of course, Chuck couldn't wait for the boys to get big enough to go out with him hunting and fishing. We'd go down to Pancho's and saddle up her gentlest horses and teach them how to ride. Chuck spent hours in that corral, teaching himself how to rope. It was funny to watch him playing cowboy; those calves would try to hide when they saw him coming. The boys loved to roughhouse with him in Pancho's pool, and he made slingshots for them, then took them hunting for lizards and kangaroo rats. He taught them the names of all the flowers and plants; I was surprised at how much he knew, but when Chuck was interested in something, he couldn't learn enough.

As young as they were, he took the boys trout fishing on the Kern River. "At least I can show them how to bait a hook and cast," he told me. But the river was deep from snow melt and he spent so much time watching that they wouldn't fall in and drown, that he tied each one to a tree, gave them a pole, and finally got some fishing done. I raised the roof when I found out about that, but the boys didn't seem to mind in the least. When they got older Chuck took them backpacking every summer for a week in the high Sierras, taking with them only what they carried in. Bud Anderson and his son, Jim, went with them. It wasn't an easy week, but they all had a good time. So, living out there had its compensations.

We lived out at the Wagon Wheel Ranch for nearly two years. In the winter of 1950, the Air Force moved us to another old ranch house on the south end of the lakebed. The airplanes took off right over our roof, but we didn't mind. Now, our nearest neighbor was only ten miles away. Colonel Boyd was now General Boyd and had moved all of Wright Field's test section out to Muroc. Chuck got permission from him to fix up the old house, which was a mess, little more than a concrete slab with a roof over it. Chuck sided the house, doing most of the work himself, although guys would drop by to help. They put down linoleum on that concrete floor, but got drunk while they were doing it, and I found more tar on the ceiling than on the floor. I didn't like being stuck off at the end of a lakebed runway, but we were assured that this was only temporary quarters until new housing was built.

The Boyds lived in a big hilltop house. Anna Lou Boyd was a virtual prisoner inside because she suffered from asthma, and the blowing sand and dust practically killed her. She was an expert bridge player and organized a bridge club. She offered to give me lessons, and I informed a certain Air Force captain that I expected him to be home by seven every Tuesday evening, so he could babysit while I took those lessons. Well, he bucked and snorted, but he knew I meant business. And I did; I stuck to it. Once a week, I played bridge like an Air Force officer's wife.

While living in that old house I saw the smoke from two or three crashes. One day Chuck called me from the base. I had wanted to see the delta-wing he was flight testing and he told me to take the kids out in the yard and watch him take off in the XF-92. I went out and saw him coming at us. That airplane got bigger and bigger. He got about fifty feet off the ground and went back down, running out of lakebed in front of me and the children. If he kept on coming, he'd plow right into us. I stood there paralyzed. I saw him try to turn the airplane, and it skidded in a cloud of dust. I took the kids and ran into the house to call the tower. They had Chuck on the intercom speaker and I could hear him talking. The airplane had lost its power, but he was all right. He had gashed his nose on the windshield, but he would be home for supper.

RESCUE MISSION

One day when I was going out to fly the XF-92, Pete Everest stopped me on the flight line. "Where are you off to?" he asked. "To fly the XF-92," I said. "No, you're not—I am." Pete was a major, in charge of the military test pilots at Muroc, and a fellow West Virginian. I was five-ten, and he was a couple of inches shorter than that, but ruggedly built and extremely strong. In a bar brawl, you could get him down on the third swing of a sledgehammer. Pete was a damned good pilot, probably my closest rival in sheer ability among the fighter test pilots. The old man picked Pete to do high-altitude test work on the X-1 after my Mach 1 flight, and I flew chase for him on the day when his canopy suddenly burst and his pressure suit saved his life; he managed to get back and land safely under great difficulty.

We had fun together raising hell hither and yon, but he was intensely competitive and not someone who willingly took second place to anybody. On the

213

job, I had to watch my step with him. So, I told him, "Well, screw it. You outrank me, and if you want to fly that thing, be my guest." I turned around and walked back to operations, leaving Pete looking a little shocked. He didn't expect me to surrender so fast, and that airplane was a tricky bastard to fly cold. If he dinged it, the old man would have him for supper. I don't know what he did because I took off my parachute and went home early.

Everest was piqued because he didn't get the X-1 supersonic flights or the XF-92, either. Those assignments came to me directly from the old man. And in late 1949, when Colonel Boyd was promoted to general and moved himself and the entire flight test division out to Muroc, that kind of petty horseshit on the flight line came to a crashing halt. Man, all of us shaped up fast. After being on our own for more than two years, we cringed knowing that the sternest disciplinarian in the entire Air Force was on his way. Fun and games were definitely over. Ridley called me at home the night before the general arrived, kind of stuttering in that high nasal voice: "Chuck, goddamn, I can't find my Air Force tie. It must've burnt with our house. You got an extra?" That damned fire had happened two years earlier.

Hell, we wore any damned thing we wanted, which wasn't very much in summer, with temperatures stuck above one hundred. We nearly forgot how to salute, and sometimes we'd joke and wonder what it was like being in the real Air Force. Well, the old man showed us in a hurry. He came roaring in from Wright Field, ordering Saturday morning inspections, lining up all of us under the baking sun. We had spent hours scraping off two years of corrosion from our belt buckles, polishing those brass buggers until they gleamed. Our shoes were spit-polished, our uniforms so starched and pressed that bread could be sliced on the creases. We had fresh haircuts and close shaves. Christ, we had never looked any better, but the old man put half of us on report. He went up and down the line, scowling, eyeing us from peaked hat to polished toe. A few of the guys began wobbling under the sun and keeled over. The general stepped right over them. He knew damned well what had been going on at Muroc and he just lowered the boom.

Within a year or two, none of us would have recognized the place. We were renamed Edwards Air Force Base in honor of Capt. Glenn Edwards, who was killed testing the Flying Wing, which looked like a boomerang. (Russ Schleeh took over the program; he was taxiing for takeoff when the nose wheel began to shimmy violently. The airplane nosed over, fell apart, and burst into flames. Russ broke his back, but managed to pull his copilot out. He was so damned disgusted with the Flying Wing that he tried to stop the firemen from putting out the flames.) With the change of name, sleepy old Muroc ceased to exist. Edwards became the Free World's center for advanced aviation research that would take us to the edge of space. By the time I left in 1954, there were ten thousand people working at Edwards. So, Muroc was an oldtimer's memory, along with unpolished shoes and belt buckles.

General Boyd arrived just as I was finishing my test work on the XF-92. In fact, I checked him out in that airplane. He crawled in the cockpit and said, "Now, Chuck, what do I have to do?" I said, "Well, I'll tell you, sir, you just go rolling down the runway, and when that airspeed indicator hits 180, you just blow a little on that stick." He laughed, but he later said I was so right, that he never worked any controls so sensitive in his life. "How in hell did you land that thing at 67 mph?" he wanted to know. Obviously he meant that question as a compliment and was very pleased with my test performance, so the last thing that either of us expected was that he would be forced to sign orders sending me back to test pilot's school. But that is exactly what happened, the result of jealousy against me.

I had no shortage of enemies in flight test, and one of them (I never learned who) discovered that I had never completed the stability and control course at test pilot school. That is, the school was in two parts. I finished the first part, then went on to fly the X-1, skipping the second part, stability and control school, a six-month course. Without a diploma from stability and control school, I could not be certified to do flight testing. Well, it was ridiculous. I had more stability and control experience than any of my would-be instructors. Performance tested how high and fast an airplane could fly; stability and control tested all of its handling characteristics by performing spins, stalls, high angles of attack. A fighter was a moving gun platform, and to be accurate in firing its weapons, it had to be a stable platform. I had literally hundreds of hours of stability and control work behind me when I was forced back to school. General Boyd's hands were tied; regulations were regulations. I was sabotaged, but it was ironic having the Air Force's big test pilot hero back in test pilot school, hitting the books.

The school was on base. The instructors made damned sure it wouldn't be easy for me. Their attitude was right out in the open: they would love to flunk me. The word got back to me that they had actually laughed at the possibility, wondering what the Air Force brass would do about it when they denied me a diploma. In class, the instructors smirked every time they called on me, as if to say, "Okay, hot shot, let's see how you handle this one." They just dumped on me. The word was out that I could be tripped up academically, so they loaded me down with extra assignments, and if I didn't complete every last equation or problem, I stayed after class until I did. If I were a minute late to class, they put me on report. I knew they wanted me to explode, so they could really nail me and maybe ruin my career. So, I did what I was told and counted to three or four hundred. But I always remembered those nasty sons

The only photos
Chuck and Glennis had
of each other
during the War.

Chuck's P-51 Mustang with ground crew.

A reunion with Madame Gabriel.

Yeager photographed
in France while
evading capture.

Wingman Bud Anderson

RIGHT:
Photographed on the day
Chuck shot down five Me-109s.

Col. Albert Boyd with the
Lockheed P-80R "Shooting Star"
in which he broke a
speed record.

LEFT:
Wedding picture.

LEFT:
Jack Ridley with Chuck.

RIGHT:
Bob Hoover and
Chuck at the
Nut Tree Restaurant.

ABOVE:
Chuck with the X-1.

RIGHT:
Pancho Barnes
and Chuck.

President Truman presents the Collier Trophy.

President Eisenhower presents the
Harmon International Trophy for men to Chuck,
and the Women's Harmon International Trophy
to Jacqueline Cochran.

Hahn Air Base: Glennis on show set done by "Squadron Girls."

Hahn Air Base: First honors in the 1956 Fighter Weapons (left, standing, Col. Fred J. Ascani).

The F-20 Tigershark,
which General Yeager thinks is the finest fighter.

The Yeager Family in 1965.

Peacetime Congressional Medal of Honor from the Congress of the United States, presented by President Gerald Ford.

Chuck advising Sam Shepard
during filming of "The Right Stuff"
with a mock-up of Glamorous Glennis.

of bitches. If they were harassing me because of a
cocky attitude or because I wasn't doing my work, I
would respect that. But this was spite. I put a little
red flag next to the name of each one of those guys,
and I nailed them the first chance I got. That's exactly what I did, and ruthlessly, too.

I was scared they were going to flunk me no
matter how hard I worked. Ridley tried to help by
tutoring me; I remember sitting up half the night,
night after night, struggling through complicated problems. I felt trapped, and I could smell disaster at the
end of the line. No diploma for this jock. But then an
amazing thing happened. General Boyd grabbed me
out of school and took me with him to France. Wham,
bam. One day I was in class, the next I was on his
wing in a fighter crossing the Atlantic. The school's
commandant was a bird colonel. He raised hell, saying
I couldn't miss three weeks of school and expect to
graduate. General Boyd's authority extended over
the school, and he told me to pack my bags. The
French government invited him over to evaluate their
first generation of jet fighters and bombers, because
we had much more experience in high-speed aircraft.
The old man chose me to go with him. He said, "I
know how disappointed you'll be leaving school to
go fly, but I thought I'd take you, anyway."

God, it was wonderful, although we worked our
butts off. We went first to French Air Force headquarters in Paris to get briefed, then flew down to
Marseilles to their flight test center. Although he was
a general officer, he always flipped a coin with me to
see who got to fly first. And if he won, you could bet
your tail he would put that airplane right on the end
of the runway, landing as pretty as any pilot could
ever do. He was so expert at evaluating airplanes
that he could fly once and write up a complete flight
test report. The general wanted to go to work very
early when the air was smooth, but the French engineers drifted in around nine in the morning, broke
out the wine and cheese. The old man wiped that out

fast. I flew the Mystère up to Paris and made the first
sonic boom over that city in a steep dive. We had a
lot of problems, but we worked well together. The
old man was like me: stick him in an airplane and
his day was made.

Maj. Gen. Albert G. Boyd

The French wanted our advice about their prototypes and which ones to put into production. The
Chief of Staff assigned this mission to me, and I, in
turn, selected Chuck to go with me. We took turns
chasing each other in an F-86, while one or the other
of us flew the prototype. We worked hard and under
very trying conditions. This was truly the unknown,
flying in foreign aircraft we were unfamiliar with,
hoping the French engineers really had made themselves understood while speaking to us in imprecise
English. We really missed having a Jack Ridley
along—our own engineering backup to help us get
through these tests on new equipment. We started by
flying the MD 450 Dassault Ouragan and ended by
flying the MD 452 Mystère jet fighter. In between, we
flew their bomber and cargo plane prototypes. I recall taking off in their four-engine jet transport. Chuck
was in the copilot's seat, and I had just put my
wheels up when someone tapped me on the shoulder.
I turned to see a little man in a striped coat with a
tray of champagne. I turned to Chuck and burst out
laughing. "Oh my God," I said, "that's all I need on
my first flight in this thing."

Chuck, of course, took up their fighters and did

everything in the world that could be done to them. The French engineers just shook their heads. He spun them, dived them, stalled them—everything. As usual, he just impressed the hell out of me with his ability to perform under pressure and his understanding of the systems aboard. It was partly innate and partly self-taught, but whatever the reason, he had more than the equivalent of an engineering degree, many times over. After ten minutes, he flew those unfamiliar airplanes as if he owned them. His quick mastery over complicated equipment was just amazing.

On the way back from France we stopped off in Madrid. At dinner, I said, "General Boyd—" but he interrupted. "Chuck, we're after-hours now. Call me 'Al.' " I said, "General Boyd, the two of us can be stuck together on a desert island for the next ten years, but you'll still be 'General Boyd.' " I could no more call my own dad "Hal" than call General Boyd by his first name. I think if I had ever tried to call him Al, my mouth would not have known how to get it out.

When we returned to Edwards, the old man marched on the test pilot school. The commandant told him, "General, there's no way we can pass Yeager. He's missed too much work." The old man handed him the stability and control reports I had prepared on the XF-92 and the French jets. "Study that," he said, "you might learn something. Yeager knows more about stability and control than you can teach him." The commandant said that might be, but rules were rules, and I couldn't get a certification diploma without completing my course work. And without the certificate, my test pilot days were over. General Boyd turned red, then purple. He slammed his fists down on the table and his voice shook that room. "Goddamn it, I'm in charge of this school. You will pass him."

And that's how I got my diploma.

FLYING IN THE GOLDEN AGE

EDWARDS AIR FORCE BASE, CALIFORNIA,
1949–1954

Being at Edwards in the 1950s, I was part of the greatest era in research flying in the history of aviation. In less than five years, a whole new air force was dumped in our laps for flight testing, including most of the prototypes of today's supersonic aircraft. The grandparents of the combat planes that fought in the skies over Vietnam in the sixties and seventies were all tested at Edwards in the fifties. I remember Jack Ridley coming back from a check flight in a new swept-wing jet bomber, his engineer's eyes bugged with excitement. "Those bastards haven't just gone back to the drawing board," he said, "they've started over from scratch." That was about it.

From first light to last light, seven days a week, the desert sky over the Mojave thundered from new and powerful afterburners, an extra kick in the butt that shot us in the sky with a blast of flame and smoke. Man, we were at the center of the world, the only place on earth to be if you loved to fly. The old

221

air force was being scrapped, and a new air force was being born right on our doorstep. Prop planes were obsolete, and the thousands of B-29s and Mustangs that had won World War II were being cut up for scrap, replaced by an air fleet of jet and rocket-propelled supersonic fighters and bombers.

The Air Force didn't have a dime for research and development when the war ended. But then the Cold War with the Russians began to heat up, and when they tested their own A-bomb in 1949, we suddenly had millions to spend to develop supersonic interceptors for air defense. One year later, war broke out in Korea, and our Sabres were dogfighting Russian-built MiGs high over the Yalu River. Combat pilots always exaggerate the performance of the enemy's equipment, and a lot of our guys were insisting that those Russian planes were flying supersonic in afterburner. True or not, the race was on among our airplane producers to build fighters that would outclimb, outspeed, outmaneuver, and outshoot the Russian MiGs. The hangars at Edwards were crammed with their prototypes.

By the mid-1950s, the one hundred twenty test pilots working for General Boyd had flight tested more than fifty prototype fighters, interceptors, deep penetration fighters, all-weather fighters, day fighters, medium and heavy bombers, helicopters, heavy-lift cargo planes, and fuel tankers. We flew straight wings, swept-wings, and triangular delta-wings. We grew up believing that an airplane's wings were supposed to be longer than its body, but prototype high-performance fighters arrived from the factory with tiny stub wings thin as razors. We wondered how in hell they would stay in the air.

Everything changed at once. I had carried maybe fifty pounds of electronics in my World War II Mustang, but now new jets had fifteen hundred pounds of sophisticated electronics. Cockpits were right out of *Buck Rogers*. My old squadron relied on my eyes and Andy's to spot a gaggle of enemy planes. Now, a

pilot who couldn't see beyond his kitchen sink saw
the enemy from fifty miles away as blips on his
cockpit radar screen. I had a couple of minutes to set
up an attack on German fighters, but a jet pilot,
closing at tremendous rates of speed, would have
only a couple of seconds. (During the late fifties at
Edwards, a test pilot, diving in a Mach 2 fighter,
actually outraced the shells from his cannons and
shot himself down.) These new jets would dogfight
by radar-locked and heat-seeking missiles. Even as
we flight tested these prototype airplanes, others were
testing its new weapons. The first batch of heat-
seekers headed straight for the sun.

How complicated could flying get? The old prop
fighter cockpits were kept simple so the average guy
could fly in it. The new cockpits, crammed with dials
and switches, caused even Jack Ridley to scratch his
head. Some Air Force brass at the time talked about
eliminating a human pilot altogether, to fly these
complex airplanes by computer. I personally didn't
think much of that idea. The practical compromise
was the two-seater, with the guy in front doing the
driving, while the guy in back worked the radar and
weapons. But what a time to be a test pilot! By the
summer of 1954, I would be test-flying Lockheed's
F-104 Starfighter, the so-called missile with a man
that could fly at Mach 2 and climb more than ten
thousand feet a minute. The oldest head among us
was a brand new learner.

I flew, flew, flew. If I wasn't flying chase for
another guy's test program, I was flying a program
of my own. I was probably logging more flying time
than the entire air force of some damned banana
republic, but all of us were. There wasn't even time
to be jealous when somebody else was assigned to
test a hot new fighter. Wait an hour, and you would
get to fly a hot new bomber or the latest X research
airplane. The competition among the manufacturers
was intense, but for every new airplane accepted into
the Air Force inventory, one or two were rejected.

Changes came so thick and fast that some airplanes were obsolete even as they arrived at Edwards. That was true of an X research airplane, the X-3, which had seemed so advanced when the Air Force contracted for it in 1945, but which was outperformed by the new jet fighters by the time I crawled in its cockpit in 1953.

There were so many new ways to bust my ass that I lost count. Every day was an adventure with the Ughknown—taking off for the first time in the X-5, with variable swept-wings that could be repositioned in flight to aid in lift or in landing, or with revolutionary pitch controls called elevons that combined the functions of elevator and aileron. I flew the X-4, which combined elevons and speed brakes; in a straight down power dive from 35,000 feet, I could not go faster than 250 mph. I did stability and control testing on that airplane, a semi-tailless research aircraft like the British *Swallow* that had crashed a few years earlier. Aerodynamicists still thought that the safest supersonic configuration was to leave off the horizontal tail surfaces, where air collides off the wings. *Wrong*. I got her out to .92 Mach when she began to spin violently. We figured that at .93 Mach she would punch a hole in the desert, so we quit right there and junked her.

I was even test flying our biggest new bomber. General Boyd flew to Edwards in the prototype of the Boeing B-47 Stratojet, our first swept-wing, six-engine bomber, capable of delivering an atomic bomb to its target at the speed of a fighter. He had Boeing's engineers thoroughly brief me on the systems, then he checked me out flying it. The bomber had two seats in tandem under a canopy, and the old man sat behind me while I took off. I did fine until the time came to land. I lined up with the lakebed, put down the landing gear, but that 200,000-pound bomber refused to land. It was so clean aerodynamically that there was absolutely no drag, and we floated forever fifty feet off the deck, while I sweated it out. General

Boyd was just chuckling to himself; he knew this would happen and wanted to see how I'd handle it. "Christ," I said to him, "this thing is like a hot-air balloon." "So I notice," he replied. "But how about putting us down on the deck while it's still daylight." I finally did. But I almost ran out of eight miles of lakebed doing it. The old man hopped out. "Okay, Chuck," he said, "it's your test program."

Over the next six months, and in between other testing programs, I did all of the stability and control tests on the Stratojet, flying with their engineers and filling out test cards on its take-off capacity with heavy bomb loads, its performance at various altitudes, and its flying range. Russ Schleeh teased me about it. "The next time there's a fight at Pancho's between the fighter jocks and the bomber pilots, I expect you to stay neutral." "Bullshit," I told him. "It'll take more than a couple of rides in the Forty-Seven to make me one of you bastards."

But it was funny. When the Forty-Seven became operational a year later, I had more time flying it than anybody else, and with my fighter training I could fly formation by second nature, so the Strategic Air Command asked me to help train their fuel tanker operators in airborne refueling of these big bombers. The KC-97 fuel tankers were filling stations in the sky that extended an attack bomber's range to targets anywhere in the world. They carried thirty thousand gallons of fuel. Airborne refueling was a brand new technique, and the boom operators aboard the tankers needed practice hooking up. For me, it was just simple formation flying, snuggling up to the big tanker and giving each operator ten practice tries. I gave thousands of hookups flying six hours a day, day after day, until it became routine for the boom operators. Not long after, a B-47 set a new record by flying twelve thousand miles during a twenty-four-hour period, refueled three times by tankers en route.

Flying formation was one of the first things I did to test a new fighter's control systems. A fighter is a gun platform, and the more stable the fighter, the easier it is to hit a target. In these tremendously fast jets, stability and control were critical performance factors. I'd crawl on somebody's wing to see how stable my airplane handled. But like anything else in life or in flying, the most difficult things become easier after you've done them hundreds of times. And a lot of the civilian test pilots working for the airplane manufacturers were barely able to stay in the sky flying the new high-performance jets. They lacked the background and experience of military pilots. We flew everything; they were limited to flying airplanes that their company produced. Many flew bombers or cargo planes in World War II, but through the seniority system became fighter test pilots who might be able to finesse testing a souped up Mustang, but who had no business in the cockpit of a modern jet fighter.

They couldn't fly in formation; they had no background or training. I flew as chase when a civilian test pilot butchered the test of the XF-85 Goblin, a tiny, so-called parasite fighter that was carried by a bomber mother ship and launched to defend it against enemy air attackers. The company's civilian test pilot was incapable of staying in formation with me, and when the time came for him to attach the XF-85 to the mother ship by means of a trapeze configuration underneath, I watched him wreck the little parasite, and I was barely able to escort him down to an emergency landing on the lakebed. The Air Force canceled the XF-85 program after only two hours of testing.

It was a shame to see a good program and good equipment ruined by bad piloting. One of the worst accidents at Edwards occurred in the 1960s when another civilian test pilot, completely out of his element trying to fly in formation, rammed his fighter into the prototype B-70 bomber, killing himself, most of the bomber's crew, and wiping out both airplanes. That accident should never have happened. We had

reached a point at Edwards where test flying challenged the best of us. There was just no room (or
excuse) for underqualified test pilots.

These new airplanes demanded proficiency or
they would kill you. By definition, a prototype was
an unproven, imperfect machine. It was usually
underpowered, had controls that were too light or
too heavy, new hydraulic or electrical systems that
were bound to fail, and more than a few idiosyncra-
cies that were certain to bust your ass if you spotted
them too late. Some defects were obvious: Convair's
Delta Dagger was completely redesigned following
the poor performance of its prototype. But other problems, like an unexpected vicious pitch up at high
speeds or a dangerous yawing tendency, might be
discovered late in a program, only after hundreds of
hours of flying time. The test pilot's job was to discover all the flaws, all of the potential killers. It was
precise, scientific flying that included stressing an
airplane beyond the most violent combat maneuvers.

Testing was lengthy and complicated, resulting
in hundreds of major and minor changes before an
airplane was accepted into the Air Force's inventory.
Even then, airplanes were constantly being changed
and improved with higher-performance engines, new
electronics and weapons systems, so that a later model
easily outperformed the original. But to stay alive
testing prototypes, you just had to know what you
were doing. You had to learn those systems, especially the emergency systems, ask questions of the
engineers, study the damned pilot's handbook that
was getting thick like a Manhattan phone directory.
But a lot of pilots, civilian and military, weren't
interested in doing homework and couldn't be bothered. And a lot of them got caught.

Arrogance got more pilots in trouble than faulty
equipment. That's what killed Dick Bong, our top
war ace in the Pacific, who became a test pilot. Dick
wasn't interested in homework. He crashed on takeoff when his main fuel pump sheared. He had ne-

glected to turn on his auxiliary pump because he
hadn't read the pilot's handbook, so he flamed out
only fifty feet up. He had no ejection seat, but stood
up in the cockpit, popped the canopy and then his
chute. The air stream wrapped him around the ship's
tail, and he went in with his airplane.

Bong at least had a reason for being arrogant.
He was a top war ace. But I never could figure why
the most arrogant bunch at Edwards were the NACA
pilots. The National Advisory Committee on Aeronautics had got into the flight test business while I
was still flying the X-1. They bought a second X-1
and hired civilian test pilots to fly it. I flew it first,
checked it out, then turned it over to them. Their two
pilots took turns cracking the gear on landing. The
X-1 demanded an experienced fighter pilot at the
controls, and those two just weren't qualified to fly
it. Both of them were later killed. Each time a new X
research plane was delivered, the Air Force would fly
it first, milk it dry of data, then turn it over to NACA.
We did that with the X-3, X-4, and X-5, completely
exhausting their capabilities. NACA would poop
around with an X airplane for two or three years
after we were done with it, acting as if they were
discovering secrets of the universe. I thought that
some of their pilots were the sorriest bunch in aviation.

By the time I left Edwards in 1954, NACA had
assembled a better crew of civilian test pilots who
would do important testing in the North America
X-15. Scott Crossfield worked for NACA and was the
first pilot to fly at Mach 2. He was a proficient pilot,
but also among the most arrogant I've met. Scotty
just knew it all, which is why he ran a Super Sabre
through a hangar.

That stupid accident would never have happened
to an Air Force pilot because he would have accepted
a few pointers about what in hell was going on with
a new airplane. But Scotty wouldn't. His attitude
was typical of the NACA bunch: there was nothing
worthwhile that a military pilot could tell them. I

had been testing the Super Sabre and delivered one to the NACA hangar from the North American plant. The crew chiefs came out with Scotty, who was scheduled to fly it. I handed him all the paperwork and the handbook on the airplane and told him, "Scotty, it will take you about a week to run an acceptance inspection on this airplane. There's a lot to learn, but when you're ready to fly it, give me a call and I'll come over and go through the various systems with you." His reply was, "It has a pilot's handbook, doesn't it? That's all I need."

Well, you look at a guy like that and say, "See ya around." A week later, I received a call from Paul Bickel, NACA's boss at Edwards, asking me to come over to their hangar. There was the Super Sabre, bashed through their hangar wall. "What in hell happened?" I asked. Paul said, "Scotty lost utility pressure." I told him, "That's exactly right! If you lose that on landing, you have no brakes or nose-wheel steering." But Scotty didn't know it, and when he tried to taxi to his hangar, he ricocheted off two parked airplanes and punched his plane through the hangar. I told Bickel, "All your pilot had to do was take five minutes to go through some of the emergency systems before he tried to fly it."

Neil Armstrong may have been the first astronaut on the moon, but he was the last guy at Edwards to take any advice from a military pilot. Neil was NACA's backup pilot on the X-15. One day, Bickel called me to say that NACA was scheduling an X-15 flight and planning to use Smith's Ranch Lake as an emergency landing site. Paul knew me from my early days at Wright, where he had been one of those flight test engineers who thought the X-1 was doomed. But he respected my judgment about the condition of the lakebeds because he knew I'd been flying them since 1945 and knew them like the back of my hand. Smith's Ranch Lake was about 250 miles away, and I told him I had flown over it recently and it was soaked from the winter rains. He said, "Well, my pilots were over there today and they said it's not wet."

I laughed. "Well, then, be my guest." But Paul had doubts of his own or he wouldn't have called. He asked me if I would fly Neil up there and attempt a landing. "No way," I said. "Would you do it in a NACA airplane?" he asked. "Hell, no. I wouldn't do it in any airplane because it just won't work." He then asked, "Would you go up there if Neil flew?" "Okay," I said, "I'll ride in the back seat."

I tried my damndest to talk Armstrong out of going at all. "Honestly, Neil, that lakebed is in no shape to take the weight of a T-33," which was a two-seat jet training version of the Shooting Star. But Neil wouldn't be budged. He said, "Well, we won't land. I'll just test the surface by shooting a touch and go"—meaning, he'd set down the wheels then immediately hit the throttle and climb back up in the sky. I told him he was crazy. "You're carrying a passenger and a lot of fuel, and that airplane isn't overpowered, anyway. The moment you touch down on that soggy lakebed, we'll be up to our asses in mud. The drag will build up so high, you won't be able to get off the ground again." He said, "No sweat, Chuck. I'll just touch and go."

And that's exactly what Armstrong did. He touched, but we sure as hell didn't go. The wheels sank in the muck and we sat there, engine screaming, wide open, the airplane shaking like a moth stuck on fly paper. I said from back, "Neil, why don't you turn off the sumbitch, it ain't doin' nuthin' for you." He turned off the engine and we sat there in silence. Not a word for a long time. I would've given a lot to see that guy's face. It was cold, and the sun was moving behind the mountains in late afternoon. Very soon it would be dark and the temperature would drop to below freezing. We were only wearing thin flying suits and the nearest highway was thirty miles away. "Any ideas?" I asked him. Neil shook his head.

Before dark, NACA sent out a DC-3 to search for us. I got on the horn with the pilot and told him to give us time to walk over to the edge of the lakebed, about a mile away. I told him to touch down, but not to stop. "Open the door and keep on moving while we jump aboard." He did a good job, and when we got back to Edwards, Bickel was still there. I don't know what he said in private to Neil Armstrong, but when he saw me he burst out laughing.

NACA was the forerunner of NASA. But whatever their initials, in the old days I rated them about as high as my shoelaces. (Today it is a new breed. I'll take my hat off to any of the NASA pilots flying the shuttle.)

I lived balls-out, flew the same way. I had my own standards, and as far as I was concerned there was no room at Edwards for test pilots who couldn't measure up to the machines they flew. I was harsh in my judgments because a pilot either knew what he was doing or he didn't. The NACA pilots were probably good engineers who could fly precisely, but they were sorry fighter pilots. I was angry at the system which gave the first crack at new airplanes to the manufacturer's own test pilots. Testing should be impartial, but each manufacturer used its own test methods that often exaggerated its airplane's capabilities. There were some excellent civilian pilots, like Lockheed's Tony LeVier and Fish Salmon, Republic's Carl Bellinger, and North American's Wheaties Welsh. Pard Hoover had left the Air Force to join North American. But there were also a lot of duds, who flew new and expensive equipment for the big bonus risk money, their only qualifications being company seniority that gave them first crack at big projects. Frankly, when guys like that drilled a hole in the desert, I felt a lot worse about the airplanes they destroyed.

I had a grudge against those who flew for the money. We military pilots flew for low pay because flying was our way of life. Those guys collected two hundred bucks for every minute they spent above 40,000 feet. What prima donnas! The civilians flew a preliminary test to insure a new airplane's airworthiness. Then the plane was turned over to us. We tested it to verify their data and to determine whether the airplane met its military specifications. Spin testing and dive tests came later on. The civilians were supposed to take those risks and collect their bonuses for doing so. But as soon as I got my hands on a new airplane in that first phase, I did everything to it that could be done. I'd spin and dive test it because I enjoyed the challenge. When the manufacturers saw my data cards, they'd call in their own pilots and say, "Why should we pay you for a spin test when Yeager already did it?" The civilian pilots complained that I was taking the bread out of their mouths, but I could care less. The system rubbed me wrong, and General Boyd finally got it changed after a long, bloody battle. I was out of the testing business when the Air Force took it over entirely.

To my mind, those company test pilots were salesmen with a license to fly. Military pilots were impartial. We could not recommend procuring or rejecting an airplane; that decision was made at the highest levels. But we did recommend that airplanes not be procured unless they were changed and improved in certain ways. For example, in 1953, North American delivered to us their new Super Sabre, the F-100, probably the most eagerly awaited new jet fighter of the postwar years, the first that could fly supersonic in straight and level flight. It became the first of what would be called "the Century series" of American jet fighters—the F-100, the F-102, F-104, and F-105, culminating in the late sixties with General Dynamics's F-111, a swing-wing two-seater that carried eight tons of bombs and rockets at 1,650 mph.

Every test pilot at Edwards drooled for the chance to crawl in that F-100's cockpit, including yours truly. After my first flight, I went over to North American's hangar to talk to Wheaties Welsh, their chief test pilot. "Hey," I said, "you can't fly in formation with this thing. It has the damned sorriest flight control system I've ever seen." Wheaties just shook his head. He was an old fighter jock who had shot down Japanese Zeros during the Pearl Harbor attack. "Goddamn it, Chuck, you're just being hypercritical," he insisted. "No, I'm not," I said. "That airplane just isn't stable." Pete Everest told him the same thing.

Welsh said, "I'll prove to you that you're nit-picking. I'm going to bring in some fighter pilots from the Tactical Air Command, guys who just know how to fight, and let them fly it." And he did. Flying chase with those TAC pilots was wild. They had a ball booming across the sky. "God, this thing really goes," they said, taking it out to 1.33 Mach. When they came in, Welsh asked them, "What do you guys think about the airplane's stability?" Those jocks looked blank. "Huh?" No, they didn't try to fly formation, they just flew balls-out. "Great airplane," they said. "Really hot."

We had a real conflict developing with North American, and Dutch Kindelberger, their board chairman, went to the Pentagon to insist that there was nothing wrong with his Super Sabre and that a few of the Edwards test pilots were nit-picking. He carried with him the statements from the young fighter jocks saying how great the airplane handled. Usually the military test pilots have the final word about whether or not a prototype should go into production. In this case the Air Force, knowing that the Tactical Air Command was panting to get their hands on that hot new fighter, decided that the deficiencies in the F-100 were in the extreme corner of the flight envelope and would be unlikely to cause pilot problems. Dutch won the battle, but, man, did he lose the war.

About two hundred F-100s had been delivered to the Air Force in September 1954, when Wheaties Welsh was killed diving an F-100 at 1.4 Mach. The

airplane disintegrated, but the flight recorders revealed it was directionally unstable. The Air Force
grounded all the F-100s in its inventory and sent
them back to North American. The modifications
necessary included a larger tail and a new flight
control system, and they almost bankrupted the company. But it took the death of their chief test pilot to
make that airplane safe to fly. Was Welsh just being
a salesman when he accused us of nit-picking? If so,
he was a fool to attempt a structural integrity demonstration dive.

Only rarely are dangerous flaws discovered in
airplanes that are already in place with squadrons
around the world. But that happened with an earlier
North American jet fighter, the F-86 Sabre. Suddenly,
and for no apparent reason, we lost three or four
pilots who were killed while doing rolls down on the
deck. Their airplanes just went right into the ground.
Investigators could not figure out why.

I flew a Sabre as a chase airplane. One day, I
flew up into the Sierras to check on a favorite fishing
lake. A buddy of mine named Dave Sheltren lived at
the edge of the lake, and I came across low to buzz
his place, did a slow roll over his house, when suddenly my aileron locked. It was a hairy moment,
flying about 150 feet off the ground and upside down.
But the moment I let off on the Gs, pushing up the
nose, the aileron unlocked. Very strange. I climbed to
15,000 feet, where it was safer to try it again, and
each time I performed that rolling maneuver, the
aileron locked. I figured that somehow the wings
were bending under stress and locking the aileron. I
called General Boyd as soon as I landed and told him
I thought I knew how those crashes occurred, but not
why.

The old man sent inspectors to take apart my
Sabre's wings. They found that a bolt on the aileron
cylinder was installed upside down. Crew chiefs in
every Sabre squadron were ordered to inspect their
airplanes' wings for that upside-down bolt, while an

inspection team went to the North American plant and found the culprit. He was an older man on the assembly line who ignored instructions about how to insert that bolt because, by God, he knew that bolts were supposed to be placed head up, not head down. Nobody told him how many pilots he had killed.

Those complex airplanes were unforgiving of mistakes, but some prototypes were so damned complicated that they never really got off the ground. We called them "hangar queens" because that's where they sat while the engineers worked them over trying to figure out why this or that was leaking. Some were so delicate that if you kicked a tire you'd probably short a circuit. Republic had a hangar queen, a combination jet-rocket prototype, that took forever getting past taxiing tests. They taxied her so often that they wore out two sets of tires, but each time her engine was ignited, something else went wrong. As a joke, a couple of us threw a rope around her landing gear and hauled her out of the hangar at the end of a tractor. A crew chief came running up demanding to know what in hell we thought we were doing. We told him we were just taking her outside for some fresh air. The Republic guys were not amused. I flew as chase when that particular airplane finally got off the ground. Her engine exploded just as her gear was raised and the pilot was almost killed.

We lost a lot of people, mostly the victims of pilot error. Nearly twenty test pilots, some of them good friends, bought the farm during those years. One guy was killed just closing the canopy to his B-47; something went wrong and it crashed down on him, crushing his skull. Guys died because they delayed too long trying to decide whether to stay or jump. A test pilot's instinct was always to try to bring an airplane back, especially a prototype carrying expensive measuring and recording devices. Nine out of ten pilots will be killed if they attempt to dead-stick back in a flamed-out jet. I only did it when I was feeling particularly good and sharp, knowing that gliding down in a jet was very tricky. Accidents occurred because all of us were flying too many different airplanes to really learn all there was to know about a specific emergency system. Flying at supersonic speeds, a pilot has a couple of seconds to take decisive corrective action when something goes alarmingly wrong. Some of the dead pilots needed more time to figure it out.

I was investigating officer on a few of the accidents. The crash site looked like a meteor-impact crater, just a smoking hole in the desert. We'd sift through the ashes searching for clues about what happened. The work was gruesome, but specially trained accident investigators almost always were able to determine the cause of a crash after a thorough job that included interviewing any eyewitnesses, recovering flight data, and analyzing bits and pieces of wreckage. But there were some fatal accidents that made no sense.

Driving into Edwards via the main gate, a visitor crossed James Fitz-Gerald Boulevard, en route to base headquarters. Fitz had been my backup pilot on the X-1 after Hoover. He was the best takeoff and landing pilot I ever saw. Nobody remembers that Fitz was the second pilot to break Mach 1 in the X-1. He was a West Pointer, with a beautiful young wife and new baby, and was destined for great things as a military pilot. In late 1948, we had flown together to the Cleveland air races. Fitz returned alone, flying a T-33 with 312-gallon tip tanks on his wings. On landing, the wing hit the ground, the airplane cartwheeled, and Fitz died of terrible head injuries. How and why such a fabulous pilot was caught that way is hard to understand.

Joe Wolfe Avenue is a main drag at Edwards. Joe was a bomber pilot and a good one. He went up in a B-47 and came down near the base housing area. Joe got caught somehow, but the wreckage provided no clues. He and I had talked about his flight the night before at my dinner table, so I know he thoroughly understood that airplane and all of its systems.

Neil Lathrop Street takes you to the main hangar complex at Edwards. Neil was a competent bomber pilot who got caught in a B-51. The old-timers at Edwards remember these guys, but in a couple of years they were just street names out there on the desert. Soon we ran out of streets to name, and in a few very special circumstances, named buildings in honor of outstanding pilots who ran out of luck. Most of them died before they had really made their mark. The real art to test flying was survival; maybe only a spoonful of more luck and more skill made the critical difference between a live test pilot and a street name.

In 1952, I drove around in a Model A Ford. I had as much fun driving it as tinkering with it. Joe Wolfe was the original owner. When he was killed, his wife, Sylvia, sold it to Neil Lathrop for one hundred dollars. When Neil was killed, his widow sold it to me for one hundred dollars. Wanting that old car overcame my fear that it was jinxed, but I told Glennis, "If something happens to me, don't sell it to another pilot—blow it up." When I left Edwards in 1954, I sold it to Pete Everest for one hundred dollars. We agreed that the car should always stay at Edwards, be sold from test pilot to test pilot, for no more than a hundred bucks. When Pete left, he sold it to X-2 pilot Iven Kincheloe. When Kinch was killed, his widow sold it to X-15 pilot Bob White. But Bob wasn't mechanical and couldn't keep the Model A running properly, so he broke the tradition by selling it to an airman, who took it with him when he left the service.

That I lived to sell that old car took nothing less than a miracle. After hundreds of hours of test flying, my luck nearly ran out flying Larry Bell's latest rocket research airplane, the X-1A. No one who saw the flight data from that ride or heard the tapes of my voice transmissions could ever figure out how I survived—and neither could I.

GIVING CHASE

Carl Bellinger

Flying chase was an art that not many test pilots bothered to perfect. There was no glory flying chase, no brownie points to score; but a skilled and dedicated chase pilot often meant the difference between a pilot's making it back or not in a dire emergency. Chuck Yeager was the best one to have flying your wing in a tight spot. Everyone wanted him to fly as chase because he had logged more rocket flying time than anyone else and knew those complex systems intimately. He was also the most skilled and experienced test pilot there, who had taken off and landed thousands of times on those lakebeds in all kinds of situations. And he had the best damned eyes of any

of us and could spot trouble before a warning light
flashed on the instrument panel.

Chasing was unselfish flying, and there were some
pilots who just didn't stay alert. Chuck was a notice-
able exception. He flew as balls-out flying chase as
he did flying the X-1. As a chase pilot, he was a ten;
by comparison, most of the others were sixes or sev-
ens. The difference was critical. I know. Yeager saved
my life.

I was testing Republic's prototype, the X-F-91, a
rocket-propelled experimental fighter, in the summer of 1951. Chuck flew chase on my first flight. We
took off at the first light of dawn; I was rolling down
the lakebed runway, getting ready to lift off, when he
came by in a Sabre and began to fly in formation
with me before I was even airborne—superb piloting
right from the start. He did a half-roll right above
my canopy to check me before I had my wheels up. I
had just lifted off the deck and retracted my gear
when Chuck radioed, "Man, you won't believe what's
coming out of your engine." A moment later I got a
fire warning light. "Christ," I said, "I think I'm on
fire." He replied, "Old buddy, I hate to tell you, but a
piece of molten engine just shot out your exhaust,
and you'd better do something quick." He meant I
should punch off my wing tanks and turn right back
onto the runway.

We were about five hundred feet over the lakebed,
heading out. He said, "Don't you hit my house with
those tanks, either." Normally, I would've laughed,
but we both knew I was in one helluva bind, too low
to eject and my cockpit filling with dense black smoke.
The fire in back was tremendous, and I radioed to
him, "Chuck, I can't see in here."

"Do a two-seventy to the right and keep it tight,"
he said in that calm voice. I followed his instructions, got my gear down, and in only a few crisp
words, he had me lined up and landing. He stayed
right on my wing as we touched down. I had that
canopy open and hit the ground the minute the ship

stopped rolling. I jumped for it just as the tail melted off. Flames and smoke poured into the sky. Chuck was right there and I climbed on his wing. His canopy was open and I just shook my head. "Damn, that was close," I shouted at him. "It *really* was," he laughed. We taxied up the lakebed with me holding on to his fuselage and met the fire trucks racing toward us in a cloud of dust from seven miles away. From the time Chuck saw my engine start burning until he talked me down took no more than ninety seconds. That's about all the time we had. The X-F-91 had burnt to ashes by the time the fire engines arrived at the scene.

I never lost a pilot while flying chase, but there were many close calls. After I had flown the X-4 research airplane, the Air Force turned it over to NACA, and I flew chase for their pilot, Joe Walker. We were climbing together through 20,000 feet, and I was listening to Joe talking with the control center, when it hit me that there was something very wrong. Joe wasn't making sense, and he was slurring his words. Hey, I thought, that guy has hypoxia. And it was going to get worse because we were climbing straight up. Without enough oxygen pilots act drunk and irrational, then black out. I flew close to his canopy and saw that his head wasn't rolling from side to side, which probably meant he was getting partial oxygen from his mask. I radioed: "Hey, Joe, be alert. Go to one hundred percent on your oxygen." He replied, "Oh, shut up, will you. I'm trying to fly a program here."

I needed to find a way to slap him back to reality. I said, "Hey, man, I just flamed out. Got me a real emergency. Follow me down." That got through to him, and he went down with me, his head clearing at the lower altitude, although he was dazed. Being typical NACA-arrogant, he was ready to readjust his oxygen mask and go back up. "No way," I said. "Get down on the ground." He finally did.

I flew a lot of chase for the Navy's Skyrocket project in 1951. Bill Bridgeman flew this Douglas rocket plane; he was a former Navy fighter pilot and a good guy. His engine system and flight profiles were identical to the X-1's, so there were dozens of ways I could be helpful during his flights. And poor Bill had some hairy moments. On one early flight he got a fire warning light and black smoke billowed out of his engine. I was right there with him. Man, I knew that terror. "Have you jettisoned your fuel?" I asked him. "No," he replied. I didn't have to ask why. He was scared to dump fuel into the burning engine. I told him to ease back on the throttle to see what happened. The smoke thinned. That meant the fire was inside the jet engine that was carrying him toward the lakebed, not inside the rocket chambers. I told him to turn off the engine and hit the CO_2 bottles (his fire extinguisher). The smoke vanished, and the warning light went off, and he was able to glide back, just barely. As we were coming in, a Douglas engineer asked him to fire up the jet again to see what would happen. Christ, we couldn't believe that idiot.

Bill had other nightmares: about to be launched from the mother ship, he saw the pressure drop on his fuel gauge and called for an abort. I heard him loud and clear. Bill turned off all the systems, but the pilot of the mother ship must've had his finger punched down on the microphone transmission key and couldn't hear Bridgeman. He started the countdown to launch with Bill screaming, "Don't drop me." It was horrifying. I was screaming at the pilot, and so were the control guys on the ground, but the Skyrocket was dropped. Bill dropped like a boulder and I dove after him, figuring he had had it. But he managed to crank up and fly right. "Goddamn it, I told you guys not to drop me," he shouted.

It was funny later, much later, as was the time when his troubles came in bunches. He lost his engine and his radio, and his canopy frosted over. I was in a frenzy. How do you talk a guy down who can't hear you? He got his radio back, and I was busy lining him up, crawling under his damned airplane to make sure his gear was down and locked, correcting this, suggesting that, so I didn't notice that the bastard had got his engine started, which immediately started his defroster. I looked and saw him sitting in there with a big grin, watching me struggle to sweat him down. He saw that I saw and began to chuckle. "You were doing so great, Chuck, I didn't want to interrupt." We were only about fifty feet off the deck. I said, "Okay, Navy, you're on your own from here. Hope you don't screw it up."

Test pilots sometimes just did screw up. Bill once stalled that thing at 30,000 feet, got to pitching violently and went into a straight down spin. The Skyrocket was known to be dynamically unstable, and spins were to be avoided. I dove down with him, stayed on his wing as he plunged seven thousand feet in ten seconds. On a deal like that I kept my mouth shut, no radio chatter, because there were dozens of people listening intently, including all of Bill's Douglas bosses on the ground, who wouldn't be pleased with his performance. But I knew that the flight data would give him away, so I purposely asked, "How are the stalls progressing?" as if he had planned a stall test. There was an investigation after the flight data was studied and both of us were called on the carpet, but we played dumb to the point where Bill's boss exploded, "You're a pretty cute pair," and slammed out of the room.

Bridgeman did more than his share of good flying, eventually achieved 1.8 Mach. He survived the Skyrocket only to be killed doing leisure flying out to Catalina. For Bill, that trip was like a motorist driving to the Seven-Eleven to pick up a quart of milk. He was probably flying complacent and without his usual alertness. That's when an airplane bites hard.

NACA also had a Douglas Skyrocket. Scotty Crossfield flew it and, in November 1953, became the first one to break Mach 2. None of us blue suiters was thrilled to see a NACA guy bust Mach 2, but as Jack Ridley said, "We'll take 'em on Mach 3." Things were happening that fast. About ten months before Scotty's big flight, Bell delivered a new rocket research airplane for testing, the X-1A. It was a longer version of the X-1, with a bubble canopy for better vision and a different fuel system to provide more sustained power than did *Glamorous Glennis*. The X-1A was scheduled to be flight tested at Edwards by one of Bell's contract civilian pilots, then turned over to NACA for high altitude research. I flew chase for Bell's pilot, Jean "Skip" Ziegler. And it was the old story: another civilian pilot in over his head.

I chased Skip in a Sabre jet and kept up with him using my afterburner. I sat right on his wing up to .93 Mach, saw the shock waves rippling across the wing's surface, and heard the fear in Skip's voice, reporting: "My ailerons are buzzing like mad." He was also getting heavy buffeting. I told him, "Everything is normal. That's exactly what happened in the X-1 at .93. Push on and it will smooth out for you."

He wouldn't or couldn't. For three consecutive flights he sat out there at .93, saw shock waves, got bounced around, and came back in. He thought the airplane was unstable, and his concern began to worry Bell's engineers, who decided to send the airplane back to the Buffalo plant for static ground testing. Skip went back with it, and while he was there, he participated in a fueling test of another Bell research plane, the X-2. Skip was inside the X-2, attached to the bomb bay of a B-50, when the LOX tank suddenly blew up at 20,000 feet. The X-2 and Skip were ripped from the mother ship and sent to the bottom of Lake Ontario. Ziegler never had a chance.

So, Larry Bell had a rocket airplane and no driver. Skip had worked on the program for months and to begin training a new pilot would create a long delay. Bell asked the Air Force to take over the test of the X-1A and requested me as test pilot. General Boyd agreed and brought together the old X-1 team to help—Ridley, Dick Frost, and Jack Russell, my crew chief. I would need those trusted old heads on this program because like the X-1 there was no ejection seat aboard the X-1A. Hell, there wasn't even a door. I was bolted inside without any way to get out in an emergency. That had worried Ziegler, too, but I told him, "It makes no difference because there's no way to survive a jump at such high speeds and altitudes." True or not, it was a naked feeling stepping into an experimental airplane with no exit.

In the past when I began a tough program, I was fired up. This time my heart wasn't in it. In fact, I probably had no business flying in that thing. I was tense, depressed, and sick with worry about Glennis, who was expecting our fourth child. Nothing had ever slowed down Glennis. During the other pregnancies she had morning sickness for the first few weeks, then perked right up and kept to her normal schedule until the day of delivery. This time she physically went to pieces and none of the doctors could figure out why. She ran a constant fever, and her joints became so sore and swollen that she could barely get out of bed to go to the bathroom. Each new day found her weaker than the last, until I really began to fear that Glennis wasn't going to make it.

It didn't take long for me to realize how much I depended on my wife's strength and how much I had taken it for granted. The foundation of our family life was knocked out from under us. Donald, our eldest, was only four. Mickey was three, and my mother volunteered to take him for a while if I could find transportation back to West Virginia. So, on my next flight east, I loaded ol' Mickey into a B-25 and delivered him to Mom. Sharon, our youngest, was a two-

year-old toddler who learned how to crawl under our
backyard fence and wandered out into the desert, so
that the air police had to send up helicopters to find
her. I got special permission for my in-laws to come
onto the base and move their trailer right next to our
house. Without them to help at home, I'd be lost.

I took out all my worry on the doctors at the
base hospital. They didn't know what in hell was
wrong. They thought Glennis might have rheumatic
fever. One specialist said she probably had a bacte-
rial infection called San Bernardino Valley fever, that
was an undulant fever common on the desert. They
ran tests up one side and down the other, then stood
around scratching their heads. I was tempted to strafe
the bunch of them. They kept her in the hospital for
three weeks, but she came home sicker than ever,
instructed to take three aspirin every four hours to
ease the pain in her swollen joints. In those days, the
more uncertain they were, the more X-rays they took.
The hazards of too much radiation were unknown,
and they kept zapping Glennis and our unborn child
every chance they got. We would pay a terrible price
many years later.

I raised such hell with those damned doctors
that the Air Force finally sent out a two-star general
who was head of the medical branch. He drove to the
house and examined Glen, scratched his head, too,
and shipped her off to Letterman, the big military
hospital in San Francisco. She was there for three
months.

It was the worst possible time for me to be involved with a risky research project. I was thirty,
recently promoted to major, and for the first time I
began to think that test flying was a young guy's
game. Glennis was always so self-reliant and efficient that I never really worried about doing dangerous work. She ran that family whether I was around
or not. I knew other test pilots whose wives went to
pieces every time they left for work. Those women
were bitchy and miserable; a few hit the bottle hard.

Their husbands were under the gun, and some were
forced out of test flying, or, faced with the choice,
broke off the marriage. I was one of the very lucky
ones, but this time, flying the X-1A, I felt I had my
neck stuck out from California to Buffalo, New York.

I talked about it with Glennis. I told her, "I'm
crazy to take this on with you so sick. I'm thinking
about backing out of it." She said, "I know you really
want to go ahead, and I think you should. I don't
worry about your flying, so don't you start worrying
or you'll get into trouble up there."

Ziegler was killed in April. The next month, Larry
Bell came to Edwards for a visit and we had a talk.
"Well, Chuck," he said, "once again you've bailed my
company out of a tough spot. We owe you a big debt
of gratitude." I said, "Well, Mr. Bell, that's fine. But
if I bust my ass in your airplane, who's going to take
care of Glennis and my kids?" He looked startled. I
said, "I'm not one of your civilian pilots who collects
a big bonus and all kinds of insurance. I'm just hanging out there with a neck stretched ten miles."

Mr. Bell said his company would take out an
insurance policy on my life. "Even though it probably isn't legal, we will pay for the high-risk premium, and I think the Air Force will look the other
way knowing the tough spot you're in." A few days
later he called me to say they had taken out a $50,000
premium on my life. It sure as hell wasn't legal, but I
felt a little less stretched.

The X-1A remained at the Bell plant for five
months undergoing testing and modifications, so it
was November before I made my first flight. By then,
Glennis had delivered Susie. The birth was normal;
Susie weighed eight pounds and was perfectly healthy.
Best of all, Glennis's mysterious ailment slowly dis-
appeared; the fever was gone and so was the inflam-
mation in her joints. She was still weak and tired
easily, but we were both tremendously relieved and
began to return to normal living. For me, that meant
climbing into the X-1A without an ejection seat.

"I'll Never Do That Again"

The purpose of those flights was to explore the consequences on man and machine of high-speed, high-altitude flying—picking up where the X-1 left off, the objective being to climb twenty to thirty thousand feet higher than previously at speeds better than Mach 2. It was damned ambitious, and Ridley and I worked up flight profiles that were almost identical to the X-1 flights. I'd be dropped at about 25,000 feet, then turn on each of the four rocket chambers during a slight climb until I reached maximum altitude. The X-1A burnt four minutes longer. Landing would once again be a powerless glide onto the lakebed.

Loaded with fuel, the ship was four thousand pounds heavier than the X-1, and I would fly it using a control stick rather than a wheel. Jack Ridley would still be with me when I got aboard, but this time I would not have to face the ordeal of climbing down a ladder into a blast of slipstream. Instead, I stepped down into an open cockpit. Then Jack would lower the canopy and bolt it into place. This time we also had more support personnel, even a flight surgeon to help me into my T-1 pressure suit—vital life support flying at such extreme altitudes. The damned thing squeezed me like a vise, cut off circulation to my arms and legs, soaked me in sweat, and caused me to walk like a mechanical soldier. The helmet fit pressure-tight to maintain its seal, pressing the sides of my face so much that I could barely talk. But that suit had already saved a couple of lives, so I didn't complain too much about the extreme discomfort, although I could hardly stand wearing it for more than an hour.

The X-1A was a lot better airplane than the X-1, although it wasn't pleasant being locked into a dangerous rocket airplane. So, I prepared for these flights knowing that my life depended on learning about every bolt and switch. Jack and I discussed the potential hazards and emergencies. We both knew I was pressing my luck because there were situations that no amount of piloting skill could overcome. An engine fire, for example. What do I do? Turn off the engine, jettison remaining fuel, and pray that the volatile liquid sprays out the back and not into burned-out fuel lines, causing an explosion. In a bad fire the only hope was to jump for it. Jack joked: "We'll give you a can opener and line your route with mattresses." Heh-heh-heh. If the ship caught fire, my pals would drive to work on Yeager Boulevard.

After umpteen hours of research flying, I became a fatalist. I was damned aware of the dangers, but I didn't dwell on them or let them spook me. Taking risks was my job, and if I were destined to be blown to pieces on the next flight, there probably wasn't a whole helluva lot I could do to prevent it from happening. All I could do was what I always had done: fly carefully and stay alert, counting on my experience and instincts to pull me through. I never took any airplane for granted, not even a Piper Cub. In a high-risk program like the X-1A, I thoroughly prepared myself, tried to cover all contingencies in planning the flight profiles, and finally just said, "Well, screw it. Let's get this goddamn program over with."

But my first flight on November 21, 1953, was beautiful, and I landed feeling much better about what I was doing. The B-50 dropped me at 25,000 feet, and I accelerated out to 1.3 Mach on three rocket chambers. The ship flew exactly like the X-1, and I felt right at home. It was only a familiarization flight, and at 45,000 feet, I ran out of fuel and glided back down to the lakebed. I told Jack, "She flew nice. Just as pretty as could be." We decided that on the second flight I would go out to 1.5 Mach, which is as fast as I had flown the X-1.

By now these rocket research flights were so routine that Jack and I were on our own, pretty well free to do our own planning and flight profiles with neither NACA nor the Air Force looking over our

shoulders. General Boyd, for example, was back at
Wright, taking charge of a missile development program. And the NACA guys now had their own test
flight program and could care less about ours. But
Ridley and Yeager had their eyes on NACA. The day
before my first ride in the X-1A, Crossfield had flown
NACA's Skyrocket up to 72,000, nosed into a shallow
dive, and registered two on his Mach meter. Jack and
I decided to sneak up on NACA and whip them in the
X-1A. The Bell engineers told us that the X-1A, because of its small tail, would probably lose stability
going any faster than 2.3 Mach. We figured the ship
couldn't go beyond 2.3, anyway. But that was enough
to better Crossfield's record.

Ridley went to work with his slide rule and figured out a flight profile that would take me out to
2.2 or 2.3 by the fourth powered flight of the X-1A. I
would climb to 45,000 feet on three rocket chambers,
then light the fourth, providing the thrust to go supersonic. I'd climb at a forty-degree angle to 50,000
at 1.3 Mach, reach 1.5 at 55,000, and continue climbing to 60,000, where I'd push down the nose (in pilot
jargon called "push-over"), reaching the top of the
arc at 72,000 feet. There, I'd level off, doing 1.8 Mach,
and take it on out until I ran out of fuel. By then, I'd
really be streaking because the ship weighed only
five thousand pounds empty, but its powerful rockets
had six thousand pounds of thrust propelling me in
the thin atmosphere, where there was little drag or
wind resistance. Jack calculated a 2.3 Mach flight
and chuckled with excitement. We nicknamed our
secret plan "Operation NACA Weep" because those
guys were really crowing about Scotty's record.

December 17 would be the fiftieth anniversary of
the Wright brothers' first powered flight at Kitty
Hawk, North Carolina, and the television networks
had scheduled special programs about Crossfield and
his Mach 2 flight. Jack said, "Aw, shit. All that fuss
for a guy who's gonna be the second fastest by the

seventeenth." Our plan was to smash Scotty's record
on December 12.

My next two flights were perfect. On December
2, I went out to 1.5 Mach, and six days later, I flew
out to 1.9. I had told our crew chief, Jack Russell,
"Hey, you sumbitch, if I get a fire warning light, I'm
gonna strap you in my lap on the next ride and let
you deal with it." Jack and his guys knew the stakes
and kept those rocket chambers so damned clean
that they claimed they were germ-free. I had a few
complaints, though. The control stick wasn't hydraulically boosted, and you needed real muscle to move
it back and forth at high speeds. I bitched about the
visor in my pressure helmet because it screwed up
my sharp eyesight. The visor contained filament wires
to keep it from fogging, which obscured my vision.
And when the sun reflected off that visor, everything
became milky white—like flying snow-blind. The ship,
though, was really behaving herself. I was actually
enjoying these flights.

Fourth Powered Flight: December 12, 1953

I was up and out before dawn to get in a couple of
hours of duck hunting before going to work. I drove
out in the Model A to the base Rod and Gun club.
The sun was just peeking over the far mountains
when I reached the blind. There were three or four
guys already in there. By eight, I was over at the
base firehouse having a sweet roll and a cup of coffee
with the firemen. The fire chief was an old hunting
buddy and kept my brace of ducks in his refrigerator.
By eight-thirty I was dressing for work in front of my
locker in the operations building. My pressure suit
needed minor repairs, which gave me time to clean
my shotgun. Several of us kept our guns in our lock-
ers, because being so damned busy, we took to hunting during a few spare hours here and there. A few
days earlier, I was landing on the lakebed and spot-

ted a gaggle of Canadian geese just sitting out there. A few of us drove out in a convertible, coming in on them in narrowing circles, so that by the time they spooked and took wing we were right under them. Man, the sky rained honkers.

By nine-fifteen, I was up front in the B-50 mother ship as she rumbled down the runway. It was a cold, crisp morning, perfect weather for speed flying. I felt real good. Ridley was flying low chase this day, keeping a sharp eye on my exhaust when I fired up. Maj. Kit Murray was high chase, going up to about 40,000 feet ahead, to give me an aiming point. Both those guys would take off in their Sabres in about twenty minutes, as we approached altitude in the mother ship. We planned the drop for 30,000 feet.

At 13,000 feet, I headed for the bomb bay of the B-50, where the X-1A was nestled directly below metal scaffolding. I stepped down into the open cockpit, strapped myself into the seat, and hooked my suit into the pressurization kit and the oxygen system. I gave a thumbs-up sign, and the crew lowered the heavy domed canopy over my head and sealed the bolts. For the next ten minutes, I checked out all my systems and started my prime to get all the gaseous oxygen out of my fuel line. It worked perfectly. Meanwhile, Jack Russell was supervising the disconnect of the liquid oxygen hose. He'd plug the fuel tank only when we reached altitude; otherwise, the pressure would build so quickly that the tank might explode. At 30,000 feet, Jack sealed the tank; a few moments later the big bomber lowered its nose and began a shallow dive to achieve 240 knots, my drop speed.

. . . four, three, two, one.

That familiar cracking sound as the shackles released the X-1A. I was lifted out of my seat by the sudden drop. Much faster than the X-1, because we're much heavier. We're right on the money—240 knots, nose-up angle. I reached for the ignition switches and lit three engines simultaneously. The impact knocked me back. They popped on clean and we

whistled upstairs. With a domed canopy I clearly
saw what Skip Ziegler wished he hadn't seen shock
waves rippling like spider webs across the surface of
my wings. Streaking up at .8 Mach to 40,000 feet, I
fired the last chamber and was rewarded with that
familiar kick in the butt. At .95 Mach we began
bumping like a light airplane flying in turbulence;
the buffeting meant I was about to cross threshold
from subsonic to supersonic. We were flying the perfect flight.

Except for the blinding sun. It was bursting
straight into my face. I could barely see my gauges,
and when I took a quick look at my wing, I saw I was
climbing too steeply because the sun glaring off my
helmet visor made it impossible to see my flight
attitude indicator. Instead of a forty-five-degree climbing angle, I was going up at fifty-five degrees. By the
time I leveled off, I'd be a lot higher than the planned
70,000-foot ceiling on this flight. I lowered my nose
going through 60,000 at 1.1 Mach, and by the time I
reached the top of the arc and began to level off, I
could've shaken hands with Lord Jesus. Eighty thousand feet. A nighttime sky with flickering stars at ten
in the morning. Up there, with only a wisp of an
atmosphere, steering an airplane was like driving on
slick ice.

My Mach meter could register up to Mach 3.
Nearing engine flameout, I hit Mr. Crossfield's mark
of Mach 2. I dropped my nose slightly to pick up
more speed and watched the meter register 2.2 and
then, 2.3. I was accelerating at 31 mph per second,
approaching 1,650 mph, the fastest any pilot had yet
flown, and the fastest that any straight-winged airplane would ever fly. In my headset I heard Ridley
ask Kit Murray whether he yet had me in sight. Kit
said, "No—too small."

The Mach meter showed 2.4 when the nose began to yaw left. I fed in right rudder, but it had no
effect. My outside wing began to rise. I put in full
aileron against it, but nothing happened. The thought

smacked me: Too high, too fast, Yeager. I might have added, too late. Christ, we began going haywire. The wing kept coming up and I was powerless to keep from rolling over. And then we started going in four different directions at once, careening all over the sky, snapping and rolling and spinning, in what pilots call going divergent on all three axes. I called it hell.

I was crashing around in that cockpit, slamming violently from side to side, front to back, battered to the point where I was too stunned to think. Terrifying.

The thought flashed: I lost my tail. I've had it. G forces yanked me upwards with such force that my helmet cracked the canopy. Without my seat straps, I probably would've been blasted right through the glass. My pressure suit suddenly inflated with a loud hiss. I was gasping and my face plate fogged. Blinded, being pounded to death, I wondered where in the Sierras I was about to drill a hole.

We were spinning down through the sky like a frisbee. Desperate to see, I groped to the right of the instrument panel trying to find the rheostat switch to turn up the heat in my face plate. But then the ship snapped violently back on itself, slamming me against the control stick and somehow hooking my helmet onto it. As I struggled to get free I had glimpses of light and dark, light and dark, through the fogged visor. Sun, ground, sun, ground. Spinning down. I had less than a minute left.

Through some sixth sense, I remembered that the stabilizer was set at "leading edge full down," and I could find that switch in the dark. Still fogged over, I reached for it and retrimmed it. Still groping, I found the rheostat and the heat flicked on. My face plate cleared and I saw more than I wanted to. I was spinning into the Sierras. Without even thinking, I set the controls with the spin. The ship flipped into a normal spin at 30,000 feet. *I knew how to get out of that!* I had spun every airplane imaginable, including the X-1. At 25,000 feet, I popped out of the spin.

I radioed to Ridley. My voice was so breathless and desperate that I doubted he could understand me. "Down to 25,000 feet over the Tahachapis. I don't know whether or not I can get back."

Jack replied, "That's twenty-five, Chuck?".

"I can't say much more. I gotta save myself."

I heard a voice from the control van say, "I don't know what's going on, but he's down from altitude." God, I didn't know what was going on, either. I was so dazed and battered, I wondered if I could still fly. And I worried if the airplane could still carry me.

"I don't know if I've torn up this thing or not, but Christ . . ." Ridley couldn't understand, and when I repeated it, I sobbed.

I barely remember the next moments. But then my head cleared and I was at 5,000 feet, lining up with the lakebed. I was gliding in from the other side of the Mojave, doing 270 mph, and I started to believe I was going to make it. I got on the horn with Ridley. "I think I can get back to the base okay, Jack. Boy, I'm not gonna do that again. Those [Bell] guys were so right [warning against going faster than 2.3 Mach]. You won't have to run a structural demonstration on this damned thing. If I hadda [ejection] seat you wouldn't still see me sitting in here."

The lakebed filled my windshield, and I put her down a little hard, with a thump and a cloud of dust, but no landing in my life was as sweet as that one. The flight data would later reveal that I had spun down fifty-one thousand feet in fifty-one seconds. I survived on sheer instinct and pure luck.

Glennis Yeager

I had no idea that Chuck had set a new speed record because when he walked in the door that afternoon my first thought was that he had been in a traffic accident. He was pale and very shaky. The way he carried himself, I could tell he was hurting, and I wondered whether or not he had again broken his ribs. But then I saw his eyes: they were bloodshot, and I knew from past experience that happened from pulling heavy Gs. So, whatever went wrong happened in the X-1A.

"Are you okay?" I asked.

"Yeah," he said. "They ran me by the hospital and nothing's broken. Just beat up some." He complained that his neck was stiff and sore. "I almost bought it today, hon," he told me. I had never seen him so shaken.

I was already dressed in an evening gown because we were going to a formal banquet at the Army-Navy Club in Los Angeles, where Chuck was to give a talk. In a moment of weakness, I agreed to go, but I told him I thought we should cancel out. "No, no, hell, no," he said. He got home around four; by five he was dressed and we took off in our car for an hour-and-a-half drive into L.A. He drove, of course. It was a posh dinner, although a little long and tedious, but he gave a nice talk. That man had been up since four to go off duck hunting. We didn't get home until two in the morning. Chuck was asleep before he hit the pillow.

Maj. Gen. Albert G. Boyd

No pilot could listen to the tape of Yeager's last ride in the X-1A without getting goosebumps. I've played this tape for audiences and the impact was awesome. One moment, we're listening to a pilot in dire circumstances, battling for his life. In less than a minute, he's back in control and cracking a joke about not having to run a structural demonstration on this airplane.

I don't know of another pilot who could've walked away from that one. Each airplane has its own stability limitations that at some point in speed and altitude registers zero on a stability curve. That apparently happened to Chuck at 80,000 feet, flying at 2.4 Mach. The X-1A began to tumble, pitch, and roll out of control. The gyrations were so severe that there was an indentation on the canopy where he struck it with his head. He bent the control stick.

Chuck knew he was going to die. That is clear from his voice on the tape. He plunged from 80,000 to 25,000 feet before somehow finding the way to save himself, and the moment that he did, he regained his composure. It's the most dramatic and impressive thing I've ever heard.

I took off for Washington around midnight on December 16 in a P-80 Shooting Star and flew all night, landing at Andrews Air Force Base around dawn. The press was waiting. Somehow the word about my new speed record had leaked, even though the secrecy lid was on. The Secretary of the Air Force was going to announce it at the Pentagon later that morning, but the press crawled all over me wanting all the details. The headlines were out. The reporters wanted to know what it was like traveling at two-and-a-half times the speed of sound. I told them I'd let them know after I did it.

After the announcement, the Bell p.r. types grabbed me and sped me all over town for various interviews. They set me up on *The Camel Caravan* and half a dozen other television shows, going balls-out to milk it dry. The NACA bunch just couldn't believe it. Operation NACA Weep really kicked their fannies. The television people were pulling out their hair, scheduled to go on the air the following day with several big and expensive salutes to Crossfield as the fastest man alive. The Air Force brass just purred like a cat being rubbed.

On the way back to Andrews to fly home, one of the Bell executives in the car handed me a big box. "Chuck," he said, "we know it would be illegal to give you a gift of gratitude, but there's nothing in the regulations that prevents us from giving a gift to your wife." Inside the box was a beautiful Persian lamb jacket. "Mr. Bell wants Glennis to have this." I took the fur out of the box and rolled it up. Before taking off in the Shooting Star, I hid it in the nose, a helluva place to hide an expensive fur jacket, but it traveled fine despite high altitude temperatures of minus sixty. Glennis was really pleased. That jacket was a thing of beauty in black and gray and she wore it for many, many years. I had finally got her a fur coat, but I nearly killed myself doing it.

After that ride in the X-1A, the Air Force decided not to try any further speed runs with it, but instead concentrate on high-altitude testing. I never again flew in it, but Ridley, Murray, and half a dozen other pilots did; Murray got it up to 90,400 feet. My speed record stood for nearly three years until Bell's X-2 began its flights at Edwards and cracked Mach 3. By then I was out of the test business.

Even before that wild ride in the X-1A, I had been thinking about doing other things in the Air Force. I wanted to get back into a fighter squadron, enjoy flying only one kind of airplane again, and experience the closeness of squadron life, so different from the dog-eat-dog rivalries in flight testing. I asked Ridley if he could calculate on his slide rule how many more flights it would take before the law of averages made it impossible for me to survive. Jack pretended to figure it out on a pad, then began to laugh. "According to my figures," he said, "Major Charles E. Yeager died three years ago."

To continue to live, a veteran test pilot needs both skill and luck. My skills were fine, but after the X-1A I had scraped to the bottom of the sack labeled luck. It really was only a matter of time before I bought it; I knew it and so did a lot of other people, including a couple of congressmen from back home, who began to pressure the Pentagon to get me away from Edwards before I got killed. It took a while for the pressure to build to the point where action was taken; the word didn't filter down to me for nearly another year. By then, I was spending one of the nastiest weeks of my life out in the Pacific, secretly testing a captured Russian MiG under conditions that made me relive the terror of the X-1A for five long days.

OUTFLYING THE RUSSIANS

KADENA AIR FORCE BASE, OKINAWA, FEBRUARY 1954

I'*m standing on the wing of a Russian-built MiG 15, hanging over into the cockpit, wiring the explosive cartridges that will blow me out of the seat if something goes wrong. It's pouring rain, and I'm wearing only a flying suit. I'm drenched. Water pours down from my hair into my eyes, making it hard to fix the seat. I'm beat and grim, just flat-out pissed at how close I've come to busting my ass during the past few days. I'm flying the first MiG 15 we've been able to get our hands on, flying it every which way but loose in a tropical storm that's been sitting over this damn island for nearly a week—heavy wind and rain and low ceilings—flying on gauges with a strange metric system, in a strange airplane, flying it higher and faster than any Russian pilot had ever dared. Those bastards know better.*

Flying the MiG is the most demanding situation I have ever faced. It's a quirky airplane that's killed a lot of its pilots. We learn as we fly, on a tight time frame, the old man pushing me right to the edge—a fraction

259

further and he will probably lose me. And he knows it.

General Boyd has brought me and Tom Collins, another test pilot, out to the middle of the Pacific because a North Korean pilot named Kim Sok Ho defected in his MiG 15. He received a $100,000 reward for giving us our first opportunity to fly the MiG. We were told to run a complete flight test on it, as if it were a brand new airplane, plot its speed, power, climb rate, and range. The MiG 15 was in combat against our Sabres over Korea, and our intelligence estimates of the Russian fighter's capabilities were the basis for how we engaged them in dogfights. We would discover that our test data matched perfectly with Air Force estimates. A shaky truce was in effect in Korea, but our people thought it could bust any moment; there was a lot of interest in our test.

A white line is painted down the center of the instrument panel. Lieutenant Ho, who is here to brief us, explained that if the MiG gets into a spin, we are to shove the control stick against that white line. If the airplane doesn't come out of the spin after three rotations—he put up three fingers to make sure we understood—then "you go," he said, flicking his hand like a guy ejecting. The MiG could not recover from a spin, and the Koreans probably lost more pilots spinning in than from American guns. So, spin testing is a big no-no. One thing I did try—I purposely stalled the sumbitch, just about a foot off the runway and with the gear down. There was no warning light, nothing. I just quit flying and wacked down on the deck.

The MiG is a pretty good fighting machine, but it lacks our sophisticated American technology. It has problems—oscillating, pitching up unexpectedly, fatal spins, no stall warning, lousy pressurization, and a particular warning from Lieutenant Ho not to turn on the emergency fuel pump. That could blow the rear off the airplane; the North Koreans lost four or five MiGs that way. Man, that thing is a flying booby trap, and nobody will be surprised if I get killed.

I'm nearly finished wiring the ejection seat when somebody taps me on the shoulder. I look up and see General Boyd. "Chuck," he says, "come down for a minute. There's somebody I want you to meet." I follow him down off the wing and run through the rain to a staff car and climb inside to meet a four-star general, Jack Cannon, head of the Air Force in the Pacific. General Boyd introduces me.

"What in hell are you doing up there, Major?" he asks.

"Putting in the cartridges for my ejection seat."

"God almighty, don't you have people who can do that for you?"

"General, the crew won't do the seat-wiring because they say they aren't 'pyrotechnics qualified.' Anyway, I know as much about it as they do, and it's my ass on the line. I'm not about to flub it."

General Cannon frowns. "We brought out all those high-priced technicians from Wright, and it's beyond me why the test pilot is out there in the pouring rain."

I tell him the truth. "Because I want to stay alive, General."

OTHER VOICES:

Maj. Gen. Albert G. Boyd

The flight tests of the Russian MiG really demonstrated what Chuck Yeager was made of. It was extremely dangerous work, flying in horrible weather. The first day Collins and Yeager flipped a coin to see who would fly first. Much to Chuck's chagrin, Tom won. We knew the MiG could outclimb the Sabre, but we really didn't know its maximum altitude.

Tom climbed to 48,000 feet and began suffering from insufficient oxygen supply. He came on down and we discussed what to do. Yeager said he believed he could take the MiG higher. So, I gave him a try. I said, "I'm going to be right with you in my Sabre and if I detect any signs of hypoxia, you are to descend immediately when you're told. I don't want any arguments. You go down."

We climbed together to 51,000 feet, which is the ceiling for the Sabre, and Chuck kept right on climbing. He got up to 55,600 feet, sat up there in the MiG and flew with no problem whatsoever. Obviously his oxygen demands were much lower than Collins's. God, it was just an amazing performance.

We learned very quickly that our Sabres were much better airplanes—superior weapons systems and equipment—although the MiG had a few advantages in its rate of climb, higher ceiling, and acceleration. As the result of our tests, we recommended to our combat pilots that they maintain a speed of at least .8 Mach while engaging the MiGs, which would give them an advantage over the MiG's greater thrust and acceleration. But still, there were combat pilots who insisted that the MiG could go supersonic, so we went all out in our testing to prove this wasn't so. Yeager got this assignment, about as dangerous as any he had ever flown.

I said, "All right, Chuck, we'll go up to 50,000 feet. I'll be right on your wing all the way. We'll go straight down. I'll read the Mach number because our instruments are probably more accurate." Hell, we knew the MiG would lose elevator control on a high Mach number dive; the Russians had an automatic speed brake at .94 Mach. The only hope to recover was at about 18,000 feet, where in the denser air control effect could be resumed. I counted on Yeager's instinctive abilities in a cockpit to get him through, but even so, it was an extremely perilous assignment. I said to him, "Well, Chuck, this is high

risk again. I wouldn't blame you if you didn't want
to do it." He replied, "Oh, hell, sir, that's why I
loaded those cartridges in the ejection seat myself."

So we took off, went up to 50,000 feet, then dove
absolutely straight down. Chuck's MiG was buffeting
like mad, and he was out of control with no aileron
effectiveness at a top speed of .98 Mach, which I'm
damn sure is faster than any Russian test pilot ever
flew that thing. He began feeling some control effect
at 16,000 and began pulling out at 12,000, right in
the middle of turbulent storm clouds. We ended that
most dangerous test by landing together in a blinding rain squall. General Cannon was just amazed at
how thoroughly we were able to test the MiG under
such awful conditions. I told him, "General, just be
thankful that the enemy doesn't have a test pilot
with the skills of Major Yeager. Because of him, we
now know more about this airplane than the Russians do."

On our final day in Okinawa, there was an amusing incident between Chuck and two combat pilots
who had flown in our Sabre chase planes from Korea. One of them, a lieutenant colonel, asked Chuck
why we didn't attempt to dogfight the MiG with the
Sabre. Yeager told him that the outcome of a dogfight depended more on pilot experience than on an
airplane's performance. The combat pilot just didn't
believe it, so Chuck asked him if he would like to fly
in the MiG 15 and dogfight Yeager, flying in a Sabre.
The colonel agreed and Chuck checked him out in
the plane's systems and off they went. Chuck easily
got on the MiG's tail and stuck there. They landed
and switched airplanes, Chuck taking off in the MiG
and the colonel flying in his own Sabre. Again, Yeager
waxed his tail unmercifully. When they landed, the
colonel was extremely abashed. He said to Chuck, "I
didn't think the pilot mattered that much." Chuck
grinned and told him, "The pilot with the most experience is gonna whip your ass, Colonel, no matter
what you're flying—it's that simple."

That colonel became known among fighter pilots because the story of how Yeager had beaten him really got around. But he lost to the best pilot I've ever seen fly.

———————————

When General Boyd was in a car, he drove it; when he was in an airplane, he flew it. One night, he drove Tom Collins and me off Kadena Air Base to go out to dinner. We sat in the back of the staff car, a major and a captain, while a two-star general drove us out the main gate. We had to stop at the guard's gate to turn in our trip ticket, and I never saw such a startled look on any human being as on the face of the air policeman. The poor guy had to ask a mean-faced two-star for his trip ticket. After we pulled away, the old man began chuckling. "He never saw a general playing chauffeur, did he?"

We flew back in a big four-engine C-124, which the old man piloted with me in the copilot's seat. We flew first to Japan, where the old man gave our evaluation of the MiG 15 at a meeting of wing commanders stationed in South Korea and Taiwan, then headed home to brief General LeMay at SAC headquarters. We sat together in that cockpit for seventeen hours, flying all night across the Pacific, talking mostly pilot's talk. He told me about the early days of his Air Corps career, when he was a flight instructor in 1930. One miserable rainy day, he took off in a DeHaviland DH-4 because he loved instrument flying, but he got lost in heavy clouds and ran out of fuel. He landed on a highway and flagged down a passing Good Gulf gasoline truck and had the driver fill 'er up. He took off, but as soon as the automobile gas got in his plane's carburetor, the engine cut out and he crashed into trees, wrecking the airplane, but leaving him unhurt to catch hell from his commanding officer.

On December 6, 1941, he was scheduled to ferry a B-17 bomber from California into Hickham Field, Hawaii, which would have put him on the runway just as the Japanese launched their attack on Pearl Harbor. But the flight was delayed by bad weather for twenty-four hours, and he arrived at Hickham on December 8, with fires still burning. That was as close to combat as he got. He stayed in Hawaii in the service command. "That's my only real regret, Chuck," he said. "I would've loved to have been flying Mustangs with you in the war. I think I would've been a damned good fighter pilot, too." I told him, "General Boyd, as far as I'm concerned, being a fighter pilot is it. I'd have given my eyeteeth to dogfight again in Korea. That's what I was trained for and what I love best."

He asked me if running a fighter squadron was something I'd enjoy doing after my test flying days were over.

"General," I said, "my bags are packed."

"You're ready to move on to other things?"

"If it means getting a squadron, you bet."

"Well, Chuck," he said, "after all we've asked of you, I personally think you ought to get what you want."

General Boyd had a lot of clout, and I've got to believe he was a big reason why a colonel from the Pentagon called me a couple of weeks after I got back to Edwards and told me I could stay as long as I wanted to at a desk job, but I could no longer do research flying, or I could take over a tactical fighter squadron of Sabre jets in Germany. He was almost apologetic explaining that the Pentagon brass decided to get me out of research flying before the law of averages caught up with me. I just chuckled and told him, "Colonel, you've given me the easiest decision of my life."

I never saw Glennis happier than when I told her we were going to Germany. We had been on the desert for seven years, and it was hard to believe that the miserable week on Okinawa was actually my swan song as a test pilot.

JACKIE

In May 1953, a pilot named Jacqueline Cochran set a new world speed record of 652 mph on a one-hundred-kilometer course at Edwards, flying a Canadian-built Sabre. Jackie's record was my project. I was her teacher and chase pilot.

I first met her in 1947, not long after I broke the sound barrier, in Secretary of the Air Force Stuart Symington's office. She was a tall, blonde woman in her forties. "I'm Jackie Cochran," she said, pumping my hand. "Great job, Captain Yeager. We're all proud of you." She invited me to lunch, acting as if I should know exactly who she was, and caused an uproar just entering the posh Washington restaurant. The owner began bowing and scraping, and the waiters went flying. During the meal she sent back every other course, complaining loudly, and even marched into the kitchen to give the chef hell.

In between pumping me for all the details of my X-1 flights, I learned a little about who she was. She was a honcho on several important aviation boards and committees and was a famous aviatrix before the war, winner of the Bendix air races; she had been a close friend of Amelia Earhart's. During the war she was a colonel, in charge of the WASPs, the Women's Air Force Service Pilots, who ferried B-17 bombers to England. Hell, she knew everybody and bounced all over the world: on VE Day, she was one of the first Americans to get down inside Hitler's bunker in Berlin, and came away with a gold doorknob off his bathroom by trading for it with a Russian soldier for a pack of Lucky Strikes. On VJ Day she was in Tokyo, playing poker with a couple of generals on Mac-Arthur's staff and conned her way on board the battleship *Missouri* to watch the surrender ceremonies. As I would learn more than once over the next couple of decades, when Jackie Cochran set her mind to do something, she was a damned Sherman tank at full steam.

Hap Arnold loved her scrambled eggs and Tooey Spaatz was a drinking buddy. She was as nuts about flying as I was. "If I were a man," she said, "I would've been a war ace like you. I'm a damned good pilot. All these generals would be pounding on my door instead of the other way around. Being a woman I need all the clout I can get." But clout was no problem for Jackie. Her husband was Floyd Odlum, who owned General Dynamics, the Atlas Corporation, RKO, and a bunch of other companies.

We liked each other right off the bat. I could talk flying with her as if she were a regular at Pancho's. She knew airplanes and said flat out that flying was the most important thing in her life. She was tough and bossy and used to getting her own way, but I figured that's how rich people behaved. When we parted that day she said, "Let's stay in touch." We sure did that. Glennis and I became Jackie and Floyd's closest friends. It was a friendship that lasted more than twenty-five years, until their deaths. I was the executor of Floyd's estate. They treated me like an adopted son. I flew around the world with Jackie, and she was right—she was a damned good pilot, one of the best. And I'm sure the reason she latched onto me was because for Jackie, nothing but the best would do, and she thought I was the best pilot in the Air Force. Hell, she'd say that to anybody, anytime. She grabbed Bud Anderson on the golf course one day and said, "Andy, isn't Chuck the best pilot you've ever seen?" And Andy said, "Yeah, except when I shave."

Jackie played a big role in my life, and I in hers. It was Jackie who got the Air Force to send that two-star general to examine Glennis when she was so sick. She did it by marching on General Vandenberg, the Chief of Staff, and telling him what a disgrace it was that the wife of his X-1A pilot was desperately ill and being neglected. Floyd, who was crippled from arthritis, heard that the doctors thought Glennis had rheumatoid arthritis, and made arrangements for her to receive an exotic drug from the pituitary glands of hogs that cost three thousand dollars a shot, but it was contra-indicated during pregnancy. It was Jackie who decided that I deserved the Congressional Medal of Honor and went to work lobbying everyone from the President on down until I got it. Jackie usually got what she wanted, and she wanted those high-speed records. I helped her get them.

I've heard people claim that Jackie got me my general's star. That just isn't so, but I have no doubt that she tried. I met two sitting presidents in her living room, Eisenhower and Johnson. Any Air Force brass that Jackie didn't know on a first-name basis just wasn't worth knowing. Wherever she traveled overseas, she was treated like a visiting head of state. Between her powerful personality and Floyd's power as an industrialist, doors flew open for her. His name and connections were all Jackie needed to blast her way in where she wanted to go, whether it was wild boar hunting in Spain with General Franco or having tea with the queen of Holland or a private audience with the pope. She was always roaring off somewhere, often flying herself in her own Lodestar, with her retinue of private secretary, maid, and hairdresser. If it was a long trip and she needed a good copilot, she'd pull the right strings and get me to go with her. She even got me excused from classes at the War College, something that had never been done before, so that I could attend an international aviation conference and help negotiate some rules regarding world speed and altitude records with the Russians.

There weren't many like Jackie back in Hamlin, for sure. I never met anyone like her, man or woman. She came on like a human steamroller, and she'd take over your life if you let her. She was forever telling me how to talk and act, what tie to wear, what pants and jacket, what speeches to give and which to refuse. Hell, she would do that with presidents. She'd read something in the papers about the Air Force or space program that she didn't like and pick up the telephone to call the White House. One time she didn't get through to Johnson. He called her back, but she told Floyd to tell LBJ she was washing her hair and call back later. Floyd wanted to strangle her, but LBJ did call back.

He also paid a visit to her ranch at Indio. Jackie fed the President lunch; General Eisenhower and myself were also invited. Johnson said to her, "Hey, Jackie, when are you gonna show me that golf course you're always bragging on?" She said, "Right now. Come on, we don't need dessert, we're both fat enough." And she grabbed him and hustled him into her car and took off. Man, General Eisenhower was furious at her. When she got back, he took her aside and blasted her. "Damn it, Jackie, you should know better than that. A civilian *never* drives a President. My God, what if there was an accident?" Jackie said, "Well, then Lyndon should've said something."

General Eisenhower was almost like family. Floyd and Jackie were his earliest supporters for the presidency, and he used their guest cottage as his office to write his memoirs. The first time she had him over for dinner as President, the White House called to say that Mamie Eisenhower expected to be asked to bring along some guests of her own. Jackie said, "Why, of course." But she turned purple when Mamie's guest list arrived showing thirty names.

For Glennis and me, Jackie's world was something we could never have even imagined. The first time we were invited down to the Cochran-Odlum Ranch was in 1950; it was a three-hour drive from Edwards, about twenty-five miles from Palm Springs, driving desert all the way, but the minute we drove through those big gates, it was like entering the Garden of Eden. Thick groves of tangerine and grapefruit trees lined both sides of the driveway, and the perfume from those blossoms made your head swim. Jackie bragged that during spring, she could fly over her ranch at night and smell those blossoms a mile up. I don't doubt it. They owned a thousand acres, and it was all green grass, shade trees, a manmade pond, date-bearing palm trees, oleander and jacaranda, a private nine-hole golf course, a skeet range, stables for a dozen Arabian horses, tennis courts, and an Olympic-size swimming pool. That first visit we two desert rats were in a state of shock. We stayed in guest house number one right next to the main house, a six-room cottage, which was always reserved for General Eisenhower. I said to Glennis, "This ain't no cabin up a holler."

Jackie Cochran didn't own a pair of shoes until she was eight years old. Compared to what she suffered as a child in rural Florida, I was raised like a little country gentleman. She never knew her real parents or why she was given away. The people who raised her lived in a shack without power or running water. As a little kid she had to forage in the woods for food to keep from starving to death. She had no education, no affection, no nothing. She was kept filthy dirty, her only clothes an old flour sack. Who knows all the things that happened to her growing up; she didn't talk about it much. But when she married Floyd in 1934, she hired a private detective to go back to Florida and find out who her parents were. She figured Floyd had a right to know about her heredity. The detective gave her a written report in a sealed envelope, which Floyd returned to her unopened. "It's still unopened," she told me, "sitting in my vault unread all these years." It was still there when she died in 1980, and was burned unopened.

Jackie was tough as nails. She learned how to become a hairdresser, got out of Florida, and finally landed in New York. She got into the cosmetics business and started her own company. She became very successful, got interested in flying, and her boyfriend at the time, named Mickey Rosen, who stayed close to her all her life, taught her how to read and write, and tutored her so that she could take her exam for her pilot's license orally, rather than in writing, because writing was a real struggle. She bought an airplane, a Waco, and entered air race competitions. Then she met Floyd, the son of a Methodist minister from Ohio, who had started out as a shoe salesman and had built himself a business empire. Floyd was a real gentleman, a tremendous human being, and he polished Jackie. Until he got clobbered by arthritis, he flew with her to all the air races. By the time we met them, Floyd was confined to a wheelchair, always in terrible pain, and spent a lot of time in the big outdoor pool that was kept heated to ninety degrees.

Over the years, Glennis and I came to consider that ranch as a second home, but, man, those first weekend visits we spent most of the time just pinching ourselves. It was the garden spot of the world with an army of servants, and it was just unbelievable for us to be there. I'd get up real early and go down to the stables. Glennis was out on that golf course until sunset. I loved shooting skeet, and Floyd had the finest collection of guns I'd ever seen. In the evening, we'd dress and go up to the main house for cocktails and a wonderful dinner party. You never knew who you might meet: wheels from all over the world. Dr. Edward Teller, father of the H-bomb, might be seated on my right and Bob Hope on my left. Jackie knew how to collect interesting people, and in her house we met African big-game hunters, dukes and duchesses, a Las Vegas casino owner, doctors, writers, movie stars, adventurers—even a Nevada sheriff. But what she liked most of all was to invite down a bunch of us test pilots from Edwards and talk flying.

She took Glennis and the other wives into her room and threw open her clothes closet and told them to help themselves to her wardrobe. She'd go over to the spring fashion show in Paris and clean out Christian Dior, come back with twenty thousand dollars in dresses, and give Glennis the clothes the models had worn. She drooled over Glennis's slim figure, really a perfect model's figure, and loved to see her wearing those expensive fashions. She gave her furs and jewels, too. She was extremely generous that way. So was Floyd. He'd hire a fleet of taxis to take all of us into Palm Springs and spend Saturday night as his guests at some posh private club.

For us military pilots at Edwards, being invited down to Jackie's was a big, big deal. She really liked Col. Fred Ascani. Jackie was a devout Catholic and so was Colonel Fred, but she gave him hell for having eight kids. They'd argue birth control all the time. She liked Jack and Nell Ridley and Pete Everest and his wife, Avis. General Boyd was a special favorite. She usually invited down the old man as her only guest. But Jackie was damned fussy about everything, including her guest list, and really put me and Glennis on the spot by asking our advice about the pilots she should invite down. But there were some guys, like Dick Frost, for instance, who politely turned down her invitation because they found her too overbearing and wanted nothing to do with her.

Jackie was a tiger. She expected to get her own way in everything, and, if you ever crossed her, you'd better duck. I remember the first time I met General Eisenhower there, we sat down after dinner and talked together for more than an hour. Hell, he remembered everything about me: how I had gone to him during the war and asked to stay with my squadron, and he even recalled the article in *Stars and Stripes* when I had shot down five Germans. He laughed and said, "How could I forget anybody who refused to go home?" Jackie couldn't stand it any more and came over to where we were seated. "General, do you realize what a famous pilot you're talking to?" she smiled. Well, the General really laid it on with a damned trowel. He said, "I've known Chuck more than twenty years. We go back together to since the war." Later, Jackie was really sizzling. She said to me, "How could you let me play the fool? Why didn't you tell me you knew General Eisenhower from day one?" I said, "Hell, you never asked." I thought she was going to punch me. She turned her back and marched out, slamming the door nearly off its hinges and didn't talk to me again for a couple of days.

General Eisenhower presented me with the Harmon Trophy at the White House in the spring of 1954 for my flight in the X-1A, and we got to know each other quite well at Jackie's place. One time I brought down a friend of mine named Delbert Moses, a big raw-boned Texan, who was a neighbor. Delbert was an electrician, a very nice and quiet guy who seldom said a word. Floyd had planted what he called "Hell's Half-Acre"—lemons that were sweet, oranges that were sour, all kinds of oddball fruits—and I took ol' Delbert over to show it to him. We began to pick some tangerines that were sour as lemons to take back to our friends. We were talking about a hundred feet from General Eisenhower's study, where he was working on his memoirs. The next moment, he was right on us, waving a walking stick. "What are you two doing here?" He thought we were thieves stealing fruit. Then he saw me and smiled. "Oh, it's you, Chuck," and invited both of us over to his study for a cup of coffee. Delbert was really flabbergasted.

Jackie was Floyd's hobby. Going for speed records cost a fortune, but he happily paid the bills, and kept pushing her to try for more. She'd say to him, "But I'm not sure I can do this even with Chuck helping me." And he'd tell her, "Of course you can, and I expect you to do it." He was damned proud of her, and really got a kick out of her. Sometimes she could be so outrageous that you just had to laugh. She got all over me about learning to play golf. I said, "No way." God, she hounded me to at least go on the course with her. She and Floyd had opened it to the townspeople of Indio, charging them five bucks to play nine holes. One day I did go out with her, and there were a bunch of people playing ahead. Jackie just said, "Coming through, coming through." One guy didn't recognize her and said, "The hell you are. What gives you the right?" Jackie got hot. "You son of a bitch, get your fat ass off my golf course and never come back." Man, that was it for me.

I'd come back from a trip with her, flop down and sigh, and tell Glennis, "Never again. Damn it, never again." Well, then she would have my mother down and make a big fuss over her, or when I was out of the country, have Glennis and the kids stay for a week. She even flew them back to West Virginia in her Lodestar for a surprise visit with my parents. If one of our kids got sick, she wanted to send for a specialist. Floyd was the same; they just couldn't do enough for us. Jackie smoked, but she would get annoyed if other people smoked around her. That was how she was. But she was a remarkable person and I respected the hell out of her for how much she had accomplished and how far she had come. She was a pain at times, but I figured she had earned that right. Jackie had paid her dues in spades.

Glennis Yeager

Jackie and Pancho Barnes had several things in common: they both wished they were men and wanted nothing to do with women. They both idolized Chuck and lived vicariously through his accomplishments. Chuck was exactly who they wanted to be if they could only have been born as men. And, of course, they were both obsessed with flying.

I could also say they were both generous, but Pancho didn't expect anything in return. Jackie tried to buy me. She couldn't, but that didn't stop her from trying. She wanted Chuck. I don't mean romantically. Jackie was all power and ambition. She wanted Chuck's time to help her achieve her records, and she wanted the prestige of having him at her side at aviation conferences and in her big living room. Colonel Ascani once said to me, "Jackie's house is the only place where Chuck can't be outranked no matter who else is there." That was true. As far as Jackie was concerned, Chuck was always the star of her show. She loved to show him off, and if she could've found a way to bottle and sell him, she'd have done it in a minute. So she gave me expensive clothes not only to keep me quiet, but to assuage the guilt she felt.

Pancho couldn't stand women and neither could Jackie. Jackie would get annoyed if any women's groups invited her to give a talk. "What do I have in common with a bunch of damned housewives?" she would complain. I got the message. I think they were both intimidated by good-looking women, although Jackie could be quite attractive when she was dressed to the nines. She was a powerfully built woman, big-boned, with strong manly hands that could belong to a steamfitter. But she also had big beautiful brown eyes and blonde curly hair. Pancho was just a mess.

Jackie was always buying me, but Pancho called a spade a spade. Her bar was little more than a desert whorehouse. She knew it and so did I. She respected me because, unlike a lot of other wives, I never made a fuss about my husband going there. If that was where Chuck wanted to be, fine by me. I never saw anyone at Pancho's that would make me feel threatened. Pancho was amoral, with the foulest mouth imaginable. Jackie at least tried to be a lady even if she wished she were a man. Pancho looked like a man and didn't give a damn, I guess.

Both of them put up with me because I was part of a package that included Chuck. The big difference between them was that Pancho was not particularly important in Chuck's life, but Jackie really was. She introduced him to the right people and gave him an opportunity to grow in ways that he never would have experienced if he hadn't known her. And she also did the same for me, through him. She'd literally tell him how to dress and act: put this tie on, not that one; don't say this, do that. She taught him a tremendous amount, doing for Chuck what Floyd had once done for her. Chuck never would have accepted that from anybody else. And Chuck was the only person on earth who could tell off Jackie. Whenever she made a scene in a restaurant (which always happened when everything was going smoothly and everybody was having a good time, because she couldn't stand tranquillity) and began to complain loudly about this and that, Chuck would say, "Goddamn it, Jackie, shut up." And she would. Those two had a real hold over one another.

She was very demanding of Chuck and tried to keep him under her thumb. He'd get mad as a hornet at the things she sometimes did or said, but he usually did what she asked, whether it was dropping everything to go off with her to some aviation meeting or make a talk to a group she was entertaining.

Bud Anderson would come back from playing golf with Jackie and say to Chuck, "That woman gives me fits, and I'm not in the front lines with her like you are." I think one reason why Chuck didn't say, "That's it, I've had enough," is that it would have crushed her. We were like adopted family.

I couldn't believe people actually lived that way. Her living room was as large as the movie theater in my home town. She had had it enlarged to fit an enormous rug she bought that was in the Yugoslavian exhibit at the 1939 World's Fair. She and Floyd each had their own private secretary and personal maid. The ranch had its own switchboard and operator, and Jackie would stay in her bedroom until nearly noon, phoning friends all over the world. The place crawled with servants, who came and went in droves. The kitchen help were always in trouble because Jackie was a fabulous cook and never satisfied with their dishes. Maybe because of her terrible childhood, she had a cleanliness fetish, took three or four showers a day, and had her bed linen changed daily. She was a good golfer and expected those she invited down to play with her; Chuck, of course, was the exception. He didn't like the game and couldn't be bothered to learn. She loved to gamble, playing penny-ante poker with the guys after dinner. Jack Ridley once played twenty-one with her and was amazed when she asked for another card with seventeen showing. "That gal adds by tapping her fingers," Jack laughed. And she could drink most of the guys under the table. She had a real wooden leg; her drink was Beefeaters on the rocks.

Everyone who came down to the ranch had to put up with her in some way. No one escaped. The Secretary of the Air Force, Stuart Symington, had to go out with her while she showed off her new Lincoln. Jackie loved to drive fast and roared off doing seventy-five over undulating hills. The car cracked down so hard that it broke the shock absorbers. Symington got out and walked back to the ranch.

"I'll never get in a car with that woman again," he said.

At first I was very intimidated by these lush surroundings and by Jackie, who charged around like a bull moose in heat. But gradually I got used to it—and her. When Chuck helped her get her speed record, she came out to Edwards and moved into our house. I moved out with the children, down to the ranch, and Chuck moved into the bachelor officers' quarters on base. I spent hours cleaning my house, waxed all the floors, and she got in there and had her maid scrape off all the wax because she was afraid that Floyd would slip on it. I was so mad I could spit. Susie came down with chicken pox, and Jackie wanted to fumigate my place. I said to her, "No way. That darned stuff will turn my drapes yellow." She was furious. "Goddamn it, if I get sick now I'll lose everything and I have all this money invested in this project." I told her, "Oh, Jackie, quit worrying. You probably had the chicken pox, and if you didn't, you'll just fly with it as well as you would without it. Forget about it." I finally convinced her after she had fifteen doctors give her the same opinion.

She didn't get chicken pox, but she sure got chickens. She and Chuck were making a low-altitude practice run out over the desert and accidentally came over a farmer's poultry shed about ten feet off the deck, and a couple of thousand broilers panicked and stampeded into a wire fence. Jackie had to pay a few thousand in damages for all the dead birds.

Floyd just doted on her. His day was made if Jackie gave him an affectionate hug or a kiss. I got to know him well when I was recovering from having Susie. Jackie insisted that I recuperate at the ranch. After being so sick, I was barely walking. She brought me down, had a nurse for the baby, bought me a motorized golf cart to get around in. She really could be very kind. Floyd insisted that I spend a lot of time in that hot pool. We were practically in the same condition. He was about twenty years older than

Jackie, his body wasted by being so crippled. He was a kind, gentle person, who kept his pain to himself, and needed to be strapped in two life preservers to stay afloat. It took a lot to get him angry, but sometimes Jackie pressed the right button, and then the back of Floyd's neck would turn crimson and he'd erupt: "Great Scott!" That was the worst you could get out of him.

Each of them lived in separate worlds; Jackie was always off and running somewhere, and Floyd was deeply involved in his business dealings. He was tough and tightfisted with everyone but her. He and Howard Hughes were close in business. Hughes was so paranoid that he refused to call Floyd at the ranch because he was sure the ranch's telephone operator listened in. So Floyd had a private line installed. All he had to do was lift the receiver and the phone would ring in Hughes's suite, wherever he was. Jackie once bragged that she could get through to Hughes whenever she wanted to. She lifted that receiver and got one of Hughes's henchmen, and that was that.

One time Howard Hughes came out to the ranch to meet with Floyd. But he wouldn't come to the house. He insisted they meet out on Floyd's golf course. He didn't say where. "Just drive around; you'll find me." I took Floyd out on my golf cart. We finally found him parked behind the bird aviary at the edge of the course. Terry Moore was with Hughes. Floyd got off the cart and walked to the car using his canes. He got in the car and had his meeting. When Floyd got out of the car, I saw Terry Moore spray the air inside, probably a germ disinfectant.

Another time, I went with Floyd to Las Vegas to help him get around when he had a meeting with Howard Hughes, who was then living at the Hilton. I took Floyd up in his wheelchair to keep the appointment. We got out of the elevator on Hughes's floor and found ourselves in a locked room. The elevator closed and we just sat there in that locked room with no way out. Somebody finally came to fetch us and

took us into another room that was very lovely, and
finally, Howard Hughes came in and greeted us. He
looked like all the newspaper photographs from his
younger days, very handsome and fit, but he was
really in bad mental shape, filled with paranoia. Floyd
introduced me, and Hughes, being so active in aviation, knew who Chuck was, and that seemed to relax
him a bit about my being there. But he stood far
back, away from my germs. Floyd could walk on a
level floor and followed Hughes into another room to
have their meeting.

Floyd became like a favorite uncle to us. Chuck
and I had a very modest savings account, and he
took some of that and invested it for us in the stock
market. He also started The Fat Cat Uranium Corporation for Chuck, Jack Ridley, Pete Everest, Bob Uhrig,
and General Boyd. They flew up to Utah and staked
out several claims. Floyd even staked them to a small
airplane that they kept out at Pancho's strip and
used to ferry up geologists to do research for them in
Utah. The corporation ultimately made quite a lot of
money; we still have our shares.

Well, Jackie lived vicariously through Chuck, and
Floyd lived vicariously through Jackie's exploits, so
it was a strange kind of merry-go-round. But we
stayed close with them. They visited us in Germany
when Chuck got his squadron. Floyd had put Jackie
up to running for Congress against the Democratic
incumbent in Indio, but she lost badly and wasn't in
the best mood. She went off flying, and Floyd and I
took a steamer up the Rhine. We each had our own
staterooms, just like a transatlantic ship, and our
seating for dinner. The food was fabulous and we
had a wonderful trip.

Later, when Chuck went to the War College for
six months and I stayed behind, Jackie invited me
and the children to stay at the ranch. Jackie pro-
fessed to love kids, and I had raised ours to be well-
behaved, but I kept my brood out of her way. Jackie
was not famous for patience. Jackie was five-eight,

wore an eight or nine shoe—a big woman, buxom, but not particularly heavy. Most of the dresses she gave me I had to take in because she was twice as big as I was.

But Jackie would stab me every once in a while. I started turning gray back in the 1960s. Jackie said I should dye my hair. "Damn it, Glennis, nobody should ever be gray." She tinted her hair gold, but I had black hair and the gray really showed. I was pulling out so many gray hairs that my hair was actually thinning. So, finally I agreed with her about dyeing my hair. She had just come in off the golf course when I approached her about it; she had been a professional hairdresser and owned her own cosmetics business. But she just erupted, "Oh, for God's sake, I've got a lot more to take care of than to worry about your hair. Do what you want with it. Shave it off if you want to." And she roared off.

I felt terribly hurt, but I got the message. She didn't give a damn what I looked like and actually hoped that I'd screw up. I got some dye that was okay except it turned my hair red when the sun shone on it. Later, when Chuck was sent to Korea, I stopped dyeing it. When he came back it was real salt and pepper. He looked at me. "I hope you like it," I said. "It cost an awful lot for them to do this." He laughed. "The hell it did. You just let it grow out." He was hard to fool with those good eyes. Chuck never wanted me to wear makeup or dye my hair. "Don't listen to Jackie," he said. "Just be yourself."

In the spring of 1953, when I was preparing for my flights in the X-1A, Jackie approached General Vandenberg about trying to set speed records in an F-86. She would use a Canadian-built Sabre, built by

Floyd's company, which had more thrust than the American jets, but, being a civilian, she needed special permission to use Air Force facilities and equipment. During a trip out to Edwards, General Vandenberg discussed Jackie's request with General Boyd, who knew her well and admired her. When the old man and I had been to France testing the French airplanes, Jackie happened to be in Paris, and he had taken her up in a two-place jet fighter, the first time she had flown over 600 mph. So, General Vandenberg approved Jackie's request, and the old man asked Colonel Ascani to make all the arrangements, which was ironic because Colonel Ascani then owned the existing low-altitude speed record. Anyway, he asked me to be Jackie's instructor on the F-86.

It was summer on the desert, and in order to get smooth air for precision flying, we had to fly early in the morning. That first day, I set us up for a six A.M. takeoff and told her she had to be there at five to get briefed on the flight, get her G suit on and so forth, in order to start engines at six. I was there at a quarter to five. At five, no Jackie. Six, no Jackie. Six-fifteen rolled around and she came bouncing in. I shut the door to the office we were using and sat her down. I said, "Look, I want to tell you something. If you want to fly this program, you're gonna be here on time. You've got fifteen people out here working at four in the morning to pre-flight your airplane and get your gear ready, while you, a single pilot, can't get here on time. Look at all the man-hours you've already wasted for the Air Force, not to mention the guys who are busting their tails for you. If you want this program, you're gonna be here when you're scheduled to be here." From then on we had no more problems. If I said be here at five, she was.

She had no jet experience and was a little apprehensive. I had checked her out in the airplane's systems the day before, teaching her the cockpit, the landing gear handle, the flaps and the throttle, the techniques for flying the Sabre—but only what she needed to know, the basics. I would be right with her on these flights and could analyze any problem that came up and tell her what to do. I didn't want to get her muddled by throwing everything at her all at once, and it made it a lot easier for her. The big thing I told her over and over: "If I tell you to do something, you do it immediately and don't ask why."

We lined up both airplanes for that first takeoff. I climbed up onto her wing and watched her start up, then ran over to my airplane and started up. We both closed our canopies, and I checked and saw that she had her flaps set for takeoff. I spoke to her on the radio. She was a little scared. "Don't get too close," she said. "Forget about me," I told her. "I'm used to this. This way I can watch you and see if you do anything you shouldn't." I remembered setting her air conditioner selector switch down to the cool position because the sun was up and blazing against her canopy. So, we took off together and about the time she broke ground, she flipped the gear handle and the gear came up. She radioed, "I've never been so hot in my life. This cockpit is burning me alive." I moved in real close to where our wings were overlapping and I could see the corners of her flying suit rippling from blowing air. The Sabre was equipped with a powerful canopy defroster that bled air right off the engine compressor and it was really hot at low altitude and full power. I could also see her hand on the throttle. I said, "Take your hand off the throttle, move it back six or eight inches. Okay. Now, raise it up a little higher and move it outboard." I was watching her hand and I could see the lever for the defroster control. Somebody had accidentally hit it when she got in the cockpit and turned it on. I told her to move back the lever. She did. Her flying suit stopped rippling and she cooled down. We flew for a while. She was always excellent at landing airplanes; nothing bothered her. After she landed, I debriefed her. She bitched and moaned about that hot cockpit.

I said, "You've got to get used to things like that. That happens in flying."

We had maybe a half-dozen of these orientation flights. Finally, General Doolittle called me and asked me to fly down to Jackie's ranch and meet with him privately. She was staying in my place at Edwards. General Doolittle was a close friend of hers, and he really put me on the spot by asking me point blank whether I thought Jackie could keep from busting her ass in a Sabre and fly proficiently to set records. "The Chief of Staff is concerned about this," he said. "The last thing we want is a catastrophe involving Jackie Cochran. If you think she can go through with this, we'll back her. If you think she can't, just say the word and we'll back off. But know this, Chuck. If you say she can, the monkey is on your back to keep her from getting hurt." I told him, "General, she's a good pilot with a tremendous background of experience in flying. She can fly practically anything, and I really think she can do this program."

So we went for it. She had a lot of confidence in me, but occasionally other pilots like Pete Everest and Tom Curtis flew chase for her, and she would be upset because I knew better than they what her capability was. Jackie hated the smell of sweat and kerosene inside the cockpit and on her parachute, so every time she flew, she carried a perfume spray. Every airplane she flew in smelled like a French whorehouse. For a year after Jackie went through there, pilots could still smell her perfume aboard those Sabres she flew.

After six or so flights in the Sabre, I figured she knew it well enough, so I took her up to 45,000 feet and told her to push her nose straight down. We dove together, wing to wing, kept it wide open and made a tremendous sonic boom above Edwards. She became the first woman to fly faster than sound, and forever after, she loved to brag that she and I were the first and probably the last man and woman team to break Mach 1 together.

Then we began practicing for the three-kilometer run. To get the maximum true speed out of the Sabre we had to fly when it was as hot as possible because the hotter the air, the higher the true speed, which is many miles an hour faster than on a cool day. But hot air means turbulence. One boiling afternoon we were about a hundred feet off the deck going at .92 Mach and the air was shaking our airplanes like a cocktail mixer. Suddenly I saw fuel gushing out of her wing and the side of her fuselage. I told her, "Hey, you've got a little problem. Shut off your throttle—stop cock it. Turn off your engine. Get your nose up." She obeyed immediately. But her fuel was still gushing out back. Meanwhile, I got on the radio, used another channel, and told tower to get the fire trucks out because we had a bad fuel leak. They scrambled. I told her, "Okay, start a gradual left turn and the minute the airspeed gets below 200 knots, get your landing gear down." She did. I was right beside her. I said, "Okay, drop the nose. Keep your airspeed up to 150." She did it perfectly and she lined up for a lakebed landing. Man, I got her out of that thing the minute we landed.

The next day Jackie broke the speed record. We came back down, and the official judges verified the data from the special recording devices, and, I swear, it was worth the effort just seeing the expression on that woman's face. She was very quiet, really surprised me. "Thank you, Major Yeager," she said, and she hugged me. The first person she heard from was Colonel Ascani, who held the previous record and sent her a warm letter of congratulations. We celebrated her achievement at the officers' club at Edwards. Jackie was so thrilled that she could hardly speak. But the person wearing the biggest smile was Floyd. Man, he practically busted with pride. I had taken him up a few days before in a two-seat jet trainer, after driving him in from the house in my Model A. He was so frail that there was no way to get a parachute on him, but I flew nice and level, and he thoroughly enjoyed going around the course we had laid out for Jackie. Privately, he thanked me for helping Jackie get through the program successfully. I told him, "It's her mark, Floyd, she did it herself." And that was true, even though some of the pilots at Edwards thought I had pulled her around the course like a dog on a leash. Bull. I chased her. That's all.

Five years later, she would prove how good she was. This time she would attempt new speed records in the Lockheed F-104 Starfighter, a Mach 2 airplane that plenty of experienced fighter pilots were scared of. And she would set records that still stand. And later that same year, she and I would fly to Russia together and have more adventures in three weeks than most people have in a lifetime. But those stories are for a later chapter. Jackie Cochran was a truly extraordinary person.

GOOD-BY

Before leaving for Germany in 1954, there was a farewell party at Edwards that became a historic occasion because I actually got Jackie and Pancho together in one room. They hated each other from as far back as the 1930s, when they competed in women's air races. Pancho would say to me about Jackie, "How can you stand that old bitch?" And Jackie would say to me about Pancho, "That disgusting bitch—how do you stand her?" I had Pancho on one side and Jackie on the other and there were no fireworks. Glennis said pulling that one off was a bigger achievement than breaking the sound barrier and she was absolutely right.

Really, the person I was saddest to leave behind was Jack Ridley. We had worked so closely together for so many years that I felt naked going out into the world without him. I said to him, "Goddamn it, Jack, how in hell do I get a squadron from point A to point B without your slide rule?" Ol' Jack was sad too, because my leaving really symbolized an end of

an era for both of us. But he stayed on for a couple
more years. He and Nell had a young son, Ronnie,
after years of thinking they couldn't have any children. Then Jack was transferred to Japan. Glennis
and I heard from them from time to time, and they
were happy to be leaving the desert. "Nell is willing
to go anywhere in the world where there is no wind
or sand," Jack wrote.

We always thought we'd get back to Edwards
again and be involved in some other hairy test programs. But it wasn't to be. We lost Jack in 1957. He
was riding as a passenger on a C-47 that hit the side
of Mt. Fuji. Whatever happened wouldn't have happened if only Jack had been in the pilot's seat. But he
wasn't.

Nell renamed young Ronnie, Jackie L. Ridley, Jr.
Jackie was Jack's legal name, but once he began to
shave, he preferred Jack. Jack's son is now a fine-
looking young man who resembles his dad. I saw
him and Nell in 1980 at dedication ceremonies for
the Jackie L. Ridley Mission Control Center at Edwards. That's the building that the flight engineers
use, and among those guys Jack was a legend. Any
Air Force flight engineer at Edwards knows all about
Jack. He was the best there was. "Well, son," he had
said, the day I left Edwards, "we had ourselves some
fun, didn't we?" Jack, we sure as hell did.

A NEW OLD MAN

EUROPE, 1954–1957

OTHER VOICES:

Emmett Hatch

The Air Force had been racially integrated only seven
or eight years by the time I became a fighter pilot. I
came up through the ranks as an enlisted man, the
same as Chuck Yeager, but it wasn't easy for me as a
black man. There were many racial incidents along
the way with no shortage of rednecks eager to shoot
me down. Only a handful of black pilots were scattered around the world in those days, and I knew I
couldn't afford to make any serious mistakes, but I
was young, full of piss and vinegar, and when Chuck
Yeager became my squadron commander in Germany,
he stood between me and guys ready to jump me.
Chuck just wouldn't tolerate that kind of crap. It's
true he grew up in West Virginia, where there are

some definite racial attitudes, but there is also a camaraderie between those who know what it is to be down and out. Without a doubt, he saved my neck on a couple of occasions. Serving with him became a highlight of my life.

Our squadron of Sabre jets was part of a three-squadron fighter-bomber wing stationed at Hahn, which, in 1955, was a brand new fighter base up on the "Houndsback," two thousand feet above the Mosel River, about thirty miles from Wiesbaden. Europe has the worst flying weather in the world, and Hahn had the worst weather in all of Europe. Heavy fog and rain were continuous, and only God knew why the Air Force decided to build a base up there. We lost a few pilots in the fog, while learning to be extremely proficient bad-weather pilots.

We couldn't believe that the famous Chuck Yeager was heading our way. We knew, of course, that he had broken the sound barrier and was a great test pilot. In fact, just before he came to us, he had been back in Washington to receive the Harmon Trophy at the White House for his flight in the X-1A. But fighter pilots aren't impressed by anything but dogfighting, which was about all we did. Anytime we took off, we knew guys were sitting upstairs waiting to jump our ass. So, there was a helluva line of eager young pilots anxious to jump our new squadron commander and see what he was made of. Testing Yeager turned out to be a massacre. He waxed everybody, and with such ease that it was shameful. The word got around that he was somebody very special.

In those days we flew the F model of the Sabre, which was slow. The Canadian fighter jocks in Europe loved to dogfight us in their own lighter, more maneuverable Mark V Sabres. They were merciless, and there wasn't much we could do about it. But Yeager took those guys on every chance he got. He flew the F like the rest of us, but he waxed those Canadians every time. We flew at maybe 90 percent of capability. Yeager flew at 101 percent. It was incredible to fly behind him in a traffic pattern because he flew with such precision. And he trained us by having us take turns flying his wing, which is really like flying his airplane because we emulated all his turns and maneuvers to keep up. For example, if he went into a tight diving turn, we went right with him even though we may not have done that before. I flew his wing when a couple of Canadian jocks bounced us. Chuck radioed to me, "Hold on," and did a tight pull up, simultaneously hitting his speed brakes. The Canadians zipped past us and we ended up waxing their tails. I was *impressed*.

Another time I flew his wing and socked in as tight as I could, thinking that was what a good wingman should do. Chuck told me to move my control stick from side to side. I saw that my airplane barely reacted. At the speed we were moving, the controls were very sluggish, and if anything happened I wouldn't have the quickness to avoid colliding with him. That's how he delivered the message that I was flying too close.

Flying with him we flew at our maximum ability because that's how he flew. We would get up in clouds and instead of flying around them, we'd maneuver in and out. You really do some complicated flying when you start playing with clouds. They have holes and unusual shapes that create tricky maneuvers—good training for aerial combat. Instead of taking a straight thirty-minute flight somewhere, we'd go down on the deck below 1,000 feet. We could get there either way, a relaxed cruise or skimming over trees and barns. The hard way we learned something. Yeager wouldn't let us get there the easy way.

We used to make bets on how close to the end of the runway his wheels would touch down on landing. Actually go out with a measuring tape. He was always a foot or two right at the end of the runway, a perfect landing every time, even in near-zero visibility.

My nickname in the squadron was "Jock" because I had played college basketball. We were flying air-to-ground gunnery in France, and after I made my pass at the target, Chuck radioed, "Well, Jock, how did you do?" I told him I thought I scored about forty percent. He said, "I beat you." I said, "I'll bet you on that." So when we landed I called the range officer to get our scores. I got forty percent. That SOB got eighty percent. I put down the phone and crawled off the base. Later, he told me, "God, Jock, that was really great. I could actually see the bullets hitting the target." I said, *"What!"* He replied, "The vortex from the shells. I saw them."

We were coming back from gunnery in North Africa when he came on the radio. "Hey, you guys, look at that tanker burning down there." We said, "What are you talking about?" We flew for another ten minutes and looked down. Sure enough, there was a ship on fire. We couldn't imagine how he could see so much better than the rest of us, and wondered if he had binoculars stashed away in his cockpit.

Chuck came to us as a major and rather quickly was promoted to lieutenant colonel. We were a good squadron and he fit right in. He operated with a twinkle in his eye, as easygoing and friendly as any squadron leader we had ever encountered; his rank was there because he wore it on his collar, but he lived to fly like the rest of us and probably flew more than the other squadron commanders in the wing. He was right in the middle of our beer busts, parties, and poker games. Being a squadron commander is all young fighter pilots ever hoped to become in this world, and we just hero-worshiped the guy. We busted our asses to please him and earn his respect. If he sent for one of us and asked a lot of questions, we knew damned well we had done something wrong and were in trouble. He would listen to an explanation and say, "You're full of shit." And, God, to get that from him was worse than a slap in the face and having your epaulets ripped off. I don't recall him ever chewing anyone out. He didn't have to. Everyone, including all the enlisted men in the ground crews, took real pride being in Yeager's squadron.

We were living with a legend and we knew it even then. We read everything we could find about him and learned he was a World War II combat ace. We'd sit with him in the officers' club, prime him with beers, and get him to talk about airplanes and flying, soaking up every damned word. Try as we might, we couldn't get him to talk about his exploits, but there was nothing about aviation that he didn't know. Whatever he really thought about our individual flying skills he kept to himself. Nobody ever heard him say, "I don't think you can hack this." His attitude was, "Here's what we're gonna do, and you'll do it just fine." He made us think we could all fly with his capabilities, which was absolutely crazy. For example, he made his personal mark in the squadron by ordering us to wear red scarves and deciding that we would fly in a diamond formation. Air Force regulations demanded that all squadrons fly in a stacked formation, but Chuck just shrugged. He said, "The acrobatic teams fly a diamond and we're as good as they are." We became "The Red Diamonds."

One day an Air Force inspector was checking out the armament switches on one of our airplanes when suddenly all six fifty-caliber machine guns began firing out over the woods toward a German village. Fortunately, no civilians were hurt, but there were investigations, and the result was that special safety pins were inserted in the trigger mechanisms that kept them from firing. Each pin had a big red tag attached to it, and we could barely fly with all the crap on our control sticks. We bitched and moaned about it, then, lo and behold, those pins began disappearing. We'd climb in the cockpit and report them missing. Colonel Yeager finally called us together and said, "Hey, you guys, leave those pins alone. Regulations are regulations." But they kept disappearing until not one airplane in the squadron had a safety pin left. In fact, we almost forgot they ever existed.

One day, months later, Chuck asked somebody to fetch something from his locker. There were all those missing pins, piled in our squadron commander's locker. He was the one who removed them all. Chuck was a free-wheeler, and the Air Force bureaucracy drove him nuts. He knew we had to live within the system and could not fight it head-on and win. But, damn, he knew how to resist.

Col. Fred Ascani commanded the entire wing. He was tough and strict, a real terror to work for. Ascani had been General Boyd's deputy, so Chuck knew him well. Even so, Ascani had bugaboos, and if anyone violated his rules, he lowered the boom. His biggest bugaboo was accidents. When he took over the wing, the accident rate was atrocious, so he staked his career on a zero accident rate. Wreck an airplane and he'd wreck you. We flew into Pisa, Italy, one day and a guy in our squadron snapped the nose wheel off his Sabre while landing. Chuck called the squadron maintenance officer and gave him a list of parts that would be needed to bolt a fixed nose gear on the airplane, and they arrived in a C-47, while Chuck pounded out the air intake with a sledgehammer. The repairs took nearly a day, then Chuck flew that airplane back to Germany with the nose wheel down and bolted, a really tricky piece of flying. It was rolled into the back of a dark hangar, quickly repaired, and never reported.

But then I crashed.

I was flying alone, coming down to refuel outside of Paris on a beautiful Sunday morning. I was feeling real good and began doing rolls coming down. But my control stick stuck and I couldn't stop rolling. I got down to 1,400 feet, more afraid of Colonel Ascani than of dying. Finally I ejected. I was so low that I did only two swings in my chute before I landed in a tree.

Ascani went out of his mind. He roared in on

Chuck: "What in hell was Hatch doing? Why was he rolling that airplane?"

Chuck said, "Hell, Colonel, he was doing exactly what he was supposed to be doing. He was doing a clearing roll."

"A *what*?"

Chuck said, "That's right. Anytime we are descending, we do a roll to make sure we aren't letting down on top of another airplane. It's a safety precaution. All my people do it."

Chuck saved my precious ass. I had no business doing those rolls, and I could've been court-martialed, my career ruined. Ascani just said, "Yeah, well, I suppose . . ." That was the end of it.

There's nothing better on this earth than to be part of a fighter squadron. You really are close and sharing. By the time my three-year tour came to an end, I was one of the old heads, an element leader, one of the guys Chuck counted on. I extended my tour for another year. Four of us senior guys did that. Chuck was gone a lot of the time, and he needed us. He was the Air Force's showpiece in Europe, and they were always sending him off somewhere on special assignment. Ascani was not pleased, but there was nothing he could do about it. The British or French would request him through the State Department, asking that he be allowed to help evaluate one of their new aircraft. The guy was a real celebrity, and he was constantly traveling all over Europe to air shows and conferences. Wherever he went he was always bumping into somebody he knew—pilots, sportsmen, princes, name it. He would meet a person only once and remember him twenty years later— everything about him, too; I've seen him do it. He'd be requested to hunt pheasants in Portugal with some dignitary. General LeMay, the head of SAC, flew into Spain and sent for Chuck to show him off to the Spanish air force brass. Then the two of them went partridge hunting with Franco. I never saw Chuck hunt, but he once went out with General Gross, vice commander of the Twelfth Air Force, hunting German roebuck deer, which are no bigger than dogs. Gross took one or two shots and missed, but Chuck bagged that deer at six hundred yards. The general couldn't believe it. He said, "God almighty, Chuck, how in hell . . ."

The guy was unbelievable. Because of him our wing won all the USAF European gunnery meets. Ascani loved him for that. He was high man in air-to-air and air-to-ground every time. The other contestants shook in their boots having to confront Yeager. One gunnery mission he flew they were firing two guns, and one of his jammed. So, using one gun he scored 85 percent—some unheard of thing like that— and he won anyway. The Air Force maintained a huge gunnery facility at Wheelus in Tripoli, and we went down there for a month at a time, living in tents out on the desert, flying and shooting night and day. One time he flew in a day after we arrived, and I sat upstairs waiting for him. As soon as I spotted his Sabre, I bounced him. I came in right on his tail and then took off with full power before he could react. I said, "Welcome to Tripoli, Colonel Yeager." He laughed. "Goddamn, Jock, if I catch you I'll whip the black off of you." Those would be fighting words from anybody else. From him, I just said, "Well, Colonel, you'll have to catch me first."

Being back with a fighter squadron was like coming home to the hollers of West Virginia—back among my own kind, who talked my language. At Hahn, we were only minutes of flying time away from possible combat with the Russians and their allies. We'd barely get our wheels up before reaching the East German border. Czechoslovakia was a half-hour flight. A week seldom passed in the 1950s when East German or

Czech pilots didn't invade our air space and cause us to scramble to intercept. They knew our Sabres could never catch up with their MiGs before they scooted back over the border. Often they staged their sweeps to coincide with our end-of-the-day beer calls, but there was more to it than just harassment. They were testing our reaction time. We were constantly on alert and kept at maximum readiness.

My squadron commander during World War II really was "the old man." He was all of twenty-five, leading a bunch barely out of their teens who thought he was over the hill. Now, I was "the old man," a thirty-two-year-old married major, commanding pilots whose average age was thirty and who were also mostly married, living on base with their families. To win their confidence I had to perform up to expectations. Once they saw I was really good, they would follow my leadership—not just obey orders—because I had proved that I knew what I was talking about.

Any new squadron commander is in a tough spot. There's a lot to learn, and being untested he is watched like a hawk by both his subordinates and his superiors. There were plenty of squadron commanders who couldn't lead a group in silent prayer. I knew I'd be watched closer than most, and by the top brass, too, because pilots with big reputations were often more trouble than they were worth, pains in the ass who threw their weight around and bugged out every chance they got. I knew plenty of guys like that. During my early years at Wright Field as a maintenance officer, one of the big war aces began parking his Lincoln Continental convertible in my hangar when he went off to fly. Nobody was allowed to park a car in a hangar, but he ignored the rule. I had the air police tow his car away and enjoyed telling him I was the one who did it. So, I told the squadron, "Hey, I'm here to have a good time. To me, a good time is flying with you guys. I'd rather do that than get laid." They laughed and got the message.

I wasn't much on spit and polish or running around with a clipboard. I had thirty pilots, twenty-five airplanes, and five hundred ground and support personnel under my command. A good squadron can run itself only up to a certain point; the commander must stay on top of things, but I wasn't about to chain myself to a desk doing it. And, man, I learned fast that if one of my people got into trouble, so did I. Both of us landed in front of the wing commander, Col. Fred Ascani, a West Pointer who hadn't served as General Boyd's deputy without a lot of strict discipline rubbing off. Forget that Colonel Ascani helped to select me to fly the X-1, and that we had spent social weekends together at Jackie Cochran's place. This was a new ballgame.

My first weekend as squadron commander he called me at home at two in the morning. "Chuck, what in hell is going on with your people?" God, I wondered if there was a riot. But he called me because the German police in town had called him. Two airmen from my squadron were arrested for being drunk and disorderly. I crawled out of bed and drove into town to get those guys out of the can. The next time I got such a wake-up call, I went straight to the barracks and woke up my first sergeant. I told him to wake up every man in the barracks. I said, "If I have to get up, so do you. This is our squadron and our guys." We all marched downtown to the jail and picked up the airmen. After that, I never got any more late night calls about my airmen.

Colonel Ascani ran a tight ship. Fighter pilots are naturally competitive, and the three squadrons in his wing even competed in Friday-afternoon beer guzzles at the club, where it was squadron against squadron. Really rough. He came in one Friday, saw the guys staggering around the bar with their shirts unbuttoned and ties undone, and took me and the other squadron commanders aside and reamed us out. "Goddamn it, I don't care how drunk they get, but we're gonna look military doing it. I want those

ties and shirts buttoned even when they hit the deck."
He sounded just like General Boyd.

I was as competitive as a college football coach
in training my bunch to be the best squadron in the
wing. I had high performance standards and because
the men respected me, they stretched to reach them.
Hell, it was like a little conspiracy. I'd teach them
tricks that none of the other squadrons knew, things
I had learned as a desert rat at Muroc. For example,
a Sabre fighter needed a big electrical cart to start
its engine. If the Russians could have found a way to
blow up those carts, they would've ruled the skies.
Sabre pilots who were forced to land somewhere
discovered they couldn't take off again because there
was no electrical cart available. That happened once
at Muroc and somebody, maybe Ridley, came up
with the idea of blow-starting a Sabre with another
jet. I showed my guys how to do it using the T-33,
the two-seat trainer version of the Shooting Star,
that started on its own battery. I moved the T-33
about fifteen feet in front of the Sabre and ran up its
engine to about eighty percent of power. The exhaust
blew directly into the front of the Sabre's engine and
began to spin the turbine blades to about six percent
revolutions a minute, enough to crank its engine. It
was like getting a car to start by coasting it in neutral down a hill. Man, those guys were speechless.
Soon everyone in the Twelfth Air Force was practicing blow-starts.

Another trick I learned back at Tonopah during
my training days in prop airplanes, when I saw a
grizzled old crew chief hammering nails around the
gun mounts in a P-39. "Help hold them guns steady,"
he explained, "and give you better shooting scores."
I figured if it worked in a P-39 it should also work in
a Sabre. And it did, although a few of my crew chiefs
were scared to drive nails into a government property airplane. One of them complained, "But, Major,
that's against regulations." I told him, "Hell it is.
There's no regulation about it because no one else

does it." When our pilots reported better gun scores over the other squadrons, we kept our little secret to ourselves.

There were dozens of little tricks that weren't in flight manuals that could mean the difference between life and death in a combat situation, and to me it was a responsibility of what pilots call "an old head," a veteran flier, to pass on tricks of the trade. There was always something new to learn up there. When Hahn received the first radar system to land aircraft in bad weather, we practiced landings in zero visibility; during those first attempts a few of our guys came down on the beam through the fog and almost landed right in the middle of the Mosel River. But we practiced with the ground operators day after day until most of them were landing safely while crews on the ground couldn't see a hand in front of their faces. All of us enjoyed being in a good squadron that was becoming even better.

Toward the end of my first year in Germany, I was promoted to lieutenant colonel, and Colonel Ascani made me the leader of our wing gunnery team. We competed against all the other fighter wings in Europe. Air-to-air shooting was my big scoring event. We fired at a target towed by a high-speed jet, our shells painted individual colors so that the holes could later be identified. Air-to-ground, we came in on the deck to shoot at large rectangular targets. The competition also included skip-and-dive bombing. My test piloting had really improved my precision as a flier so that I lined up early on the targets and let my good eyes take it from there. I was usually high man overall in the competitions, and our wing won the finals. Gunnery contests were a big deal; we were gone for months practicing and competing.

But I wasn't the only Yeager having fun. For the first time since we were married, Glennis was enjoying an Air Force assignment as much as I was. We had a German housekeeper to help take care of the kids, and unlike the majority of Air Force couples who spent the weekends at the club and base movie theater, we were eager to make the most of living in a foreign country. Every weekend that we could get away, we were gone. We became friends with the burgomaster of a nearby village called Traben-Trabach. Dr. Melscheimer was also a wealthy wine merchant, who owned the rights to several large hunting areas. Nobody in Germany just arbitrarily went out hunting. You had to be invited by somebody who had purchased hunting rights on a given piece of property called a *revier*. We became regulars at Dr. Melscheimer's hunting lodge, where the other weekend guests were businessmen and industrialists from Hamburg and Berlin. German hunting weekends are very aristocratic and social, and while Glennis's kitchen-deutsch was a helluva lot better than mine, I got by speaking the hunting language. Dr. Melscheimer was elderly, but his son Carl Armin was my age, and also an avid hunter. So was Carl's wife Siegrid, who was almost as good with a gun as Glennis.

While we were still at Ramstein, our quarters were located next to the base skeet range. One afternoon a few officers were out shooting and Glennis grabbed my shotgun and asked if she could shoot a few rounds. Those guys looked at her as if she had dropped out of the sky. Wives never shot skeet. Glen whacked out twenty-five straight hits. Between the two of us, we were no slouches on a hunt. We'd go out early in the morning, stalk game through deep forests of pine and beech, hunting stags, wild boar, or small deer. By late afternoon, we were back at the lodge for four o'clock tea, then after dinner, we often hunted by moonlight.

Soon, Dr. Melscheimer was trusting me to act as *jaeger*, or "hunting guide," for an important guest. I followed all the customs and learned their hunting traditions. I wore *lodencloth*, the green hunting uniform of a guide, a green shirt and tie, and a green felt hat with a boar's hair shaving brush in the back. When we killed an animal, I gave it the traditional

letzter bissen, a "last bite," by placing a twig in its
mouth, a symbol of respect to the animal. I also took
a twig off an evergreen shaped like a cross, dipped it
in the animal's blood, and wore it in my hat as a
trophy of that day's hunt. The cross-shaped twig honored St. Hubertus, patron of hunting.

Carl Armin and I competed as guides, each of us
trying to lead a guest to the day's biggest head. But I
had an advantage: The day before the hunt I flew
over the *revier* and carefully mapped it out, much the
same as I had done at Edwards, picking out fishing
holes and good hunting areas. So my party usually
beat Carl Armin's by bringing in the day's biggest
head, and the guests raved about me to Dr. Melscheimer, who smiled and nodded, saying, "Yes, I've
trained that American well." He made me a master
hunter on his *revier*, a real honor that meant, among
other things, that I could go out and hunt alone; and
he invited me to join the guild of German hunting
guides, the only foreigner in that outfit.

Glennis didn't sit around waiting for me to get
back if I was off flying somewhere. She and Siegrid
took off in our four-wheel drive jeep station wagon
and hunted on their own. They once joined a party of
German boar hunters and bagged the day's only kills.
While those German men grimly watched, they had
their pictures taken by the local newspapers, and
then they had to buy drinks for all the other hunters—
the price for having beaten them.

The kids had a ball, too. They enjoyed the snow
in winter, not having seen much of it out on the
Mojave. Hahn, high up in the mountains, brought us
drifts right up the lower windows and a white Christmas was guaranteed every year. About the only thing
that slowed them down were a couple of bad accidents. Susie, who was then four, stuck her finger in a
light socket and electrocuted herself. The housekeeper
saw it happen, grabbed her, almost getting zapped
herself. Glennis got the power turned off and saw
that Susie had stopped breathing. She gave her

mouth-to-mouth resuscitation and got her heart
started, then raced her to the base hospital, where
they slapped oxygen on her. She was okay in an hour
or so, but it took Glennis a couple of days to stop
shaking. Then Mike, who was six, almost lost an eye
going up concrete stairs on a pogo stick, while Susie
tumbled off a bike and broke an arm. Her arm was
still in plaster when she fell and broke her leg, and I
began to think it was more dangerous being Susie
than flying the X-1.

About ten months after I arrived at Hahn, life
became more complicated and dangerous for all of
us. The wing received new airplanes—a bigger and
more powerful version of the Sabre, called the H
model, which gave us much faster acceleration. The
MiGs discovered that fact when a couple of them
wandered over our small gunnery range at Fürsten-
feldbrück, outside of Munich. I scrambled, leading a
flight of four model Hs, and shocked the hell out of
those MiGs by catching up with them before they
reached their border. We just sat on their wings,
eyeball to eyeball with those Czech pilots, who were
taken completely by surprise. We escorted them back
where they belonged and gave them plenty to report
in their mission briefings. The new Sabres had greater
range and could carry heavier loads, and our mission
was suddenly changed from air defense to "special
weapons." We became fighter-bombers carrying nuclear weapons.

Base security was increased to guard the bombs
that were stored in special underground bunkers,
and we began to train in techniques for dropping
them. Each Sabre carried one Mark XII tactical nuclear bomb, which in those days was still heavy and
cumbersome, about the size and shape of one of our
wing tanks. The bombs were low-yield, but we didn't
know whether or not we could really survive the
blast after dropping one on a target. We practiced
various techniques using dummys. We came in low
on the deck until we were about ten miles from

target, then we raised our nose about forty degrees and fired off the dummy bomb in a shell-like trajectory. Or, we'd come in on the deck, then climb straight up over the target, release the bomb, then flip over backwards in an Immelmann and race to get the hell out of there. The bomb, meanwhile, continued to climb to about 10,000 feet before nosing over and dropping to earth. We also practiced high-altitude dive bombing, releasing the bomb at about 18,000 feet. All we had to do was drop it within twelve hundred yards of our target. And that was a low-yield weapon. None of us was happy about coming in on the deck, exposed to enemy ground fire, with an atomic bomb strapped to our belly. We just hoped to God we would never have to really prove the effectiveness of those techniques.

The wing now had a big intelligence section that supplied each pilot in all three squadrons with his own personal target in Russia and East Germany. Each pilot kept his flight plan folder stashed in his cockpit until he had it memorized and practiced flying his profile so often that he could do it in his sleep. Our Sabres could not be refueled from airborne tankers, and we could keep flying only for a couple of hours before our tanks ran dry. All of our targets were deep inside the Soviet sector and included radar and other communications sites. Our attack was meant to pave the way for the main strike force of long-range Strategic Air Command bombers, but unlike those guys, we had no way of making it a round trip mission. To get to the target and back would take longer than our fuel supply. So, a big part of our training was E and E classes—escape and evade—because all of us would be forced to parachute down in enemy territory. Man, missions didn't get more serious than that, but the guys just accepted it as their job.

During the 1956 Hungarian uprising, when Russian tank divisions began moving all over Eastern Europe, our wing went on the highest priority alert.

At two in the morning, our pilots were roused and
assembled in the briefing room and given their targets, while real atomic weapons were attached to
their airplanes. The guys climbed into their cockpits
around three A.M. and sat all night on the flight line
waiting for the word to take off. By the first light of
dawn, the alert was called off. Not many guys dozed
off that night; it was as close to the real thing as any
of us ever wanted to be.

Because we were now a nuke squadron, the powers that be decided to move us out of Germany in
order to disperse targets of potential Soviet attack.
They ordered our wing into France, and, God, none
of us wanted to go from our comfortable brand new
base into a make-ready strip just across the German
border in Toul, that was little more than a sea of
mud with some trailers and Quonsets trucked in overnight. Glennis and the kids got there a week after I
did and just rolled their eyes. It was the pits. Just
miserable. Everyone hated every minute being there,
and to make it worse, the strategic move became a
joke when General de Gaulle decided that no American nuclear weapons could be stationed on French
soil.

At that point we should have packed and gone
back to Hahn. Instead, we just sent our bombs back
there; now, if there were nuclear alerts, we would fly
to Hahn to load our bombs, then take off and fly to
the target. Whoever approved that plan deserved to
be stationed at Toul for life. To make it worse, tensions were really high with the French. We were
limited to flying in a narrow corridor around our
base, and Mirages flew real aggressive against some
of our flights. On one occasion, the French actually
dropped their wing tanks and our guys did, too, usually a sign of aerial combat. In the mood I was in, if I
had been in the sky that day, I might have started a
war.

The only thing good about the place was that it
was close enough to Germany so that if Glennis and I

drove most of Friday night, we could at least spend all day Saturday and most of Sunday at Dr. Melscheimer's hunting lodge. I had expected to spend a three-year tour at Hahn; instead, we suffered more than a year in the mud at Toul.

But in spite of the bad conditions, I commanded the best performing squadron in the wing. I had come to Germany as a green and untried major and left France as a light colonel with good marks as a TAC squadron commander. There were plenty of ambitious colonels who always wanted more than what they had. I was never ambitious in terms of career moves. I just wanted to keep doing what was fun, and when I was offered command back in the States of a squadron of F-100 Super Sabres, an airplane I had helped to test fly at Edwards, I grabbed the offer before I even asked where my new squadron was located. Being a gypsy was part of the military life, so, I really didn't care that this new assignment took me back practically to where I started from three years before—out on the California desert at George Air Force Base. Glennis wasn't thrilled going back to the wind and sand again. "Make it short and let's get back to Germany," she said. I agreed. But neither of us would bet on our chances.

Other Voices:

Maj. Gen. Fred J. Ascani

It was sheer coincidence that Chuck and I served together in Europe, he as squadron commander of his first tactical unit, and myself as group commander. Chuck was just outstanding in every way. For example, I had my own way of measuring a squadron's morale. His squadron held parties once a month, and I couldn't help noticing that the wives ran the show and were much more active than the men in making the evening a success. That, to me, was a good indication of high morale because the men couldn't force their wives to go all-out that way and do extra things that made their squadron parties special. That came from enthusiasm and group togetherness. If the husbands were working closely among themselves and enjoying their tour, the wives mirrored that fact in how they worked together. Those evenings among Chuck's men were warm and happy, and that's really how I remember his squadron.

He didn't have to flex any muscles to be a leader. Being Chuck Yeager was impressive enough. My God, I wasn't exactly a stranger to his skills, but when he led our wing at gunnery meets, the guy claimed he could actually see the flight pattern of his shells, and I don't doubt it. His scores were phenomenal, and with those eyes of his he could set up and position himself before the rest of us even saw the target. Great eyes, but also instant depth perception that was just uncanny. I could be looking directly at a target from a great distance (and often I actually was), but I couldn't see it until Chuck pointed it out to me. By Air Force rules, the wing commander had to participate in these meets, and I flew as number three man, but frankly, I wasn't in Chuck's league. Not many of us were. And we were all veteran pilots. The kids in his squadron just worshiped the ground he walked on because he really was that exceptional with a control stick in his hands.

When we received the H model of the Sabre, Chuck and I decided to test it against the older model, which he flew. We agreed to go wingtip to wingtip and then go balls-out. We stayed even for a while and I thought, "Well, this new model is no more powerful than the older one." Suddenly, that bastard began creeping ahead and I couldn't catch up. I thought, "My God, the Air Force has given us a lemon." It couldn't be, though, because I knew from others who had flown the H model that it was faster than the old F. When we landed I did some nosing around and discovered that Yeager had told his crew chief to crank in the tabs on the tailpipe, giving him increased exhaust gas temperature and that much more thrust. That's how he managed to stay in front.

I had to laugh because that ploy was so typical of Chuck. He knew that by cranking in the tabs he was exceeding the red line temperature for the exhaust gas escaping from the airplane's nozzle. But with his world of experience, he also knew that when the engineers designed that engine they calculated into it a margin of safety, so that flying above the red line was not particularly dangerous, provided you did it only in brief spurts, which is exactly what he did to beat me. The guy was really sophisticated and insightful about airplane engineering. And that's why he was always a helluva competitor. It was obvious that test or not, he'd cheat to make sure that nobody flew faster than Chuck Yeager, and it really was unfair because nine out of ten pilots wouldn't dare to exceed that red line.

At Hahn we lived down the street from Chuck and Glennis, and our kids became friends. Our two eldest sons decided to run away together. As I recall, they left a note telling us what they had done. They weren't in trouble, but just having an adventure. We found them out in the German woods about a mile away. They stayed away two days and nights, when Chuck and I decided to go check on them. We crept up close without giving ourselves away, and I whispered, "Goddamn it, that's not good for them to be out here, Chuck." Yeager put a grin on that face of his and replied, "Aw, hell, Colonel, they can't get lost. They just think they're real he-men. Let's leave them alone." The boys returned home the next day.

Damn, I was sorry when Chuck left the wing, and he and Glennis were disappointed, too. They

loved being in Europe. We had a real farewell bash
for them, and, really, everyone was sorry to see him
leave, even some on the staff who complained that he
was gone too much of the time on personal appearances, or that he was underhanded in some of his
wheelings and dealings to get things done for his
squadron. There was a constant shortage of spare
parts because his maintenance people hogged them.
And that was because Chuck went out and got them
everything they needed and more. But, hell, that was
Chuck. What a character. There was just no one else
like him.

WHAT GOES UP MUST COME DOWN

A fighter pilot doesn't care where in the world he is stationed as long as the flying is good. Outside of actual combat, which is the ultimate flying experience, most of us oldtimers stayed in the military because we loved to fly fast airplanes, and the Air Force owned them. Once my test piloting was over, it was the luck of timing that made being a squadron commander as interesting as test piloting. In Germany, we had flown with nuclear weapons and learned how to deliver them. Back on the Mojave at George Air Force Base, my new squadron was the first in the Tactical Air Command to be armed with air-to-air Sidewinder missiles. In the early 1950s, I had helped test the airplanes that created the modern air force; in the late 1950s, I was in on the ground floor of the operational deployment of these new airplanes and their sophisticated weapons systems that would receive their first combat testing a decade later in Vietnam.

My squadron at George was made up of super-

sonic F-100 Super Sabres, whose powerful engines
gulped tremendous amounts of fuel, but which could
be flown nonstop anywhere in the world, refueling
from airborne tankers. Between learning to dogfight
with missiles and traveling five thousand miles nonstop on training exercises, all of us felt we were
flying right into the future. Air warfare would never
be the same.

George was only fifty miles from Edwards. Glennis
wasn't too thrilled living again in a sandbox, but like
most Air Force wives, she was more interested in the
quality of the local schools, and whether the base
had a well-stocked commissary and a decent hospital. Her equivalent of having a good airplane to fly
was decent on-base housing; on that score, the Air
Force was still in the damned dark ages, so she dipped
into our savings and made a downpayment on a
three-bedroom place in Victorville, a couple of miles
from the base. Our street had shade trees and was
only a block or two from the local school. There was
still sand in our coffee mugs after a hard night's
blow on the desert, but at least the family was comfortable. I had warned her, "Hon, we better settle in
fast because I have a feeling I'm gonna be off and
running."

When I reported in at George, April 1957, long-
range deployments were a new art. Only the year
before, as leader of our wing gunnery team in Germany, I had flown the ocean in an F-86 Sabre that
had no airborne refueling capability. We flew back to
the States to compete in the finals in Nevada by
hopscotching across Europe to land and refuel until
we reached Scotland. There, extra wing tanks were
added, and we raced our fuel gauges across the Atlantic, hoping to reach Greenland before our tanks
went dry. Then we hopscotched across North America to Nevada, an exhausting two-and-a-half-day trip.

Airborne refueling was developed for the big SAC
bombers, and I had helped train their first tanker
boom operators years before. But until a fighter could

hitch onto a filling station in the sky, crossing the Atlantic in a single-engine airplane was as awesome as when Charles Lindbergh first did it, thirty years before. The ability to refuel without landing was as revolutionary to military aviation as the invention of the jet. In World War II, it had taken a full six months to transport and establish an operational fighter squadron in England. Now, we could fly anywhere and set up for combat in a matter of days.

My outfit was the first daylight air defense squadron of 100s in the Tactical Air Command, so they were an elite group, like being handed a Rolls-Royce. They were the best bunch I ever flew with, and my two years with them was the most fun I had as a squadron commander. TAC gave us the first Sidewinders, eager to discover how quickly their best pilots could become proficient learning to fire weapons that cost fifteen thousand bucks each. At those prices we didn't waste many practice shots. Firing those Sidewinders really impressed us about how well we would need to fly to survive future combat. All we had to do was wax a tail, turn on the system and get a rattling tone in our headsets, which meant that the heat sensors were locked on the hot-air exhaust of another jet, turn on our gunsight radar that locked us on target, then fire and watch that missile streak right up the tail of a drone, blasting it to pieces. Until evasion tactics could be developed, the price of getting your fanny waxed in future combat would be a high-explosive missile rammed up your behind.

But before that could happen some sumbitch would have to stick on your tail long enough to close in and get a lock on your exhaust. Dogfighting with missiles would really be survival of the fittest, but the new technologies were already weeding out weak sisters. For example, any fighter pilot who couldn't hack formation flying was in a tough spot hitching up to a refueling tanker high above the ocean. If he couldn't maneuver himself into position to fill his fuel tank, he was going to swim. Good pilots learned to master these new challenges; the others got out. It really was a black-and-white situation. The good ones had few problems adapting to the changes.

Until my squadron deployed to Spain in 1958, the Tactical Air Command had never enjoyed a perfect deployment and were beginning to wonder whether fighter aircraft were capable of extended range flying without suffering numerous aborts. We made it to Spain and back with all our airplanes. The next year we flew to Japan, then later, deployed from the States back to Spain and on to Italy. And we maintained a perfect deployment record, unique in TAC. I felt almost as good about that as breaking the sound barrier because a transoceanic deployment was how the TAC brass rated a squadron's leadership and ability. A lousy bunch lost half their airplanes to aborts en route.

Commanding an elite group eager to bust their tails to please me was a wonderful position to be in. We practiced airborne refueling under every kind of weather condition until we could do it practically in our sleep, and it was a pleasure watching a squadron of really proficient fighter pilots flying crisp and precise. In-flight refueling was actually used in the 1920s when an airplane named *Question Mark* set an endurance record by flying back and forth between Los Angeles and San Diego for 150 hours, being refueled in the air by pumping fuel through a hose from an airplane flying overhead. Our technique wasn't too different. It was called "probe and drogue." The four-engine tanker, holding about thirty thousand gallons of fuel, ran out a long hose with a funnel attached at the end. Our airplanes had probe outlets on the side and we positioned ourselves to push in the funnel against the probe. The tankers could refuel three fighters at a time from drogues dangling from each wing and its tail. For an experienced formation flier it was not difficult, although bad-weather refueling could get rough. Even then, it was a matter of squadron pride to do things right.

So when the order came to deploy to Spain, I told them, "We're gonna do this the TAC way—we get where we're going, every damned one of us." I didn't get any arguments. There wasn't a pilot there who didn't *know* he'd make it wherever he was sent, even to hell and back. Transoceanic flying didn't intimidate that bunch. They knew their airplane and its systems and could cope with any problem. If a good pilot knew what he was doing, flying to Spain was no more difficult than flying to Indianapolis. Maintenance was the heart of a squadron, and our crews had everything they needed to keep our airplanes in top shape. I just told the crew chiefs, "You guys are in charge. When you tell a pilot that his airplane is ready, that's all he needs to know. So, you'd better make damned sure you know what you're talking about."

I never applied pressure to keep all of our airplanes in the air; if two or three were being serviced, we just lived with an inconvenience, rather than risking our lives with aircraft slapdashed onto the flight line. I wouldn't allow an officer-pilot to countermand a crew chief-sergeant's decision about grounding an unsafe airplane. A pilot faced with not flying wasn't always the best judge about the risks he was willing to take to get his wheels off the ground. And it paid off. My pilots flew confident, knowing that their equipment was safe.

Other squadrons suffered aborts because pilots got uptight once land was left behind, becoming supercautious if anything went wrong. Fighter pilots had much less experience flying over oceans than bomber pilots, who had been doing it in their big birds since the war. There were some damned good reasons to turn back from a mission, including a fuel leak, but to be able to make a sound judgment about whether to stay or abort meant knowing what was a manageable problem. There were dozens of ways to circumvent malfunctions, but the guys knew that I wouldn't risk their lives to avoid an abort. Squadron commanders who lacked experience and were unsure about their airplane's systems often agreed to aborts simply to play it safe over water. But the best way to fly safe was to know what in hell you were doing.

To get to Spain, we had to rendezvous successfully with two sets of tankers en route. Navigating to the rendezvous points was my job as flight leader. The longest leg of the trip was six hours to the Azores, where we would land, refuel, then fly to Spain on our extra 275-gallon wing tanks. On the first leg, eighteen Super Sabres in our squadron left California and flew to Langley Field in Virginia, where we refueled and took off for the Azores in flights of six.

Ocean weather was changeable, and we encountered strong head winds at 35,000 feet, that slowed us and increased fuel consumption, so we climbed a couple of thousand feet at a time, until the winds decreased at about 40,000. At the two-hour mark we made our first tanker rendezvous, and the refill operation was perfect. But two hours later, the weather turned murky and it became damned near impossible to visually sight those big birds. We only carried gunsight radar, which is why we were limited to day flying. No radio contact either. Nuthin. I began to sweat it. As far as I could figure we were right on time and on the mark, and those tankers were probably in our vicinity; but that wasn't good enough with fuel gauges edging toward empty. I was practically straining the eyeballs out of my head, until by sheer luck I came in right on the tail of a big lumbering shadow in the middle of a dark cloud. Those guys had been calling us on the wrong channel frequency. The last of our airplanes to refuel had about two minutes of fuel remaining.

Other than that one moment, the flight was a piece of cake. Not one problem. We landed at the Azores, refueled, and headed for Spain, twelve hundred miles away. All eighteen landed safely a couple of hours later at the big SAC base at Moron, near the southern coast, the first perfect deployment of a TAC fighter squadron. It was a long day of flying, but we weren't too tired to keep from having a helluva party that night. The TAC command center in Washington tried to phone congratulations, but the SAC switchboard in Spain couldn't find us.

We stayed in Spain four months providing air defense for the SAC B-47 bombers that had also deployed from their base in Arkansas. Mixing my guys with those SAC pilots was fun to watch. My pilots were ten feet tall after that deployment, and they were aggressive jocks. We all wore our red scarves and took real pride in our squadron. The SAC crews came limping into Spain looking as if they had crawled all the way. I hadn't seen such low morale this side of a prison camp. We offered to give them rides in our fighters to perk them up, but they got sick riding in back. The "Colonel Bogey" song was on the jukebox at the officers' club, and we sang our own words: "SAC, it makes the grass grow green." The base commander was a SAC bird colonel who didn't know what in hell to do with us. I was in charge of my squadron and took my orders from TAC. I got away with murder.

Gibraltar, Tangier, Seville, and Málaga were easy half-hour flights on weekends. My guys loved life and never got homesick. We had our Sidewinder missiles with us over there, and I worked out a deal with the gunnery range commander in Tripoli, where they were firing Matador ground-to-ground missiles that sometimes got away from them. We flew down and chased out-of-control missiles, hammering them with our Sidewinders—really good practice.

TAC was delighted with our performance and perfect deployments. We were singled out as a show squadron, and other TAC commanders visited us at George to be briefed on our deployment procedures, especially in the maintenance section. I felt damned good and never would have imagined that my days

as a TAC squadron commander were numbered, or
that I was about to get clobbered and barely escape
court-martial.

In the winter of 1959, we were ordered to deploy
to Aviano, Italy. We flew from California to England
Air Force Base, Louisiana, refueled, and took off again
at two in the morning. We hit our first set of tankers
off the North Carolina coast, then two more sets
before arriving back at Moron, in Spain, around five
in the afternoon—an eleven-hour flight. All eighteen
Super Sabres deployed perfectly. We spent the night
at Moron, a Saturday night, and were scheduled to
fly into Italy the next morning. Having spent four
months at Moron the year before, my guys knew
where to go to unwind. When I drove back on the
base at seven the next morning, I found TAC Maj.
Gen. Karl Truesdell waiting to see me. He had flown
all night from Texas to personally congratulate us on
another perfect deployment, but stood around in the
cold dawn talking to himself because all of my pilots
were in town. An hour before the briefing for our
flight to Aviano, they all showed up in their flying
suits. The general couldn't believe they could live
that way, but that's how it was.

We took off on time for Aviano. The weather
turned bad over France and Germany and got worse
as we started our approach into Aviano in six hundred feet of overcast and heavy rain. It wasn't a good
situation; the Super Sabre is a tough airplane to
land under perfect conditions, but the weather was
miserable all over Italy and Europe. It was Sunday
morning, and the only base radar operators on duty
were Italian air force guys who could barely speak
English. Either their radar wasn't working or they
didn't know how to operate it properly, so we let
down using a low-frequency radio beacon. Christ, it
got hairy. I came in under the clouds only to look a
cliff in the eye, and turned just in time. The guys
were following me down, locked in tight, and I was
sure I was going to lose some people.

I had never been to Aviano, didn't know the terrain, but we finally found the field by the grace of God, and I landed furious at the controllers' poor performance. If it hadn't been for experienced flight leaders in each of our three elements, we would probably have killed some pilots. I found the base commander, a bird colonel, and really lit into him for having those Italian operators in the tower. His excuse was he thought we had our own cockpit weather radar, as did the last squadron of F-100s to deploy to Aviano, and could make our own let-down. So we got off on the wrong foot. The next day he came down to the flight line and asked if he could fly with the squadron. I was still steaming. I said, "You aren't going to fly with my squadron because that's the way it is." He turned purple and stomped off.

Our first weekend in Aviano, Col. Pete Everest flew up from North Africa, where he was in charge of the gunnery range. I hadn't seen Pete since Edwards, so we had a squadron party in his honor. We started at the club on base at five in the afternoon, and by eight we were feeling no pain. Pete and I and a few others drove in a staff car to a restaurant in Pordenone. We had trouble finding the place; the streets were narrow and winding, and we busted a headlight and dented the fender. When we got back to the club around eleven, the party was still in full swing. The guys who were still standing were outnumbered by the guys who weren't. The jukebox was turned over and some wine bottles were broken. I took the club manager aside and paid for the damage. I figured one of my mechanics could do some body work on the staff car, and I would pay for a new headlight, and that would be the end of it. Man, was I wrong.

By the time I woke up the next morning, I had more to worry about than a hangover. The base commander had laid for me and had me nailed. He had called his superior, the commanding general of the Seventeenth Air Force, in Germany, to complain that we had wrecked his club, and he wanted me out of there. I went to see him. "Colonel," I said, "we paid for all the damage." He said, "I don't care. You're getting out of here." I had been nasty to him, and he was paying me back in spades by ruining my career. I just looked that guy in the eye, thinking, "You rotten, petty son of a bitch." I was mad at myself, too. I should've known to watch my ass around a guy like that. He had me dead to rights, and I felt sick.

I tried calling the commanding general of the Seventeenth, hoping to tell my side of the story. I had reason to hope he would want to help me out because he was Russ Spicer, my old wing commander in the Second World War, who was shot down the same day I was, when he came down too low to light his pipe. But General Spicer refused to take my call. Instead, I received a terse wire from TAC headquarters back in the States. It was signed by Gen. Frank F. Everest, no relation to Pete, unfortunately. It said: "Assign command of your squadron to your deputy and report to me immediately." I had heard that General Everest was a terror, and I was really scared. I told Pete Everest, "Jesus, my career is wiped out." He felt terrible, but tried to put the best light on things when he saw how upset I was. I was being relieved of command and ordered home. Pete said, "Well, hell, it was only a fighter pilots' party. General Everest knows all about them. He'll probably just chew your ass and send you back here." I said to Pete, "If they only wanted to chew me out, ol' Russ Spicer could have done that." The guys in the squadron were in a state of shock; so was I. All of them thought I'd come back, but the base commander set them straight. He told them, "Yeager is through."

That flight across the Atlantic took forever. I sat hunched in my seat too miserable to eat, sleep, or even think clearly. One minute I thought there was no way the Air Force would let me go down the tubes, and the next, I was sweating all the enemies I had made by being famous, who would love to lynch me. The Air Force was the only job I ever had, and the possibility of being forced out in disgrace was almost more than I could handle.

I had never met General Everest, but I sat in his outer office sweating bullets. His secretary, a Women's Air Force lieutenant colonel, finally came out and asked, "Are you Colonel Yeager?" The way she looked at me, I figured I had had it. I said, "Yes, Ma'am." She took me in to see the general.

I saluted as smartly as I knew how, and he invited me to sit down next to him on a leather couch. Then he asked, "What in hell were you doing in Aviano?" I said, "General, we were just having a fighter pilots' party." I told him about damaging the staff car, overturning the jukebox, and breaking some bottles of wine. "We paid for everything. The guys were just happy. We have a good outfit." He asked if Pete Everest had been involved. I said, "Yes, sir, he came up from Wheelus."

Finally he smiled. "Sounds like you two had a pretty good time. Well, Chuck, you've done a helluva good job with that squadron, but I pulled you out of there to save your career. They were getting ready to court-martial you. You did damage government property, and they had a strong case to convict. Having that on your record would be the end of it for you. Now, I want you to go back to George and cool your heels for the next couple of months. We're going to send you to the Air War College. There's no way to send you back to Aviano, so we have to give your squadron to someone else. But go on home and try to forget about what happened. It won't be held against you in any way."

TAC bailed me out but I had almost augered in. I couldn't believe how close I had come to a court-martial that would have shot me down once and for all. A conviction would have meant the end of promotions and any future command. But General Everest was true to his word. I was assigned to the next class at the War College in Montgomery, Alabama, and while I was there, the promotion list was pub-

lished of those who had made full colonel. My name
was on it. I was still in good standing, although my
promotion meant that my squadron commander days
were finished. Bird colonels command entire wings,
which is a lot more authority and responsibility and
a lot less fun. But I sure as hell wasn't complaining.

TO MOSCOW WITH JACKIE

In 1959, Jackie Cochran was elected president of the Federation Aeronautique Internationale, the most prestigious international organization in aviation, and it was scheduled to hold its annual meeting in Moscow. Jackie decided to fly to that meeting in her own two-engine Lockheed Lodestar, a private passenger airplane that Floyd had bought for her a few years before. I had flown it with her a couple of times, but she had never before flown as far as Russia and wanted to take me along to navigate and be her copilot. So, the summer before my squadron flew to Aviano, Jackie made her pitch to the Chief of Staff, and I was granted permission to go on special assignment with her to Russia. The Air Force thought it was a rare opportunity to get an experienced military pilot in there to nose around. They gave me intelligence briefings, aeronautical charts and maps, long-range cameras, and plenty of film.

Playing James Bond, I wore civilian clothes and

carried a civilian passport, hoping to pass myself off as Jackie's hired civilian copilot. Jackie was at her New York apartment getting ready, and by the time I caught up with her she was supervising last minute details at LaGuardia's private terminal. She never traveled light, but she outdid herself this time. As passengers we carried her private secretary, her maid, and her hairdresser, as well as a woman from the State Department to act as her Russian interpreter. The baggage compartment bulged. I crawled in next to her in the copilot's seat and just shook my head. That airplane must've weighed as much as a B-52, but she got us into the air with at least a couple of feet of runway to spare, and we climbed into the midnight sky.

Gen. Tommy White, the Air Force Chief of Staff, had written to base commanders along our route, ordering them to assist Jackie in any way. We planned to refuel at the air base in Presque Isle, Maine, and around two in the morning I called the tower and gave them our civilian identification number, November one three victor, the number on her tail. The tower refused to allow us to land, even when I told them that Jackie had permission. "Oh, sure," they replied, "so does Lana Turner." I told Jackie to set up her landing approach and told the tower: "I'm declaring an emergency. You can't refuse permission under these circumstances." Hell, we were almost out of fuel. The tower informed me that if we tried landing, they would turn off the runway lights.

Jackie grabbed the mike: "This is Jacqueline Cochran. I am landing." As soon as we stopped rolling, the airplane was surrounded by air police, who clomped aboard, ordered us out, and escorted us under guard to base operations. Finally the base commander arrived, a bird colonel who obviously didn't read his mail, because Jackie's name meant nothing to him. "You people will leave immediately," he said. "This base is closed to all civilian traffic." I just waited for Jackie to blow, but she surprised me by

smiling sweetly and asking, "Sir, may I have your
permission to make a phone call? I have a credit
card." The colonel nodded and Jackie began to dial.
It was two-thirty in the morning. She said, "Tommy,
sorry to wake you, but I've just landed at your base
at Presque Isle, and I'm getting the idiot's treatment.
Yes, sir, he's standing right here." She handed the
receiver to the colonel. He was the first guy I ever
saw talk on the phone while standing at attention.
His face turned to chalk, and he muttered "Yes, sir"
over and over as he got Roto-Rootered long distance
by the Chief of Staff. When he hung up, he managed
a small smile and said to Jackie, "Miss Cochran, you
can have anything you need or want, including this
air base."

Jackie signed for the fuel and left five bucks for
the coffee we drank. And that's how our trip began.

Four days later we flew into Yugoslavia, after
spending three hectic days in Spain, where Jackie
was wined and dined as FAI president. From Belgrade, it was on to Hungary, and we flew through
the Iron Curtain for Budapest. The Communists were
strict about where we could overfly. A Russian navigator joined us in Belgrade to fly with us behind the
Iron Curtain. They insisted on putting him aboard
over their territory, and we were all ready for him.
He sat down in the copilot's seat and the minute our
wheels went up, I left the cockpit and locked the
door behind me. We had rigged Jackie's cockpit gyro
to deviate it. Up front, it appeared as if we were
going straight ahead, when actually we were flying a
great circle route. My maps showed all their airfields
and I could control the cabin gyro from the master in
the rear of the airplane. I got some great pictures of
MiG bases before we landed.

When we finally flew into the Soviet Union, camera work wasn't on my mind. The weather was so
rotten that we had to battle our way in. Over the
Carpathian Mountains the Lodestar began to ice, and
our navigator looked a little green. We were follow-

ing his damned flight plan. He had diverted us to
Kiev, instead of following our schedule into Poland,
where, he said, the weather was terrible. Kiev was
an alternate and it couldn't be worse than Poland.
The weather was so awful that we couldn't make
radio contact with Kiev, and I began to wonder if
maybe the navigator's bosses weren't setting us up to
splat. Jackie did all the driving, while I studied the
approach charts into Kiev. The navigator's English
matched the damned weather, but he took the chart
and pointed to a route different from what was
printed, insisting that was the way to get in.

It was no time to argue, and we followed his
route, Jackie lowering us through black clouds into
pouring rain and heavy winds. Visibility was zilch, a
really rough deal, with crosswinds blowing at 40
mph. But ol' Jackie laid that airplane down right at
the end of the runway, on one wheel—a great piece
of piloting—and set us down on a grass strip! The
Russians must've really been surprised that we made
it. I was sure they wanted to wipe us out. I figured
that strip hadn't been used since World War II. But
their guy on board looked even more relieved than
the gals in the passenger section when we pulled up
to a small shed and Jackie turned off the engines.
Then she put on fresh lipstick, powdered her nose,
and combed her hair. She always left an airplane
looking as if she had been to the hairdresser's.

I didn't say anything to Jackie. She was already
paranoid about the Russians, worrying they would
kidnap me if they found out who I really was. I
thought she was nuts, but Floyd had planted that
seed by remarking to her that he was surprised the
Air Force had allowed me to go. I knew too much as
a test pilot and TAC squadron commander. "Goddamn it," she said, as a couple of Russians in uniform approached our airplane in the wind and rain,
"I'm not gonna let you out of my sight." But the next
day we flew into Moscow, and as soon as we landed,
Jackie was swept up in flowers and formal welcomes

and whisked away. The rest of us had our passports taken away. They also took away our airplane; we wouldn't see it again until we left the country three weeks later. Meanwhile, the Russians made such a fuss over her, and she kept all of them hopping by changing schedules and adding dinners and receptions, that it was easy for me to go unnoticed, while passing myself off as her hired copilot.

I forget how many countries sent delegations to the convention, but she entertained them all. When she ran short of money, she wired her New York bank to send more via the American embassy. Those poor gals in her entourage could have used ten more in help because Jackie fired off as many phone calls, cables, and letters daily as our embassy down the street. Being a perfectionist, Jackie was stuck in the wrong country. The Russians did things their own way, and she was usually hopping mad. I'd try to get her mind on other things.

One day as we were leaving the hotel I teased her: "Hey, Jackie, did you know you had bow legs?"

She stopped in her tracks. "I *do*!"

"Yeah, I'm surprised I never noticed it before." There really was nothing wrong with them, but for days afterwards I'd crack up seeing her sneak looks at her legs.

The Russians found out who I really was at their official banquet at the Kremlin. All their aviation honchos attended, and I sat across from Colonel Mikoyan, their chief test pilot, whose brother Arem designed the MiG, and whose father Nikolai was Soviet foreign minister. Ol' Sergei Mikoyan overheard somebody say, "Mr. Yeager, please pass the vodka," and perked right up. *"Yeager,"* he said, *"the test pilot?"* I admitted it gladly because up to then Russia had been a boring experience, mostly tagging around after Jackie, and I almost welcomed being kidnaped if it would be interesting. Mikoyan became very animated and pointed me out to the people with him. He introduced me to Andrei Tupolev, their famous bomber designer, and said, "We must meet and have a long talk."

The Russians sent a car for me the next day, and we met at an ice-skating hippodrome, not far from the Kremlin. There was a conference room upstairs with Kvass, their bottled soft drink, next to each chair at a large table. There were two guys with Mikoyan, "colleagues," he said. I noticed that every fifteen minutes one or the other of those two would get up to go to the bathroom—changing the tape in their recorders.

I was amazed at how much Mikoyan knew about me, even that I had test flown the MiG 15 at Okinawa. I told him, "Yeah, when I dove that thing, I sure wished you people had learned about a moving tail." He laughed. "My God, you actually *dove* in it? Anytime that nose dropped, my heart would stop."

It was interesting for me to learn how little flying time their test pilots logged compared to someone like me, who flew anything and everything all the time. Their total flight time wasn't a tenth of mine. But ol' Mikoyan was surprisingly knowledgeable about our new airplanes and their systems. He knew, for example, that I was leading a squadron of F-100s, and began pumping me about its range and performance, and I told him only what had already appeared in *Aviation Week*. He was really eager to learn whatever he could about the F-104, our Mach 2 fighter, the so-called missile with a man in it, and the sumbitch actually knew that I had done the military test flying on it. I said, "Colonel, as long as I'm in your country, how about giving me a ride in your new MiG 21?" He laughed. "Colonel, I will do it if you give me a ride in your 104."

At one point, he became very confidential and asked me what we were doing about trying to solve the problem of engine compressor stalls—shock waves forming inside the engine, causing flameout. The way he asked it was clear that they hadn't solved it, and I wasn't about to tell him that our engineers had. I just looked mournful the way he did. When I left I kind of searched myself to make sure my own pocket wasn't picked, that I hadn't accidentally told him something valuable. I was sure I hadn't, and those two tough-looking guys with him did not seem very pleased.

I never did get to ride in any of their military airplanes, but Tupolev and Mikoyan staged a dinner in my honor, and many of their top pilots and brass attended. Pilot talk is pilot talk the world over, and a lot of those guys had flown against the Germans in World War II, using our lend-lease airplanes. We had given them the good ol' P-39, the airplane I had trained in, and which, alone in our squadron, I had really enjoyed. So, we swapped P-39 stories, and they were delighted that I had flown hundreds of hours in an airplane they loved. They sure as hell didn't think we had sent them a dog.

Jackie had a half-promise that we could fly out of Russia via Siberia, over the Aleutian chain into Alaska. She wanted to end up at her California ranch, and that route would save us three thousand miles. But as the time came to leave, the Russians changed their minds. Jackie was a tough old tiger, and she snarled and snapped at a couple of high-ranking Soviet generals to the point where I got nervous. Civilians just don't yell at generals and call them idiots. I grabbed her and took her aside and whispered, "Shut up, damn it, before they fly you to Siberia, not over it." But they did give her permission to fly out via Rumania. By then, I think, they were just glad to see the back of her. When we got to the airport, the KGB were crawling all over our airplane. They even took off some outside panels—looking for stowaways, I guess. They never did find my film and cameras.

A few days later I got some great shots of a MiG base as we were letting down over Sofia, Bulgaria, and that evening, I met most of those MiG pilots at the home of one of our embassy people. That's when I learned that a drunken diplomat is a bigger pain than hemorrhoids. Our guy laid on the vodka to loosen the Russians, but succeeded only in hammering himself and became obnoxious. He told the Russians, "I've seen you guys fly, and you're really not much. Colonel Yeager can take on six of you at once and wax you right out of the sky." Those Russian pilots plonked down their glasses and left without saying so long. I didn't blame them. Jackie was livid and I'm sure she complained about the diplomat's performance as soon as she got back. The guy was a fool, and a potentially interesting evening was ruined.

The next day was Jackie's turn to play the fool. She almost got herself clapped in prison. She wanted to fly on to Turkey, but the Bulgarians and the Turks are not exactly kissing cousins. Both countries prohibit direct flights, and the Bulgarians told her, "You can't go into Turkey from here. They won't permit it." Jackie picked up the phone and got a call through to the Turkish air force Chief of Staff, a pal of hers, and said, "Will you please tell these idiots that I can come into your country from anywhere?" Unfortunately, the Bulgarian air marshal understood English well enough to know that being called an idiot was not something he'd take from his wife, much less a rich American woman. If the guy had been carrying a pistol, I really thought Jackie would've been blasted. The air marshal snarled at her, "Madam, you have exactly one hour to leave this country. And you will fly via Yugoslavia." I got us the hell out of there.

By then I had had enough, but Jackie had her second wind. We flew back to Spain, arriving late at night over Madrid in some of the worst weather I've ever seen. St. Elmo's fire danced along our wings, and Jackie gave me the controls and went back to the passenger compartment to tell her worried entourage, "Don't worry. The best pilot in the world will get us down." Man, I had to be the best that night. When we landed there were six inches of hailstones on the runway.

We spent three days resting, then flew back to Paris for the annual air show. On our last night there we ate at a four-star restaurant, and Jackie got edgy watching the rest of us enjoying a perfect meal and excellent service. That's when she really got dangerous because complacency drove her nuts. But then, she saw her opening: a woman at a nearby table was feeding scraps to her poodle, and Jackie, who had a cleanliness fetish, went into a rage. The French love to bring their dogs to restaurants, and who in hell cared. Jackie called for the owner. "You're not going to allow *that*, are you?" When told that he sure as hell was, Jackie staged a big scene and stormed out.

On the homeward leg, we headed north to the Arctic Circle, and flew along the ice cap at 10,000 feet on a sparkling clear day, one of the most beautiful sights I've ever enjoyed in my years of flying. It was a tough but interesting trip, with a lot of hard flying and navigating, and when I got home, having been gone nearly two months, I told Glennis: "Goddamn it, that's it. Never, ever again." But I always said that after going on a trip with Jackie.

COMMANDANT
FOR SPACE

Glennis Yeager

When I was ill carrying Susie, my folks came to Edwards to help out and stayed several months, until Chuck finally began to complain about a lack of privacy. I told him, "I'll make a deal. If you'll do the grocery shopping, I think I can manage on my own." He agreed. To this day, he still does a lot of our shopping. That is, he kept his word as long as he was at home to do it. But especially during his years as squadron commander, he was gone a tremendous amount: three months in Spain, two months in Tripoli, two more at the gunnery meet in Nevada, and several months flying all over the place with Jackie. I wasn't happy about it, although I certainly couldn't blame him for being away so much. That was the nature of his job.

332

Being gone, Chuck might be the one who missed out the most—watching his kids grow up—but he probably didn't realize it. The kids accepted the fact that he was always gone because they lived around military bases where most of the other fathers were away a lot too; so, it wasn't one of those deals where the boys would complain: "Jimmy's dad was at my game, why couldn't my dad be there?" Heck, Jimmy's dad was probably off flying somewhere with Chuck. On the other hand, my children were exposed to so much more than the average kid, in travel, living in foreign countries, and some childhood memories that are really unique. For example, when Jackie moved into our place to go for her speed record, I took the kids down to her ranch, with the exception of Don, who was still in school. He stayed with neighbors until school was over, then his dad sneaked him in a P-84 jet fighter, strapped him in his lap, and flew him down to Indio. Chuck taxied to a deserted part of the field where nobody would see and handed Don to me. That boy's eyes were like saucers. He told me, "Dad flew us right over the trees."

But I'd get mad because when Chuck came home he was like a favorite house-guest. The kids would say, "Hey, Dad's back! Great! Now we can have some fun." Mom wasn't so great; I was the one stuck with all the disciplining. But fathers who are absent a lot try to make up for lost time, and Chuck must've seemed like Santa Claus, taking them out hiking and fishing, building things with them, and doing what I didn't have the time to do. Then, too, he kind of lost touch with the kids' capabilities, and especially when the boys were very young, expected too much of them at times. When he said no to something they wanted to do, that was it. No appeals. And he never changed his mind. If he said he wouldn't take them fishing unless they cleaned their rooms in fifteen minutes, and it took them twenty minutes, they were out of luck. But they lived through it. The kids understood him, knew his faults, shortcomings, attri-

butes, the whole nine yards. Their Dad was just
stubborn as a mule.

Chuck never had a game plan for his career.
When the time came we just went where he was sent.
A few times he bitched and moaned about a particular assignment, but he never tried to get his orders
changed, and was happy as long as he could keep
flying. Before his career ended, we had some wonderful experiences overseas, meeting new people and
learning their ways. Chuck was always the catalyst
for doing things. In the Philippines, for example, he
learned that some farmer was growing a new kind of
rice and had to go out in the boonies and see for
himself. Once I got out, I enjoyed it, but getting me
to go was like pulling teeth. I was just cautious and
methodical. With him, it was always a wild-goose
chase to try something different, and he would goad
me into going along. Just like his Air Force career:
had it been my career, I would have planned each
step of the way. Chuck just let it happen, and somehow things always fell into place.

But an Air Force wife's life is an emotional
rollercoaster. The military life is rough on marriages,
and fighter pilots are not ideal husbands. I got to
know the wives in Chuck's squadrons and helped
them handle personal problems. The men were away
an awful lot and many took advantage of the situation. The wives told themselves it didn't mean anything and went along by keeping their mouths shut,
until something happened they couldn't ignore—
maybe a perfumed letter arrived for a husband, or
lipstick discovered in the wrong place and the wrong
shade. They had to convince themselves it wasn't
important or get out. That's what it came to.

Over the years in the military, I saw a heck of a
lot of wrecked marriages. I've seen wives dropped by
the wayside; I've known some who had affairs of
their own, either because they were lonely or wanted
to get even. I've also known of three suicides among
abandoned wives who had no place to go and no

prospects. I couldn't understand women who put themselves in that kind of helpless position. If you raise a man's children and run his household, you're an equal partner and deserve to share equally in his income. I just decided, half is half and that's how it's going to be. I insisted on having my own savings account and had property in my own name. It wasn't much, but if I had to I could hack it on my own. I didn't expect to be dumped, but I couldn't stand the idea of being helpless and beholden.

I knew wives who went into a deep depression whenever their husbands flew off on a long deployment somewhere because they knew what would happen. True, the men were probably going to shack up every chance they got, if they were inclined to do that. But there was a big difference between having a fling and getting seriously involved with another woman, and the wives most fearful of desertion were those who didn't even know how to write a check, who let their husbands do everything for them. They were literal balls and chains around a husband's neck. They probably guessed right that he was of a mind to dump them, and they would find themselves out on the south forty.

I was only twenty-one when we had our first child, and twenty-six when the last one was born. I was only forty-three when the last one left home to go out in the world. When the kids finally left, I aimed to start a whole new phase of my life. I wanted to complete my education, really get into my music, maybe establish a small business. Chuck had his career, and I wanted a part of my life to be separate from my marriage and family. I would do it for me, not for some kind of insurance or security. Chuck respected me for that.

The kids were in school when Chuck was sent to the War College, so I stayed behind in Victorville. He flew home practically every weekend, so, in some ways it was just like the early days of our marriage when I was back in West Virginia. He was gone for ten months. He made full colonel while he was there, and when the course ended, the Air Force appointed him as commandant of the Aerospace Research Pilots School at Edwards.

Going back was really the most pleasant period of his career. One reason was that Eleanor and Bud Anderson were also stationed there and lived right down the street from us. This was the first time since the war that those two were stationed together. Also, because of Chuck's rank, we finally got good base housing for the first time. The children were in high school, and I took up golf and duplicate bridge. Jackie gave me one of those electric golf carts, and I was out on the course the minute the kids were off to school. Bud and Chuck would sneak off hunting and fishing every chance they got. The kids were happy and thriving, and it was an enjoyable time for all of us.

All told, we spent seventeen years living at Edwards, but those six years were the best of them. Chuck was happy and productive, too, even though for the first time, his primary assignment wasn't flying, but running a school. Heck, I had paid my dues years before out on the Mojave as a captain's wife living in a shack, wringing out diapers in the bathtub. Being a colonel's wife was a lot more pleasant, and I didn't let anyone or anything get in the way of my lifestyle.

Most of the students at the Air War College spent their spare time playing golf. I came out on top in the class because golf didn't interest me. There were all kinds of airplanes available to fly, but only a couple of us took advantage of the opportunity. Flying was our golf. But, then, in the middle of the academic year, Jackie went to the Chief of Staff and asked him if I could go to Spain with her to negotiate with the Russians on the rules of the Sporting Committee, the FAI group that sanctioned aviation records, like one-hundred-kilometer closed courses and straight-away courses for absolute speed records that would be recognized by all nations. She said, "Yeager is the only one who the Russians respect for his experience in high-speed airplanes. He can explain the problems and get them to agree." So, Gen. Tommy White said, "I don't see why Chuck can't go." He sent a wire to the War College, saying he wanted me excused to go to Spain for a week. The War College was outraged; the commanding general said, "Our classes have the highest priority. Colonel Yeager isn't going anywhere." It was the old man versus test pilot school all over again. General White was furious and gave them a direct order to let me go. He said, "Publish orders on Yeager in my name and send him." The school never forgave me for that. But I went with Jackie to Madrid and we got everything jelled on the FAI records, including a Russian agreement to recognize fifty-miles-high as space.

That week in Spain may have helped me to land a wonderful job, because after completing War College, I was appointed to head the new Air Force Aerospace Research Pilots School to train military astronauts. The school was getting started at Edwards. Here was an opportunity to pioneer the next frontier in flying. The Air Force had hoped to be the ones to put the first men into space, but the Eisenhower administration chose NASA, a civilian agency, which, ironically, selected all military pilots for its first group of astronauts. The Air Force wasn't interested in going to the moon. We had had plans on the boards since 1947 for orbiting military space stations manned with our own astronauts. We knew damned well the Russians had similar plans, and we aimed to beat them to it. All we needed was the green light from Congress and the White House.

Our school was a historic first step for putting the Air Force into space. At that point, little was known about the rigors of space travel and the ability of astronauts to sustain long periods of weightlessness. These unknowns awaited future testing and evaluation, but in the meantime, we decided to train a first generation of military aerospace test pilots in the highly precise and disciplined flying demanded by orbiting space labs and transportable shuttles. The course work was high-powered engineering and flight mechanics, and the training would preview the new techniques demanded by piloting in space.

The work was certainly different from anything I had done previously. It was my first nonflying job, and unlike my years as a squadron commander, where I was constantly flying with young pilots, teaching them combat tactics and gunnery proficiency, I now left most of the instruction to our expert staff, half of whom had Ph.D.s, and like our students, were among the best and brightest pilots in the Air Force. Hell, most of the kids in our school could bury me academically, although there was plenty I could teach them about precision flying, and I made it a point to fly with each student once a month to monitor his progress. But basically I was an administrator and manager—the fate of being a bird colonel. I never would've believed I could be happy in that kind of role, and I probably would not have been, if the work had been less important.

But the school was laying the foundation for the nation's new commitment to space. I procured and helped to develop a six-million-dollar space simulator, far advanced for its day, that provided every facet of a mission into space, except for the experience of weightlessness. Our kids were the first generation of Air Force pilots to be proficient using computers.

All of us involved in starting the school knew we were breaking important new ground. Flying the X-1A, I had flown to the edge of space and was one of the pioneers of extreme high-altitude flying. I was famous, and my name lent weight to the new project.

Having been used as the Air Force's showpiece for so many years, I knew most of the big brass in Washington, and I wasn't shy about pounding on their doors to get what I needed. I was a good salesman because I really believed in the product. No blue suiter wanted to surrender space to NASA, and the Air Force backed me to the hilt. In seven or eight years, we hoped to have manned labs in orbit, experimenting with lasers and particle beam weapons, and be ready to fly the X-20, the Dyna-Soar, a lifting body airplane that was the forerunner of the space shuttle. Our graduates would be in the cockpits.

As a veteran test pilot, I couldn't wait to fly weightless. To me, the promise of the Space Age was even more exciting than the transition from propellers to jets. I plunged into the new job, going full-throttle. I flew back and forth to Washington so often that I began to feel like a damned lobbyist, which is really what I was. We needed money to find cheap ways of exposing a student to a space environment. I got Gen. Bernard Shriever, head of the systems command, to authorize the money for our computerized space mission simulator. We received four million dollars to convert three Lockheed Starfighters, the F-104, with six-thousand-pound thrust rocket engines and hydrogen peroxide reaction controls on the nose and wings—the cheapest way we knew to give a student a minute and a half of zero Gs. The airplane would get him up to 100,000 feet in an inflated pressure suit, and he could practice maneuvering with his reaction controls just as if he were in a space capsule.

I had a faculty and staff of thirty, which included Frank Borman, Tom Stafford, and Jim McDivitt before they joined NASA to become famous astronauts. Even before the doors opened in 1961, we were swamped with applications; I was on the selection board that met several times a year at the Pentagon, and we picked the top one percent. Initially, we had room for only eleven students; that was all

the airplanes we had for them to fly, and we picked
only graduates of the Air Force test pilots' school.
After two classes, we ran out of test pilots and put
our students through six months of test pilot training
and then six months of space training. And we had
the cream of the Air Force enrolled. For example, in
one class we had Maj. Mike Adams, who was so
damned good he had his choice between flying the
new X-15 or becoming a NASA astronaut—an envi-
ous position to be in. He chose the X-15 and was
killed in it several years later. Col. Dave Scott was
his classmate, and he chose NASA. He was with Neil
Armstrong over the Pacific when the reaction controls got out of phase in the capsule. David took over,
righted that thing, and got them back safely.

I remember one really impressive moment with
David and Mike at the school. They were up flying
together in a two-seat version of the Starfighter, running low-lift drag ratio landings, meaning they came
in at a very steep angle and needed to flare the
airplane, give it power, and go around and shoot
another steep landing. On one of these runs, they lost
their engine. The airplane hit the ground with a
bash. Mike Adams in the back seat ejected just before
that thing hit, but David Scott didn't. It was amazing to me: both guys made a split second decision
that was absolutely correct. And both were opposite
courses of action. The rear cockpit crunched, and if
Mike had stayed he would have been killed. If David
had punched he would have been killed because when
he hit, his seat was cocked sideways. To me, that
incident indicated their capability and future.

NASA's Mercury astronauts had been chosen before our school geared up. But over the next six
years, the space agency recruited thirty-eight of our
graduates to their corps of astronauts. Because we
had the most advanced experimental test pilot school
going, NASA relied heavily on our recommendations.
But some of our guys turned them down flat. They
came back from their interviews in Houston and told

me, "Colonel, we're overqualified for their program.
All we get to do is take a ride like one of those
damned chimps they sent up. We don't want to get
involved because everything is controlled from the
ground and there is nothing to fly." I said, "Hell, I
don't blame you. I wouldn't want to have to sweep
off monkey shit before I sat down in that capsule."

But as time went on, NASA made its program
damned attractive to recruits. They were in a tough
spot, needing outstanding pilots who were little more
than Spam in the can, throwing the right switches
on instructions from the ground. Even then, they had
trouble landing precisely and it sometimes took half
the Navy to locate a capsule bobbing in the Pacific,
miles from where it should've been. Also, they had
many more astronauts than available rides, and a lot
of guys never flew or had to wait for years to get
their opportunity. So, they sold their program like
one of those fly-by-night land developers selling tracts
in the desert. For signing up, a guy got a free expensive house, donated by a local realtor in Houston,
and a cut of a lucrative contract with Time-Life. The
glamor, splash, and money made it attractive to some
pilots. The guys came back from their interviews and
told me, "All the talk in Houston is about how much
money we are going to make."

My attitude was they shouldn't get a dime for
being selected for the space program, especially when
the risks involved weren't half as great as some of
the research flying done at Edwards over the years.
It rubbed me wrong and I said so: "Forget that crap.
Don't ever make a decision whether to be an astronaut based on damned perks. Either the program is
right for you or it isn't. And if it isn't, stay the hell
out of it."

After a couple of years, the Navy and Marines
began sending us pilots to train, as did several NATO
countries. By then we had room for twenty-six students, and NASA, feeling the political heat for picking too many blue suiters, was relieved that we were

teaching pilots from other branches. But I had my own political problems. From the moment we picked our first class, I was caught in a buzz saw of controversy involving a black student. The White House, Congress, and civil rights groups came at me with meat cleavers, and the only way I could save my head was to prove I wasn't a damned bigot.

In late 1961, we were ready to start screening applicants for our first class at the space school, and because they would be the first bunch, the screening process was particularly thorough. We wanted only the very best pilots, and our first couple of classes consisted of experienced military test pilots, who had graduated from Edwards's test pilot school, and whose abilities and academic background were demonstrably outstanding. Our space course was six months of intensive classroom work and flight training. My staff at Edwards culled the applications, pulled out the most promising student candidates, conducted preliminary checks of their records, and forwarded their recommendations to a selection committee at the Pentagon, which carefully reviewed the background of each applicant, conducted personal interviews, sought evaluations from their superiors, and further winnowed the list.

I was a member of the final selection committee, and after several months of interviewing and tough deciding, we published our list of the first eleven students. Actually, we had twenty-six names in order of preference, but we didn't publish our list that way: we just named eleven guys alphabetically as the members of our first class, and listed the first three or four alternates, in case any of them dropped out.

The quality of those selected was such that they added tremendously to the prestige of our new school, which was our intention all along. I was thrilled with the choices. But when our list was published I received a phone call from the Chief of Staff's office asking whether any of the first eleven were black pilots. I said, no. Only one black pilot had applied for the course and he was number twenty-six on the list. I was informed that the White House wanted a black pilot in the space course.

The Chief of Staff was Gen. Curtis LeMay, probably the most controversial personality in the Air Force, since his days as the tough, cigar-chewing head of SAC. I knew him pretty well. I remember briefing him at SAC headquarters after I had tested the MiG 15 on Okinawa, and he was very interested in the MiG's directional instability while climbing. "Yeager, how bad is that snaking motion?" he asked. I told him, "Well, sir, just about right to hit a B-36 wingtip to wingtip if you were shooting at him." My answer really tickled him, and he told it all around. And during my tour in Germany, he sent for me while he was in Spain, to show me off a little during a hunting trip with Franco. General LeMay wasn't what I would call a smoothie. He was blunt: you didn't have to read between the lines dealing with him.

He got on the phone and said, "Bobby Kennedy wants a colored in space. Get one into your course." I said, "Well, General, it's gonna be difficult. We have one applicant, a captain named Dwight, who came out number twenty-six. We already published our list with the fifteen who made it, and it's going to be embarrassing to republish the list with Dwight's name on it because now everyone knows who the first fifteen are." He said: "Okay, I'll just tell them they're too late for this first class." But a 150-millimeter shell came ripping in from the White House, and LeMay was told: "By God, you will have a black pilot in that program—now!" He called me back: "Do what you have to do, Yeager, but get that colored guy in." I said, "Okay, General, but what I think we ought to do is take at least fifteen students in the first class, instead of eleven, and make him number fifteen. Give me a little more money and I can handle this many in the school."

He agreed, and we brought Dwight in. Ed Dwight was an average pilot with an average academic background. He wasn't a bad pilot, but he wasn't exceptionally talented, either. Flying with a good bunch in a squadron, he would probably get by. But he just couldn't compete in the space course against the best of the crop of experienced military test pilots. In those days, there were still comparatively few black pilots in the Air Force, but Dwight sure as hell didn't represent the top of the talent pool. I had flown with outstanding pilots like Emmett Hatch and Eddie Lavelle; but unfortunately, guys of their quality didn't apply for the course. Dwight did. So we brought him in, set up a special tutoring program to get him through the academics because, as I recall, he lacked the engineering academics that all the other students had.

Hell, I felt for Dwight, remembering my own academic problems in test pilot's school. It's really a rough situation, and he didn't have a Jack Ridley working with him—a genius in explaining the most complicated problems in understandable language. He worked hard, and so did his tutors, but he just couldn't hack it. And he didn't keep up in flying. I worked with him on that, and so did other instructors; but our students were flying at levels of proficiency that were really beyond his experience. The only prejudice against Dwight was a conviction shared by all the instructors that he was not qualified to be in the school.

So we had a problem. General LeMay had asked me to keep him informed about Dwight's progress and knew what was happening at Edwards. About halfway through the course, I flew to Washington to attend an Air Force banquet and was seated next to General LeMay. He asked me if there was any improvement with Dwight. I said, "No, sir. We're having a lot of trouble just trying to keep him from getting so far behind the others that it will be hopeless. He's just not hacking it." The general grunted. Then he looked me in the eye and said, "Chuck, if you want to wash out Dwight, I'll back you all the way." I about fell out of my chair.

But it didn't come to that. Dwight hung on and squeezed through. He got his diploma qualifying him to be the nation's first black astronaut, but NASA did not select him and a few powerful supporters in Washington demanded to know why. The finger of blame was pointed at the school and I was hauled on the carpet to answer charges of racism raised by Dwight and some of his friends.

All hell broke loose. A few black congressmen announced they would launch an investigation of the incident, and the Air Force counselor, their chief lawyer, flew to Edwards from the Pentagon to personally take charge of the case. Man, I was hot. I told that lawyer, "You do have a case of discrimination here. The White House discriminated by forcing us to take an unqualified guy. And we would have discriminated by passing him because he was black." Maybe "discrimination" was the wrong word, but I made my point. Anyway, the decision was made to fly in a group of black civil rights attorneys and a few congressmen and show them Dwight's school records.

I met with them. I said, "I'm the commandant of this school, but the truth is that I lack the college education to qualify as a NASA astronaut. It so happens, I couldn't care less. But if I did care a lot, there isn't a damned thing I could do about it because the regulations say I must have a college degree. Captain Dwight may care a lot about getting a diploma from this school, but the fact is he lacks the academic background and the flying skill to do it. Anyone with his grades deserved to be washed out, or it would be discrimination in reverse. Now, here are his complete school records from day one. Let's review them page by page."

The group had no idea that he had received special tutoring and was shocked to see his poor grades; they were satisfied that prejudice was in no way involved in this case. But that wasn't quite the end of it. I was so damned mad that I told the Air Force lawyer, "Hey, I want to file some charges of my own. I'm a full colonel and he's a captain, and I want to charge him with insubordination. If he brought charges against me and couldn't make them stick, I want that guy court-martialed." I was told, no way; the Air Force would not allow that to happen because they had taken enough heat over this matter already.

I was disgusted. I knew damned well that Dwight had taken a cheap shot at my West Virginia accent to try to save face. Hell, if I had been from Philadelphia or New York, he wouldn't have even tried. He was prejudiced against *me*, figuring that anyone from my part of the world was a redneck bigot. Many Southern whites who are honest will admit having problems about race in a general sense, but I didn't have to be the type who thought of all blacks as niggers to flunk Ed Dwight. And what really hurt was that the guy called into question not only my professional integrity, but also my most basic loyalty to the Air Force, which had allowed me, an undereducated country boy, to climb as high as my talents would take me. Ignoring the fact that I was a raw kid, often made fun of as a hillbilly, they gave me a chance to crawl in the cockpit of an expensive airplane and prove that I had what it took to fly that thing. I knew prejudice. I ran up against officers who looked down their noses at my ways and accent and pegged me as a dumb, down-home squirrel-shooter. But, damn it, the Air Force as an institution never let me down for an instant. In spite of where I came from or what I lacked, they trained me and gave me every opportunity to prove myself. Nowadays, it has become fashionable for some companies to advertise themselves as "equal opportunity employers." The Air Force practiced that with me right from the start, and I would never deny to anybody else the chance to prove his worth, no matter who or what he is. There never were black pilots or white pilots in the Air Force. There were only pilots who knew how to fly, and pilots who didn't.

OPERATION
GOLDEN TROUT

Gen. Irving "Twig" Branch was my kind of commander. Twig had a sense of perspective about running the flight test center at Edwards; he worked hard and efficiently, but when fish were biting or ducks were flying, there was no holding him back. Friends in Texas would call him in California and say, "Hey, Twig, we got so many doves in the air we can't see the damned sun." Buddies down in Louisiana saved him a place in their duck blind. Pals in Wyoming had his horse saddled and waiting for the next antelope hunt. Twig's office was like a command post for *Field and Stream*. And because he ran the base, getting to these far-away places was no problem. He'd order up a B-57 bomber and use the bomb bay to load his gear going, and carry back the game. Twig was a general and ran the show, so what could a couple of colonels like Anderson and Yeager do, but go along on these trips whenever General Branch told us to? And because we were as fanatic as he was about the outdoors, and damned good at it to boot, he never went anywhere without us. As Andy said, "Twig is *muy simpatico.*"

To say that General Branch made my years as commandant of the space school more enjoyable is a weak understatement. Twig made it heaven, and I made up for a lot of years when test piloting and squadron commanding got in the way of rod and gun. But once the space school was really launched and humming, there was just no excuse for hanging around when Twig gave marching orders. He'd call me at the school: "Hey, Chuck, how's your schedule? I got us booked to give a talk and hunt ducks down on the Gulf next Tuesday."

As commandant I had a dozen airplanes at my disposal. Andy was operations officer of the flight test division, so he had anything he ever needed to get somewhere. And Twig, of course, had it all. In my case I was constantly traveling somewhere on Air Force business, doing a lot of speech-making and personal appearances, and if a trip took me to good hunting-and-fishing territory, I figured I'd earned the right to take advantage of the situation. I remember flying down to a Confederate Air Force convention, where I was asked to appear in a B-57. Capt. Joe Engle flew down with me, and we stopped off in Albuquerque on the way home to pick up a couple of elk that Twig and I had shot the weekend before. We loaded our game in the bomb bay. As we were taking off to go back to Edwards, a fire warning light came on from one of the engines, and as I cut back on the power, I had to laugh. I told Joe, "Hey, if we auger in with all this elk meat, they're gonna think we had the biggest knucklebones they've ever seen." And when it was grapefruit harvest season, I'd fly down to Jackie's ranch in Indio and load up her fruit in a six-hundred-pound drop tank baggage pod. I bent all the regulations and I'm sure I could've been court-martialed a dozen times over.

Andy and I were in the shape of our lives. Hell, we crawled all over the Sierras every chance we got, working higher and higher into the mountain lakes, some of them so inaccessible there were no trails. It was an ordeal getting up there—we'd call them "four blister treks"—but, man, it was worth it because that's where we fished for golden trout. Not many people knew about these gold-colored trout; they're so delicious that once you eat some, you'd crawl halfway to heaven to have more. Ridley, Russ Schleeh, and I discovered goldens by accident while fishing a cold mountain stream during the X-1 days. Jack hooked one and said, "Look at this little bugger. Looks like he's been eating gold nuggets." We caught a batch, fried them up, and just rolled our eyes to heaven. Golden trout are indigenous to the Sierra, but because they're found mostly in the coldest water at the highest elevations, most fishermen couldn't be bothered packing in and out fifty to one hundred miles. But I could.

Looking back, I'd say it was probably a mistake to let Twig Branch in on the secret of the golden trout. Andy and I took him up to one of our fishing holes and cooked him up a batch. The general's face just lit up. Hell, I could see wheels spinning and turning in his head. He had a lot of friends in New Mexico and planned to retire there, and the idea of being a thousand miles from golden trout did not please him. The next thing that happened was Andy, looking damned worried, coming to me and shaking his head. "Jesus, Chuck, I don't know. The guy is a general and he did give me a direct order, but I've got to sign for the airplanes and my neck is really stuck far out." I said, "What in hell are you talking about?" And that was the first I heard about Operation Golden Trout.

If *I* say General Branch might have gone too far, you can imagine. He decided to transplant the Sierra golden trout into the mountain streams of New Mexico. And he had cooked up his scheme with pals in the New Mexico Fish and Game Department. He authorized Andy to fly up to New Mexico in a four-engine C-130 cargo airplane used to transport troops and vehicles to pick up his pals in their four-wheel drive that carried special oxygenated containers to hold the golden trout. The trip probably violated half a dozen Air Force, federal, and state regulations; but a general is a general, and we were ordered into action.

And it was top-secret stuff. Andy flew back with the cargo plane in the dead of night, parked in a deserted part of Edwards, and when the cargo doors opened out rolled a New Mexico State Fisheries vehicle. We took off by chopper into the snows of the Sierra high country. We carried special containers to load up baby goldens that hopefully could be nursed to maturity in New Mexico and fed into their streams by spring. We camped for the night in subfreezing temperatures. Here we were, two colonels and two New Mexico game wardens, fishing illegally in a California stream, hoping that a California game warden didn't wander our way and clap us in jail. Andy and I filled three big containers with baby trout and hid them under a footbridge, until the two game wardens discovered what we had done. "Goddamn it," they said, "you guys are out of your minds. That's the first place a California game warden would look."

We choppered back, transferred the babies into oxygenated tanks, loaded them aboard the four-wheel drive which drove up the ramp back into the cargo airplane, and whisked off to New Mexico. General Branch's plan worked perfectly. The fish did fine in a winter nursery and were released into the lakes in the spring. And that's why golden trout can be fished in New Mexico. The sad part is that Twig never lived to enjoy fishing for them there in retirement. He was killed the following year, when his airplane hit a tree in bad weather, coming into Seattle.

But before that tragedy there was almost another, involving me. This occurred a few months after Operation Golden Trout. I had taken General Branch up to Rocky Basin Lakes, about eleven thousand feet up in the Sierra. Andy and I had fished there a lot, but it was a tough haul in by foot and the general arranged with some Army friends to have a Huey chopper drop us off. We stayed a couple of days, and it was *cold* up there, way below freezing. We had skim ice on the lake even at midday. The Army came back for us, and we loaded up the chopper with an icebox full of fish and all our gear. There were three guys on board, pilot, copilot, and crew chief, when General Branch and I crawled into that Huey. I guess we were overloaded for such a high altitude because I no sooner strapped myself into a jump seat in the middle, when we took off, went up about eighty feet, began shaking to pieces, and came down upside down in the middle of that icy lake. I remember seeing water, foam, and stars. The next thing I recall is swimming toward shore, half-frozen to death. The lake was a mass of foam and debris. I saw the ice chest pop to the surface. Next, the crew chief; then the copilot; then the pilot. It seemed like I was treading water for three or four minutes, before General Branch bobbed up to the surface, gasping for air, his eyes bulging. He had been trapped inside that chopper and had to break the plexiglass and go out underneath. He was saved by an air pocket.

We swam to shore and huddled together, shivering. Twig looked at me kind of funny and said, "Do you feel all right?"

I said, "Yeah, not bad. Except my head is burning."

He said, "I don't wonder. I can see your brains, for chrissake."

I said, "What are you talking about?"

"Your whole head is laid open and I can see your brains."

"That can't be," I said, but the blood was pouring down my face.

I had been scalped blasting through the plexiglass of that Huey, the skin from my skull cap laid back in five places. It would later take 138 sutures to close up that mess. He was looking at the gray bone of my skull and thought it was my brains. He got me to lie down and the crew chief found a first aid kit floating in the wreckage and bound up my head as best he could. But lying down made my head bleed profusely. When I stood up, the bleeding would ease, but I was freezing in my wet clothes. Twig said, "We're about nine miles from Tunnel Meadows airstrip. I'm going on down and call for a rescue chopper. You guys wait here."

Man, it was cold. The three other guys could at least sit down and bunch up, but I had to keep standing or my head would bleed bad. Finally, I said, "Let's get the hell out of here. I can make it down to Tunnel." I had just been up to this lake two weeks before on a backpack trip with Andy and was in real good shape. So we began to trek out. After about four miles, the other guys began to lag, so I went on without them. The trail was all down, which made it tough on the legs but easy on the wind. I did the nine miles in about two-and-a-half hours and arrived at the airstrip just as General Branch had stepped into the phone booth outside the small operations building. He was starting to dial when I tapped him on the shoulder and said, "General Branch." He wheeled around and dropped the phone. He thought I had died up there and that he was confronting my ghost. Finally he blurted, "What in hell are you doing here?" I said, "I just got tired of standing around up there so I walked out."

Edwards flew a Husky H-43 up and I got to the base hospital around five that afternoon. Talk about somebody with a sore head. They shaved the hair off those cuts and I looked like the world's largest baseball. I walked in the door around seven like a damned sultan in a turban. Glennis took one look and didn't even bother to ask what happened. She ran to the telephone because we were about to have a dinner party for six couples, and she wanted to catch them before they left to come over. "At least you could've called me," she said as I stumbled into bed.

That was my humorous accident. The next one wasn't half as funny.

GOING FOR
ANOTHER
RECORD

Lockheed's Starfighter, the F-104, was the first Mach 2 fighter aircraft, and the first to break the sound barrier in a climb. I had flight tested it for the Air Force back in 1954. The airplane had a bad pitch-up problem. Flying it at a thirty-degree angle of attack, its short, thin wings blanketed its T-shaped tail, causing the nose to suddenly rise dramatically. The next thing a pilot knew he was in a flat spin toward earth, pushing the throttle forward as far as it would go, high engine rpms being the only way to recover a 104 out of a flat spin.

The special rocket-powered 104s we had at the space school had the same pitch-up problem. Lockheed delivered three of them to us in 1963 for use in high-altitude, zero G training. Before our students began flying them, I decided to establish some operating parameters to learn at what altitude the aerodynamic pitch-up forces would be greater than the amount of thrust in the hydrogen peroxide rockets installed on the nose. We had two 250-pound thrusters to train for maneuvering in zero G conditions. We thought we would encounter pitch up somewhere around 95,000 feet. And while I was at it, I wanted to establish an altitude record in the rocket version of the 104. I flew it on the morning of December 12, 1963, and had the airplane up to 108,000 feet. It had gone beautifully, and I was scheduled for a second flight in the afternoon. Mom was visiting us, and Glennis drove her over to base operations. We had a quick lunch; I was still wearing my bulky pressure suit because once you get sweaty and take it off, you can't get it back on. Then they took off, and so did I.

I climbed to 35,000 feet, about one hundred miles from Edwards at the foot end of the San Joaquin Valley near Fraser Peak, and headed for Rogers Dry Lake at 37,000 feet in afterburner. I was traveling at better than Mach 2 when I fired the six-thousand-pound-thrust rocket in my tail that burned a mixture of hydrogen peroxide and jet fuel. By then, I was climbing at a steep seventy-degree angle, whistling through 60,000, feet and the afterburner flamed out, oxygen-starved in the thin atmosphere. That was expected. Later, I planned to go into a shallow dive to allow the engine blades to windmill in the rush of air, working up the necessary revolutions enabling re-ignition in the lower air, at about 40,000 feet. So I shut down the engine and let the rocket carry me over the top. I had to watch my tailpipe temperature, because at my steep climbing angle it would overtemp even though I was on idle.

I went over the top at 104,000 feet, and as the airplane completed its long arc, it fell over. But as the angle of attack reached twenty-eight degrees, the nose pitched up. That had happened in the morning flight as well. I used the small rocket thrusters on the nose to push it down. I had no problem then. This time, the damned thrusters had no effect. I kept those peroxide ports open, using all my peroxide trying to get that nose down, but I couldn't. My nose was stuck high, and the damned airplane finally fell off flat and went into a spin.

I was spinning down like a record on a turntable, and because I couldn't get into a shallow dive and drive air through the engine turbine, my rpms were falling off drastically. I had no hydraulic pressure because that operated off the engine, which had wound down to the point where it stopped and locked at about 40,000 feet. I was feeling kind of hopeless about this ride. The data recorder would later indicate that the airplane made fourteen flat spins from 104,000 until impact on the desert floor. I stayed with it through thirteen of those spins before I punched out. I hated losing an expensive airplane, but I couldn't think of anything else to do.

OTHER VOICES:

Bud Anderson

Chuck likes to say that I was flying with him every time he was forced to bail out of an airplane. The first time was during squadron training in Wyoming, while staging a simulated attack against a box of B-24s, and I saw this P-39 whipping past, upside down, trailing smoke, and thought, "Man, they make these exercises realistic." Then I saw that the guy jumping for it was Chuck. The second time was in the skies over France. Technically he is right: I was flying with him with a bunch of other P-51s, trying to shoot down Germans. I didn't learn that he had been shot down and jumped for it until I got back to England. The third time was flying chase for him when he flew in the NF-104.

I happened to be flying in a T-33 as he was taking off on his second flight of the day in the rocket-powered 104. I knew he was going up, so I had my radio on his frequency, and I heard his chase pilot abort because of a wheel shimmy while he was taxiing for takeoff. Chuck took off anyway. But he had to have a chase plane or the flight would be canceled, so I called over to them and said, "Hey, I'm right over the field and I'll chase you." Hell, there wasn't much a chase plane could do in this case, but try to follow the guy and eyeball him as long as he could. I knew he was going up to 100,000 feet, so I'd try to keep him in sight to be in the area where he came down and offer any assistance, if necessary. So, Chuck continued with the flight, with me as his chase. And God, I saw that airplane coming down just like an autumn leaf off a tree. As a matter of fact, it was falling so flat and so straight, that I could circle him, kind of corkscrewing down with him. We went through about 14,000 feet and I said, "Hey, Chuck, that's enough. Get out."

He punched out a few seconds later, much to my relief, because I was beginning to think he was going in with the airplane in the effort to save it. I circled around and watched him float down on the deck and hit. It seemed like a perfect chute deployment, and I came in low over the deck to check on him. I expected to see him up, chute gone, waving at me. Instead, he was just lying there. I thought that was strange. I came around a second time and he was still lying there, but this time I saw an arm wave. So I said, "Hell, no problem." By then I was talking to the base, and a chopper was enroute to get him. So I went back, but Chuck didn't come in. I found out they had flown him directly to the hospital. I got in the car and drove over. I went into the emergency room, and there was Glennis looking really grim. I said, "What's up?" She told me he was very severely burned. I thought she got it wrong and went inside and the doctor told me the same thing. I said, "*Burns!* What are you talking about, burns? How can a guy get burned bailing out?"

I went ahead and punched out. My pressure suit was inflated and a rocket charge underneath blew me and my seat straight up at 90 mph. An automatic device unhooked my seat belt and released the parachute ring from the seat. A seat-butt kicker, another small charge, kicked me out and straight down. I began falling, picking up speed, tumbling headfirst toward earth, and I saw that damned seat tumbling with me, somehow becoming entangled in my chute lines. There was still residual fire in the back of that seat from the rocket charge and my shroud lines began smoldering. Christ, I saw that clearly. The chute popped, jarring me, and I sweated that those lines hadn't burnt through. I had a quick sense of relief, though, because the popping chute dislodged the seat. Then the seat smashed into my face. I got clobbered by the tube end of the rocket, glowing red hot.

It just knocked the shit out of me. It hit me so hard that I really didn't know what happened. Busted the faceplate out of my helmet; I saw stars. Suddenly there was a roar. Burning stuff on that seat ignited the rubber seal around my helmet and in the pure oxygen environment, it erupted like a blow torch. My head was engulfed in flames and smoke. I couldn't breathe. I couldn't see out of my left eye where the seat had bashed me. I was choking to death on smoke, gasping to draw a breath. I stuck my hand inside the open faceplate and tried to scoop in air to breathe. My gloved hand caught on fire. I thought, "What a way to go!" I was still hooked to an emergency oxygen bottle, feeding oxygen to the flames. By instinct, I pushed up the visor on what was left of my helmet. That automatically shut off the oxygen. By then, I was very close to the ground and there was still residual flame, smoke, and soot pouring out of my helmet. I hit the ground hard.

I could hear Andy buzzing me and managed to wave at him on his second go-round. I finally got up and took off my parachute harness, pulling apart the scorched shroud lines with my bare hands. Then I pushed the release locks on the neck ring connected to my pressure suit helmet, rotated it, and took off my helmet. Until then, I don't think anyone had ever taken off a pressure suit helmet without help. It is literally impossible to get all those latches unlocked by yourself; I don't know how in hell I did it. I recall glancing at my helmet with my good right eye, and it really looked like war. It was bloody and burned and smashed.

I was dazed, standing alone on the desert, my helmet crooked in one arm, my hand hurting so bad that I thought I would pass out. My face didn't hurt at all. I saw a young guy running toward me; I had come down only a mile or so from Highway 6 that goes to Bishop out of Mojave, and he watched me land in my chute, then parked his pickup and came to offer his help. He looked at me, then turned away. My face was charred meat. I asked him if he had a knife. He took out a small penknife, unfolded the blade, and handed it to me. I said to him, "I've gotta do something about my hand. I can't stand it any more." I used his knife to cut off the rubber-lined glove, and part of two burned fingers came off with it. The guy got sick.

Then the chopper came for me. I remember the medics running up. I asked them, "Can you do something for my hand? It's just killing me." They gave me a shot of morphine through my pressure suit. They couldn't get the suit off because it had to be unzipped all the way down, and then I'd have to get my head out through the metal ring, but my face was in such sorry condition that they didn't dare. At the hospital, they brought in local firemen with bolt cutters to try to cut that ring off my neck. It just wouldn't do the job. Finally, I said, "Look in the right pocket of my pressure suit and get that survival saw out of there." It was a little ring saw that I always carried with me, even on backpacks, and they zapped through that ring in less than a minute.

I began dozing off from the morphine, only half-aware that Glennis was there, but Doc Stan Bear, the flight surgeon, kept shaking me awake. He was probing into the blood caked over my left eye, where there was a deep gash. The blood was glazed like glass from the heat of the fire, and Doc kept poking through it asking me if I could see anything. I said, no. I heard him mutter, "Christ, I guess he lost it." But suddenly I saw a ray of light through a small hole. I told Doc and he smiled. "That dried blood saved your sight, buddy," he said. Then he let me pass out.

They had me on an IV, and I was so groggy the next day that when General Branch came by and I tried to tell him what happened, I fell asleep in the middle of a sentence. Glennis, Andy, Bob Hoover, and test pilot Tony LeVier came to visit, but I was hardly aware. They were keeping me on pain killers.

So, it was several days before I realized how bad things really were. My face was swollen to the size of a pumpkin, badly charred from being blowtorched. Ol' Stan Bear came in and sat down. He said, "Well, Chuck, I've got good news and bad news. The good news is that your lungs have not been permanently damaged from inhaling flame and smoke, and your eye looks normal. The bad news is I'm gonna have to hurt you like you've never hurt before in your life to keep you from being permanently disfigured. And I'm gonna have to do it every four days."

I stayed in the hospital a month, and every four days, Doc started from the middle of my face and neck, scraping away the accumulated scab. It was a new technique developed to avoid horrible crisscross scars as the skin grew beneath the scabs. And it worked beautifully. I have only a few scars on my neck, but my face healed perfectly smooth. The pain, though, was worse than any I have ever known. I remember Jackie insisting that I recuperate at her ranch after I was discharged from the hospital. She said, "I was once a nurse and if something comes up, I'll know how to handle it." Doc Bear flew down there, too, to do scraping, and told her, "Jackie, you might want to leave. This is pretty rough." And she huffed, hell, no, she was a nurse, and all that. Man, she lasted twenty seconds and had to leave the room. How I wish I could've gone with her. In the end, though, I came out no worse than losing the tips of two fingers, and I'd call that getting away cheap.

OTHER VOICES:

Glennis Yeager

Chuck's mother had arrived the night before his accident. We had gone to lunch with him between his two flights in the 104, and because it was a gorgeous December afternoon, I decided to take her around the golf course on my cart. We saw a helicopter fly overhead and land on the hospital pad. We could even see the patient being helped out; he was wearing an orange pressure suit, same as Chuck's, but I never made the connection somehow. We went on home and the phone was ringing. It was Jackie

Cochran calling me from New York. She was hysterical. "What happened to Chuck?" she asked. I said to her, "What on earth are you talking about?" She said, "He's been hurt. General LeMay was notified at the Pentagon and his office just called me." I yelled, "I'll call you back," and hung up on her just as she was shouting for me not to.

At the hospital, Doctor Bear met me and said, "Basically he's pretty good considering he has first-, second-, and third-degree burns." I asked to see Chuck and he hesitated. "He looks pretty bad." Heck, I had seen plenty, but when I walked inside and saw them trying to saw through his neck ring, I had to steel myself. It was horrifying. And I saw that he saw me. I said, "How do you expect to be asked to dance, looking like that?" I got a smile, but I didn't know what to say. Every human being has some vanity. I remember Chuck getting upset as he started losing hair up front. I was worried about getting gray so young. But I thought there was no way to keep him from being horribly disfigured, and I thought, how unfair, how much he didn't deserve it. I was just sick.

Jackie wanted to send her personal physician, Dr. Randy Lovelace, who was also a friend of ours. To her, Randy was Jesus Christ. I asked Chuck what he wanted to do and he said, "I'll stick with Doc Bear. He knows what he's doing." How true, although there were moments when I wanted to punch him for how he was forced to hurt Chuck while peeling the scabs off his face. But he worked a wonder, and we owe him deep gratitude.

A SPACE
LEGACY

By the end of my sixth year as commandant, the space school was the most advanced facility of its kind in the world. The school was a major employment agency for both the military and civilian space programs. Our kids constituted nearly half of the NASA astronauts, all of the Air Force team selected to fly in the first orbiting space labs and Dyna-Soar shuttle programs, and I couldn't help but feel damned good about our contribution to the next big revolution in flying.

Mostly because of our high-powered staff and a demanding academic and test flying program, a student graduating with our diploma could practically call his own shot for the future. Each of our graduating classes was pounced on by both the Air Force and the civilian space agency. About half the class chose to go with NASA; the others were among those selected to be the first Air Force astronauts, destined to fly the X-20 Dyna-Soar, then under development with Boeing, the forerunner of the reusable space shuttle.

he Air Force had also created a new Manned Or-
ital Laboratory Command to test experimental weap-
ns and military hardware from permanently orbiting
abs in space. Most of their astronaut recruits came
rom our school.

I had flown the prototype of the new M-2 Lifting
Body reentry vehicle, on a brief suborbital flight,
aking off from the lakebed, so the new technology
was at hand, and the training in our classroom prepared future space pilots for developments twenty
years down the road. Our school was at the cutting
edge of a new age of flight. Flying in space was a part
of a logical step-by-step advance since my sound
barrier flight in the X-1.

Once the feasibility was established, it was only
a matter of time for the hardware to be developed to
get us there. The X-1, crude as it was, led directly to
the X-1A, that had carried me up to the dark, dark
part of the sky and the edge of space. Those of us
involved in extreme high-altitude testing at Edwards
twenty years earlier were the first human beings to
see the earth's curvature from an airplane. These
pioneering flights led directly to the development of
the X-15 rocket airplane that carried test pilots right
to the edge of space, 295,000 feet and higher. NASA's
Gemini flights were also crude, little more than orbiting a guy around the earth inside a tin can, but
those flights proved the feasibility of orbiting space
stations and reusable shuttles. So, the trained astronauts we graduated each year at our school knew
that future space missions and hardware were inevitable for them.

But unexpectedly we got clobbered. The Johnson
administration, which previously had approved the
seed money for a military space start-up, suddenly
reversed itself. The increasingly costly war in Vietnam probably had a lot to do with their decision to
cancel the Air Force Dyna-Soar program and scrub
our manned orbiting laboratory plans, and keep space
for peaceful purposes. This 1966 decision came just

as I was preparing to leave the school as commandant and become a wing commander in Southeast
Asia.

Man, I was shocked by Secretary McNamara's
decision. There we sat with a school that had trained
the first generation of military spacemen, who now
had no missions to fly. My first reaction was that all
our hard work had been for nothing. Yet I really
didn't believe that. Our school had been too successful, our graduates spread all over, into important
ongoing programs. Joe Engle, for example, one of our
brightest graduates, was flying the X-15. And many
of our guys were now NASA astronauts, several of
them destined to fly the Space Shuttle, whose systems and uses were right on target with the training
they had received years before in our classroom.

I never did get a chance to fly in space, but
starting up that space school was the next best thing.
We developed a space mission capability for the Air
Force and provided trained manpower for future space
efforts, civilian or military. Our school's legacy was
the great pilots we turned over to NASA, many of
whom are still making their mark. In the end, though,
the space training function was wiped out and the
school reverted to its original role of training military test pilots.

I wasn't around when the space school closed its
doors. By then I was half a world away, overseeing
the operations of five different squadrons of combat
aircraft engaged in more earthly matters—waging
war in Vietnam.

VIETNAM

Glennis saw much worse than my burned face at the big hospital at Clark Air Base in the Philippines, where she was working as a volunteer in the lab, as our most seriously wounded guys were being airlifted in from Vietnam. I was commander of the 405th Fighter Wing, headquartered at Clark, in charge of five squadrons scattered across Southeast Asia: a squadron of fighter-bombers on Taiwan, armed with nuclear weapons targeted into China, in case the war spread; two squadrons of B-57 Canberra bombers at Phan Rang; an air defense squadron at Da Nang, both in Vietnam; and a detachment of fighters in Udorn and Bangkok, in Thailand. The logistics involved were awesome, and it was tough having my people dispersed over tens of thousands of miles of real estate, but I managed to squeeze in 127 combat missions.

I became a wing commander in 1966, but I had been to Vietnam for the first time a couple of years earlier, when Gen. Hunter Harris, commander of the

Pacific Air Forces, called me at the space school and asked me to take a trip to Vietnam and Thailand. He said, "I want you to give a talk to each of our fighter wings. We're having trouble getting those men to do any good over there. They're releasing their bombs too high and pulling out, missing a target by five miles."

Evidently, we were losing a lot of people while trying to knock out heavily-defended bridges. I spent a month going from base to base and talking to the pilots. I told them, "Damn you guys. You drank the best booze, had the best-looking women, flew the hottest airplanes—now you're gonna have to pay for your reputation. If you have a bridge to knock out that's your job. I know the ground fire is lethal. I know that if you really press home and go down on the deck, you'll be lucky to come through it. But that's war. That's your mission, and you've got to start doing it."

I was a forty-three-year-old colonel talking to pilots who were ten or more years younger, but I think I made an impression because they knew I wasn't some middle-aged desk jockey, but a guy who put his own ass on the line more times than they ever would. I wasn't anxious to see a lot of young guys go out and die, but, damn it, not one of them had been drafted into the Air Force. They had chosen to become military pilots, knowing it was a high-risk profession. Maybe they joined because flying was fun, but all of their training and flying time was geared to make each of them a skilled professional killer. That's what gunnery ranges and dogfighting were all about. In combat, they were expected to go balls-out and accomplish their mission, no matter what, which was why we lost many of our best, aggressive pilots.

Whether or not a guy wanted to be in Vietnam was irrelevant. Personally, I didn't have any philosophical problem about it and didn't know many pilots who did. All of us did have problems with the

way the war was being stage-managed from the White
House, but hobbled as we were, we obeyed the rules
and did the best we could. Every G.I. knows the old
expression: "Ours is not to reason why. Our is but to
do or die." That says it all.

I spent two years commanding the 405th. Being
a wing commander was a huge job as well as a
logistics headache. I was used to being in the thick of
things, but my guys were scattered over thousands of
miles. I was responsible for the morale, performance,
and well-being of five thousand men under my command, and if something went wrong, if there was a
screw-up or a major failure in operations, yours truly
would take the heat. Somehow, I had to find a way
to stay on top of my men and their equipment.

I scratched my head wondering how. The obvious answer was there was no way I could involve
myself in the daily nitty-gritty of squadron life; a
wing commander was a manager, forced to rely on
his squadron commanders to keep up morale and
operational performance. I knew some wing commanders who demanded that their squadron commanders report to them almost hourly, but that didn't
seem a very practical way to try to run five combat
squadrons simultaneously. Being a bird colonel meant
surrendering the old squadron intimacy. Instead, I
was like a judge in a tennis match, perched up on a
high chair, overlooking the court and the players. I
was above daily activities, but the trick was not to be
so high above that I missed what was really happening below.

I had to trust my five squadron commanders to
get the job done. The personnel under my command
flew five different airplanes from six separate bases,
and the only way I could figure to get a handle on
what they were doing was to work closely with the
squadron commanders. So, I brought them all into
Clark regularly to review their problems and needs. I
told them, "I'm here as a listener. I'm not able to
stay on top of everything that's going on under my

command, so I have to trust you, my commanders, to set me straight. I'm not a second-guesser, and you can run things your own way for as long as you get good results. If I see you making some of the same mistakes I made when I was a squadron commander, I won't hesitate to point them out. Otherwise, you won't find me breathing down your neck. Hell, this is a learning process for me as well."

But I was a regular visitor. I made it a point to fly in for a day or two at each of my squadrons' bases at least once every ten days. I'd spend the night, attend their briefings, and go out on a mission with them. That way I could accurately monitor their performance, notice any changes in their proficiency or morale from one visit to the next, and stay informed about what was happening. We were the lucky ones because we did most of our combat flying in the south. The outfits that were really catching hell were hitting up north in the teeth of the most intense ground fire in the history of warfare, dodging everything from rifles, machine guns, hundred-millimeter cannons, and SAM missiles, to MiG 21s.

The list of what they couldn't hit was three times longer than what they could, and it was damned frustrating not to be able to fire on shipping offloading arms and ammo in Haiphong harbor, or to nail SAM missile sites or MiG bases, power plants, and fuel tank farms. All were on the forbidden list. The rules of engagement even forbade attacking a MiG while it was taking off or landing.

Vietnam was the first modern air war. We used "smart bombs," guided by laser beams and sophisticated electronics, developed a new weapons system in a tactical fighter aircraft called Weasel because its job was to ferret out and destroy enemy radar and missile installations, and armed some aircraft with secret electronics that could jam and disrupt North Vietnamese radar and communications. Meanwhile, the Russian-supplied North Vietnamese were no slouches, either. Their surface-to-air missiles were murderous, and their radar was able to counter many of our sophisticated measures with countermeasures of their own.

But you could get hurt flying in the south, too, where ground fire was intense at times, especially around the Ho Chi Minh trail. So, we always took off on a mission knowing that it would be either kill or be killed—one of the two was certain to happen—the same as any other combat situation in war. And I quickly learned that the kids flying in my squadrons fought with the same intensity that Andy and I had fought in World War II. Despite the uproar about the war back home being reported in the *Stars and Stripes*, those guys flew balls-out to do their jobs. There was no holding back, even when all hell broke loose.

I flew a Martin B-57 Canberra, a twin-engine bomber. It was perfect for our work, mostly air-to-ground bombing and strafing. It carried eight 750-pound bombs, had four twenty-millimeter guns for strafing, and a range of more than eight hundred miles. Although the airplane was vulnerable to ground fire, and you had to be adept at "jinking"—weaving and twisting to avoid gunfire on the deck—it was damned effective as a light bomber. I flew with a copilot, taking part in close air-support operations, mostly at night, firing flares and hitting troops and supplies coming down the Ho Chi Minh trail. We had specially equipped recon airplanes that carried infrared detectors that could locate heat sources beneath the thick jungle canopy, as well as image intensifiers—low-light television and radar—that picked up troops and vehicles moving on a moonless night. We also had special "people sniffers" that detected sweat or urine traces down below. When any of these detection devices made contact, we'd be called in and hammer them.

In the south, a typical operation was responding to a call from a forward air controller, operating either on the ground with our troops, or flying in a small single-engine prop airplane, to launch an air strike on a specific point where Vietcong or North Vietnamese troops were spotted. The target was indicated for us by white phosphorous rockets, and then we'd hit it with heavy bombs or do strafing work.

Strafing was always dangerous because it meant coming in on the deck and drawing ground fire, especially over villages occupied by the V.C. A rifle bullet in the right spot could bring down a jet, and although we accumulated plenty of bullet holes on these missions, fortunately, few were lethal. We hit only villages where the V.C. had moved in, slaughtered the local leaders, and taken over the rice fields. They were expanding their cadres, raising food for their forces, and when they saw us coming half of them ran and the other half opened fire. That's the way the war was fought over there: bombing, strafing; strafing, bombing.

A lot of our strikes were directed against the fourth tree from the right because most of the real estate in the south was thick rain forest and jungle. On one occasion, we were ordered into an air strike against a suspected V.C. ammo dump. Christ, there was nothing down there but a thick canopy of trees, so thick we could barely see the bomb blasts, until one of the guys laid in a five-hundred pounder and the whole damned jungle blew up. The same thing happened to me.

The V.C. did a lot of tunneling, setting up whole battalions underground in a series of intricate tunnel networks that ants might have envied. Our intelligence could never tell where they were. But in the summer of 1967, a combat battalion of American troops was moving across a valley about 150 miles from Saigon, when they began drawing heavy mortar and rifle fire from a particular ridge. My B-57 squadron was called in. I led a flight of four, carrying eight low-drag, delayed-action, five-hundred-pound bombs.

The forward air controller pinpointed the ridge as the most probable location of the hidden V.C.

They figured it was just honeycombed with underground tunnels. We went in and dropped one bomb at a time. I had a wingman with me, rolled in, picked a point where the ridge seemed most likely to be hiding the V.C., and dropped my bomb. I pulled up, but failed to see an explosion. I thought it was a dud. Suddenly, I saw an eruption of red-brick dust and smoke from either side of the ridge. We later discovered that my delayed-action bomb had gone right down the main entrance of the V.C. tunnel, shored with red bricks. So we went to work on that ridge, and about every other bomb would result in red dust blowing out the side. Two days later, we received a report from Army intelligence that we had killed a tremendous number of V.C. troops. As a wing commander, I was credited with killing fifty V.C. soldiers. And it was pure chance, like a blind man pitching a ringer in horseshoes.

For me, the craziest part of Vietnam was back at Clark. I was in charge of the pilots in my wing, most of whom were married and had their families living at Clark, so Glennis had the rotten job of consoling and helping new widows. We lost about one guy a week. I owned the pilots, but the 6200 Materiel Wing owned my maintenance and airplanes. Mine was not to reason why, and it was a screwed-up mess. A squadron under my command would be inspected five thousand miles away, and I would get a bad inspection report saying our bomb racks didn't work. Hell, nothing worked on our airplanes, including the nuclear weapons delivery system on our fighters in Taiwan. But as wing commander, I was responsible. And it did me no good to complain that I had no control over the maintenance because Gen. Jim Wilson, head of the Thirteenth Air Force at Clark, devised that system and insisted on sticking with it. He ran things his way.

Every Wednesday afternoon, he would come down to my wing, get behind my desk, and sit down. He operated on a card item system of control, and I

would have as many as two hundred card items—
meaning gigs—against my wing in a single week,
which really wasn't so bad considering there were
five thousand guys under my command. So, I had to
flip through these cards with him: "Beer can on front
lawn of barracks. Beer can removed." "Airman caught
out of uniform. Airman reprimanded." On and on,
through more important things like gigs against supply status and operational readiness. Each gig card
had to have remedial action. It took me a couple of
hours to go through these cards with the general.
One of the combat support groups had sixteen hundred cards, and it actually took a day and a half to
brief him. It was a helluva way to run an outfit, but
General Wilson was effective; I'll admit that. Everyone, including yours truly, was scared to death of
him.

General Wilson had one policy that could have
been borrowed from one of those antiwar comedies.
All of the airplanes due for maintenance in my wing
were on a tail number schedule. That meant I had to
predict one month in advance, and in the middle of a
damned war, exactly when a particular airplane would
be needing maintenance. If an airplane was shot up
or shot down, the schedule went to hell. General
Wilson would park his staff car at the taxi strip and
read off the tail numbers of airplanes parading past
him from a master list. If fighter 397 failed to show
up at the precise time and date when I said it would,
he wanted to know why. Man, he was driving me
nuts. I couldn't schedule an airplane to get shot down.
Maybe 397 was hit by a SAM three days before, and
that's why 399 was taxiing out instead.

Finally, in desperation, I got together with another colonel named Ernie White, who ran the maintenance for my wing, and we devised a plan to beat
Wilson's system. By God, if he expected to see 397
leave our maintenance hangar exactly when we said
it would, then we would give the general what he
wanted. Before an airplane left the maintenance han-

gar, we repainted the tail number to conform to the general's master list. That way, 397, which may have been blasted out of the sky a week earlier, came sailing past the general's sedan and was checked off. General Wilson never did catch on and later gave me one of the best officer-effectiveness reports I ever received. I'm sure the records never did get straightened out, but I got out of there with my whole skin.

Bud Anderson was also over there as a wing commander, stationed at Okinawa, but he spent most of his time with his squadrons based in Thailand, where the living conditions weren't exactly posh. So, whenever I flew in to visit, I loaded about two thousand pounds of fruit, grain, and vegetables into the bomb bay of my B-57, and when I landed his crews would laugh and say, "Here comes Yeager in that C-57," which was a cargo plane. As soon as I opened the canopy, the guys would shout up, "What's today's special, Colonel?" I'd say, "Avocados, papayas, and rice. And you bastards better eat it all."

Andy and I had earned our share of medals in World War II, so we became kind of cynical about medal awards ceremonies in Vietnam. Christ, that country was about to sink under the weight of bronze and brass. If we flew ten missions in World War II—a six- or seven-hour combat mission each—we earned an Air Medal. If a Vietnam helicopter pilot flew ten combat missions—meaning ten takeoffs and landings with forays into combat zones in between—he also received an Air Medal. And because those pilots could take off and land a dozen times a day, some of them were collecting enough Air Medals to become scrap merchants. Lots and lots of people got many, many medals for accomplishing less, if you care to look at the end result. As Andy put it, "Vietnam was a place where you could get a medal or a court-martial quicker than any place else."

Man, that was true. Not long before my tour ended, the Air Force filed court-martial charges against a bird colonel named Jack Broughton, who was a

deputy wing commander of F-105 Thunderchiefs that
were fighting in the north. Jack was a helluva commander and a great combat pilot. His guys loved
him. A couple of them had come in over Haiphong
harbor as a Soviet freighter was off-loading weapons.
The Soviets opened fire on them with a deck gun,
and Jack's guys fired back. When they returned to
base, they told Jack what they had done, and he, in
turn, made a serious mistake. He destroyed their gun
camera film—the evidence—and told his pilots to
keep it quiet.

Meanwhile, the Russians filed a formal complaint,
claiming American jets had attacked one of their
ships without provocation. The White House queried
General Ryan, then Air Force commander in the Pacific, and he launched an investigation. When the Air
Force finally confronted Jack, he confessed, and the
brass decided to court-martial him and his two pilots. When it came down to finding a colonel who
was senior to Jack to head his court-martial board,
every bird colonel in Southeast Asia ducked for cover.

Four or five colonels begged off, claiming they
were too close to the war, flying up north themselves, to be objective. It was a damned mess and no
bird colonel, hoping to be promoted to general some
day, wanted to be involved. Everybody from the Joint
Chiefs down wanted to nail Broughton and his pilots
to make them examples. Nobody wanted to displease
the Chief of Staff, but nobody wanted to nail Jack,
either, because most of us sympathized. They finally
came to me. I had no excuse. I wasn't flying in the
north, and my date of rank preceded Jack's by several months. I wouldn't have minded being a general, and I didn't want the Chief of Staff mad at me,
either, but somebody had to give Jack a fair shake.

Nobody was proud of his cover-up, but I didn't
think he should be made the Air Force's whipping
boy. The punishment should fit the crime. And the
punishments in this case could range from the ultimate disgrace of a dishonorable discharge to a fine

and a letter of admonishment. To me, the heart of the matter was not what Jack had done, but what his pilots had done, and why.

Fighter pilots would go crazy with frustration watching Russian freighters unloading SAM missiles in Haiphong harbor, knowing that the rules of engagement prevented them from doing a damned thing about it. If those two guys in Jack's outfit had just said, "Screw the rules," and hit that ship out of sheer anger, then Jack was really stretching things trying to protect guys like that. But if it could be proven that the Soviet ship fired first and Jack's pilots fired back in self-defense, then Broughton was guilty of bad judgment rather than being part of a conspiracy to cover up a serious violation of the rules of combat engagement. There wasn't a responsible officer in the Air Force who didn't believe that a pilot had every right to defend himself, if fired upon, under any circumstances.

Years before, I had got myself caught in the middle of a controversy involving the B-36 bomber. The Air Force wanted it, but Martin Aircraft lobbied hard against it, siding with the Navy, because it was too vulnerable in daylight bombing. General Boyd sent me to Washington to meet with a group of Air Force lobbyists preparing to testify in behalf of the bomber before Congress. I had flown against it as a test pilot in test exercises. In fact, I had made about twenty successful passes against a B-36 with Russ Schleeh at the controls. But an Air Force general tried to get me to say it was a good airplane. He asked, "What if you had tried to get at it at night or in bad weather?" I said, "I probably couldn't find that thing without radar." The general got angry and said, "Then why don't you change your testimony?" I told him that wasn't the way it happened. The weather was good and I never missed finding the B-36. It was a piece of cake. At that point the general gave up in disgust: "You're doing more damage to us than the Navy." I was upset and called General Boyd.

He told me to come on home. "Never compromise
your integrity," he said. "Tell it the way it is."

That's exactly what I did in the Broughton case.
A court-martial is not run by civilian rules of law,
but by the military code of justice. Together with
four other officers, we sat as a five-judge panel, with
a representative from the Judge-Advocate General's
office on hand to advise us on the rules of procedure.
The Air Force had conducted a thorough investigation, and the two-star general in charge appeared for
the prosecution to recount the details of how Jack
had destroyed the gun camera film. But when the
young captain defending Jack tried to question the
general about other matters, including making the
entire investigation available to the court, the two-
star refused. I said to him, "General, we're here to
conduct a fair trial. You can't pick and choose what
information you are willing to share with this court."
The general reared up and said, "The hell I can't." It
was that bad on the Air Force side. I said, "The
entire Air Force report must be submitted to this
court." Not only did he refuse, but he got up and
stomped out.

I figured I knew why. The investigation would
have revealed overwhelming evidence that the two
pilots had been fired on first. That came out in the
courtroom. We had good, solid data, including audio
tapes of the mission that weren't destroyed. The pros-
ecutor tried to argue that it was irrelevant to the
charges against Broughton whether his guys were
attacked first. A cover-up was a cover-up. Bull. It
made all the difference in the world. Based on the
evidence, we dismissed all charges against the two
pilots. And it took the five of us on the panel only a
few minutes to decide on a fair punishment for Jack.
I said to the others, "If I were in Broughton's place, I
would have laid it right out on the table. I would've
gone up the chain of command and said, 'Here's
what my pilots did and I back them one hundred
percent.' Nobody would've punished a pilot for de-

fending himself, and Jack would've been off the hook. But Broughton didn't do that. He took it on himself to protect guys who probably didn't need protecting, and in my opinion, we can't dismiss all the charges against him." The other judges agreed.

We found Colonel Jack Broughton guilty of destroying government property—the gun camera film—and ordered him to pay thirty-five dollars in damages, the cost of the film he destroyed. He also received an official letter of admonishment. It wasn't one of those stiff letters, but it was enough to follow him around in his personnel folder. In that sense, it was a kiss of death because the only way for a senior officer to survive a scandal of that magnitude was to have all charges against him dismissed.

Jack knew he was finished, his career destroyed. He loved flying and loved the Air Force, but he would never again have a command, and to a guy like that a desk job is a jail sentence. Jack was bitter, and I didn't blame him. He was relieved of his duties in Thailand and sent home. He resigned from the Air Force not long after. And I never heard a peep of criticism that I had been too lenient. In fact, General Ryan later mentioned the case to me and was complimentary. He said, "You got Broughton out of that mess as gracefully as possible. I was glad to see him retire rather than receive a dishonorable discharge. He didn't deserve that." He sure didn't.

Not long after that trial ended, I was recommended by Air Force headquarters in Washington to become a wing commander of tactical fighters in Vietnam. The wing was located at Phan Rang, where I had a squadron of B-57s, and it would be a natural for me. I would get to fly up north and meet some of those MiG 21s. Glennis began packing to go back to the States with the kids and stay at Jackie's in Indio until I got back in twelve months. I got word that orders were being published on the assignment, and we shipped all of our household goods back into storage. At Clark, I had been under the command of

the Thirteenth Air Force, headed by General Wilson.
My new assignment would place me under Gen. William Momyer, who headed the Seventh Air Force. I
had never met him, but I heard he was a brilliant
tactician. And just as I was about to leave for Phan
Rang, the word came back that Momyer didn't want
me. He told the Pentagon, "I choose my wing commanders, not you people. Send Yeager somewhere
else."

General Ryan, who had approved my transfer,
went to bat for me with Momyer, who worked for
General Ryan, but had the right to pick his own wing
commanders. One of Ryan's deputies told me he heard
the two generals arguing about me over the squawk
box and that the conversation got pretty damned
nasty.

It was degrading being the center of a squabble
between two high-powered generals, one of them
trying to shove me down the other's throat. I hadn't
asked to go to Phan Rang; the colonels' assignment
branch at the Pentagon had ordered it. If it had been
my idea, I wouldn't have been so upset, because a
guy who tries to pull strings to get something can't
bitch if those strings wind up tight around his neck.
General Ryan acted on his own taking up the cudgels
for me because he knew, as I did, that I was the
perfect guy to lead combat squadrons flying in the
north. At that point, feeling really hurt at how I was
being treated, I seriously thought about packing it in
and calling it a career. I was a full colonel with
twenty-six years under my belt and could have retired at two-thirds of my pay.

I had seen senior officers sticking around long
after their careers had ceased to be enjoyable to
protect their career investment and retirement dollars. I didn't worry about money. I figured I could
make a living on the outside flying as test pilot for an
airplane manufacturer. I used my own simple formula: either the Air Force was still fun for me, or it
wasn't much fun anymore. If it wasn't fun, why hang

around? Lt. Gen. Bennie Davis had replaced General Wilson at Thirteenth Air Force at Clark, and I really liked and respected him. I went to him for advice. I said, "General Davis, honest to God, I'm ready to throw in the towel. I'm exactly the guy they should want for that job. My people would be aggressive because that's how I do business. Instead, I get poked in the eye with a stick. I think it stinks, and right now I feel like I've about had it."

General Davis said, "Chuck, I know exactly how you feel. I thought about quitting once or twice myself. Being the highest-ranking black man in the Air Force hasn't been the easiest climb. But, hell, man, you've got to expect to get sandbagged every once in a while. I agree, you would have been perfect for the job, but Momyer will never take you now. No way. Why? Because Ryan wants him to. The fight isn't about you, but which of their wills is strongest. These battles go on all the time. Among generals, it's like a workout in a gym. So, stay cool and patient. I'm certain the Air Force won't let you go to waste. They'll make it up to you."

I took General Davis's advice and dropped the idea about early retirement. I figured I still had a few more bumps and bruises left to give to the cause. Meanwhile, the Pentagon assigned me to take over a TAC wing of F-4 Phantoms at Seymour Johnson in North Carolina. We were the first deployed to South Korea during the *Pueblo* crisis, when the North Koreans captured a Navy boat, and were over there for six months. By then, my oldest son, Donald, was fighting out in the boonies of Vietnam. I could fly from Korea and visit him. I would have to sneak in because Momyer was still in command, but it would take more than that guy to keep me from seeing my son.

OTHER VOICES:

Glennis Yeager

I probably overprotected all of my children. I wouldn't let them see spooky movies or watch violence on TV. I didn't let them get drivers' licenses until they were eighteen or a senior in high school. They turned out to be fairly nice kids; oh, they were roughnecks and whatnot, but they wouldn't pull the wings off a fly. What I'm trying to say is that I raised them to be kind and gentle. Don graduated from high school before we left for the Philippines. Chuck very much wanted him to be appointed to the Air Force Academy, but when Don went for his physical, he couldn't pass the red lens test, meaning, his two eyes didn't focus simultaneously. My grandmother was cross-eyed, and I blamed my heredity. Here was Chuck with the most perfect eyes in the world, and I had worked so hard to get that kid to agree to go—I just was devastated. Don didn't care, but both of his parents sure did. Jackie offered to pay for an operation to have Don's condition remedied, but we got conflicting opinions about whether or not it really would work. Jim Anderson, Bud's son, was also disappointed because he and Don were friends and Jimmy made it into the Academy. But Don went instead to Redlands University and then to the University of West Virginia. He was drafted after completing his sophomore year and became a paratrooper.

It was really a rough moment for me. Here was my first-born, and I tried to do the best for him all the way, and he turned out a darned good kid. And they sent him over there. You've spent all this time teaching him not to do anything unkind to anybody or anything, and then he is taught how to kill. One of the hardest moments in my life was writing to Don and telling him that he had to do what he had to do.

So, I had both my husband and my son in that war. I didn't worry about Chuck; he could take care of himself. But Don was also like a willow, who could bend and accept anything. He was a paratrooper and was on point guard with his platoon when they were ambushed. I guess he must've killed a bunch—he never would tell me, although he told Chuck—but they gave him the Bronze Star with a V for valor. When the general was about to pin it on him, he said, "Here's one that I bet your dad doesn't have." Don said, "Yes, sir, he does." I have Don's medals now. He gave them to me when he got home and said he never wanted to see them again. But I think he'll change his mind someday.

I'd fly into Vietnam from Korea in my Phantom while General Momyer was still commanding the Seventh Air Force over there. I knew he wouldn't let me into the country just to visit my son, no way. In fact, he probably would have court-martialed me for · trying. A full colonel couldn't fly into the country without his personal permission, and I wasn't about to receive that. So, I bluffed my way through the communications net by using a call sign—Blue Bird One—that I had used when I was flying B-57s over there.

Meanwhile, I had arranged to fly into Cam Rahn Bay, where the Army picked me up in a chopper and flew me out to Bong Son, where Don was flown in from the bush to visit with me. A few times, I choppered out to his outfit bivouacked in the central highlands and spent the day with them. He was in the 173rd Airborne Brigade. I flew back to the air base in a chopper with Don as a gunner, kind of riding shotgun for the old man. I got a kick out of it.

On a few of these sneak visits, Seventh Air Force

headquarters almost caught up with me. The operations officer at the base was a friend, and he tipped me that Momyer's guys wanted to know the name of the pilot who had flown in in an F-4. The general had those bases wired, but I managed to stay about an hour ahead of him. So I got the hell out, but not before coming in over the trees at 600 knots where Don was, then pulling up and doing slow rolls. Don later told me it was something to be seen: guys hit the deck like it was the end of the world. He enjoyed those visits, and so did I. It was really something for a guy like me to see my son in that environment, doing the things he was doing. Once I even went out with them on patrol, which was an interesting experience for an Air Force colonel.

I noticed he was using just about everything I had taught him about hunting and fishing and living in the wild. He and his platoon were wiping out V.C. left and right because they knew their habits, ambushing them at night with starlight scopes and claymore mines. Don would set a mine on the rope bridges across a jungle river, and it would be so black at night, that he would stay right at the end of that bridge until he knew their point man was just about across it. He said he waited until he could smell the garlic on the guy's breath before detonating the mine. That kind of war was an eye-opener for me; those were really brave kids. Later in his tour, Glennis and I took his girlfriend and went to Hawaii to visit him during his leave. Don came out of it without a scratch.

Andy also went out with his son, Jim, who was flying a single-engine prop airplane for psychological warfare. Jim would scoot over the jungle canopy and turn on his big loudspeakers that blared a propaganda message while a second guy kicked out thousands of leaflets. He took up Andy on one of his missions and said, "Hey, Dad, would you mind doing a little work here?" So, Jim, a second lieutenant, had a bird colonel kicking out leaflets.

Once Andy and I flew a combat mission together.

He flew in the back seat of my B-57, and we went out and bombed a bunch of trees at the direction of a forward air controller, who thought V.C. were hiding down there. It was no big deal to either of us, and only later did we talk about the fact that it was our first mission together in twenty-two years. Considering all our close calls since then, it was amazing that two old jocks were still around to do it.

A MIRACLE STAR

In the fall of 1968, the time came to deploy from Korea back to our base at Seymour Johnson in North Carolina, and all three of my F-4 Phantom squadrons made it back as neat and clean as a pin. No aborts, no problems. I maintained a perfect deployment record in TAC that was unique. General Disosway, TAC's commander, wrote a glowing commendation, calling me his outstanding wing commander. But a couple of months after I returned to the States, TAC got a new commanding general and I told Glennis, "Better pack our bags. I may not be around long." Gen. William Momyer came back from Vietnam and took over.

Forget the compliments from others; I figured I was in for a rough ride. Not long after he took over, the general came down to Seymour Johnson and we finally met. He looked me over, stepped into my staff car, and never said a word on the ten-minute ride to wing headquarters. I briefed him on my wing, our activities in Korea, and our current status. He nod-

ded and left. We were together more than an hour,
and I can't recall him saying a word.

A month later, I took my outfit down to Puerto
Rico and staged a firepower demonstration. Momyer
was there. I led the wing on the bombing exercise,
and laid in a snake-eye bomb right in the box. The
general ignored it. The guy was allergic to me, and
because he was my boss and a four-star general, I
had a bad itch. He had his opinion about me, and I
had mine about him, but his was the one that counted.

Not long after, an assistant secretary of the Air
Force came down to Seymour Johnson with an entourage to see a typical TAC base in operation, and
the escorting general wheeled them in my direction.
The secretary (whose name I've forgotten) said, "I'd
love to go up in one of your fighters." Hell, why not?
I'd flown VIPs around dozens of times, given them a
nice smooth ride, and they had always enjoyed it. So,
I took this guy up, even hit a tanker with him in the
back seat so he could see how we refueled, then went
out and fired some rounds for him on the gunnery
range. He was really delighted and flew back to Washington around two in the afternoon. About five-thirty,
I was pulling into the driveway of my house when
the radio in my staff car informed me that General
Momyer was calling. I said, "Just a minute. I'll get
on my hot line in the house."

Hot line it was. That damned receiver practically melted to my ear. Momyer was in a rage. I had
never before been exposed to such verbal abuse: "How
dare you fly that secretary without my permission?
Who in hell do you think you are? Yeager, I'm telling
you this—there isn't enough room in this command
for both of us." On and on, until I finally said, "General, I don't know what you heard, but the Pentagon
people brought him down and wanted to impress
him and handed him over to me. I thought I had
impressed him fine." Momyer banged down the
receiver.

I was slightly concerned, about the way I'd feel if

a wing fell off. I called a few of the senior officers on Momyer's staff to get some feedback about what went wrong. I was told, "Don't worry about it. You know how the boss can get. You did a good job with the secretary. Don't worry about a thing." But, hell, I knew better. There was no way I was going to survive that kind of chewing out by a four-star general who ran TAC. I was one of his senior employees, and if this were a civilian corporation, I'd already be heading for unemployment. My days as a wing commander under that guy were in a quick countdown. He was going to get rid of me as fast as he could. I never knew what his grievance was, but the boss doesn't have to explain himself. For all I knew I was already gone, but the paperwork just hadn't caught up with the decision.

And that's how it turned out, although not quite in the negative way I expected. A couple of days later, when I returned from lunch and found a telephone message to call Lt. Gen. Gordon Graham, TAC's vice commander, I knew damned well what the message was going to be. Gordy was a friend; he came on the line and said, "Well, Chuck, you're not gonna like part of what I've got to say."

I sighed. He said, "You know, generals are not allowed to fly their own airplanes except under special circumstances. I'm sure that won't make you happy, but if I know you, you'll find a way to wiggle around it." I said, "What in hell are you talking about?" He replied, "Congratulations, General Yeager."

I came damned close to fainting. "Jesus, Gordy, are you kidding me?"

"No, I'm not. I've got the promotion board list right in front of me and I see the name Charles E. Yeager as brigadier general, U.S. Air Force."

It was a miracle. That board of generals met annually to consider the names of colonels recommended for promotion to general officer by each of the major commands. Each command submitted five or six candidates, making about twenty-five to thirty new generals from the ranks of five thousand full colonels, and I knew General Momyer didn't name me among the six colonels from TAC recommended for promotion. But my perfect deployment record was well known throughout the Air Force, and one of the generals on the board remarked about the absence of my name from TAC's list. I found out that the board asked for my records from the Pentagon, saw the evaluations I had received from General Wilson and General Disosway, and concluded that I deserved promotion. Momyer wasn't even consulted. The board of ten generals published their list and sent it to the Secretary of the Air Force, who, in turn, forwarded it to the Senate to be ratified. The President had to sign it because the number of general officers is controlled by law.

I was just stunned. And elated. Hell, yes, I wanted to become a general before I retired, but I thought my lack of education would probably screw my chances of making it someday. And I sure didn't expect it to happen while I was under Momyer's command. For a guy who came in as a private and worked his way up through the ranks, it was one hell of a wonderful honor. I called Glennis and said, "Hey, you think you can stand living with a general officer around the house?" She said, "It depends. Who do you have in mind?" When I told her, she let out a big whoop.

I remember thinking, "Well, the system never has let me down. In spite of everything, the system is fair and just." Outside of Glennis, the first people I told were my maintenance crews. I went down to the flight line and gave them the word. In the past, if we had a Saturday night wing banquet or party at the officers' club, I would take some of the guests, especially those who had good-looking wives, load them in a staff car, and go down on the flight line to show them the airplanes. The kids working night shift really appreciated it, particularly if the wives wore miniskirts. So, I went down and told them, "You guys really helped me get this thing. You're the reason we have the best deployment record in TAC."

I never heard a word from General Momyer. No note of congratulations, nothing. I guess silence was his message, although it was highly unusual for a commanding general not to congratulate a new general in his command. To this day, I really don't know what caused his hostility, and I was nervous that he could somehow get me off that promotion list. But friends at the Pentagon reassured me that the general's hands were tied. I just hoped those ropes were strong.

A few days after learning of my promotion, I flew to Washington to lead the fly-by over the Capitol at President Eisenhower's funeral. The weather was bad, but the guys flying with me were good and we had no problem. That night I went to dinner with some friends from TAC command, and we celebrated my promotion. I said, "That's the way politics can be in the Air Force. You can really get wiped out unless people are pulling for you."

The first time I was referred to as "General Yeager" really was a thrill. It happened a few months later, when Glennis and I boarded a C-141 to fly to Germany to start my new assignment as vice commander of the Seventeenth Air Force. By law, there can be only a limited number of generals, and a newly promoted general can't pin on his star until a vacancy exists. But because of my new assignment, I was authorized to wear my star to Germany, although I would not begin to draw general's pay until the effective date. So we boarded that airplane and the crew chief saluted and said, "Welcome aboard, General Yeager." That really sounded nice. Glennis said, "Well, it took us ten years to get back to Germany, but at least we're going back in style."

We picked up right where we left off with our German friends. In the year-and-a-half we were there, I got to the point where I not only could speak some German, but I could actually make myself understood.

My job was interesting. I worked closely with the Sixth Allied Tactical Air Force and the West Germans in organizing joint NATO exercises and training. Glennis and I were just in hog heaven. But during Christmas of 1970, I received a call from Air Force headquarters alerting me to a new assignment. The job title was, "U.S. Defense Representative to Pakistan." I asked, "What do we have in Pakistan, and why me?" The answer was I would fly with their air force, help them to train and advise them, especially in the use of Sidewinders. Why me? I had been personally requested for the job by a fellow West Virginian, our ambassador Joe Farland, through the State Department; the Pentagon had kicked it around and finally consented to let me go there.

Hell, I didn't know a thing about the country. I'd been there once, very briefly, stopping off when I rotated into Turkey. I knew it was very primitive and rough country and Moslem. Glennis knew even less. She said, "Where is it on the map?" Susie, who was twenty, was working in the library. I asked them if they wanted to go. They both kind of shrugged. I said, "What the hell, it will be an adventure for all of us." And it really was: I landed in the middle of the Pakistan-Indian war, while Glennis helped to dream up a device that swept the country—colored condoms.

PICKING UP
THE PIECES

OTHER VOICES:

Glennis Yeager

We were in Pakistan eighteen months, and it took me
nearly that long to get over the shock of being sent
there. I had barely heard of the country, and the next
thing I knew, I was living in Islamabad, the capital
city, in a seventeen-room house with eight servants,
rapidly going out of my mind in boredom and frustration. I thought to myself, "Boy, would Jackie
Cochran love this mess." Those servants about drove
me to drink. All of them were men. I had one to cook,
one to sew, a driver, a gardener, and a bodyguard. I
had one to wash from the floorboards down and one
from the floorboards up.

And they were all absolutely useless. Of course,
the country was extremely poor, with annual aver-

age earnings of about seventy-five dollars, and we were the rich Americans who had everything, so those servants wanted only to be fed. They spent the day lining up for meals in the kitchen. For a big house like that, I could've used a couple in help, I suppose, but all day long, I tripped over servants who didn't do anything but eat all day. Each day was a new hassle about who was supposed to do what and why. I had a head bearer and I finally said, "Okay, this is it! If you want to keep your job, you tell the rest of them what to do every day, and if I don't find it done when I come home at night, that's it."

Those guys made an ugly American out of me, and I was so mad at them that I didn't give a damn. I could've gladly had them shot, and one night I actually had my chance. Chuck was a great people-collector, and during his hunting, he met a tribal chief named Malik Atta and invited him home to dinner. The chief accepted and pulled up in front of our place with six bodyguards armed to the teeth. Our servants were so scared serving dinner, they almost dropped the platters. Their knees were knocking, and I made the mistake of complaining about one of them to the chief. I said, "He's lazy and he steals."

The chief jumped from his chair. "Be so kind, Madam, to point out the culprit and I will shoot him on the spot. This instant. He's dead. Then you shall take one of my servants who will serve you loyally and lay down his life for you."

Chuck and I were really concerned. The chief took out a pistol while our servants huddled in a corner, already practically dead from fright. I said, "No, no, chief, I didn't mean 'steal.' He must've been thirsty because he drank an entire pitcher of cream." We got the chief sufficiently calmed down to put away his gun, but it was close.

I was a grouch about servants because I had absolutely nothing to do from sunup to sundown.

Chuck was out and busy. Susie was working at the international school and was gone most of the day, and there I was, staring out my bedroom window at the distant Himalayas. Ambassador Farland and his wife were down-home folks and had us over several times a week. Joe and Ginny were West Virginians, and we became good friends. But outside of embassy functions there was nothing to do. At a party one night with the Farlands, I was talking to Bob Grant, the head of the population section of our Agency for International Development, and I said, "God, I'm so bored, I'm about to jump out of my skin. I can understand why many of the women who come over here don't last long." He said, "Why don't you come to work for me? I can use some help." I said, "You must be kidding. I don't know beans about population planning." He said, "Well, give it a whirl. I'll put you on a contract." I started working four hours a day and ended up working eight to ten hours a day and enjoying every minute of it.

Our job was to help the Pakistanis cut back on their enormous population growth. Birth control was not popular and seldom practiced. I wrote pamphlets that were distributed in villages all over the country, and set up a library and catalog system on the subject that could be used by local officials involved in population planning. As for the condoms Chuck was always laughing about, most of the Pakistani men wanted nothing to do with them. We told each other, well, it is just a matter of getting the message across. But one of the male secretaries said to me, "The color makes it too embarrassing." I asked what he meant. "To a Moslem," he said, "white is the color of purity." I asked him, "What if they were orange or red or purple? Would that make a difference?" He thought it would. So, we ordered those darn things in every color of the rainbow.

I remember Chuck stopping by one evening when a bunch of us were packing them up for distribution.

He said, "What the hell are you guys doin'? Is there a party or something?" He thought they were colored balloons. We distributed orange, green, blue, red, and yellow rubbers by the thousands, and they became popular throughout Pakistan. Orange was the favorite color. We couldn't keep any orange condoms in stock.

Shortly after we had returned to Germany to start our tour, we became grandparents. Our son, Mike, who was an enlisted man in the Air Force, sent us a cable telling us that his Linda had delivered a healthy baby boy. We hadn't seen the little guy, and he was now fourteen months old. By then, we were in the middle of an India-Pakistan war, and Mike wired us that little Jason had cancer, that the outlook was uncertain, and the baby was going to be operated on.

I had to get back to be with them, and the ambassador pulled every string in the book to get me on the first plane out of there. By then, the Indians were shooting up the airport, so it wasn't easy. But I got to Denver to be with them, and Mike met me at the hospital and said the baby wasn't going to live. Jason had a huge neuroblastoma (cancer) on his adrenal gland. God, what a shock. I stayed the whole time he was in the hospital, more than a month, during which he received radiation treatments, the whole bit. Then I flew back.

One month later, they operated on Jason again. That time, Chuck flew back to be there in case something happened. But they opened up that little dickens, and the tumor was dead. They just peeled it off his insides. We called him our miracle baby.

When we arrived in Pakistan in 1971, the political situation between the Pakistanis and Indians was really tense over Bangladesh, or East Pakistan, as it was known in those days, and Russia was backing India with tremendous amounts of new airplanes and tanks. The U.S. and China were backing the Pakistanis. My job was military adviser to the Pakistani air force, headed by Air Marshal Rahim Khan, who had been trained in Britain by the Royal Air Force, and was the first Pakistani pilot to exceed the speed of sound. He took me around to their different fighter groups and I met their pilots, who knew of me and were really pleased that I was there. They had about five hundred airplanes, more than half of them Sabres and 104 Starfighters, a few B-57 bombers, and about a hundred Chinese MiG 19s. They were really good, aggressive dogfighters and proficient in gunnery and air-combat tactics. I was damned impressed. Those guys just lived and breathed flying.

One of my first jobs there was to help them put U.S. Sidewinders on their Chinese MiGs, which were 1.6 Mach twin-engine airplanes that carried three thirty-millimeter cannons. Our government furnished them with the rails for Sidewinders. They bought the missiles and all the checkout equipment that went with them, and it was one helluva interesting experience watching their electricians wiring up American missiles on a Chinese MiG. I worked with their squadrons and helped them develop combat tactics. The Chinese MiG was one hundred percent Chinese-built and was made for only one hundred hours of flying before it had to be scrapped—a disposable fighter good for one hundred strikes. In fairness, it was an older airplane in their inventory, and I guess they were just getting rid of them. They delivered spare parts, but it was a tough airplane to work on; the Pakistanis kept it flying for about 130 hours.

War broke out only a couple of months after we had arrived, in late November 1971, when India attacked East Pakistan. The battle lasted only three days before East Pakistan fell. India's intention was to annex East Pakistan and claim it for themselves. But the Pakistanis counterattacked. Air Marshal Rahim Khan laid a strike on the four closest Indian air fields in the western part of India, and wiped out a lot of equipment. At that point, Indira Gandhi began moving her forces toward West Pakistan, and President Nixon sent her an ultimatum: An invasion of West Pakistan would bring the U.S. into the conflict. Meanwhile, all the Moslem countries rallied around Pakistanis and began pouring in supplies and manpower. China moved in a lot of equipment, while Russia backed the Indians all the way. So, it really became a kind of surrogate war—the Pakistanis, with U.S. training and equipment, versus the Indians, mostly Russian-trained, flying Soviet airplanes.

The Pakistanis whipped their asses in the sky, but it was the other way around in the ground war. The air war lasted two weeks, and the Pakistanis scored a three-to-one kill ratio, knocking out 102 Russian-made Indian jets and losing thirty-four airplanes of their own. I'm certain about the figures because I went out several times a day in a chopper and counted the wrecks below. I counted wrecks on Pakistani soil, documented them by serial number, identified the components such as engines, rocket pods, and new equipment on newer airplanes like the Soviet SU-7 fighter-bomber and the MiG 21 J, their latest supersonic fighter. The Pakistani army would cart off these items for me, and when the war ended, it took two big American Air Force cargo lifters to carry all those parts back to the States for analysis by our intelligence division.

I didn't get involved in the actual combat because that would've been too touchy, but I did fly around and pick up shot-down Indian pilots and take them back to prisoner-of-war camps for questioning. I interviewed them about the equipment they had been flying and the tactics their Soviet advisers taught them to use. I wore a uniform or flying suit all the time, and it was amusing when those Indians saw my name tag and asked, "Are you the Yeager who broke the sound barrier?" They couldn't believe I was in Pakistan or understand what I was doing there. I told them, "I'm the American Defense Rep here. That's what I'm doing."

India flew numerous raids against the Pakistani air fields with brand new SU-7 bombers being escorted in with MiG 21s. On one of those raids, they clobbered my small Beech Queen Air that had U.S. Army markings and a big American flag painted on the tail. I had it parked at the Islamabad airport, and I remember sitting on my front porch on the second day of the war, thinking that maybe I ought to move that airplane down to the Iranian border, out of range of the Indian bombers, when the damned air-raid siren went off, and a couple of Indian jets came streaking in overhead. A moment later, I saw a column of black smoke rising from the air field. My Beech Queen was totaled. It was the Indian way of giving Uncle Sam the finger.

I stayed on in Pakistan for more than a year after the war ended, and it was one of the most enjoyable times of my life. From 1972 until we came home in March 1973, I spent most of my time flying in an F-86 Sabre with the Pakistani fighter outfits. I dearly loved the Sabre, almost as much as I enjoyed the P-51 Mustang from World War II days. It was a terrific airplane to fly, and I took one to see K-2, the great mountain of Pakistan and the second highest mountain in the world, about an hour's flight away at over 28,000 feet.

It's a fabulous peak, as awesome and beautiful as any on earth, located in the middle of a high range that runs the length of the Chinese-Pakistani border. We actually crossed over into China to get there, and I've got some pictures of me in my cockpit right smack up against the summit. I made two or three trips up to K-2—real highlights. I also did some big-horn sheep hunting in the Himalayan foothills. Susie owned a little Arabian mare. She took her horse when I went hunting and actually learned some of the Urdu language of the mountain people.

Mumtaz Hussain was a village chief I got to know very well because his village was in good sheep hunting country. One morning, shortly after dawn, I drove up and noticed quite a few villagers standing around in mourning dress. I was told that during the night the grandmother of Mumtaz's wife had died. She was a woman of very high standing in the village, and Mumtaz said this meant he had to go into forty days and nights of mourning. I remembered that forty days and nights bit from Sunday school, so I told Mumtaz that out of respect for his wife's grandmother I would cancel my hunting that day. "Oh, no," he said, "you are my guest, and it would grieve me if you did not hunt this day."

So, I went on out in the desert with the *shikari*, the guide, hunting sheep and chucker partridge, and came back late that afternoon. By then all two hundred men in the village were seated in a big circle in the village square, all in mourning. Mumtaz was at the head. They drank tea and gossiped, but every few minutes one of the villagers would hold up his hand and say, "Let us pray for the old woman." They'd pray for about ten seconds and go back to their tea and talk. Nearby were steaming pots of curried rice, barbecued goat and sheep. A visitor would be invited to eat and drink tea with them and join in the ten-second prayers.

I returned the next weekend to see how Mumtaz was doing in his mourning, and I took Susie with me. This was during the war, and she was afraid her mare would be killed by the bombing and strafing, so I said, "Okay, we'll see if Malik Atta will take your mare and care for her." Malik Atta was Mumtaz's nephew and raised the most beautiful stallions I have ever seen. In Pakistan, men only rode stallions. No way they'd even climb up on a gelding, much less a mare.

We drove to the village, and I saw that the mourning circle of villagers was still intact, with more than thirty days and nights still to go. I got out of the car and told Susie to go over to Mrs. Mumtaz's house. In well-to-do families, the woman had her own house and her own women servants, while the men had their own houses and male servants. I didn't want Susie to be exposed to the tribesmen because they had never seen a Western girl before. However, Mumtaz came down the steps and took her and said, "No, Susie, come with me."

He led her up on the platform of the village square where the two hundred men all sat visiting and drinking tea, and when they saw Susie, they all stood up and bowed to her. Then each of them came up and shook her hand. Through me, they had heard a lot about her and knew she loved to ride. She had on jeans, boots, and a blouse and scarf because she had planned to ride her mare, but Mumtaz led her to the head chair and sat her down on his right. One of the men brought her some tea and they all stood there, gazing at her for five minutes. They couldn't take their eyes off her. It was very unusual for the tribe to see a girl without a veil over her face, especially a Western girl dressed as she was.

Finally I told Mumtaz I thought it best for Susie to go over to Mrs. Mumtaz's house because then I could visit with him and the rest of my friends in the village. He agreed. When it came time to leave we sent for Susie. She got in the car, and on the way home she chuckled about the scene at Mrs. Mumtaz's house. About fifty women were sitting around drinking tea and socializing while a couple of professional mourners wailed loud and long. She said it just about drove her nuts listening to these pro mourners screeching and wailing. The rest of the women, including Mrs. Mumtaz, just ignored them. In Susie's opinion, the men in the village had the better deal. They prayed for ten seconds every few minutes, but they didn't have to listen to all that wailing.

Malik Atta sent a stableboy to fetch Susie's mare, and he rode her back to the village, a distance of fifty miles.

THE FLYING GENERAL

Bud Anderson

Chuck and Glennis came back out to the desert in 1973. Chuck was stationed at Norton, just down the dusty old trail from Edwards. His new assignment was safety director of the Air Force, which made him, in effect, the only general officer who was allowed to pilot an airplane. Of course, like all generals, he had to have a pilot along with him, but Yeager never in his life sat in the second seat. He argued with the Pentagon, "Look, how in hell can I be in charge of Air Force safety if I can't fly airplanes myself to see if they are safe?" So, he was the exception to the rule and loved every minute of it.

He traveled constantly, going around to all the bases to hold safety inspections, and when he got to where my son was stationed, he asked for him to fly in the cockpit with him. He said, "I hear Captain Anderson is one of your best young pilots." Jim didn't know what in hell was happening when he was ordered to go fly with some general. When he saw it was Chuck, he burst out laughing. But Chuck told me, "Hey, ol' Jim can really fly."

I know he had had his heart set on his son Don becoming a pilot, but Don really wasn't that interested, and although it pained Chuck a lot when Don couldn't get into the Air Force Academy because of some minor thing with his eyes, he eventually saw the light about it. He told me, "Hell, I went to test pilot school with Jimmy Doolittle, Jr., and I remember the pressure on that guy trying to live up to his dad's reputation. Same thing would've happened to Don. No matter what he would've done, people would expect him to do as much as me, and there was no way, because those kinds of opportunities are long gone." My son Jim didn't have the famous father problem. I was only "famous" as Chuck's friend.

In fact, I was responsible for Chuck's last airplane ride on active duty. He was running out of time, and so was I. He had thirty-four years in and I had thirty. Five years was the limit he could serve as a brigadier general, although if he got a second star, he could serve seven more years because he wasn't commissioned until 1944, and the law allowed him to serve thirty-five years of commissioned time. He was really of two minds about it. He was only fifty-two, very young to retire, especially as a general officer. It was one of those deals where he would've liked to be asked to become a major general, for the honor of it. He and Pete Everest had always been rivals: both from West Virginia; both great test pilots, and both one-star generals. I'm sure he would've enjoyed edging Pete out, but he knew damned well a second star would mean serving at the Pentagon. Chuck just rolled his eyes about that. He said, "Shit, there won't even be any flying to speak of." When the time came, he was ready to hang it up.

So 1975 was it for him. And a few weeks before he was scheduled to retire, he came to Edwards to hold a safety inspection, and the officers involved came to me for advice about the best way "to please General Yeager." I laughed. I told them, "Get him an airplane to fly and stick a pilot in the back seat, and you won't hear any complaints out of him." And that's what they did. But before he took off, he called me at my office and said, "Listen, I'm too damned old to bail out. I don't want you within a hundred yards of that flight line. Hell, I don't want you to even look out your goddamn window."

I wasn't in the sky with him that day, so he didn't have to bail out of that F-4 Phantom. But before he landed, he came down right over the deck at 500 knots and did a couple of beautiful slow rolls. I know because I peeked.

In the end he logged ten thousand hours flying in 180 different military aircraft, including foreign or experimental rocket aircraft. And to another pilot, that was the most enviable thing about Yeager's career; no matter what he was doing, he never stopped flying. Being Chuck, he made damned sure that retirement wouldn't keep him from continuing to fly military airplanes. Dave Scott, who was a student at his space school and took over NASA's high-speed flight research center at Edwards, called him and said, "Chuck, how would you like to be a NASA consultant for no pay? All you have to do is fly 104s when you want to." Chuck said, "Hell, yes." The Air Force also made him an unpaid consultant at Edwards for the same reason.

Before he retired, he was enshrined in the Aviation Hall of Fame in Dayton, the youngest member ever to be inducted. Jackie enshrined him in the ceremonies down there, and then Edwards honored him by unveiling a huge oil painting of him and the X-1 in the lobby of the base officers' club, directly opposite the front door. Hell, parking spot one was reserved there for him; the second spot was for the base commander.

But the retirement ceremonies were at Norton, where he was headquartered. General Boyd, who was long retired, flew all the way from Florida in his own Bonanza, and said, "Chuck, there are damned few people in the world that I would do this for." He conducted the retirement ceremonies on the stage. General Doolittle and his wife Jo were there, and Jackie and Floyd Odlum. Most of the guys he had flown with in flight test were there, as well as guys he commanded in his squadrons, and a bunch of us from World War II, including Obie O'Brien, Don Bochkay, and Chuck McKee. It was a typical Yeager crowd: fighter pilots, test pilots, a few generals, and a couple of millionaires, sheepherders, and drunks. General Boyd read the special orders retiring Chuck and then there was a pass-in-review parade in his honor.

After the ceremonies, he came up to me with tears in his eyes. He said, "Jesus, not one damn piece of equipment in the sky." Bob Hoover was going to fly by in a P-51 Mustang to honor Chuck, but he got socked in in fog back in L.A. Chuck was really upset. He said, "I spent my life flying and there wasn't even a pigeon in the air when I said good-by."

A SUMMING UP

$\mathbf{T}$he person I am is the sum-total of the life I've lived. So, I have very deep emotions about the blue Air Force uniform that I wore most of my adult life. The Air Force molded and trained me, and who I am and whatever I've accomplished, I owe to them. They taught me everything I needed to know to do my job. There is no such thing as a natural-born pilot. Whatever my aptitudes or talents, becoming a proficient pilot was hard work, really a lifetime's learning experience. For the best pilots, flying is an obsession, the one thing in life they must do continually. The best pilots fly more than the others; that's why they're the best. Experience is everything. The eagerness to learn how and why every piece of equipment works is everything. And luck is everything, too.

Many pilots are killed because they get into situations where it is impossible to survive, while others, because of luck or knowing everything about their emergency gear, slip between the raindrops. I made my share of critical mistakes that nearly cost me my life. I climbed too steeply in the X-1A and paid for it by being bashed around the cockpit and scared out of my senses knowing I was going in. To survive took everything I knew and had ever experienced in a cockpit, so that maybe one hour less flying time could have been the difference between drilling a hole or landing safely. I saved myself by sheer instinct, but a knowledgeable instinct based on hundreds of previous spin-tests. Experienced at spinning down to earth, I was less disoriented than others who had done it many fewer times, and was more likely to make the right moves to save myself.

And luck. The most precious commodity a pilot carries. How can I explain surviving the million-to-one odds against me when my ejection seat tangled in my parachute shroud lines and set them smoldering, to the point where after I landed I pulled those burnt lines apart with a slight tug? I can't explain it. Nor can I explain surviving intact after getting clobbered by the rocket-end of that chair and having my face set on fire. To survive, fly again, and have no facial scars? Luck, pure and simple.

Ever since Tom Wolfe's book was published, the question I'm asked most often and which always annoys me is whether I think I've got "the right stuff." I know that golden trout have the right stuff, and I've seen a few gals here and there that I'd bet had it in spades, but those words seem meaningless when used to describe a pilot's attributes. The question annoys me because it implies that a guy who has "the right stuff" was born that way. I was born with unusually good eyes and coordination. I was mechanically oriented, understood machines easily. My nature was to stay cool in tight spots. Is that "the right stuff"? All I know is I worked my tail off to learn how to fly, and worked hard at it all the way. And in the end, the one big reason why I was better than average as a pilot was because I flew more than anybody else. If there is such a thing as "the right stuff" in piloting, then it is experience.

The secret to my success was that somehow I always managed to live to fly another day. To be remembered for accomplishing significant things, a test pilot has to survive. Hell, I could've busted my ass a dozen times over and nobody would have heard of me. I would have been Yeager Boulevard carrying military housewives to the commissary at Edwards. Popson Drive is a nearby street from the flight test center, but who remembers poor Ray Popson, a fine pilot and a wonderful guy, who ran out of luck? Who remembers my old friend Joe Wolfe? How many know or care that Edwards is named for Glenn Edwards? And what did Glenn Edwards do for a living? These young guys augered in before they could make their mark. Some of them might have been better pilots than I, but I made it into a rocking chair and managed to accumulate a lifetime of work and luck to be at the right place at the right time.

I don't deny that I was damned good. If there is such a thing as "the best," I was at least one of the title contenders. But what really strikes me looking back over all those years is how lucky I was. How lucky, for example, to have been born in 1923 and not 1963, so that I came of age just as aviation itself was entering the modern era. Being in my early twenties right after the war was the key to everything that happened in my life, placing me smack in the Golden Age of aviation research and development, allowing me to participate in the historic leap from prop engines to jets, and from jets to rockets and outer space. To make his mark on history, Christopher Columbus had to be born at a time when the world was believed to be flat. To make mine, people had to still think the sound barrier was a brick wall in the sky. To have reached my twenty-first birthday in the age of the Concorde would have done me no good at all.

Not that flying today isn't fascinating; but technology has removed much of the stress and dangers that made test piloting similar to being a matador. I've also been lucky to retain my health, stamina, and skills so I can stay current with the latest generation of military airplanes. I can because guys at Edwards are kind and bend regulations every once in a while and allow me to crawl aboard the latest equipment. I'm sixty-two and still flying the latest jets. Often I think about ol' Jack Ridley and the charge he'd get flying some of these new birds, remembering how excited he was every time a prototype was rolled out in the 1950s. What would Jack think now of our "fly-by-wire" control systems?

Today's fighter pilot flies by computer. Through his controls he instructs the on-board computer: "Give me so many G turns," or, "Give me this specific rate of roll or yaw," and the computer analyzes his flight data and moves the control surfaces to obey his commands. Now we can build very unstable airplanes at lower speeds to make them more maneuverable at high speeds because the computer will keep the airplane within its stability envelope at any speed. The result? Airplanes performing almost beyond human limits.

For example, the F-16 jet fighter had the first "fixed force" sidearm control. The pilot didn't move the stick; pressure from his hand produced electrical impulses that entered the computer through a so-called strain gauge. It was a problem for new pilots because human beings aren't calibrated in force, and they were never sure exactly how many pounds of pressure they were applying when they gripped their controls. So, that was changed to a movable force stick—moving it about one inch back or forward.

The F-16 had no back-up system for its computer flight controls, and in the development phase, we lost some airplanes and pilots. But the F-18 and F-20 have back-up systems and use digital computers that are more finely calibrated than the older analog computers. These new airplanes have "Head-Up Display,"

which projects all the flight data a pilot needs on the
windshield: angle of attack, airspeed, altitude, even
what weapons are on the airplane. In the old days,
less than a decade ago, the first onboard computers
working inertial navigation and weapons systems
needed about four minutes to power up. Now, a pilot
crawls in his cockpit, turns the power on, starts his
engine, and in twenty-two seconds he's ready to go
with a full bank of reference data. And, boy, what a
ride!

The new fighters are designed to sustain nine Gs
of constant maneuvering at low altitudes. My old
World War II Mustang pulled four Gs in banking
from a 400 mph dive, and we pilots were four times
our normal weight. If we pulled more than four Gs,
we began to lose vision and ultimately lost conscious-
ness. My squadron wore the first "anti-G suits," which
had a bladder against the stomach, thighs and calves
to keep the blood from draining into the lower body.
That suit is pretty much what is still being worn
today. Wearing it, we can withstand those nine Gs
the new aircraft demand.

We spent years and billions of dollars research-
ing and building fighters that were capable of more
and more speed, until we finally realized that we
didn't need blinding speed. Most dogfighting is done
at speeds ranging from .9 to 1.2 Mach. Anytime you
operate out beyond 2.2 Mach number, about all you
are doing is using fuel. If a guy is running, you can
launch a missile that travels about two Machs faster
than your launch speed and catch him. In the old
Mustangs, the object of a dogfight was to try to get
on the other guy's tail. But with the new air-to-air
missile systems, we no longer need tail-end position.
The new ones don't home in on hot engine exhausts.
The guy who wins a dogfight today is the first to
rotate, aim, and shoot. So, the newer fighters like the
F-18 and F-20 have engine systems that are limited
to Mach 2 speeds; they remind me of those durable

airplane engines of the 1940s—simple, few parts, easy to maintain, very strong.

I have flown in just about everything, with all kinds of pilots in all parts of the world—British, French, Pakistani, Iranian, Japanese, Chinese—and there wasn't a dime's worth of difference between any of them except for one unchanging, certain fact: the best, most skillful pilot had the most experience. The more experienced, the better he is. Or, for that matter, *she* is. I'm thinking of Jackie Cochran, who was really outstanding, much better than many, many male pilots I have flown with, but only for one reason—she had more flying time. It is that simple. If I had a choice between dogfighting a less experienced pilot in a better airplane than mine, or a more experienced guy in an airplane that wasn't as good, I know how I'd choose.

Fortunately, the U.S. Air Force produced both the best equipment and the best training in the world. Fighter pilots fly and fight because that's their job. Guys like Andy never backed off for a moment in going down to the deck to press home and finish off a smoking Me-110. My squadron in the 1950s never blinked about their potential targets so deep into Russia that they'd run out of fuel before getting back. The way the best of us fought in Europe so many years ago is how the best of us fought in Korea and Vietnam. World War II may have been the last popular war, but that made no difference to guys who flew balls-out in Korea or up north in Vietnam. Military guys don't get to veto what wars we fight. Once a policy is decided, we are sent to enforce it. Sure, there are some wars that are easier to get behind than others, but for the most part, the guys fighting are only concerned with two things: winning them and staying alive while doing it.

Dogfighting is unbelievably impersonal. You never think, "Gee, I wonder if the guy I'm about to shoot down has a wife and kids." You're thinking, "Okay, if I break left and he rolls out, he's got me." If you've got to go down on the deck and hit a bridge, you don't worry about whether or not people happen to be crossing it. When a forward air controller points you in the direction where your bombs should be dropped, you don't think, "Hey, wait a minute, what do I have against the Viet Cong? What have they ever done to me?" You might debate the pros and cons of the war with your buddies over beers, but your job is to go on in and drop those bombs accurately, no matter how lethal the ground fire. Military pilots go balls-out and risk their precious lives whenever they are asked. Loyalty and dedication are the only ways I can explain it.

I've met very few military pilots who were war-lovers, but also very few who weren't excited by the challenges of combat situations. That part is true enough. For a fighter pilot, combat is the ultimate flying experience, but no one who has lost close friends or witnessed the awfulness of bombing and strafing, or has had a live nuclear bomb loaded onto his air-plane in a maximum alert situation, would ever want to repeat those experiences. But if, tomorrow, the pilots from the Air Force Academy's last year's grad-uating class were ordered to war, they would go out, strap in, and take off to do their jobs exactly the same way that I took off to go fight the Nazis more than forty years ago. That willingness to risk every-thing in behalf of a mission hasn't changed, in my opinion, from the day I won my wings. To me, that's what made the Air Force so special and why I loved it so much.

I was always afraid of dying. Always. It was my fear that made me learn everything I could about my airplane and my emergency equipment, and kept me flying respectful of my machine and always alert in a cockpit. Death is the great enemy and robber in my profession, taking away so many friends over the years, all of them young. Facing death takes many different kinds of courage. There's battlefield cour-age, for example, where a guy, hopelessly trapped,

suddenly decides to take as many of the enemy with
him before he himself is killed. Many Congressional
Medals of Honor were awarded for those kind of
heroics. Posthumously, of course. Then, there is a
more calculated kind of courage that comes when
you are strapped inside a bullet-shaped rocket airplane to fly at speeds where many experts think the
ship will disintegrate. Does that kind of courage merit
the Medal of Honor? Jackie Cochran thought so, and
the year after I retired, she set out in typical Jackie
style to beat down every door in Washington to win
that medal for me. At the time, I wouldn't have bet
on her chances, but the nicest part about winning
that medal was that I'd receive it standing up.

OTHER VOICES:

Dick Frost

A few months after Chuck got out, I received a phone
call from Jackie Cochran, asking my advice about
her plan to win for Chuck the Congressional Medal of
Honor. She said she had discussed the matter with
Gen. George Brown, who was then the Air Force
Chief of Staff, and that General Brown was very
enthusiastic and promised her that the Air Force
would back her all the way. She asked me and several others who had worked on the X-1 to send letters to General Brown stating our view about Chuck's
courage in attempting those flights. I told her, "Jackie,
I helped design that airplane and knew more about it
than anyone, yet I could not say with any certainty
that it could make it safely through Mach 1. Courage
is right."

Well, she proceeded and got to the point where the Air Force drafted a recommendation for General Brown to submit to the Joint Chiefs of Staff. To get this proposal to Congress needed a unanimous recommendation by all the other branches. But the Army, Navy, and Marines decided not to go along with the Air Force because the X-1 program was conducted in peacetime, and the Congressional Medal of Honor was for wartime exploits against an enemy.

So, the Air Force backed off, regrouped, and redrafted a proposal to give Yeager a special peacetime Medal of Honor. They sent it on to Congress, and it was approved.

Jackie certainly was the impetus for the medal, but a lot of us thought that the reason Chuck didn't get the regular Congressional Medal was that Jackie had made too many enemies over the years. Had it been somebody else pushing his case, the outcome might've been different. But, hell, what difference? It was a tremendous honor, the nation's highest tribute to a guy who deserved it. President Ford presented it to Chuck at the White House in 1976. And a lot of us who have known Chuck for nearly thirty years couldn't help being misty-eyed about it: glad for Yeager, sad to see the end of an era that produced his kind of pilot. He was, without question, the best pilot this country has produced.

A FAREWELL
TO ARMS

OTHER VOICES:

Glennis Yeager

When the time came, I was ready to get out, and I think Chuck was, too. His retirement was the Air Force's loss, and although I don't think he would have been happy serving seven years longer without being able to fly, in my opinion—prejudiced of course—he should have received a second star. We spent our first month in retirement at Jackie's place in Indio because the house I bought for us in Grass Valley wasn't ready—a big, sprawling house with redwood siding in a forest of madronas and Douglas firs, with a big pond out front where mallard and wood ducks brood in season. We planned to stock it with trout and bass. Grass Valley is in the California Gold Rush country, in the foothills of the Sierra, and my family has lived there for three generations. The house was really the house of our dreams.

Starting our new life at Jackie's was a good idea, a way to just unwind with not much to do but horseback ride and soak up the sunshine. While we were in Pakistan, Jackie had suffered a serious heart condition and now wore a pacemaker. During our time at Norton, Chuck did weekly grocery shopping for Floyd and Jackie, who, as a retired Air Force colonel, was entitled to use the commissary. He bought about three or four hundred dollars' worth of groceries every week and drove it down to them.

She and Floyd were really in poor health, and it was sad to see. Jackie just couldn't accept growing old. She hated it passionately—couldn't stand it, mostly because she was forced to retire from competitive flying, and finally had to sell her Lodestar, which really crushed her. She was in her middle sixties. But I'll hand it to her, she decided Chuck should have the Congressional Medal of Honor and went chasing after it and nailed it down. It was a wonderful honor that might not have happened if not for her. But after all her work, she felt so poorly that she couldn't make it to the ceremonies in Washington. Neither could General Boyd, who died only a few weeks later from cancer. That news was really a depressing shocker.

We were Floyd and Jackie's closest friends and saw a lot of them in the last years. Floyd died at age eighty in 1977, and Chuck was named executor of his estate. Floyd asked that his ashes be scattered over the ranch to nourish his plants and flowers. Chuck and another friend took care of that, but some ashes were blown back inside the airplane. Chuck and I agreed that was the way to do things when our time came—only be neater. And no services, nothing; we had had enough of those during our years in the military, although it was impossible to get Chuck to go to any of them. He'd say, "What difference does it make? The guy won't know whether I was there or not." I'd say, "That's not why you go. You go to lend support to his survivors." The only one I could get him to attend was when Eleanor Anderson's mother died; he did that out of respect to Bud and Eleanor, and he put on a suit, too.

After Floyd died, Jackie began to rapidly decline. I think she just gave up and wanted out. She suffered heart and kidney failure, became swollen and had to sleep sitting up in a chair. It got to the point where friends didn't want to visit her because she became so impossible. Chuck continued to visit and was about the only one on earth who could get her to smile. She died in August 1980, in her seventies, living in a modest house because the ranch was sold to a condominium developer.

I started my own little business, buying properties around Grass Valley, and kept very busy, but it took Chuck a while to adjust to retirement. He kept a sixteen-pound sledgehammer in the garage that his dad had used in the gas fields of West Virginia, and used that to break up firewood. It was great exercise, but it meant he was bored. He chopped mountains of firewood. He'd putter around, building cabinets, chopping wood, wondering what to do with himself from one minute to the next. He drove me crazy, he drove Bud crazy, and I thought, "How·many years is it going to be like this?"

Gradually he got into the swing, and, as always with Chuck, things began to fall into place. He had invitations to go out and make speeches—that had never stopped since the sound-barrier flight—and he began accepting. Friends invited him to hunt antelope in Wyoming, and he and Bud hunted dove and quail in the fall, and still, every July, they go on a two-week backpack into the Sierra. Those two carry in fifty-pound packs and trek about 125 miles up to a lake where the golden trout spawn, at thirteen thousand feet.

Somewhere along the trail he discovered hanggliding, and took up that. Then some West Virginia

Republicans came along and tried to get him to run for the Senate against Robert Byrd. Chuck just laughed and said to me, "Can you imagine me doing that?" I said, "Nope." A Hollywood movie director named Hal Needham asked him to work on a rocket car speed record and on the movie, *Smokey and the Bandit II*. They raced at Rogers Dry Lake and got the car up to Mach 1.

And, of course, he couldn't keep away from Edwards; he went down there to fly every chance he got. Northrop also hired him as a consultant, which gave him a chance to fly their F-20 and F-5 airplanes. The amazing thing about Chuck is that his eyes are still perfect. I can't even thread a needle with my glasses, but he does it for me in a flash. Of course, he can't hear worth a darn. He and Bud both, from all those years of roaring jet engines, but Chuck says he just turns up the radio in his headset so that it rattles the whole cockpit and he gets along fine.

Over the years, I was much more apprehensive about his driving than his flying. But now, when we go somewhere, he sets that darned cruise control at fifty-five and that's it. It's so boring I actually complain. But Chuck really hasn't changed. He's off and charging as much as ever. The publicity over *The Right Stuff* turned up all the burners, and that phone rings off the wall. He could be traveling every day of the year, but Chuck does what he wants to do, when he wants to do it. We have an agent to handle the commercials he does on television. A.C. Delco's sales went through the roof after Chuck began appearing. The nicest part is knowing that his accomplishments are appreciated out there. We could use a couple of secretaries to handle all the mail, but you know who does that chore.

We've had a good life. I wouldn't change a whole heck of a lot, even if I could. I have my routines. I feed the ducks out on the pond and take care of our pet, TDB, which stands for "That Damned Bird." TDB is a male quail that we found while walking in the woods. Its mother was killed by a hawk. I took him home, and he thinks I'm his mother now. He has the run of the house and follows me around pecking at my shoe. But he'll allow only Chuck to pick him up and pet him. He has been with us for five years.

My mother lived with us for four years, until her death in November 1983. She was an invalid from a stroke and needed my constant attention. So, the nine years since Chuck's retirement have just zipped by. This year we celebrated our fortieth wedding anniversary, which hardly seems possible because we're still relatively young. I figured we had it all because we had our health and were active. Chuck is probably in better shape today than he was years ago because he gave up drinking, watches his weight, and walks two to three miles every day. But my annual physical examination last year was a shocker. I felt fine, no complaints, but they discovered cancer in my pelvic and abdominal area, possibly the result of all those X-rays back when I was carrying Susie. I spent some time worrying what would happen to my family, thinking "Why me?" I was angry. But after thinking it over, I decided to fight. Will and determination can sometimes defy the odds. Having lived with Chuck so long, I know that's true.

When Glennis got sick, friends said to me, "If anyone can beat cancer, she's the one." That's exactly right. I had seen guys doing all they could to survive in an airplane out of control, but their best just wasn't good enough. Glennis did her best and won. They kept zapping her with chemotherapy past the point where many people just couldn't take any more, and in the end, when the surgeons opened her up, they found the cancer destroyed. It was her tremendous victory. She toughed out the long ordeal and wouldn't allow herself to be defeated. My wife would have been one helluva great pilot.

I travel around the country more now than ever before. Business and civic groups constantly invite me to give talks. People are hungry for heroes, and I've long ago got used to being credited with a lot more than I really accomplished. My appeal is courage: even those who are not particularly interested in aviation are fascinated by a guy who strapped his fanny inside a dangerous airplane. It's the kind of one-on-one situation, like a cowboy who rode a furious bull and didn't get thrown, that people can relate to. They can't imagine themselves in such a scary situation, and yet, as Glennis proved, there's all kinds of courage that's no less admirable.

I'm glad to see a reawakened patriotism in the country and that plays a part in why this old pilot is still asked to make speeches. We military pilots did our jobs out of dedication, not for money or stock options. Hell, we believed in what we were doing, and in this complex and often impersonal world, it's easy to get confused about what we are doing and why we do it. I don't find that kind of confusion when I go to reunions of my old fighter squadron, or the fighter pilot aces' group, or the test pilots' association. Guys who have been tested under extreme adversity know damned well where they are coming from and what they believe. We get together and lie to each other about our exploits in the old days.

My first months out of the service, I felt kind of lost. For the first time that I could remember, there were absolutely no demands on my time. I could do anything I wanted to do, when I wanted to do it. Or, I could do nothing. It made no difference. So all that freedom looked kind of empty. Then, too, there was the feeling that I had been dumped off the merry-go-round and left behind.

For example, what does a lawyer do who has done lawyering all his life and is now out to pasture?

The Air Force was my life, and it was tough to just walk away from it. Being able to stay current and fly their latest equipment certainly helped my morale during this transition period. But then it began to dawn on me that I had the best of that world—the continual joy of flying without the headaches and responsibilities of command.

People don't change just because they grow older. What was fun at twenty-four is still fun at sixty-two, and I fly, hunt, and fish every chance I get. As a young test pilot, I lived to the hilt, and I haven't slowed down a whole helluva lot. I don't try to jump off a fifteen-foot fence because I'd probably break a leg; I'm not as limber as I was, but I can still pull eight or nine Gs in a high-performance aircraft, just as I did years ago. And I'm not alone: the two best pilots I've known, Andy and Bob Hoover, fly as much as they can. Bob is still giving air shows around the country every weekend, just as he did back at Wright in the early 1950s.

Given our backgrounds and experience, we aren't doing anything extraordinary. We still have our eyes, reflexes, and good health, so strapping us inside an airplane's cockpit is no different from a sixty-year-old driver turning on his car engine. When he turns the key, puts that car in gear, and drives off somewhere, he's doing exactly the same thing we do. He's been driving for a long time, and I've been flying just as long. I don't extend myself beyond my physical capabilities, but I still fly demonstrations.

Life is as unpredictable as flying in combat. If the day comes when a flight surgeon tells me I can't fly anymore in high-performance jets, I can always sneak out back and fly ultra-lights. Just like when the day dawns that Andy and I can't manage our treks into the Sierra to fish for golden trout—hell, there are still nearby lakes and plenty of rowboats. You do what you can for as long as you can, and when you finally can't, you do the next best thing.

You back up but you don't give up. I'm one of the fortunate retirees who has plenty of reasons for wanting to extend my longevity.

I get a lot of personal pleasure out of flying an F-20, but I know too many people who have erected barriers, real brick walls, just because they have gray hair, and prematurely cut themselves off from life-long enjoyments by thinking, "I'm too old to do this or that—that's for younger people." Living to a ripe old age is not an end in itself; the trick is to enjoy the years remaining. And unlike flying, learning how to take pleasure from living can't be taught. Unfortunately, many people do not consider fun an important item on their daily agenda. For me, that was always high priority in whatever I was doing.

My concession to aging is to take better care of myself than I did when I was younger. There are still so many new experiences and challenges, like hang-gliding or fooling around with ultra-light aircraft. Not long ago, the Piper Aircraft people asked me to fly one of their airplanes nonstop from Seattle to Atlanta, to try to establish a new distance speed record. I did it shaving a couple of hours off the old record. Nobody needs to remind me of how lucky I am.

Nowadays, I hunt as much for the exercise—traipsing for miles through hill and dale—as for the sport. As long as I can put one foot in front of the other, I'll be out there ten years from now. I don't still fly high-speed jets out of some nostalgia for the past: I do it because I love it. If it wasn't fun, I'd drop it in a minute, including the consultancy jobs I have with a couple of manufacturers. My lifestyle doesn't demand much money. But I'm definitely not a rocking-chair type. I can't just sit around, watch television, drink beer, get fat, and fade out.

And there's so much more I want to do; I've never lost my curiosity about things that interest me. Fortunately, I'm very good at the activities I most enjoy, and that part has made my life that much sweeter. I haven't yet done everything, but by the time I'm finished, I won't have missed much. If I auger in tomorrow, it won't be with a frown on my face.

I've had a ball.

INDEX

ABOUT LEO JANOS

LEO JANOS is a prize-winning author who has written extensively on a broad range of subjects for *The Atlantic Monthly*, the *Smithsonian Magazine*, *The New York Times*, *Science*, *People*, *Cosmopolitan*, and the *Reader's Digest*. Janos was a *Time* correspondent for nine years, where he served as Washington correspondent, then as Houston bureau chief, covering the Apollo space flights. A former White House speechwriter for Lyndon Johnson, Janos was recipient of the 1981 American Institute of Physics–United States Steel Foundation science-writing award. He is the author of *Crime of Passion*.

THE PRIVATE LIVES
BEHIND PUBLIC FACES

These biographies and autobiographies tell the personal stories of well-known figures recounting the triumphs and tragedies of their public and private lives.

☐	05110	**FERRARO: My Story**—Geraldine Ferraro w/Linda Bird Francke (A Bantam Hardcover)	$17.95
☐	25147	**IACOCCA: An Autobiography** Lee Iacocca w/Wm. Novak	$4.95
☐	25045	**OUT ON A LIMB** Shirley MacLaine	$4.50
☐	25234	**"DON'T FALL OFF THE MOUNTAIN"** Shirley MacLaine	$4.50
☐	24511	**GIANT STEPS** Kareem Abdul Jabbar & Peter Knobler	$3.95
☐	25985	**'SCUSE ME WHILE I KISS THE SKY** David Henderson	$4.50
☐	25484	**AN UNFINISHED WOMAN** Lillian Hellman	$4.50
☐	05094	**DANCING IN THE LIGHT** Shirley MacLaine (A Bantam Hardcover)	$17.95
☐	25453	**CITIZEN HUGHES** Michael Drosin	$4.50
☐	34241	**TRAPPED:** Michael Jackson Dave Marsh A Large Format Book	$9.95

Prices and availability subject to change without notice.

Buy them at your local bookstore or use this handy coupon for ordering:

Special Offer
Buy a Bantam Book
for only 50¢.

Now you can have an up-to-date listing of Bantam's hundreds of titles plus take advantage of our unique and exciting bonus book offer. A special offer which gives you the opportunity to purchase a Bantam book for only 50¢. Here's how!

By ordering any five books at the regular price per order, you can also choose any other single book listed (up to a $4.95 value) for just 50¢. Some restrictions do apply, but for further details why not send for Bantam's listing of titles today!

Just send us your name and address and we will send you a catalog!

We Deliver!
And So Do These Bestsellers.

DON'T MISS
THESE CURRENT
Bantam Bestsellers